D0340113

Origins and Evolution of Behavior Disorders

FROM INFANCY TO EARLY ADULT LIFE

Origins and

Evolution of

Behavior Disorders

FROM INFANCY TO EARLY ADULT LIFE

Stella Chess, M.D.
Professor of Child Psychiatry
New York University Medical Center

Alexander Thomas, M.D.
Professor of Psychiatry
New York University Medical Center

BRUNNER/MAZEL, *Publishers* • New York

Library of Congress Cataloging in Publication Data

Chess, Stella.
  Origins and evolution of behavior disorders.

  Bibliography: p.
  Includes index.
  1. Child psychopathology — Etiology — Longitudinal
studies.   2. Child psychopathology — Longitudinal studies.
3. Adolescent psychopathology — Etiology — Longitudinal
studies.   4. Adolescent psychopathology — Longitudinal
studies.   I. Thomas, Alexander, 1914–   . II. Title.
[DNLM: 1. Adjustment Disorders — diagnosis.   2. Adjustment
Disorders — psychology.   3. Child Behavior Disorders —
diagnosis.   4. Child Behavior Disorders — psychology.
5. Longitudinal Studies. WS 350.6 C524o]
RJ499.C4728   1984   618.92′89   84-14227
ISBN 0-87630-368-8

Copyright © 1984 by Stella Chess & Alexander Thomas

Published by
BRUNNER/MAZEL, Inc.
19 Union Square
New York, New York 10003

MANUFACTURED IN THE UNITED STATES OF AMERICA

Every limit is a beginning as well as an ending. Who can quit young lives after being long in company with them, and not desire to know what befell them in their after-years? For the fragment of a life, however typical, is not the sample of an even web. Promises may not be kept, and an ardent outset may be followed by declension; latent powers may find their long-awaited opportunity; a past error may urge a grand retrieval.

George Eliot, *Middlemarch*

Contents

Foreword by Judd Marmor, M.D.   ix
Preface   xi

PART I. THE NEW YORK LONGITUDINAL STUDY

Chapter 1. The Need for Longitudinal Studies   5
Chapter 2. Theoretical Framework   10
Chapter 3. Sources of Data and Methods of Data Collection   24
Chapter 4. Subject and Parent Ratings   41
Chapter 5. The Clinical Sample Over Time   52

PART II. QUANTITATIVE ANALYSIS

Chapter 6. Approach to Quantitative Data Analysis   61
Chapter 7. Multiple Regression Analyses: Correlations Between
            Three-Year Ratings and Early Adult Adaptation   68
Chapter 8. Set Correlation Analyses: Correlations Between
            Childhood and Early Adult Ratings   81
Chapter 9. Sex Differences   89
Chapter 10. Summary and Overview of the Quantitative Analyses   96

PART III. QUALITATIVE ANALYSIS

Chapter 11. Approach to Qualitative Data Analysis   103
Chapter 12. High- and Low-Risk Subjects at Three Years and
             Early Adult Outcome   110
Chapter 13. Childhood Antecedents of Early Adult Adjustment 130
Chapter 14. Six Cases of Depression in Childhood
             and Adolescence   148
Chapter 15. Three Cases of Brain Damage   164
Chapter 16. Origins of Behavior Disorders   183
Chapter 17. Evolution of Behavior Disorders   203
Chapter 18. Symptom Choice   218
Chapter 19. Adolescent Issues   229

PART IV. PRACTICAL AND THEORETICAL IMPLICATIONS

Chapter 20. Parent Guidance   251
Chapter 21. Continuity–Discontinuity and Developmental Stages:
             A Life-Span Perspective   261
Chapter 22. The Goodness of Fit Model: Theoretical and
             Practical Implications   273
Chapter 23. Overview: What We Know; What We Don't Know   287

PART V. APPENDICES

A. Early Adult Life Interview Protocol for Subjects   297
B. Adjustment Rating Scale from 3-Year Parent Interview   302
C. Global Adaptation Score—Early Adult Age Period   306

Bibliography   309
Index   319

Foreword

Advances in psychiatric theory and practice during the past half century, although less dramatic than those in medicine and surgery, have nevertheless been significant and noteworthy. Leaving aside the important developments in neurochemistry and psychopharmacology, perhaps the most important paradigmatic shift has been the one from a linear to a systems-oriented conceptual framework. Within the latter paradigm, causality is no longer attributed to a single factor or isolated "trauma," but rather to the interaction of multiple biopsychosocial variables.

The present volume by Chess and Thomas, like their 1980 work on *The Dynamics of Psychological Development*, is a noteworthy example of this new way of thinking about personality development and mental disorder. Step by step, in logical and orderly fashion, and buttressed by numerous illuminating case examples, they explicate the complex pluralistic dynamics that are involved in both normal and abnormal developmental patterns.

Moreover, earlier theories (including those of Sigmund Freud) about these issues were based mainly on retrospective reconstructions of early life histories — recollections that we now know had to be biased, not only by the inevitable lacunae in individual memories, but also by the fact that no one who is immersed in a system can possibly perceive all the variables involved in the dynamics of that system. Theories based on such retrospective data almost inevitably tend to become reductionistic, selectively emphasizing certain factors at the expense of other still unknown or unrecognized ones.

An important way of obviating at least part of this methodological prob-

ix

lem is the technique of anterospectively following the course of human development from birth to adult life as an outside observer, and with as much conceptual validation as possible from other observers. Chess and Thomas sagely chose this approach when they began their historic New York Longitudinal Study in 1956, and then continued to observe their subjects from infancy to adult life. Their findings, as described in this volume, make fascinating and instructive reading, and the practical implications for therapeutic intervention that follow from their studies are far-reaching. In particular, their pioneering contributions to a better understanding of the role of temperament in personality development, and their elaboration of the "goodness of fit" model are valuable and important additions to the clarification of how and why mental disorders originate. The authors are wise enough to know that many unsolved problems still remain, but they have taken us all a giant step forward, and for that we can be grateful.

Judd Marmor, M.D.

Preface

This volume reports our methods of data collection, quantitative and qualitative data analyses, findings, and their implications for the New York Longitudinal Study (NYLS) into the early adult age period. Earlier stages of the study were detailed in three previous volumes: *Behavioral Individuality in Early Childhood* (1963); *Temperament and Behavior Disorders in Childhood* (1968); and *Temperament and Development* (1977). In addition, we explored a number of theoretical implications of our findings from the NYLS and our other research studies, as well as from the relevant research literature, in the volume *The Dynamics of Psychological Development* (1980).

The analyses reported in the present volume not only utilize the data from our recent early adult-life follow-up of our subjects, but also integrate this information with our prospective data going back to early infancy. This has been our approach to both the quantitative and qualitative analyses, so as to exploit the special value of sequential, prospective information obtained in the course of a long-term, anterospective longitudinal study.

The title of the present volume emphasizes our focus on the origins and evolution of behavior disorders. This issue has been a major focus of the NYLS from its inception. A prospective longitudinal study, which minimizes the distortions of parental or subject report so frequently found in retrospective studies, has a special opportunity to explore the issues of the origins and evolution of behavior disorders. We have also examined our data for the subjects whose development has proceeded in a healthy direction, and have attempted to define some of the factors responsible for healthy versus psychopathological development in our subjects.

From its outset in 1956, the NYLS has been inspired by the concept that the child's own characteristics played a significant role in the processes of psychological development. In this regard, we have concentrated on the child's behavioral style, or temperament, an influential factor which had previously received little systematic attention in the research or clinical literature. At the same time, we were also committed to an interactionist model, in which temperament could not be studied by itself, but only as one factor in the constantly evolving interactionist interplay, which also included the child's abilities, motivations, other special attributes, and the whole complex, shifting array of intrafamilial and extrafamilial environmental influences. As we proposed these formulations in the 1950s and 1960s, they ran counter to the dominant, one-sided environmentalist views and drive-reduction and stimulus-response models of the time. Naturally, it has been especially gratifying to us over the past decade to see these concepts, which had been advocated by us and a small minority of other workers, enter the mainstream of developmental theory.

In our own analyses of the developmental course of individual subjects, whether this took a healthy or pathological direction, we have found the concept of "goodness of fit" to be a most useful model for the identification of the significant organismic and environmental factors and their dynamic, interactional interplay. It is of interest that in recent years a number of other developmental psychologists and psychiatrists have begun to use this model, though some of them may not use the term "goodness of fit" itself.

A number of young research workers have asked us to describe our methods of approach to a longitudinal sample that have contributed to our very high rate of sample maintenance and to the breadth and scope of the data we have been able to collect. This we have done in various parts of Section I of this volume, The New York Longitudinal Study.

Our acknowledgment is expressed to the National Institute of Mental Health, whose generous support (NIMH Grant MH-31333) enabled us to carry through this follow-up into early adult life and provided the resources for the quantitative and qualitative analyses reported in this volume. We are grateful to the *American Journal of Orthopsychiatry* for permission to reprint in Chapter 2 portions from our article, "Current Trends in Developmental Theory" in their October 1981 issue; to the *American Journal of Psychiatry* for permission to reprint in Chapter 4 portions from our article, "Genesis and Evolution of Behavior Disorders" in their January 1984 issue; to the *Journal of Nervous and Mental Disease* for permission to reprint in Chapter 14 portions from our article, "Depression in Childhood and Adolescence, A Prospective Study of Six Cases" in their July 1983 issue; and to the *Archives of General Psychiatry* for permission to reprint in Chapter 15 portions from our article, "A Longitudinal Study of Three Brain-Damaged Children" in their April 1975 issue.

Our thanks are extended to Drs. Richard Lerner and Sam Korn, whose careful and thoughtful editing of previous drafts of this manuscript served to clarify and sharpen a number of our formulations. Above all, we and the scientific community are deeply indebted to the families and subjects of the New York Longitudinal Study, whose unstinted and unfailing cooperation over these many years has made this study possible.

Stella Chess, M.D.
Alexander Thomas, M.D.

Origins and Evolution of Behavior Disorders

FROM INFANCY TO EARLY ADULT LIFE

PART I

The New York Longitudinal Study

CHAPTER 1

The Need for
Longitudinal Studies

There is certainly no dearth of theories offering to explain the origins of behavior disorders in childhood and adolescence. Most prominent and influential have been those advanced by the psychoanalytic movement. Some analysts have remained committed, with little or no modification, to traditional Freudian concepts. Others, such as Jung and Adler in the past, and Horney, Sullivan, Fromm, Erikson, Winnicott, Rado, Marmor, Kohut, among others in recent years, have offered varying types and degrees of change for psychoanalytic theory and practice. In some cases the modifications of classical Freudian formulations have been relatively minor, even if they have aroused intense controversy within psychoanalytic circles. In other instances, the proposed revisions of theory and practice have been so radical as to raise the question of whether they could still be legitimately considered to fit within a psychoanalytic framework.

A major attraction of psychoanalytic theory, whether orthodox or revisionist, is that it has offered a systematic and comprehensive formulation of both normal and pathological psychological development from early infancy onward. The theory has also given serious attention to the complexities and significance of ideas and emotions, and especially to their motivational aspects.

By contrast, behaviorism, the other major contender in providing a systematic explanation of the origins and evolution of behavior disorders, has suffered from an overly simplified conceptual scheme of the pertinent biological and environmental influences and the nature of the interactional processes

5

between them. Behaviorism has also, by deliberate decision, ignored the subjective intrapsychic factors which are so central to human psychology, brushing them aside as an "unknowable black box." Contemporary social learning theory has attempted to remedy some of these deficiencies of traditional behaviorism, but with only limited success (Thomas and Chess, 1980, Chapters 1 and 2).

Psychoanalytic theorists, behaviorists, and social learning theorists, as well as advocates of other conceptual schemes, have relied heavily, and even primarily, in their formulations of psychopathology on data obtained from patients and their families who have come for professional help. The behaviorists have also utilized animal models derived from neurophysiological research, but their relevance to the subjective intrapsychic phenomena so crucial in understanding human psychopathology is highly debatable. For a number of decades, the assumption that retrospectively obtained histories of early childhood events, feelings, and fantasies represented a valid body of data on which to base theories of child development went virtually unquestioned. In the past two decades, however, a number of studies have revealed significant distortions in the accuracy of mothers' retrospective reports on the early developmental history of their children, even when the child's development has been normal (Haggard et al., 1960; Robbins, 1963; Wenar, 1963).

If retrospective parental reporting of the child's normal development can be unreliable, this problem will undoubtedly be even greater when the child presents symptoms of a behavior disorder. In such cases, the potential for inaccuracy of parental recall will be magnified by defensiveness, by the search for plausible explanations, or by the influence of popular theories about the causes of psychopathology. The accuracy of retrospective parental histories describing the development of behavior problems in their children was tested in the New York Longitudinal Study (NYLS) by comparing them with the information collected prospectively in the course of the longitudinal study (Chess, Thomas and Birch, 1966). Significant distortions of retrospective recall were found in one-third of the cases and included: 1) revisions of timing to make the sequence of events conform to prevalent theories of causation; 2) denial or minimization of the child's problem in the past; and 3) inability to recall pertinent past behavior on mother's part, such as overprotectiveness. Of additional interest was the lack of systematic relationship between the degree of internal consistency on the one hand and fluency of the parent's retrospective report, and the correlation of this report with the corresponding anterospective data on the other hand.

The potential for distortions of retrospective recall is even greater for an adult patient than for the parent. The same reasons influencing inaccuracies of recall will exist, but are intensified by the much greater lapse in time. The classical illustration of this phenomenon, of course, was Freud's discovery that his adult patients' reports of traumatic sexual experiences in childhood all too often had no basis in fact.*

Even when the adult recalling his childhood experiences is not a psychiatric patient, significant distortions of memory may still occur. Thus, one of our NYLS subjects had a severe behavior disorder resulting primarily from the rigid and punitive demands of her father, which temperamentally she could not meet. When she was 9–10 years of age, however, she blossomed forth with artistic talents which brought approval from teachers and peers, and also ranked high in her father's hierarchy of values. His attitude and behavior toward his daughter changed dramatically for the better, and her symptoms disappeared in the next few years. When interviewed routinely at age 22 in the NYLS follow-up, she recalled her childhood as a happy one, remembered the mutuality of her interests with her father, and had no recollection of her father's antagonistic and punitive attitudes and behavior toward her in early childhood.

Vaillant, in reporting similar findings of retrospective distortion of recall in the adults of the Harvard Grant longitudinal study, asks, "How then may we obtain truth about the adult life cycle? Clearly, it must be studied prospectively. It is all too common for caterpillars to become butterflies and then to maintain that in their youth they had been little butterflies. Maturation makes liars of us all" (1977, p. 197).

It is true that the clinician must, on many occasions, utilize retrospective data obtained from patients and parents. He must evaluate the patient's problem and institute treatment on the basis of whatever information is available. In addition, the issues emphasized by a patient or parent in retrospective recall, even if factually incorrect, may provide useful clues to special concerns and preoccupations. On the other hand, the research worker has a different responsibility. His obligation is not patient care or other types of immediate action, but the accumulation of pertinent and accurate data. In this task, retrospective histories, if utilized at all, must be evaluated with great caution.

Furthermore, a number of possible explanations for a deviant developmental course are always available after the fact, and the absence of information gathered prior to the onset of the disorder makes it difficult, if not impossible, to choose among these alternatives. Freud himself was aware of this

---

*Freud assumed that these sexual fantasies had been present in the patient's childhood. He apparently did not consider the possibility that they had developed at some later period or during treatment itself, and then were projected backwards by the patient to the early childhood years.

problem. In a rarely quoted comment, he pointed out that "So long as we trace the development [of a mental process] backwards, the connection appears continuous, and we feel we have gained an insight which is completely satisfactory and even exhaustive. But if we proceed the reverse way, if we start from the premise inferred from the analysis and try to follow up the final result, then we no longer get the impression of an inevitable sequence of events, which could not have been otherwise determined. We notice at once that there might be another result, and that we might have been just as well able to understand and explain the latter" (1959, p. 226).

Psychoanalysts and behaviorists have argued that the validity of their theoretical systems, based as they may be on retrospective data, are validated by the effectiveness of the treatment procedures based on their concepts. However, each theorist makes a similar claim for his special formulations. Furthermore, the success of a specific treatment does not by itself prove the validity of the theory. The fact that if individuals living in a malarial endemic area showed a significantly lower incidence of malaria if they kept their windows shut at night did not prove the theory that malaria was caused by the "bad night air." The effectiveness of a psychotherapist's advice may depend not on his theory, but on the positive transference which makes the patient responsive to his interpretations and suggestions.

THE NEED FOR PROSPECTIVE LONGITUDINAL STUDIES

An adequate data base from which existing theories of the origins and evolution of behavior disorders can be tested and new hypotheses generated requires, therefore, the systematic collection of pertinent information anterospectively. Such a body of data documenting significant behavioral characteristics and environmental influences as they occur, and especially prior to the onset of symptoms, can avoid the potentially serious distortions of retrospective recall which occur in clinical studies.

Long-term longitudinal studies are expensive and time-consuming, run the risk of significant sample attrition over time, and also present special problems of data analysis. But these methodological problems have to be accepted, given the unique capacity of such longitudinal investigations to explore the developmental course of individual subjects over time (Wohlwill, 1973). Group studies conducted at one point in time, the so-called cross-sectional studies, can give valuable data on the relationship between functionally significant variables for a population as a whole. But they cannot trace the dynamic interplay of such factors in any single person over time, nor identify and analyze patterns of continuity and change in a behavioral attribute in a given individual. And it is this type of analysis which is crucial to the study of the origins and evolution of behavior disorders.

THE NEW YORK LONGITUDINAL STUDY

A number of longitudinal studies have made significant contributions to our understanding of the sequences and dynamics of psychological development (Kagan and Moss, 1962; MacFarlane, 1964; Murphy and Moriarty, 1976; Vaillant, 1977; Werner and Smith, 1982). However, our New York Longitudinal Study (NYLS) represents the one study with prospective longitudinal data starting in early infancy and antedating in all cases the onset of behavior disorder, with a substantial sample size and no loss of subjects over time, with detailed clinical evaluations of all cases at all age-periods to early adulthood presenting possible symptoms of a behavior disorder, and with periodic follow-up of all cases identified as showing a behavior disorder.

For these reasons, the data from the NYLS have provided a special opportunity to investigate the origins and evolution of behavior disorders through the childhood and adolescent periods and into early adult life. Information from our other longitudinal studies and from clinical practice have served to sharpen and expand a number of the findings of the NYLS. The findings to be reported in this volume will therefore derive from the analysis of the NYLS data alone, with the contributions from these other sources indicated specifically when pertinent.

CHAPTER 2

Theoretical Framework

Any study of the origins and evolution of behavior disorders rests upon some system of theoretical formulations as to the nature of human psychological development. The hypotheses to be tested, the procedures for data collection, and the methods of data categorization and analysis all will reflect the implicit or explicit conceptual framework of the researchers. Our own study has been guided by a number of interrelated theoretical formulations, which we have tried to make explicit and to put in testable form (Thomas and Chess, 1980).

First and foremost, primary emphasis must be given to the special and unique human characteristics in the evolution of individual psychological characteristics. In Eisenberg's words, human development must be understood in terms of "the *human* nature of human nature" (1972, p. 123). Animal models, whether based on instinct and drive-state concepts or conditioned reflex systems, are clearly inadequate when applied to human psychology. The influence of genetically predetermined instinctual patterns dwindles as one ascends the evolutionary scale from organisms with simple to those with complex nervous systems. The more highly developed the nervous system, the greater the capacity for learning and modification of genetically given behavior patterns: *i.e.,* the capacity to modify behavior as a consequence of previous experience.

Also, the conditioned reflex in the human is not the same as in the dog or other animals. In the latter, once established, the conditioned reflex remains essentially unchanged over time. It may become linked with other reflexes, it may become attenuated or reinforced, but the association with the original environmental stimulus which led to the conditioned reflex formation remains essentially unchanged. In a three-year-old boy, a water phobia may start, as it might in a dog or other animal, as a simple conditioned reflex after a frightening experience at the beach. But very quickly the anxiety symptoms create reactions in the parents, sibs, and other children and adults, which modify the original conditioned reflex and give it symbolic meaning. A developmental interactional process is set in motion. When the boy is 10 years old, the same phobia has developed new aspects, new meanings, and new influences on his functioning and social relations. And again, at 20 years, or 40 years, the same phobic symptom may be present, but its significance for the individual and his family and friends will be different at these stages.

A HUMAN DEVELOPMENTAL MODEL

If animal models are insufficient, what then is a human model for psychological development?

On the biological side, a human model must emphasize those structural and functional characteristics of the brain that are special and even unique in the human being—those attributes that make learning, language, the use of tools, and abstract thought possible. These characteristics will have emerged through the evolutionary process of natural selection: "Natural selection can select for specific ways of being sensitive to experience, or for phenotypic structures that make experience possible, just as readily as it can for any other characteristics" (Lehrman, 1970, p. 73). The geneticist Dobzhansky has spelled out this fundamental concept: "We do not inherit culture biologically. We inherit genes which make us capable of acquiring culture by training, learning, imitation of our parents, playmates, teachers, newspapers, books, advertisements, propaganda, plus our own choices, decisions and the products of reflection and speculation. Our genes enable us to learn and to deliberate. What we learn comes not from the genes but from the associations, direct and indirect, with other men" (1966, p. 14).

A human model must also emphasize the second system of inheritance unique to humans, the extragenetic inheritance of culture. "Man has something that is essentially new and which makes him human, *culture* . . . culture affects not only the general structure and dynamics of a society but also the nature of interindividual relationships. Thus, while social status and social role in the lower primates are determined by individual skill and biological structure, in human societies status and role are determined by genealogy, property or other institutional forms. Because of these differences, it is inadvisable to seek for direct analogues of human social life in primate society" (Birch, 1954, pp. 473–474).

Cultural evolution, unlike biological evolution, is transmitted immediately and cumulatively to succeeding generations through social institutions. Biological change is slow and gradual. Cultural change can be gradual or rapid and sometimes dramatic in its sudden shifts.

It is fruitless to pose the question of whether biology or culture is more important in individual psychology, just as the argument over heredity versus environment is fruitless. Psychological development occurs in a biosocial matrix through a continuous dynamic interaction of the biological and social. Mental functioning, whether adaptive or maladaptive, is always simultaneously biological and cultural. Operating as a dialectical unity, they cannot be separated mechanically from each other: "Human evolution is now the resultant of the interaction between biological and sociocultural forces, and it involves a constant feedback between them. In this respect also man differs qualitatively from the rest of the animal creation" (Dubos, 1965, p. 13).

THE NEONATE AS A HUMAN BEING

In the past, "it was thought that in the early weeks of life a baby's senses were not yet capable of taking in any information from the outside world, so that to all intents and purposes he was blind and deaf. Unable to move much either, he seemed a picture of psychological incompetence, of confusion and disorganization. Only the regularity of his experience, provided principally by his parent, was thought to bring order to the baby's mind. Until that was achieved, all he could do was feed and sleep" (Schaffer, 1977, p. 27).

Research studies of the last 20 years have dramatically changed this view of the neonate's functioning. Careful, detailed, naturalistic observations and inductive data analysis, combined with the use of new experimental techniques, have by now provided convincing evidence of the neonate's capacities. A leading researcher has summarized the conclusions to be drawn from the recent explosion of knowledge: "A newborn thus begins life as an extremely competent learning organism, an extremely competent perceiving organism" (Bower, 1977, p. 35).

The newborn infant not only recognizes visual patterns, but gives preferential attention to such patterns and to complexity, movement, and three-dimensionality over plain visual stimuli (Fantz and Nevis, 1967). The neonate is responsive to sound, can localize the direction from which a sound comes (Wertheimer, 1961), and demonstrates a capacity for "a spatially relevant, functional relation between audition and vision" (Mendelson and Haith, 1976, p. 57).

Brazelton (1973, 1978) has studied the neonate's range of behavioral integrative processes and found significant evidence of cortical control and responsiveness with 22 items, which now comprise the widely used Brazelton Neonatal Behavioral Assessment Scale. These items include, among others, response decrement to repeated sensory stimuli, orienting responses to inanimate stimuli and to examiner's face and voice, quality and duration of alert periods, responses to being cuddled, defensive reactions to a cloth over face, consolability, and self-quieting activity. Turkewitz and Birch (1971) have also reported a series of studies indicating a wide range for the neonate's level of neurobehavioral organization. The findings included responses to simple and complex auditory stimuli, habituation to auditory and somesthetic stimuli, and correlation between intensity of auditory stimulation and direction of eye movements.

Learning, as demonstrated by the formation of conditioned reflexes, starts actively at birth (Connolly and Stratton, 1969; Lipsitt, 1969; Papousek and Papousek, 1975). Learning by imitation has also been demonstrated in the first few weeks of life: "If the baby's mother, or some other adult, sticks out her tongue at the baby, within a relatively short time the baby will begin to stick his tongue back at her" (Bower, 1977). This same sequence of imitation can be demonstrated with the adult's fluttering her eyelashes, opening or closing her mouth, or other facial and manual gestures (Meltzoff and Moore, 1977; Field et al., 1982). As early as two weeks of age, the infant can differentiate between two live female faces, discriminate between voices, and begin to associate face with voice (Carpenter, 1975).

Recent research has also revealed that the newborn is capable of active social communication, that most basic element of social exchange. Condon and Sander used a refined technique of microanalysis of sound films of interaction between neonate and caretaker to demonstrate that ". . . as early as the first day of life, the human neonate moves in precise and sustained segments of movement that are synchronous with the articulated structure of adult speech" (1974). The precise synchrony occurred with both American and Chinese speech, but not with disconnected vowels or tapping sounds. Condon and Sander suggested that their study ". . . reveals a complex interaction system in which the organization of the neonate's motor behavior is entrained by and synchronized with the organized speech behavior of adults in his environment" (1974, p. 101). This interactional synchrony between neonate and caretaker has also been identified in sucking behavior (Kaye and Brazelton, 1971). The infant's cry, in addition, is an active and effective form of social communication from the moment of birth on, and this receives powerful reinforcement with the development of the smile in the first weeks of life.

Thus, the biological endowment of the newborn infant provides the perceptual and learning capacity for the neonate to begin immediately to claim its cultural nongenetic inheritance. With the first fondling, the first feeding, the first perception of the human face and human voice, the newborn responds to and integrates inputs from the environment that have both cultural and sensorimotor significance. In turn, the active responses of the infant influence the character of the caretaker's attitudes and handling. The nature of this influence is again culturally determined.

The human newborn's social being is qualitatively different from that of social organisms such as bees and ants, who are born with an elaborate, fixed, preprogrammed, instinctual structure of social functioning. How different the human being is at birth from other mammals can be a matter for debate. What is clear, however, is that the uniquely human aspects of social interaction begin to operate at birth so that the human infant very quickly becomes a different social being from other mammals. From an evolutionary point of view, the perceptual, learning, and social competence of the human neonate is intimately linked to the long period of nurturance and dependency of infancy and childhood. These neonatal capacities make possible the maximum transmission of the cultural heritage of humanity, the adaptive mechanism that is so uniquely developed in homo sapiens.

THE ACTIVE ROLE OF THE CHILD

In the mid-1950s, when we began the NYLS, theories of the origins of psychopathology and of individual differences in personality development were dominated by environmentalist views. Whether the concepts came from psychoanalysis, learning theory, or behaviorism, the young infant was considered a *tabula rasa*, a clean slate on which the environment inscribed its influence until the adult personality was etched to completion. Innate biological factors were hypothesized by many, such as instinctual drives in the Freudian system, or central nervous system typologies in the Pavlovian scheme, but *individual differences* in development were still presumed to reflect primarily individual differences in environmental forces.

While recognizing the vital contribution that the child's environment — conditions of life, relationships with parents and other family members, and extrafamilial sociocultural influences — made to the course of psychological development, we could not find in our clinical cases or the research literature the direct correlations between such environmental factors and individuality in patterns of development that these environmentalist views demanded. This dissatisfaction with the prevalent theories of the time was a major reason in our decision to investigate the active role played by the child's own characteristics, and specifically his temperament, through the intitiation of the NYLS.

In subsequent years, evidence accumulated from a number of sources confirming the judgment that the infant's development was not related in any linear fashion to parental characteristics (Beiser, 1964; Schaffer and Emerson, 1964). Our thesis on the importance of the child's own characteristics, which are independent of parental attitudes and practices, was then buttressed by an influential article by Bell (1968). In the past decade this concept has become firmly established through the weight of research and clinical evidence (Thomas and Chess, 1980; Greenspan, 1981; Lerner and Busch-Rossnagel, 1981).

THE GOALS OF BEHAVIOR: TASK MASTERY AND SOCIAL COMPETENCE

A fundamental characteristic of all living organisms is that their functioning serves some goal. For all species, survival and reproduction of the species are basic goals. Beyond this generalization, how can we conceptualize the primary motives of human behavior? Consideration of the motives and goals of human behavior has been a prime concern of the psychoanalytic movement from the beginning. No other developmental theory has given comparable attention to this issue. One of Freud's basic contributions has been this emphasis on goals, with the elucidation of how much in human behavior that superficially appears to be aimless or accidental actually involves purposive functioning. However, Freud's conceptualization of motivational forces always remained within the framework of drive satisfaction or its frustration. The inadequacy of this concept for human psychology has been abundantly documented by numerous workers, both within and outside the psychoanalytic movement (Marmor, 1942; White, 1959; Dobzhansky, 1962; Lewis, 1981). This has led many psychoanalysts such as Horney, Sullivan, Rado, Hartman, Erikson, and Kohut to propose a number of modifications or radical revisions of traditional libido theory. Their formulations have been influential in emphasizing several basic developmental phenomena. A number of psychological characteristics, such as perception, language, and cognition, cannot be encompassed within an exclusively motivational framework. Development occurs within a social matrix; highly significant phenomena, such as exploratory behavior, curiosity, and pleasure in problem-solving, cannot be explained by instinct and drive-reduction theory.

With our present-day empirical knowledge of the capacities and behavioral patterns of the young infant, it is now possible to go beyond these modifications of psychoanalytic theory, and propose an alternative formulation of the

primary goals of human activity from birth onward. Two striking characteristics of the child's behavior in the first weeks of life are his interest in mani-
pulatory-exploratory behavior and the active social exchange with his care-
takers. As described by the Paupouseks, "External change which is contingent
on the infant's own activity elicits the most intensive of orienting reactions:
approach and manipulatory explorations of various types. These reactions
all tend to be remarkably resistant to habituation and usually cease only after
trial and error or other operant forms of learning have shown the infant how
to get the relevant environmental changes repeated" (1975, p. 249). Other investigators have reported similar observations and conclusions as to the interest and competence of very young infants in exploring and manipulating
their environments (White, 1959; Bower, 1977).

The active social exchange of the neonate and young infant with his care-
takers is also conspicuous. Whether it is in learning by imitation (Carpenter,
1975), the synchrony of movement with adult speech (Condon and Sander,
1971), the interactional synchrony with the caretaker in sucking behavior
(Kaye and Brazelton, 1971), or the social communication effected through
smiling and crying, the human infant shows a remarkable competency, even
in the first few weeks of life, for beginning to achieve the goal of establishing
social attachments and relationships. "The infant comes into the world bring-
ing formidable capabilities to establish human relatedness. Immediately he
is a partner in shaping his first and foremost relationships" (Stern, 1977, p.
33).

Bruner has defined these abilities of the young child in broad terms. "For
convenience, the forms of early competence can be divided into those which
regulate interaction with other members of the species and those involved in
mastery over objects, tools, spatially and temporally ordered sequences of
events. Obviously, the two cannot be fully separate, as witness the importance
of imitation and modeling in the mastery of 'thing skills'" (1973, p. 1).

Along these lines, we have suggested that the primary adaptive goals of the
neonate and young infant, for which he is biologically equipped, can be conceptualized as the development of social relations and the mastery of skills
and tasks—i.e., *social competence* and *task mastery*. Both are specially developed in the human being with his unique capacity for learning. Both proceed developmentally as the individual's capacities mature, as learning takes
place, and as the environment makes successive new demands and presents
new opportunities. Both proceed by a constant mutual interaction. Task
mastery facilitates social relationships, and increasing social competence pro-
motes the capacity to master the environment. Most activities, such as play,
school work, sex, and athletics, contain both social and task features.

It is of interest that Freud put the goals of the healthy adult as "work and love," indeed highly similar to the concepts of task mastery and social competence. Restated thus, these goals apply to the neonate just as they do to the adult.

EARLY SOCIALIZATON

The conceptualization of the goals of behavior determines how the process of early socialization is interpreted. The establishment of regular feeding and sleep schedules, of successful weaning and toilet training, and of effective safety rules are major early socialization areas. For theories in which drive reduction is a primary focus, the acquisition of these socialization skills is equated with a continuous series of frustrations. Freud conceptualized this clearly: "civilization is the fruit of the renunciation of instinctual satisfaction" (1924, p. 297). Erikson, in his most influential work, says of weaning that "even under the most favorable circumstances, this stage leaves a residue of a primary sense of evil and doom and of a universal nostalgia for a lost paradise" (1950, p. 75). Regarding toilet training, his view is "bowel and bladder training has become the most obviously disturbing item of child training in wide circles of our society" (p. 77).

Despite their demonstration that the degree of sucking activity results not from innate oral drive but from opportunities to suck (Davis et al., 1948), the same investigators have also placed emphasis on weaning as a frustration: "the weaning process, except under the most fortunate circumstances, is bound to be frustrating to the child" (Sears, Macoby and Levin, 1957, p. 83). When toilet training and weaning are viewed as advances in task mastery and social competence, quite a different concept emerges. These skills now can be viewed as sources of satisfaction, achievement and enhancement of social relationships, rather than as frustrating experiences, as drive reduction theory would have it. Thus the child can have, by use of a cup, a control over the process of liquid intake that is not possible when sucking at a nipple. Toilet training gives control over the time and place of bowel and bladder evacuation. With weaning and toilet training, as with the establishment of regular sleep and feeding schedules, the child takes important steps in the process of social integration into the family group.

The positive aspects of weaning and toilet training are indicated from the NYLS data, in which detailed accounts of each child's behavior preceding, during, and following weaning and toilet training were obtained (Thomas et al., 1961b). Evidence of disturbance related to either of these procedures occurred in only a few children, and were related to rigid or inconsistent parental practices and attitudes. In some of the families, weaning was accomplished when the child spontaneously rejected the bottle. A few of these mothers attempted to continue bottle feeding, desisting only when it was clearly doomed to failure. These mothers openly expressed their apprehensions, based on their reading of presumably authoritative professional sources, that early weaning and toilet training might be traumatic. This was the late 1950s when child care literature was dominated by such statements. Views were also expressed during maternal interviews of feelings of uneasiness and discomfort that friends who were aware of the child's early weaning would conclude that outdated, rigid and harmful child care practices were the rule in these mothers' daily handling. With respect to toilet training, this scenario was much the same. With the exception of one case, toilet training was accomplished uneventfully and had been initiated by a number of the children — frequently by imitating an older sib.

These data indicate the positive and gratifying nature of socialization for the child as opposed to speculations that they represent deprivation and frustration. Be it toilet training, weaning, walking, self-feeding, achieving dressing skills or acquiring language, normal children are highly motivated to attempt these tasks. At the appropriate developmental level, they carry them to completion. This process of mastery is often accompanied by stress; this is true of mastery in general whether it involves a 12-month infant learning to walk or an adult writer or scientist struggling with a play or a scientific experiment. Healthy psychological development includes stress at times, and it is a misinterpretation to judge it as harmful, regrettable and a necessary evil. It is only when a quality and level of performance is demanded that is inappropriate and excessive for the individual that the stress and accompanying tension may become pathogenic. When demands are within capacity and stress is resolved by mastery, the consequences are in fact positive and lead to self-esteem. Actually, misguided efforts to protect the child from stress and tension may in fact prevent successive experiences of success, and such overprotection may rather have unfavorable consequences.

THE CONCEPT OF INTERACTIONISM

In the past, concepts of development were dominated, as were other areas of thought, by Aristotelian categories, in which opposites were mutually exclusive. Behavioral phenomena were ascribed either to heredity or to environmental influences, depending on which theory was dominant at the time. The newborn infant was considered either a *homunculus*, an adult in miniature who already possessed all the physical and psychological attributes that would characterize him as an adult, or a *tabula rasa*, a clean slate on which the environment would inscribe its influence until the adult personality was etched to completion. Where opposites operated together, as heredity and environment in shaping an individual's characteristics, it was presumed that the contribution of each category could be parceled out — so much for heredity and so much for environment, so much for biology and so much for culture.

Such linear, static models, in which biology and culture are dichotomized, have proven increasingly inadequate as frameworks for developmental theory. "For an adequate perspective in the methodology of research and theory, we cannot accept a priori definition of behavioral development either as an unfolding of the innate, with gains through learning presumably superimposed in superior phyla, or as a continuum expanding mainly through the pressure of environmental forces, with the genes merely contributing an initial push to the process. Rather, a defensible generalization is that a species' genetic constitution contributes in some manner to the development of *all* behavior in *all* organisms, as does milieu, developmental context or environment" (Schneirla, 1957, p. 79).

For human psychological development, both Freud and Pavlov formulated the beginnings of an interactionist approach. One of the major achievements of the psychoanalytic movement has been the demonstration of how much that had previously been labeled as hereditary or constitutional was really the result of the interaction between the young child and his effective environment. Pavlov, on his part, showed how biology and life experience are integrated in the formulation of the conditioned reflex. But neither Freud nor Pavlov could develop the logic of a dynamics of interactionism. With the very limited knowledge of human development available in their time and the necessity for them to rely on animal models, only the first steps were possible for them.

In subsequent years, a number of developmental psychologists suggested conceptualizations which gave some emphasis to an interactional model (Stern, 1927; Lewin, 1935; Murphy, 1947; Sears, 1951; Schneirla, 1957; Vygotsky, 1978*). We ourselves, from the beginning of the NYLS study of temperament and its functional significance, found an interactionist approach essential. Thus in our first paper (Thomas and Chess, 1957), we suggested that "total personality characteristics at any age-period develop out of the interaction of the specific reaction pattern [i.e. temperament] with all other determinants of psychological development" (p. 356). By 1961 we had formu-

---

*This is an English translation of a work by Vygotsky from the early 1930s.

lated this approach definitively: "Behavioral phenomena are considered to be the expression of a continuous organism-environment interaction from their very first manifestations in the life of the individual. This overall approach may be designated as interactionist (Thomas et al., 1961a, p. 723).

In recent years, this emphasis on an interactional model (or transactional, as some prefer to call it) has swelled to a consensus among leading research workers in human development psychology and psychiatry (Bell, 1968; Kagan, 1971; Rutter, 1972; Sameroff, 1975; Murphy and Moriarty, 1976; Clarke and Clarke, 1976; Eisenberg, 1977; McCall, 1977; Vaillant, 1977; Spanier et al., 1978). Most compelling for the acceptance of the interactional model has been the repeated demonstration in one research project after another, and especially in long-term longitudinal studies, that simpler models are inadequate to conceptualize sequences of human development and the transformation of psychological attributes over time.

The interactionist concept, as we have spelled it out recently, "demands that behavioral attributes must always be considered in their reciprocal relationship with other characteristics of the organism and in their interaction with environmental opportunities, demands and stresses. This process produces consequences which may modify or change behavior. The new behavior will then affect the influence of recurrent and new features of the environment. New environmental influences may develop independently or as a consequence of previous or ongoing organism-environment interactive process. At the same time, characteristics of the organism, either talents and abilities, goals and motives, behavioral stylistic characteristics, or psychodynamic defenses, may be modified or altered as the result of this continually evolving reciprocal organism-environment influence. Development thus becomes a fluid dynamic process which can modify and change preexisting psychological patterns. At the same time the potential for reinforcement of the old exists with the same or greater strength as does the possibility for change. Continuity over time does not imply that a reified structure, insulated from change, exists intrapsychically. Such continuity can be more parsimoniously conceptualized as the result of consistency in the organism-environment interaction" (Chess, 1979, pp. 104–105).

GOODNESS OF FIT

In our analysis of the dynamics of the origins and evolution of behavior disorders, we have found the concept of "goodness of fit" and the related ideas of consonance and dissonance to be very useful. These formulations represent a specific application of the general principle of interactionism.

When the organism's capacities, motivations and style of behaving and the demands and expectations of the environment are in accord, then goodness of fit results. Such consonance between organism and environment potentiates optimal positive development. Should there be dissonance between the capacities and characteristics of the organism on the one hand and the environmental opportunities and demands on the other hand, there is poorness of fit, which leads to maladaptive functioning and distorted development. Goodness of fit and consonance, poorness of fit and dissonance are never abstractions. They have meaning only in terms of the values and demands of a given socioeconomic group or culture.

There is no implication in the concept of goodness of fit that stress and conflict are absent. Quite the contrary is true. Stress and conflict are essential aspects of the developmental process in which new demands and expectations for enhanced levels of functioning occur continuously, keeping step with the ever-increasing capacities of the growing child. When these enlarging stresses, demands and conflicts are in harmony with emerging developmental capacities and potentials, then the consequences of such stress are constructive, rather than harbingers of behavioral disturbance. It is rather excessive stress due to poorness of fit that results in behavior problems.

The concept of goodness of fit cannot be applied abstractly but only in terms of clearly defined end results. As an example, a child may develop behavioral distress as a reaction to a new social situation in which functioning of a new kind is required. This is not an automatic signal to the parent to restore immediate comfort by withdrawing the child from the new demand. Rather, the parents should evaluate the best strategy which will make it possible for the child to master this new situation. This requires a judgment, based on the child's past experiences and an estimate of his current abilities and motivations, that the child can cope with the new expectations; with this, his efforts should be encouraged and assisted if necessary. However, if a judgment is made that the limitations of the child's capacities and/or the complexities and special demands of the new situation would result in poorness of fit, so that mastery cannot be achieved at the particular time, then a different strategy is in order. A delay in the intrusion of the new social situation until the child's level of functioning has expanded, or introduction of the individual elements of the complex social aggregate one at a time may bring about a goodness of fit and mastery, even if more slowly. Thus, the concept of goodness of fit is not a homeostatic principle of behavior aimed at stability, but rather a homeodynamic one with the aim of change in the direction of expanded competence. At times, stasis is appropriate for the consolidation of gains, and at such times restriction of new demands is in fact an essential prerequisite for constructive functioning. In other circumstances, stasis is undesirable if change and new levels of mastery are necessary for psychological reorganization and growth.

The concept of goodness of fit is similar to that employed by Kagan in studying perceptual schemata in infants and their interaction with new environmental stimuli. He emphasizes that excessive stress and distress will depend on a discrepancy from an established schema that the infant cannot assimilate, and not from the novelty or change in stimulation as such. "The emphasis is placed on the relation between his schemata and the events in the new environment, not on the absolute variability or intensity of the new situation. . . . If disruption is seen as a product of lack of congruence between schema and environment, one examines the distinctive qualities of the environment" (1971, p. 11). Stern also spells out this concept. "Very slight degrees of discrepancy provide very slight stimulation and produce low levels of attention. Increasing degrees of discrepancy produce progressively more attention up to some maximum threshold beyond which the infant finds the experience unpleasant and avoids it" (1977, p. 60).

Greenspan, in his study of psychopathology in early chldhood, formulates a primary focus of preventive intervention and treatment as the transformation of "a growth-inhibiting environment into a growth-promoting environment in the context of the individual needs of the infant" (1981, p. 61). Translated into our terms, this approach involves transforming a poorness of fit into a goodness of fit.

On the cognitive level, Hunt (1980) has emphasized what he calls "the problem of the match" between the child's cognitive capacity and the demands made on him. If the demand is dissonant with his cognitive level, the child shows "withdrawal and distress, and often tears"; if consonant, the task is performed with "interest and joyful excitement" (pp. 34–35).

The concept of goodness of fit has also been applied by Dubos as a measure of physical health. "Health can be regarded as an expression of fitness to the environment, as a state of adaptedness . . . The words health and disease are meaningful only when defined in terms of a given person functioning in a given physical and social environment" (1965, pp. 350–351).

Several studies have recently been reported which have utilized our goodness of fit model. One by Gordon (1981) indicated that "the level of adult control or demands is indeed an important component in the concept of 'fit' between parent behavior and child characteristics" (p. 175). Lerner (1984) assessed the expectations for behavioral style, in an eighth-grade classroom, of each subject's classroom teacher and peer group. Those subjects whose temperaments best matched each set of demands had more favorable teacher ratings of adjustment and ability, better grades, more positive peer relations, and more positive self-esteem than did subjects whose temperaments were less well matched with teacher and/or peer demands.

The goodness of fit model is a formulation which facilitates the application of the interactionist approach to specific counseling, early intervention and treatment situations. The formulation structures a strategy of intervention that includes an assessment of the individual's motivations, abilities and temperament, his behavior patterns and their consequences, and the expectations, demands and limitations of the environment. The specific potential or actual dissonance between individual and environment can then be proportioned. The continued application of the interactionist model to developmental study at all age-periods will certainly result in progressively increasing knowledge of the behavioral outcomes of the interaction of specific characteristics of the individual with specific features of the environment. As this happens, it will make the application of the goodness of fit formulation to preventive intervention, counseling, and treatment increasingly useful.

CHAPTER 3

Sources of Data and Methods of Data Collection

The types of data gathered and the methods of collection are determined by the goals of a study. These decisions are especially vital in a long-term longitudinal study, in which the investigator cannot go back in time to retrieve pertinent information that was overlooked at the time the behavior or environmental events occurred. Paradoxically, this problem has pressured some longitudinal studies into trying to achieve a safety net by gathering the widest variety of data possible, whether or not these data are relevant to the hypotheses and goals of the particular study. This only results in the accumulation of vast amounts of undigestible information. Furthermore, the lack of focus of such an enterprise inevitably leads to an insufficient concentration and probing in depth for the truly significant data. In addition, parents and subjects tend to be alienated and to drop out of such a study which makes extreme demands on their time and energy, and does not provide them with a clear, coherent picture of the rationale for their participation.

Especially seductive are the well-meaning suggestions from colleagues and friends that the project would be enhanced if this or that additional variable were measured. This was our experience repeatedly in the early years of our longitudinal studies and we developed a stock reply, "That's a fine idea, and we mean it, and we would be delighted if you or someone else would do that study."

GOALS

Our aims were set by the hypothesis that children showed individual differences in behavioral style or temperament from birth onward, and that this behavioral individuality played a significant role in the course of normal and deviant psychological development. Our goals, therefore, included:

1. The development of a method of data collection from which specific types of behavioral individuality in early childhood could be classified, in terms of objectively describable and reliably rated categories of temperament.
2. The study of consistencies and inconsistencies of temperament in the course of development.
3. The analysis of the pertinence of early temperament to later personality characteristics.
4. The dynamic of temperament in the mastery of environmental demands and expectations at succeeding age-stage levels of development.
5. The identification of those subjects who developed behavior disorders, and the study of the ontogenesis and course of these disorders in terms of a continuously evolving child-environment interactional process.

SOURCES OF DATA

In the pursuit of these goals, we have utilized a number of sources of data. First and foremost has been the New York Longitudinal Study, the core sample for our analysis of the origins and evolution of behavior disorders.

In the NYLS, the behavioral development of 133 subjects from middle- or upper-middle-class families, with almost all the parents born in the United States, has been followed from early infancy to early adult life. The sample was gathered through personal contact during pregnancy or shortly after birth, with parents who were willing to cooperate in a long-term study of normal child development. Only one mother who was approached refused to participate. All resided in New York City or one of its suburbs, and the method of contact ensured families of middle- or upper-middle-class background.

The cumulative collection of subjects was started in March 1956, and completed over a six-year period. Eighty-seven families were enrolled, and all children born to the families during the six-year period were included in the study. The total initial sample comprised 138 children, with 47 families contributing one child each, 31 contributing two children, 7 contributing three children, and 2 with four children.

Five children from 5 families were lost to the study in the first 3 years because of long-distance changes in residence. Our resources at that time were insufficient to continue active contact with families outside the New York City area. No further sample attrition has occurred since then, even though the families have been characterized by a great deal of geographical mobility. We have thus been able to follow 133 subjects since early infancy. (Previous reports gave this figure as 136, and the original sample as 141 due to a mechanical tabulation error).

The 84 families retained in the study are predominantly Jewish (78 percent) with some Protestant (15 percent) and Catholic (7 percent) families. There is one black and one Chinese family. Almost all parents were born in the United States. Forty percent of the mothers and 60 percent of the fathers had both college and postgraduate degrees, and only 9 percent of the mothers and 3 percent of the fathers had no college attendance. With only 3 exceptions, all the fathers worked in one of the professions, or in business at a management or executive level. Eighty percent of the mothers had similar occupations, and the remaining 20 percent were secretaries or general office workers. At the time of the birth of their first child enrolled in the study, half of the mothers were less than 31 years of age, with an age range from 20 to 41 years. The median age of the fathers was 33.6 years; the youngest was 25 years and the oldest 54 years of age.

Expressed parental attitudes were permissive and child-centered and Spock's manual *Baby and Child Care* (1957) was uniformly though not rigidly utilized as a source of child-care practices. Educational goals for the children were high, and almost 90 percent of the subjects were enrolled in private nursery schools at 3 or 4 years of age. In spite of the homogeneity of expressed parental attitudes, considerable variation existed from family to family with regard to child-care practices and expectations of the child at different age-periods.

Sex distribution of the sample is equal, with 66 boys and 67 girls. The mean IQ score at 6 years was 127, with a S.D. of 12.1.

It may be argued that the NYLS sample has special socioeconomic and ethnic characteristics which may make any generalizations from its findings difficult. In reality, however, any sample will have special demographic attributes and will also be influenced by specific sociocultural norms and values of the periods in which data are collected. The issue is to specify the characteristics of a sample sufficiently so that comparisons with other samples with different attributes will be possible.

With regard to the NYLS, we opted for a socioculturally homogeneous sample so as to minimize the effect of this variable on the findings on behavioral individuality or temperament, which has been from the beginning a major focus of the study. The question of the generalization of the findings has then been explored by comparisons with our other longitudinal samples - the working-class Puerto Rican, the mentally retarded, and the physically handicapped congenital rubella groups.

To obtain a population of contrasting socioeconomic background, a population of 98 children of working-class Puerto Rican parents was followed longitudinally from early infancy to age 6 years. In addition, single behavioral evaluations and I.Q. scores were obtained on 116 of the older sibs of these subjects, who ranged from 6 to 16 years of age.

These families were mostly intact and stable; 85% lived in public housing projects in New York City. Over 85% of the parents were born in Puerto Rico and came to New York in their late teens. Fewer than 25% of the parents had completed high school. Over 95% of the fathers were employed at the time of the study, and almost two-thirds were unskilled workers. Fewer than 10% of the mothers worked, either full or part-time (Hertzig et al., 1968).

In addition, two longitudinal samples of deviant children have been gathered and followed. One comprised 52 children with mildly retarded intellectual levels but without gross evidence of motor dysfunction or body stigmata. This group was followed from age 5 to 11 (Chess and Hassibi, 1970). The second sample comprised 243 children with congenital rubella resulting from the rubella epidemic of 1964 (Chess et al., 1971). This group was studied when they were two to four years of age, again four years later, and a third time five years later. This group has been of special interest because of the large numbers with physical, neurological and intellectual handicaps, including many with multiple handicaps.

Finally, additional pertinent data were obtained from children and adolescents seen and treated in clinical office practice.

MAINTENANCE OF SAMPLE

Maintenance of sample over time is a crucial methodological issue in any longitudinal sample. If any significant degree of sample attrition were to occur, there would be no satisfactory method of determining whether those subjects lost to the study had any significant characteristics which would have altered the results of data analysis. Indirect methods of checking, such as comparing the lost with the retained subjects on specific variables, such as age, sex, social class, initial ratings, etc., may be reassuring to the investigator. But this cannot check on the critical issue of comparability of outcome variables.

To minimize sample attrition in the NYLS, a number of guidelines were meticulously followed. The purposes of the study were carefully and clearly explained to each set of parents at the outset, and the reasons for each procedure spelled out. All interviews and test procedures were set at times and places of the parents' convenience. If a parent missed or forgot an appointment, this was accepted cheerfully as of no moment, even if it occurred more than once. Though the interviews were detailed and probing, and sometimes provoked anxiety, any type of stress interview was avoided. If a particular area of questioning evoked sharp resistance or anxiety, the direction of questioning was immediately changed, though a note was made of the parent's reaction. No unexpected procedures were introduced that had not been agreed upon initially. For example, in the special study of our twin subjects, the member of the research staff involved in this project wished to draw blood samples from the children to determine zygosity. We vetoed this otherwise reasonable desire, because we had never mentioned this possibility to the parents, and judged that this intrusive and potentially painful procedure might alienate some of them. So our staff member had to be content with data on fingerprints, height and weight, and hair texture.

The professional staff also made themselves freely available to parents whenever they had any concern over their child's behavior. This included telephone discussions, office appointments, clinical evaluation of the child, arranging for special testing or consultations when indicated, parent counseling and guidance, and regular follow-up of all clinical cases. Parents' requests for letters to schools, special psychometric testing, or advice regarding sibs not in the study were also granted immediately.

We were fortunate in having continuity of staff over the years, and, as a result, most parents felt a personal relationship and an ease of communication with their staff interviewer.

The same strategies were followed with regard to the subjects themselves, when it came to the adolescent and early adulthood interviews. At the end of the latter interview, they were invited to read their childhood records, if they so desired. All responded positively, and most found the descriptions of their early feeding, sleeping and bathing behavior fascinating, which we would not have predicted for such a relatively sophisticated group.

STRATEGIES OF DATA COLLECTION

In the pursuit of the goals of our longitudinal studies, as outlined earlier in this chapter, data have been gathered on the NYLS subjects' behavioral characteristics at succeeding age-periods, on parental attitudes and practices, and on the details of special events and experiences in the subjects' lives. Clinical evaluations and follow-ups have been done in all cases showing behavior suggestive of psychopathology. Our data-gathering procedures were shaped by a number of strategic considerations:

1. The behavioral data for each subject at any age should be gathered from a wide range of daily activities. This assures that judgments of temperament

or other behavioral characteristics would not have to rely on single or unusual situations in which the subject's typical behavioral style might be distorted by some special influence.

2. Description of the subject's behavior should be linked to the environmental context at all times. Thus, if a mother reported that her child cried when put to bed at night, after obtaining the details of the bedtime routine, the next question would be, "What did you do when he cried?" Then, "How did he respond to what you did?" Then, "What did you do then?", and so on until the sequence of interaction was completed. Or, if a teacher reported that a child hung back at the periphery of the class during free-play periods at the beginning of the year, the same sequence of questioning would be pursued. Or, if a 19-year-old described himself as anxious on going away to college, he would be asked where, when and how this anxiety manifested itself, and how he tried to cope with the anxiety. The chain of these sequences was traced until a stable response pattern was established.

3. Special attention should be given to the details of the subject's responses to new and potentially stressful situations. While his behavior with any one such experience might not be typical for him, the data from a number of new situations will illuminate coping mechanisms and aspects of temperamental individuality which might not be as evident in daily routinized life activities.

4. Interviewer data, whether from parent, teacher or subject, and direct observer reports should not be considered satisfactory if they consist primarily of interpretations of subjective intrapsychic states. Such statements may constitute valuable information on the attitudes or special concerns of the reporter, and may even be accurate, and should therefore be recorded. However, such interpretations of subjective states are frequently unreliable. Therefore, if a parent says, "My child is jealous of his baby sister," or a teacher comments, "This youngster is anxious and insecure with his peers," or a young adult states, "I have a conflict about my relationships with the opposite sex," in all cases the question should be raised, "What in his or her behavior leads you to this conclusion?" and the inquiry pressed for objective factual items of behavior.

NEONATAL DATA

Originally, we explored the possibility of obtaining data from the neonatal period onward. A pilot study showed that the newborn infant's behavior varied significantly from day to day, even from hour to hour, and that data collection and analysis would be an exceedingly demanding and complex process. Further exploration indicated that, in general, the infant's behavioral characteristics usually began to show definiteness and consistency of patterning between the fourth and eighth weeks of life. (In a recent study by Torgersen and Kringlen (1978), the genetic component of temperament, in terms of a comparison of homozygotic versus heterozygotic twin pairs, was evident at 2 months of age, but more markedly so at 9 months.) Therefore, the initial interview with the parents was scheduled when the child was 2 to 3 months of age. Initially, some children were accepted into the study at a slightly older age to accelerate the development of the project.

This is not to negate the existence of behavioral individuality in the neonate, which has been documented by a number of workers (Brazelton, 1973; Katcher, unpublished data; Korner, 1973). But the functional significance of these individual differences in the newborn, and their relationship to later temperamental characteristics, remain to be determined.

THE PARENT AS A SOURCE OF DATA

To obtain information on the child's behavior from a wide range of daily activities, and to trace sequences of responses to new situations, the parent potentially represents the most valuable source of data, especially for the early childhood period.

The reliance on parental reports has been the source of much discussion in the research literature in recent years, especially with regard to the rating of the child's temperamental characteristics. Several studies have indicated a low level of correlation of parent temperament ratings derived from standardized questionnaires with ratings derived from direct observations (Vaughn et al., 1981; Sameroff and Seifer, 1982) and suggested that these parent questionnaires may tap subjective parental attributes as much as, if not more so than, the actual objective characteristics of the child. A number of other studies, however, have reported at least moderate correlations between parent temperament questionnaire or interviews and observer rating (Bates and Bayles, 1984; Carey, in press; Dunn and Kendrick, 1980).

In any case, it cannot be assumed that a direct observer's rating of a child's behavior is necessarily more accurate than the parent's report. Direct observations have their own methodological problems. These include potential intrusiveness of the observer and potential subject reactivity to this intrusiveness; limited access to the subject with a limited sample of the subject's behavior; and the theoretical bias of the observer leading to a circumscribed range of behavior that is sampled. As one researcher has put it, a time-limited sample of direct observation suffers from "the unknown effects of the presence of the observer, the representativeness of the sample of interaction observed, and the coding of the flow of interaction into units for analysis . . . a mother's behavior probably varies in important respects as a function of whether father, grandparents, siblings, or guests are present; the other stressors in her life; and, most important, the immediately preceding child behavior" (Martin, 1975, p. 470). Direct observers may also have their own biases, whether of racial, religious, class, or sex origin. A high level of interobserver reliability may indicate that the observations are accurate, or else that the observers share the same bias. Beyond these potentially distorting effects of the observer's or tester's theoretical focus and special prejudices, specific idiosyncratic patterns of behavior may have significant effects on the child's functioning (Thomas, Hertzig et al., 1971).

A number of standardized and tested parent temperament questionnaires from early infancy to adult life have been developed (Thomas and Chess, 1981; Lerner et al., 1982; Thomas, Mittelman et al., 1982; Carey, in press). But no comprehensive standardized protocols for assessing temperament by direct observation have yet been worked out. The development of such standardized protocols would make possible the systematic study of the relationships between parental reports and direct observation ratings.

As of now, it is clear that the parents constitute a prime source of data on their child's behavioral characteristics, as well as on the details of special life events and the child's reactions to such events. Information obtained by interviews is apt to show greater correlations with direct observations than do data obtained by questionnaires (Thomas, Chess et al., 1963; Dunn and Kendrick, 1980). However, the time-consuming demands of interviews often make them impractical for any large-scale study. As a result, it becomes necessary to use the more economical questionnaire technique. There is no evidence for a systematic source of bias in parental reports (Lyon and Plomin, 1981; Thomas, Chess and Korn, 1982). More precise and reliable parental data are obtained from specific objective questions than from requests for overall general ratings (Carey, 1970).

OUR PARENTAL INTERVIEWS

In line with the above considerations, we have utilized detailed parental reports obtained by interview as a primary source of data for the early childhood period. At older age-periods, as the range of the child's functioning expanded, the parental reports were supplemented by school observations, teacher interviews, and behavioral observations during the course of psychometric testing.

Our parent interview protocols for sequential age-periods always focused on obtaining detailed objective descriptions of behavior in the daily routines of living and the responses to environmental change and special life events.

Subjective judgments by the parents were recorded as potentially useful information, but were not utilized in the scoring of temperamental traits. In many families both parents participated in the interviews, and in the others only the mother. Where both parents were present, there was consistency and agreement between them as to the facts of the child's behavior, though there frequently were disagreements in their interpretation of the "meaning" of one or another behavioral characteristic.

To minimize distortions of retrospective recall, the parent interviews were conducted frequently, and emphasis was placed on descriptions of events and behavior close to the time of the interview. During the first 18 months of the child's life, the parent interviews were scheduled every 3 months, then every 6 months until 5 years of age, and yearly thereafter until 7–8 years. At each age-stage, the range of questions was expanded to obtain behavioral information concerning the child's development and utilization of new modes of functioning. These included characteristic patterns of learning, problem-solving and social interactions, responses to success and failure, and the form and content of adaptive behavior.

Limitations in funding then made continued parent interviews of the entire sample impossible, except for systematic evaluations and follow-ups of all subjects showing evidence of a behavior disorder. Most of the parents were interviewed again when the subjects were 16 years of age, and all surviving parents interviewed again when the subjects were 18–22 years old, as detailed below.

SCHOOL OBSERVATIONS AND TEACHER INTERVIEWS

Almost 90 percent of the children attended nursery school, starting at either 3 or 4 years of age. A yearly 1–2 hour period of observation of each child was conducted in nursery school, kindergarten and the first grade, and scheduled to include, whenever possible, a free-play period. The observations were made by a research staff member who had no previous knowledge of the child's history or behavior. The observer sat unobtrusively in a corner of the schoolroom, and made a running account in concrete descriptive terms of every observable verbal, motor and gestural interaction of the child with materials, other children, and adults. The child being observed had no knowledge that this was being done.

The teacher interview was conducted by a staff member other than the observer, who also had no knowledge of the parent interviews with the child. The interview protocol was modelled on the parent interview form, and emphasized descriptive details of the child's day-to-day behavior with respect to routine events, play activity, responses to people, mood and emotional responses. Detailed accounts were obtained of the child's first reaction to starting nursery school, and the sequence of responses until a stable adaptation was achieved. These interviews were done at yearly intervals through the first grade, and constituted a rich source of data on many aspects of the child's behavioral characteristics and adaptive patterns.

PARENTAL PRACTICES AND ATTITUDES INTERVIEW

When the child was 3 years old, a special structured interview to elicit information regarding parental practices and attitudes was held with each mother and father separately but simultaneously. These interviews were conducted and taped by two staff members who had had no previous contact with the parents. Immediately following the interview, each parent was rated on a number of categories pertaining to the characteristics of the home and to specific parental practices and attitudes.

IQ TESTS AND BEHAVIORAL OBSERVATION

IQ testing was done at 3 and 6 years, using the Stanford-Binet, Form L. All children were tested, except those few whose families were out of New York for an extended period at those ages. At 9 years, IQ testing was repeated, using the Wechsler Intelligence Scale for Children (WISC). Because of limited resources, only those 9-year-old subjects were tested who had by then not moved from the New York City area. This comprised 50 subjects.

Direct observations of the child's behavior preceding, during, and immediately following the testing at 3 and 6 years was also done. A separate observer sat in a corner of the testing office, stationed there before the child and psychologist entered, and made a detailed factual written running account of the child's behavior and verbalization in the pretest warm-up period, the testing procedure itself, and the final period of free play and clean-up after the test itself was completed.

CLINICAL EVALUATION

Inasmuch as a primary objective of the NYLS involved the influence of temperamental individuality on the development and evolution of behavior disorders, special attention was paid to ensure that each case with evidence of behavioral deviation was identified and fully evaluated clinically. We were not content with data which relied exclusively on the reports of symptoms by parents or teachers, but used these reports as the initial step in a detailed standard clinical psychiatric evaluation.

At the time each infant was admitted to the NYLS, as well as to our other longitudinal studies, the parents were told that the research staff included a child psychiatrist (S.C.), who would be ready to provide a psychiatric evaluation and recommendations if behavioral difficulties of any kind occurred at any time in the child's development. The parents also knew that the research staff included a clinical psychologist who could, as required, participate in the evaluation of the problem.

Parents reported their concerns over the child's behavior to the staff interviewer, either during the regularly scheduled interviews or in the intervening periods by telephone or letter. Teacher reports of difficult behavior were obtained during the regularly scheduled yearly interviews through the first grade. In one case, the existence of deviant behavior was first identified for us by the clinical psychologist in the course of her psychometric testing of the child at 3 years of age.

Not every child whose behavior was brought to notice in one of these ways was then scheduled for a psychiatric evaluation. The information in each case was referred to the child psychiatrist, who then decided whether clinical diagnostic intervention was required. In many instances, the reported problems represented age-specific behaviors that, though troublesome, were not suggestive of pathological deviation. In still other cases, it appeared clear that the issue was a simple one involving inappropriateness in the routines which the parent had adopted to manage the given child. In these instances, the psychiatrist transmitted her judgments and suggestions to the parents through the staff interviewer. If the problem behavior then disappeared, no further action was taken, though special attention was given to the subsequent reports by parents and teachers to ensure that the original benign judgments had been accurate. In other cases, however, a desirable alteration in the child's behavior did not occur, and a psychiatric evaluation was then advised.

In other cases, the symptom patterns reported by the interviewer were of such a nature as to arouse immediate psychiatric concern. In such cases, a direct immediate clinical evaluation was advised instead of attempting to remedy the disturbances through indirect transmission of parent guidance.

In all cases where clinical psychiatric evaluation was recommended, the parents responded positively and cooperated fully in all the necessary arrangements.

All the psychiatric evaluations in childhood and adolescence were made by one of us (S.C.). In the early adult period, the clinical evaluations were made primarily by the other author (A.T.), as detailed below under Early Adult

Life Interviews. In one case, the parents had gone on their own to another psychiatrist, and a full report was obtained from this therapist. The evaluation consisted of a full clinical history from the parents, followed by a play session with the younger children and a focused interview with the older ones, and ending with a second discussion with the parents (Thomas, Chess and Birch, 1968, pp. 32–33).

Special sensory, neurological or psychological studies were undertaken when a youngster's history and the psychiatric findings suggested the need. If the presenting complaint and findings involved aspects of school functioning, additional data were obtained by focused teacher interviews and school observations.

In the final discussion, the parents were advised of the diagnosis and presented with recommendations for management (this was not done once the subjects had reached early adulthood). The parents were also encouraged to raise questions and to react to the recommendations. Their reactions and queries provided a rich source of information on their liking for the child, their responses to his qualities as a person, and the manner in which they approached their responsibilities for helping with his difficulties.

In some cases, of course, the clinical psychiatric evaluation resulted in the judgment that no significant behavior disorder in fact existed. In those cases, the parents and, in the cases in adolescence or early adult life, the subjects themselves were so advised. Any appropriate suggestions for desirable change in behavior, whether on the part of the parents or subjects, were offered in addition. Special follow-up of these cases was pursued to check on the accuracy of this initial judgment. In several cases, the subjects developed increased or additional symptoms, and on a second clinical study clear-cut evidence of behavior disorder was found.

Detailed follow-up of all subjects with behavior problems was carried out at all age-periods through information obtained from parents and teachers, and, when necessary, further direct clinical interviews with the subjects themselves.

A number of the subjects consulted one of us directly either in later adolescence or early adult life because of their own concerns over their behavioral functioning or the existence of disturbing emotional reactions. In all cases, interviews were arranged immediately and sufficient discussions carried through to define the problem and to formulate an appropriate plan of management or treatment.

Where direct psychotherapy of a clinical case was required, in some cases the parents or subjects made their own arrangements, and in others we made appropriate referrals. In a handful of cases, one of us took the responsibility for treatment, either because of the parents' insistence or the inabilitity of the subject to pay for therapy. In those subjects in treatment with another therapist, we obtained relevant data from the therapist, if given the parents' and/or subjects' consent to make this request.

The question has been raised with us several times whether we were contaminating the objectivity of our research data by this active involvement in the treatment of the behavior disorder cases, either through parent guidance or direct psychotherapy. This therapeutic service, however, was necessary for maintenance of the sample. Otherwise, a number of parents would certainly have felt that we were concerned only with our research project and indifferent to the welfare of their children, and would have lost their interest in cooperating with us. Beyond this, through our therapeutic involvement we were aware of the specifics of advice and counseling given to the parents of behaviorally disturbed children, as well as of the parental responses to these guidance procedures. This information provided very valuable data in a number of cases, which would have been unavailable in accurate and sequential details if the parents had been receiving therapeutic help elsewhere.

SUBJECTIVE INTRAPSYCHIC DATA IN CHILDHOOD

We considered it important to gather data on the subjective state of our subjects at all age periods—their moods, thoughts and goals; their feelings about people and activities; their imagination and flights of fancy; their understanding and confusion of the meaning of events, words and the behavior of others; their fears, hopes and disappointments. Important realities may be unappreciated by children, while ominous spectres may be constructed out of trivialities.

In infancy, before the development of effective communication through language, it is clear that feelings and thoughts must be inferred from observable behavior. If a new mobile is hung across the crib of a 6-month-old baby and the baby cries when it begins to move and tinkle, we infer that he is frightened or startled. Should he laugh or smile, pleasure could reasonably be deduced. Should he turn his face away, disinterest could be inferred. If an initial response of crying should be changed to smiling and touching on subsequent presentation of the same mobile, we could interpret the first negative response to a temperamental withdrawal reaction, or to a difficulty in assimilating a stimulus which was highly discrepant to an already established intrapsychic schema. We can infer that the pleasurable response could have a number of components—the shape or the sound of the mobile, or the evidence that the child himself could produce such special movements and noises by his own activity. Perhaps he gradually gives his preferential attention to one aspect of the toy. Although we cannot probe verbally for the reason, we can note the fact.

As language develops, one can have long conversations with children. Some youngsters even as young as 2 years can give accurate and detailed reports of events. Yet if such a young child is asked how he felt or what he thought the incident meant, one draws a blank. He may say, "I cried" or "I liked it," but will not elaborate further on the nuances of mood and thought that we can assume must have been present. Of course, a young child may make statements of strong feelings, especially to a parent. "You never give me anything," "You're a bad mommy," "I'll flush you down the toilet." Yet moments later, even if the parent has stood firm with the frustrating prohibition, the child may become engaged in other tasks with clear enjoyment, and communicate happily with the parent he has just finished denouncing. Thus, the fact of age appropriate verbal fluency in the preschool child does not at all involve the ability to report more than immediate feelings and thoughts.

At age 6 years we considered the possibility of obtaining significant subjective data from our subjects. We judged that the use of projective tests would be most promising, and incorporated two such procedures into the 6-year IQ testing session. One was the so-called Despert Fables, in which a number of incomplete allegorical stories are told to the youngster, and he is then asked to complete the tales. For example, a baby bird falls to the ground, and on two nearby tree branches at equal distance from the little bird the mother and father birds are sitting. The youngster's elaboration of the story is then presumed to reflect his feelings and thoughts about his family relationships. The second projective test was a series of pictures, for each of which the subject was asked to make up a story. We decided not to use the children's version of the Thematic Apperception Test because of its emphasis on problems and pathology, but devised our own set of neutral pictures. One, for example, showed a group of boys playing ball and a solitary youngster watching. Another showed a girl reading a book and an adult looking over her shoulder.

The results with these two projective tests were most disappointing. To the Despert Fables, the replies were variants of "baby stuff," "who cares," "that's a stupid question." To the pictures, the responses were primarily factual descriptions of the depicted scene with scanty imaginative elaboration. It must be remembered that this paucity of subjective data came from youngsters who were at the same time highly cooperative and interested in the task items of the IQ test. It was clear that, while with persistent questioning we might obtain more extended elaborations of the fables and stories, these would be unreliable indicators of significant aspects of the child's feelings, thoughts, and special preoccupations. We, therefore, did not make this attempt.

When our oldest subjects were 9 years of age, we explored again the feasibility of obtaining a reliable body of subjective data. One of us (S.C.) interviewed a group of 9-year-olds drawn from our friends' children and a group of children without psychiatric problems on a pediatric unit. Questions were asked such as, "What do you want to do when you grow up?", "Do you have any special feelings or thoughts that bother you?", "Tell me three wishes you want to come true," "What is the nicest thing that could happen to you?", "What is the worst thing that could happen to you?", etc. Again, the answers were for the most part noncommittal, formalistic, or even evasive. These negative findings were not surprising, given the frequent experience in clinical practice in which the parent alerts the therapist to a special meaningful experience that has just occurred, and yet the child does not bring this up spontaneously in the sessions.

By contrast, it was often possible to obtain significant subjective data in the clinical psychiatric interviews. Here the psychiatrist knew ahead of time from the parent interview what was bothering the child and how he was expressing this verbally and behaviorally. But it was still necessary for the psychiatrist to bring this information up directly to the child to stimulate expressions of feelings and thoughts—at least in some cases.

In the 16-year-subject interviews the responses were highly variable as to subjective content. Some youngsters talked freely about their hopes and plans, their self-evaluation, and their special concerns and worries. Others were noncommittal and even wary in these areas, and others were evasive or used denial. For example, one subject who later described periods of depression and self-condemnatory fantasies in adolescence, had presented herself in the adolescent interview as cheerful and happy with no special worries.

In the early adult life subject interviews a great deal of information on subjective states was communicated freely by most, though by no means all, subjects. Though these data appeared meaningful, we would not assume that they represented a comprehensive inventory in depth of the subject's feelings, ideas, fantasies and special concerns.

ADOLESCENT INTERVIEWS

When the subjects were 16–17 years old, semi-structured interviews were conducted separately with them and their parents in 107 cases. Primarily, those not interviewed were the youngest group, who were interviewed at 17–19 years of age at the time of the early adult life follow-up project. Three parents and 7 subjects refused to be interviewed. (All of these did agree for the subsequent early adult follow-up, and were interviewed then.) In 8 families who had moved out of the New York area, the interviews were done by mail.

The interview questions covered self-image, relationships with parents, sibs and peers, school functioning, special interests, sexual activity, plans for the future, substance use and abuse, and any special emotional reactions or problems. In each area, an overall general statement was obtained and then elaborated through detailed specific questioning. Discrepancies between subject and parent accounts were rare, but were noted when they occurred.

EARLY ADULT LIFE INTERVIEWS

All the subjects and parents were interviewed in person. (Adequate travel funds made it possible to interview in person even those who now lived at a distance from New York.) There were several subjects who initially refused the interview, but agreed later on, and cooperated fully once they agreed.

Age of subjects at time of interviews was as follows:

Age	Male	Female	Total
24.0 - 24. 11 mos.	3	1	4
23.0 - 23. 11 mos.	8	3	11
22.0 - 22. 11 mos.	18	19	37
21.0 - 21. 11 mos.	9	10	19
20.0 - 20. 11 mos.	16	18	34
19.0 - 19. 11 mos.	4	9	13
18.0 - 18. 11 mos.	4	5	9
17.8 - 17. 11 mos.	3	1	4
17.4 - 17. 5 mos.	1	1	2
	66	67	133

The early adult interview represented an expansion of the adolescent protocol, with questions reworded to make them age-appropriate, and with additional emphasis on subjective issues (self-evaluation, expressiveness and communication) and questions designed to identify temperamental characteristics. Questions were added on medical history and work functioning.

The early adult subject interview is reproduced in Appendix A.

The interviews were completed in 2–3 hours, in almost all cases at one sitting. A few subjects showed reluctance to pursue a specific area in depth, though they were otherwise fully cooperative. With these few limited exceptions, all the subjects answered all questions freely, though the extent and character of the elaboration of answers showed a wide range of variation.

In about 60 percent of cases, the interview was conducted jointly by the staff interviewer and one of us (A.T.), to establish interrator reliabilities. No subject objected to this procedure. In the other cases, this joint procedure was not possible, as with an interview outside the city, and the subject was interviewed by a single interviewer.

Two-thirds of the subjects were easily agreeable to having the interviews audiotaped. In these cases, the tapes were rated by an experienced clinical psychiatrist, who had no knowledge of the subjects.

For the 133 subject interviews, there were 3 raters in 50 cases, 2 in 29, and one in 54.

The interviews with the parents covered the same range of questions as did the subject interviews. In some areas, such as sexual activity and substance use, the parents varied widely in their knowledge of their youngsters' functioning.

MISCELLANEOUS DATA

Information on complications of pregnancy or delivery was obtained from the mothers during the first interview. Special events, such as divorce, parental death, major illnesses and accidents, were recorded in an ongoing fashion.

The 50 subjects whose IQ scores were obtained at 9 years were also given the Wide Range Achievement Test (WRAT). Achievement test scores were also obtained from the schools for reading and arithmetic through the sixth grade for 116 subjects.

The Offer Self-Image questionnaire was administered to 50 subjects at the end of the early adult interview. The final form of the early adult temperament questionnaire (Thomas, Mittelman et al., 1982) then became available, and was administered to 70 subjects at the end of their interviews. It was not considered desirable to give both questionnaires at the same sitting following a long interview. In the remaining 13 subjects, time pressures made it undesirable to administer either questionnaire.

CHAPTER 4

Subject and Parent Ratings

A number of quantitative subject and parent ratings were developed so that the power of appropriate statistical analyses could be utilized to the maximum possible extent.

a) *for the subjects*—temperament scores based on the parent interviews for the first 5 years of life; temperament scores based on the early adult life interviews; global adjustment scores at 3 and 5 years based on the parent interviews, and at 5 years from the teacher interview; adjustment score in early adult life from the subject interview; presence or absence of a psychiatric diagnosis (clinical case) at various age-periods.

b) *for the parents*—ratings of parental attitudes and practices from the special structured interviews held when the child was 3 years old.

TEMPERAMENT AND ITS RATING IN CHILDHOOD

Our definition and categorization of temperament have been reported in a number of publications (Thomas, Chess et al., 1963; Thomas, Chess et al., 1968; Thomas and Chess, 1977) and will be summarized briefly.

For the purposes of the analysis of behavioral phenomena, it is often empirically useful to conceptualize behavior in terms of abilities (the *what* of behavior), motivations (the *why* of behavior) and temperament (the *how* of behavior). Two children may dress themselves with equal skillfulness or ride a bicycle with the same dexterity, and have the same motives for engaging in these activities. Two adolescents may display similar learning ability and

41

intellectual interests, and their academic goals may coincide. Two adults may show the same degree of technical expertise in their work, and have the same reason for devoting themselves to their jobs. Yet these two children, adolescents or adults may differ significantly with regard to the quickness with which they move, the ease with which they approach a new physical environment, social situation or task, and the effort required by others to distract them when they are absorbed in an activity. In other words, their abilities and motivations may be similar, yet their temperaments may be different. Or, in other instances, temperaments may be similar, and abilities and/or motivations differ.

Nine categories of temperament were established by an inductive content analysis of the parent interview protocols in the infancy period of the first 22 NYLS subjects. A quantitative item-scoring method was developed and all parent and teacher interview protocols at succeeding age-periods could be scored for these categories. The 9 categories of temperament and their definitions are:

1. Activity Level: the motor component present in a given child's functioning and the diurnal proportion of active and inactive periods.
2. Rhythmicity (Regularity): the predictability and/or unpredictability in time of any biological function.
3. Approach or Withdrawal: the nature of the initial response to a new stimulus, be it a food, toy, place, person, etc. Approach responses are positive, whether displayed by mood expression (smiling, verbalizations, etc.) or motor activity (swallowing a new food, reaching for a new toy, active play, etc.) Withdrawal reactions are negative, whether displayed by mood expression (crying, fussing, grimacing; verbalizations, etc.) or motor activity (moving away, spitting new food out, pushing a new toy away, etc.)
4. Adaptability: responses to new or altered situations. One is not concerned with the nature of the initial responses, but with the ease with which they are modified in desired directions.
5. Threshold of Responsiveness: the intensity level of stimulation that is necessary to evoke a discernible response, irrespective of the specific form that the response may take, or the sensory modality affected.
6. Intensity of Reaction: the energy level of response, irrespective of its quality or direction.
7. Quality of Mood: the amount of pleasant, joyful and friendly behavior; as contrasted with unpleasant, crying and unfriendly behavior.
8. Distractibility: the effectiveness of extraneous environmental stimuli in interfering with or altering the direction of the ongoing behavior.
9. Attention Span and Persistence: two categories which are related. Attention span concerns the length of time a particular activity is pursued by

the child. Persistence refers to the continuation of an activity direction in the face of obstacles to its continuation.

Each category was scored on a three-point scale—high, intermediate or low—from the parent and teacher interviews. Item scoring was used (Thomas, Chess et al., 1963) and the item scores transformed into a weighted score for each category on each record. To avoid contamination by "halo effects," no successive interviews of a given child were scored contiguously. High intra- and interscores reliability, at the 90 percent level of agreement, was achieved.

For purposes of analysis, the temperament scores for all the parent interviews in any year were pooled for each child. Thus the ratings for year 1 represent all the scores from birth to 1 year; for year 2 all the scores from 1 year, 1 month to 2 years, etc. For each category, the range of scores was from zero to two.

EASY, DIFFICULT AND SLOW-TO-WARM-UP TEMPERAMENTS

Three temperamental constellations of functional significance have been defined by qualitative analysis of the data and by factor analysis (Thomas, Chess et al., 1968). The first group is characterized by regularity, positive approach responses to new stimuli, high adaptability to change, and mild or moderate mood intensity which is preponderantly positive. These children quickly develop regular sleep and feeding schedules, take to most new foods easily, smile at strangers, adapt easily to a new school, accept most frustration with little fuss, and accept the rules of new games with no trouble. Such a youngster is aptly called the easy child, and is usually a joy to his parents, pediatricians, and teachers. This group comprises about 40 percent of our NYLS sample.

At the opposite end of the temperamental spectrum is the group with irregularity in biological functions, negative withdrawal responses to new stimuli, non-adaptability or slow adaptability to change, and intense mood expressions which are frequently negative. These children show irregular sleep and feeding schedules, slow acceptance of new foods, prolonged adjustment periods to new routines, people, or situations, and relatively frequent loud periods of crying. Laughter, also, is characteristically loud. Frustration typically produces a violent tantrum. This is the difficult child, and mothers and pediatricians find such youngsters difficult indeed. This group comprises about 10 percent of our NYLS sample.

The third noteworthy temperamental constellation is marked by a combination of negative responses of mild intensity to new stimuli with slow adaptability after repeated contact. In contrast to the difficult children, these youngsters are characterized by mild intensity of reactions, whether positive or negative, and by less tendency to show irregularity of biological functions. The negative mild responses to new stimuli can be seen in the first encounter with the bath, a new food, a stranger, a new place or a new school situation. If given the opportunity to reexperience such new situations over time and without pressure, such a child gradually comes to show quiet and positive interest and involvement. A youngster with this characteristic sequence of response is referred to as the slow-to-warm-up child, an apt if inelegant designation. About 15 percent of our NYLS sample falls into this category.

As can be seen from the above percentages, not all children fit into one of these three temperamental groups. This results from the varying and different combinations of temperamental traits which are manifested by individual children. Also, among those children who do fit one of these three patterns, there is a wide range in degree of manifestation. Some are extremely easy children in practically all situations; others are relatively easy but not always so. A few children are extremely difficult with all new situations and demands; others show only some of these characteristics and relatively mildly. For some children it is highly predictable that they will warm up slowly in any new situation; others warm up slowly with certain types of new stimuli or demands, but warm up quickly in others.

It should be emphasized that the various temperamental constellations all represent variations within normal limits. Any child may be easy, difficult or slow-to-warm-up temperamentally, have a high or low activity level, distractibility and low persistence or the opposite, or any other relatively extreme rating score in a sample of children for a specific temperamental attribute. However, such an amodal rating is not a criterion of psychopathology, but rather an indication of the wide range of behavioral styles exhibited by normal children.

GENERALIZATION OF TEMPERAMENT CATEGORIES

It has been possible to rate each of the 9 categories of temperament in each subject at different age-periods in our NYLS, Puerto Rican working sample, and mentally retarded and congenital rubella groups. The 9 categories and the 3 constellations (easy, difficult and slow-to-warm-up) have also by now been identified in a large number of studies from many centers in this country, as well as in various European and Asian countries (Thomas and Chess, 1977; Ciba Foundation, 1982). Other categories and constellations of temperament have been suggested by various workers (Buss and Plomin, 1975;

Matheny, 1980, Rothbart, 1981), but their replicability and functional significance have yet to be demonstrated.

A number of questionnaires to rate temperament in the various age-periods of childhood, adolescence and early adult life have now been developed (Thomas and Chess, 1977; Carey, 1982; Lerner, Palermo et al., 1982; McNeil and Personn-Blennow, 1982; Thomas, Mittelman et al., 1982). A protocol for obtaining temperament data in clinical practice has also been developed (Thomas and Chess, 1977, Appendix D).

TEMPERAMENT RATINGS IN EARLY ADULT LIFE

Temperament ratings for each of the 9 categories on a 7-point scale were made by each of the 3 raters from the subject interviews. For the 132 subjects included in the quantitative analyses, there were 3 raters in 50 cases, 2 in 29, and one in 53. (One subject who had been out of the country was interviewed too late for inclusion in the quantitative analyses.)

Interrater reliabilities for the 9 categories were calculated on 16 subjects and then adjusted for systematic interrater differences. All the ratings for each of the first 25 subjects were pooled and the reliability of the mean scores determined. (In these first 25 subjects, rater 1 rated 25 subjects, rater 2 did 18, and rater 3 did 23 from the audiotapes).

As can be seen from Table 1, there was marked variability in the reliability levels for the 9 categories, with sensory threshold and intensity being espe-

TABLE 1
Interrater Reliabilities Early Adult Temperament

Category	Reliabilities	Adjusted for Systematic Differences	Pooled Ratings
Activity	.71	.80	.66
Rhythmicity	.62	.68	.76
Adaptability	.58	.59	.75
Approach/ Withdrawal	.84	.84	.71
Threshold	.15	.23	.72
Intensity	.00	.01	.33
Quality Mood	.37	.48	.68
Distractibility	.61	.59	.54
Persistence	.43	.46	.75

cially unsatisfactory. Adjustment for systematic interrater differences showed a marginal improvement, while the pooled ratings showed a substantial improvement in reliability levels for four categories, a modest improvement for two, and a modest decrease for three categories. In all analyses the average scores of the pooled ratings were used.

The possible reasons for the very poor interrater reliabilities for sensory threshold and intensity were explored with the 3 raters. For threshold, the reasons remained obscure. For intensity, impressionistic judgments by one of the raters of the subject's "depth" of feeling rather than a reliance on the subject's statements and overt behavior appeared partially responsible. In addition, the rater who rated only from the audiotapes felt that it was especially difficult to evaluate this category without the aid of facial expressions, gestures and body movements.

GLOBAL ADJUSTMENT SCORES AT 3 AND 5 YEARS

The interviews with parents and teachers in the child's first 5 years of life emphasized detailed descriptive accounts of the child's functioning in the activities of daily life, such as sleep, feeding, elimination, play, reactions to new situations and people, etc. In addition to item-scoring for temperament, these data also made it possible to develop rating schedules for the child's overall behavioral adjustment. A survey of the literature was first undertaken to determine whether the adjustment rating scales developed in other studies could be applied to our protocols. In general, either the rating criteria were too broad and encompassing to be applicable to our parent and teacher interviews or the categories of pathology were too severe for our sample. We therefore decided to develop our own rating scale by an inductive analysis of our own data.

Ratings of level of adjustment on a 5-point scale were formulated for the 3-year parent interviews in 11 areas — sleeping; eating; elimination; fears, tics and rituals; speech and communication; motor activity; relationship with parents; discipline; relationship with sibs; nonfamily relationships; and coping and task mastery. For each area, a number of specific items of behavior are listed and rated separately, and an average is then obtained. A 12th category, relationship to school, was added for the 5-year parent interview. A similar rating scale, with appropriate modifications, was developed for the 5-year teacher interview. Global adjustment scores were calculated by adding up the average score for each category and dividing by the number of categories. A copy of the adjustment rating scale for the 3-year parent interview is attached as Appendix B.

Interrater reliabilities for the 3-year scale were above .80 for 7 of the 11 categories, .75 for sleep, .68 for fears, .64 for eating, and .32 for coping. The category of coping showed very little variation in scores, and this may account for its low reliability level. For the 5-year parent and teacher interviews, the interrater reliabilities were substantially higher, all being above .88.

ADJUSTMENT SCORES AT EARLY ADULT LIFE

As with our 3- and 5-year adjustment ratings, a survey of other scales for rating early adult adjustment indicated problems in applying them to our data. We therefore developed a 7-point rating scale with 13 items for assessing adjustment from an inductive analysis of the first group of early adult life subject interviews. The 13 items included self-evaluation, relationship with family, school functioning, social functioning, sexual functioning, goals, implementation of goals, patterns of coping, communication, and emotional expressiveness, as well as several items reflecting personality attributes rather than levels of adjustment — person orientation, task orientation, and routines of daily life. Areas of defensiveness (sex, physical appearance, school functioning, etc.), symptoms such as anxiety, depression, aggressiveness, psychosomatic complaints, etc., and any clinical psychiatric diagnosis were also recorded.

Interrater reliabilities were determined on 16 subjects as with the temperament scores, and then adjusted for systematic interrater differences. All the ratings for each of the first 25 subjects were pooled and the reliability of the mean scores determined.

As with the temperament interrater reliabilities, these reliability levels show a great deal of variability, with only a marginal improvement when adjusted for systematic interrater differences, and a modest or marked improvement when pooled ratings are used.

A global adaptation score on a 9-point scale was also developed for rating each early adult subject interview. This score was derived from a qualitative composite judgment of the subject's level of adaptation in the significant areas of functioning. A copy of the global adaptation scale, with criteria for scoring, is attached as Appendix C.

Interrater reliabilities for the global adaptation score were calculated from the first 41 subject interviews which involved 2 or 3 of the raters. Rater 1 was involved in all 41 interviews, rater 2 in 28, and rater 3 in the 35 which were audiotaped.

The intraclass correlation was calculated from these 41 subject interviews. This calculation results in an estimate of per rater reliability, i.e., how close

TABLE 2
Interrater Reliabilities Early Adult Adjustment

Category	Reliabilities	Adjusted for Systematic Differences	Pooled Ratings
Self evaluation	.79	.82	.83
Family relationship	.62	.62	.76
School	.77	.76	.87
Social	.39	.40	.83
Sex	.60	.62	.74
Goals	.60	.65	.75
Implementing goals	.62	.80	.81
Coping	.45	.72	.77
Person orientation	.31	.33	.72
Task orientation	.59	.58	.71
Routines	.23	.30	.63
Communication	.25	.27	.67
Emotional expression	.39	.46	.68

would one of these 3 raters come to a typical other rater if he were interviewing subjects on his own. The intraclass correlation as calculated was 0.77.

Pearson product-moment correlations were also calculated. These product-moment correlations were as follows:

- Rater 1 with Rater 2 — 0.83
- Rater 1 with Rater 3 — 0.82
- Rater 2 with Rater 3 — 0.87

The high level of these intraclass and product-moment correlations indicate that the global adaptation score is a reliable instrument for rating our early adult life subject interviews.

Bootstrap score: For the determination of the final behavioral adjustment score in early life to be utilized in our quantitative analyses, the bootstrapping technique was used (Goldberg, 1970). With this technique, a set of elements (the specific areas of adjustment) is first subjected to an overall clinical judgment (the global adaptation score). Then, using that judgment as a criterion in a multiple regression analysis with the element scores as independent variables, the regression equation is generated that estimates the overall judgment. The data finally used are not the actual judgments, but their regression estimates. These estimates have been found to be superior in several fields. The rationale for their superiority is that the regression equation distills the implicit rating policies that are implicit when the overall judgment is made, but unlike the latter, are not subject to day-to-day variation in rater judgment, or the intrusion of irrelevant factors into the judgment.

A multiple regression analysis was performed for each of the 3 raters, in which the early adult global adaptation score for each subject of that rater was the dependent variable, and the independent variables were the 13 specific categories (self-evaluation, school, social, etc.). Each of these analyses produced two results: a) a "bootstrapped" or predicted global adjustment score for each rater and each subject, and b) regression coefficients for each adjustment category for each rater.

The regression coefficients associated with each rater's assessment of the individual adjustment categories did not differ significantly, as determined by Marascuilo's significance test (1966).

The averages of the 3 raters' "bootstrapped" or predicted global scores were the final early adult adjustment ratings utilized in the various quantitative analyses.

CLINICAL PSYCHIATRIC DIAGNOSES

The details of the clinical psychiatric evaluations are reported in Chapter 3.

All the psychiatric diagnoses throughout childhood were made by one of us (S.C.), on the basis of a standard clinical diagnostic study. The clinical evaluations in adolescence were done jointly by the two of us (S.C. and A.T.), from a detailed analysis of both the subject and parent adolescent interviews, as well as from the special data available in a number of cases. This latter information included such items as clinical evaluations, either as follow-up sessions in adolescence for earlier diagnosed clinical cases, or as new evaluations for subjects presenting symptoms or deviant behavior for the first time in adolescence, as well as school reports and special psychological test results.

Clinical diagnoses in early adult life were made from the subject interviews by the 3 raters. All three were experienced mental health clinicians; one had had no previous contact with the NYLS and a second not since the early childhood period. Interrater reliability for the clinical evaluations was determined for the first 67 subject interviews. In 19 of these subjects clinical evaluations were made by 3 raters, in 23 subjects by 2 raters, and in 25 by one rater. Of the 19 subjects with 3 raters, there was complete agreement in 17 cases. In one case there was agreement as to the presence of severe psychiatric disorder, but disagreement as to specific diagnoses. In one case, 2 raters agreed on no psychiatric disorder, and the third made a diagnosis of personality disorder. Of the 23 subjects with 2 raters, there was agreement in 21 cases. In the other 2 cases there was disagreement, with one rater's evaluation being no psychiatric disorder and the other's being personality disorder.

In the 4 cases of disagreement, the clinical evaluation made by one of us (A.T.), who had been one of the interviewers in all 4 cases, was chosen. All diagnoses for age periods have been converted to DSM-III categories (Diagnostic and Statistical Manual of Mental Disorders, Third Edition, American Psychiatric Association, 1980).

PARENTAL ATTITUDES AND PRACTICES RATINGS

These ratings were made from the special structured interviews with both parents, simultaneously but separated, done when the subjects were 3 years old by 2 interviewers who had no other contact with the NYLS.

Immediately following the interview, the interviewer rated the parent on a wide variety of parenting variables. Also recorded were data on typical demographic and background variables. In total, 99 items of information were rated from each interview.

These ratings were subjected to a detailed statistical analysis by Cameron (1977). Of the 99 ratings, he selected 70 as meeting basic statistical criteria for use in correlational analyses. Only the ratings of the mothers were used, since in the overwhelming majority of cases both parents gave identical responses. The 70 items were subjected to cluster analysis by means of the Tryon system. Eight clusters were extracted: 1. parental disapproval, intolerance and rejection; 2. parental conflict regarding each other, together with tendency to negative mutual perceptions; 3. parental strictness vs. permissiveness; 4. maternal concern and protectiveness; 5. depressed living standards. (Since the NYLS parents were of middle- or upper-middle-class status, high scores on this cluster cannot be equated with poverty); 6. limitations on the child's material supports. (This dimension correlated significantly with cluster 5); 7. inconsistent parental discipline; and 8. large family orientation in terms of planning for more than 2 children.

These 8 clusters were used as measures of parental attitudes and practices in the child's preschool age-period.

At the end of each interview, the parents also completed the Parent Attitude Research Instrument (PARI), a questionnaire widely used in the late 1950s. The analysis of the PARI responses showed it to be unsatisfactory for identifying idiosyncratic parental issues and practices in our population. This confirmed the conclusions reached at the time by Becker and Krug (1965) that "the bulk of the evidence suggests that the PARI does not predict much very well." The PARI ratings were therefore not utilized in any of the data analyses.

IQ SCORES

IQ scores were obtained on almost the entire sample at 3 and 6 years, using the Stanford-Binet, and on 50 of the subjects at 9 years, using the WISC. The mean scores and S.D.s are as follows:

Age	Mean IQ Score		S.D.	
	Male	Female	Male	Female
3 yrs.	120.1 (60)*	126.0 (64)	15.8	16.0
6 yrs.	127.0 (57)	124.5 (61)	14.4	13.4
9 yrs.	122.6 (31)	122.3 (19)	15.3	13.0

*The figures in parentheses represent the Ns.

The IQ scores were not utilized in the quantitative analyses. They were included in the qualitative analyses of individual subjects.

CHAPTER 5

The Clinical Sample Over Time

As reported in the previous chapters, we were at all times concerned with the identification of the cases of behavior disorder as they arose in the NYLS sample, with the full clinical evaluation of these cases, with their diagnostic categorization, and with their systematic follow-up.

The detailed quantitative and qualitative analysis of this body of clinical data will be pursued in subsequent chapters. In the present chapter we are concerned with the tabulation of the behavior disorder cases according to age of onset of symptoms, diagnostic categories, severity of symptoms, and outcome in adolescence and early adult life. This tabulation permits the consideration of a number of questions for this sample with its specific demographic characteristics. Does the onset of symptoms in early childhood presage a more unfavorable prognosis than in those cases arising in later childhood? Or, on the contrary, does the normally rapid rate of both physical and psychological development in early childhood make the behavior disorder cases arising in this age-period more amenable to treatment or to spontaneous recovery? What are the differences in incidence of behavior disorders at various age-periods in childhood and adolescence, and what are the factors that may account for these differences? What are the differences in prognosis for the different diagnostic categories? And, finally, what do the findings suggest as to the need for therapeutic intervention?

CHILDHOOD CASES

The childhood cases of behavior disorders are tabulated according to age of onset of symptoms, diagnostic categories, and severity of disturbance in Table 1.

As can be seen from Table 1, the four diagnostic categories into which our childhood clinical sample fell were adjustment disorder, conduct disorder, organic brain syndrome with adjustment disorder, and recurrent major depression. The least severe type of disturbance is adjustment disorder, which is defined in DSM-III as "a maladaptive reaction to an identifiable psychosocial stressor, that occurs within three months after the onset of the stressor. The maladaptive nature of the reaction is indicated by either impairment in social or occupational functioning or symptoms that are in excess of a normal and expected reaction to the stressor. It is assumed that the disturbance will eventually remit after the stressor ceases or, if the stressor persists, when a new level of adaptation is achieved" (*Diagnostic and Statistical Manual of Mental Disorders, Third Edition*, p. 299). Conduct disorder, a more severe disturbance, is defined as "a repetitive and persistent pattern of conduct in which either the basic rights of others or major age-appropriate societal norms

TABLE 1
Age of Onset of Symptoms of Childhood Cases

Original Diagnosis	Age of Onset (Years)				
	Less than 3	3–5	6–8	9–12	Total
Adjustment Disorder					
Mild	2	16	7	0	25
Moderate	1	7	2	0	10
Severe	0	3	1	1	5
Conduct Disorder					
Mild	0	1	0	0	1
Moderate	0	1	0	0	1
Severe	0	0	0	0	0
Organic Brain Syndrome with Adjustment Disorder					
Mild	0	0	1	0	1
Moderate	0	0	0	0	0
Severe	1	0	0	0	1
Recurrent Major Depression	0	0	1	0	1
Total	4	28	12	1	45

or rules are violated. The conduct is more serious than the ordinary mischiefs and pranks of children and adolescents" (*DSM-III*, p. 45). The diagnostic category of organic brain syndrome with adjustment disorder has been utilized for cases of adjustment disorder associated with organic brain syndrome, the latter defined as "a psychological or behavioral abnormality associated with transient or permanent dysfunction of the brain" (*DSM-III*, p. 101). Finally, major depression is defined as "either a dysphoric mood, usually depression, or loss of interest or pleasure in all or almost all usual activities and pastimes. This disturbance is prominent, relatively persistent, and associated with other symptoms of the depressive syndrome" (*DSM-III*, p. 210).

The great majority of the clinical cases in childhood (40 out of 45), as tabulated in Table 1, were adjustment disorders, with the mild cases predominant. The largest number of these cases appeared in the 3–5 year age-period (26), with the next largest at 6–8 years (10), with 3 cases with onset before 3 years, and only one appearing at 9–12 years. The number of cases in the other three more severe diagnostic categories were too few to define any age-period distribution trend.*

Although the total number of clinical cases in childhood seems high, this is a cumulative figure. At any one age-period, the total would be appreciably lower due to the number of recovered cases. Also, a substantial proportion of the adjustment disorder cases might have recovered spontaneously and not come to psychiatric attention if they had not been subjects in our longitudinal study. With these considerations in mind, our figures approximate those of some prevalence studies (Lapouse and Monk, 1958; Rubin and Balow, 1978), though they are higher than those of others (Rutter, Tizard et al., 1976).

OUTCOME OF CHILDHOOD CASES

The outcome of the childhood clinical cases in adolescence are tabulated in Table 2, and the outcome in early adult life in Table 3.

As can be seen from Table 2, the majority of the adjustment disorder cases, 24 out of 40, had recovered and 2 others improved by adolescence. The percentage of recovered and improved cases was not significantly different for the initially mild, moderate or severe cases, being 60, 70, and 60 percent respectively.

---

*The one case of recurrent major depression had been originally diagnosed as a mild adjustment disorder when symptoms first appeared at 8 years, and was included in this diagnostic category in our earlier reports. His subsequent clinical course made for a revision of diagnosis to recurrent major depression. His clinical history is detailed in Chapter 14 (Case 1, Harold).

TABLE 2
Outcome Childhood Disorders in Adolescence

Original Diagnosis	Recovered	Im-proved	Un-changed	Mild-Moderately Worse	Markedly Worse
Adjustment Disorder					
Mild	16	0	3	6	0
Moderate	6	1	0	3	0
Severe	2	1	0	1	1
Conduct Disorder					
Mild	0	0	0	1	0
Moderate	1	0	0	0	0
Organic Brain Syndrome with Adjustment Disorder					
Mild	0	1	0	0	0
Moderate	0	0	0	0	0
Severe	0	0	1	0	0
Recurrent Major Depression	0	0	1	0	0
Total	25	3	5	11	1

As to the predictive significance of early onset of symptoms, 72 percent of the mild adjustment disorder cases had onset of symptoms at 5 years or younger, as compared to 80 percent of the moderate cases, and 60 percent of the severe cases (from Table 1). These figures do not indicate any predictive significance of early symptom onset with regard to severity of the adjustment disorder. A tabulation was also made of the average age of onset of symptoms for those adjustment disorder cases with recovery or improvement as contrasted with those unimproved or worse in adolescence. The average age of the former group was 6.3 years, of the latter 4.0 years, indicating that the cases with earlier onset of symptoms were less likely to show improvement or recovery by adolescence.

As can be seen from Table 3, the number of recovered adjustment disorder cases in early adult life had risen to 29, with 5 additional improved from adolescence. All the 24 cases evaluated as recovered in adolescence remained so in early adult life, except for 2 subjects who showed recurrence of severe symptoms. (The detailed clinical course of one of these cases, Bruce, is presented in Chapter 13). The two cases with improvement in adolescence went on to recovery in early adult life. Thus, a favorable clinical course of a childhood adjustment disorder into adolescence was highly predictive of a con-

TABLE 3
*Outcome Childhood Disorders in Early Adult Life**

Original Diagnosis	Recovered	Im-proved	Un-changed	Mild-Moderately Worse	Markedly Worse
Adjustment Disorder					
Mild	20	3	1	0	1
Moderate	7	1	0	2	0
Severe	2	1	1	0	1
Conduct Disorder					
Mild	0	1	0	0	0
Moderate	1	0	0	0	0
Organic Brain Syndrome with Adjustment Disorder					
Mild	0	0	1	0	0
Moderate	0	0	0	0	0
Severe	0	1	0	0	0
Recurrent Major Depression	0	0	1	0	0
Total	30	7	4	2	2

*The column "Recovered" represents the total number recovered. The other columns (Improved, Unchanged, etc.) represent outcome in comparison to adolescent status.

tinued positive developmental course into early adult life. On the other hand, the majority of those cases who did not recover or improve in adolescence tended to grow worse rather than retain the same degree of disturbance, and this same trend was evident into early adult life. This pattern was evident in the mild and moderate adjustment disorder cases, as well as in the severe ones.

The number of cases in the more severe diagnostic categories — conduct disorder, depression, and organic brain syndrome — were too few to define any overall trends in outcome.

ADOLESCENT CASES

After the lull in new cases in later childhood, a number of new cases appeared in adolescence. These cases are tabulated in Table 4.

As can be seen from Table 4, as a group these cases presented more severe disturbances than those arising in childhood. Out of the 12 cases, however, 6 were considered to be recovered in early adult life, 2 improved, and 4 unimproved or worse. It is of interest that 3 of the 6 recovered cases had severe disturbances in adolescence. The special issues of adolescence as reflected in these 12 cases, as well as in the other NYLS subjects, will be discussed in Chapter 20.

No new cases of psychiatric disorder have been identified as yet in adulthood. Thus far there have been two cases of recurrent major depression, but none of autism, childhood or adolescent schizophrenia, or attention deficit disorder. There have also been no suicides or serious physical illness in the overall NYLS sample. Three cases have required psychiatric hospitalization, one in childhood and the other two in early adult life, because of severity of symptoms.

DISCUSSION

In this series of cases, onset of symptoms in early childhood did not appear to have predictive significance with regard to the severity of the adjustment disorder, but such early onset did tend to presage less likelihood of im-

TABLE 4

Cases With Onset in Adolescence

Case - Age, Onset	Adol. Diagnosis	Outcome Early Adult Life
1. (female) 13	Major Recurrent Depression, Moderate	Worse; diagnosis unchanged
2. (female) 13	Depressive Neurosis, Severe	Recovered
3. (female) 13	Antisocial Personality Disorder, Severe	Recovered
4. (male) 13	Adjustment Disorder with Depressed Mood	Improved; Narcissistic Personality Disorder, Mild
5. (female) 15	Generalized Anxiety Disorder	Worse; diagnosis unchanged
6. (male) 15	Adjustment Disorder with Atypical Features, Moderate	Recovered
7. (male) 15	Organic Brain Syndrome with Adjustment Disorder and Mental Retardation, Moderate	Unchanged
8. (female) 16	Borderline Personality Disorder, Severe	Recovered
9. (female) 16	Conduct Disorder, Mild	Recovered
10. (male) 16	Antisocial Personality Disorder, Moderate	Recovered
11. (male) 16	Schizoid Personality Disorder, Moderate	Unchanged
12. (male) 16	Conduct Disorder, Moderate	Improved; diagnosis unchanged

provement or recovery by adolescence. Furthermore, those cases with improvement or recovery by adolescence were very likely to maintain this favorable course into early adult life. On the other hand, those who did not improve tended to grow worse in adolescence rather than remain the same, and this same trend continued into early adult life.

These findings suggest that if a poorness of fit between the child's characteristics and capacities and the demands and expectations of the environment is sufficiently severe to produce a behavior disorder (see discussion of goodness of fit concept in Chapter 2) by early childhood, such a poorness of fit may be less amenable to spontaneous change or therapeutic intervention as the child grows older. This issue will be considered in the detailed examination of the clinical course of a number of the subjects in subsequent chapters.

The high rate of recovery of the mild cases, those with adjustment disorders, corresponds to that of other reports in the literature (Chamberlin, 1976; Glavin, 1972). However, a significant number did not improve or even grew worse in adolescence and early adult life, and it was not always possible to predict the developmental course of the disorder in the early period after its identification. Hence, we would suggest active *appropriate* therapeutic intervention in all cases (See Chapter 20, *Parent Guidance*).

Finally, there is the finding that only one new behavior disorder case appeared in the 9–12 age period, to be followed by a number of new cases in adolescence. This corresponds to other reports (Lapouse and Monk, 1958; MacFarlane et al., 1962). Does this finding confirm the psychoanalytic concept of a "latency period" in the middle childhood years, in which a sort of "psychosexual moratorium" and desexualization of libidinal drives are presumed to occur (Freud, 1924; Erikson, 1968)? The decrease in behavior disorders in these middle and later childhood years can then be explained as the reflection of the diminished sexual drives and conflicts as contrasted to the earlier childhood years and adolescence.

A more parsimonious explanation, not requiring the hypothetical construct of a "latency period," is that the middle-class child meets a lesser number of new environmental demands and expectations in this age-period. The demands for routinization and socialization—toilet-training, regular sleep and feeding patterns, adaptations to rules and regulations, etc.—had been made in the preschool years. Most of the children attended nursery school, so that the demands for adaptation to a new structured extrafamilial situation, for adaptation to a peer group, and for working with educational materials all came early in life. The term "latency," bound up as it is with a particular theoretical framework, could best be abandoned, and the descriptive terms "school-age period," "middle childhood" and "later childhood" utilized instead (Thomas and Chess, 1972).

PART II

Quantitative Analysis

CHAPTER 6

Approach to Quantitative Data Analysis

Both of the authors were trained and grew up professionally in the psychiatric tradition of qualitative and clinical studies. This tradition was a rich one, and resulted in a host of fundamental formulations which have enlarged and deepened our insights into the origins, dynamics, sequences of development, and methods of treatment in a variety of psychopathological conditions. To mention only a few, the research studies of Kraepelin, Freud, Bleuler, Meyer, Levy and Kanner were based on careful clinical studies and creative, systematic generalization from the data they had accumulated. These pioneers in no way felt restricted and frustrated by their inability to utilize various statistical strategies, such as correlation coefficients, analysis of variance, or factor analysis.

This qualitative tradition in psychiatric research was not peculiar to psychiatry, but dominated other areas of biological and medical studies. Whether we look at the work of Darwin, Pasteur, or Virchow, this tradition of the derivation of scientific generalizations from the intensive qualitative study of clinical data was dominant. (For recent years, we can add Piaget to the list of investigators in this tradition.)

But, inevitably, this tradition had its limitations—in some cases inconsequential, in other instances, serious. As we sat in our clinical case conferences or read clinical reports, time after time we became uneasy at the broad sweeping generalizations that were being drawn from a small series of cases. It was clear, at least to us, that other interpretations were possible, and that the clinical studies as such did not allow for a judgment of the relative validity of the competing ideas. Frequently, recourse was made to "my clinical experience" as a presumably decisive argument, when all too often this simply amounted to making the same mistakes for 20 or 30 years. And when tabular material was presented, it was assumed that if a particular symptom or other behavioral characteristic was present in 60 percent of cases of Syndrome A, and only in 30 percent of Syndrome B, then this symptom must have a significant correlation with Syndrome A. But it always seemed to us that this type of presentation did not rule out the possibility of an adventitious relationship.

We began in the early 1950s to formulate our own concepts of the active role of the child's own characteristics in influencing his developmental course, rather than it being entirely a case of the influence upon the child of the mother and other influential members of the child's environment. Our own clinical anecdotes, which seemed persuasive to us, were countered by anecdotes by some of our colleagues with contrary implications which seemed entirely convincing to them. Also, as we gathered the behavioral data on our first group of infants, we realized that our own qualitative ratings and categorizations were fraught with our own biases, and a later rating could also be influenced by our knowledge of an earlier rating on the same child. Finally, it became clear to us that only through a scheme of objective quantitative ratings could we hope to trace effectively the consistencies and changes in any child's characteristics over time and determine systematically the influence of these characteristics on the child's developmental course.

We expected that an expert developmental psychologist trained in quantitative methods would not find it difficult to transform our body of detailed qualitative data into sharply defined categories which could be rated quantitatively. To our surprise, several such psychologists consulted found this task too complicated and difficult, in spite of their expertise. Finally we approached our friend Dr. Herbert Birch, who at that time was turning from a brilliant career in animal behavior research to the study of neurobehavioral patterns in the young infant. He succeeded where others had failed and developed a set of 9 categories from an inductive content analysis of the parent interview protocols of our first 22 subjects in the infancy period. These categories could be scored continuously throughout the protocols, and the distribution of scores in each category was sufficiently wide to permit differentiation among individuals within each category (see Chapter 4). Although various amounts of data were available for additional categories of temperament, their distributions failed to satisfy either the requirements of ubiquitousness (being scorable and present in all protocols) or of sufficient variability to permit interindividual comparison.

It is of interest that almost all the nine categories defined independently by Dr. Birch corresponded closely in their definitions to the categories we our- selves had formulated by our qualitative inspection of the parent interview protocols. However, Dr. Birch added several categories of interest which we had not identified, such as rhythmicity and sensory threshold. Beyond this, his categorizations also involved a precision of definition and criteria for quantitative item scoring (Thomas, Chess, Birch et al., 1963) which allowed us to transform the narrative behavioral reports of the parents (and, later on, of teachers) into precise quantitative ratings. This made it possible to apply the power of quantitative methods to a determination of: interrater reliabil- ity; the identification of the range of individual differences for any one cate- gory; the study of consistency over time; the determination of levels of correla- tion among the categories; the identification of significant relationships among the categories by factor analysis; or the study of the functional sig- nificance of the nine categories of temperament for the developmental course of the study sample as a whole.

The breadth and depth of the analysis of our behavioral data which be- came possible with the application of quantitative methods led to the commit- ment to collect our raw data in ways which made it possible to derive quantita- tive ratings — whether the issue concerned temperament at various age-periods, adjustment scores in childhood, adolescence and early adult life, parental at- titudes and practices, or clinical diagnosis (as detailed in Chapter 4).

We also became aware of an additional highly valuable consequence of the various quantitative analyses.The identification of statistically significant cor- relations also made it possible to give special attention to those cases that dem- onstrated developmental trends in an opposite direction. Thus, for example, if the quantitative analyses indicated significant correlation between the dif- ficult temperament pattern and subsequent emergence of behavior problems, it then became of interest to analyze qualitatively the developmental course of those temperamentally difficult children who did not develop behavior dis- order. This approach, which combines both quantitative and qualitative methods, has proven most useful, as detailed in various subsequent chapters of this volume concerned with different types of qualitative analysis.

METHODS OF QUANTITATIVE ANALYSIS

Our earlier quantitative analyses, primarily of the correlations between tem- perament and behavior disorder development (Thomas, Chess and Birch, 1968), relied on a simple analysis of variance. Our recent more extensive quan- titative studies have utilized the more generic techniques of multiple regres- sion/correlational (MRC) analysis (Cohen and Cohen, 1975). In hierarchical multiple regression analysis, one can assess the effect of a variable (or set of variables) over and above the effect of another variable (or set of variables) on a dependent variable by entering these sets into the analysis, one at a time, and looking at the amount of variance in the dependent variable explained by the second set, over and above that explained by the first set. The total amount of variance explained by the two sets of independent variables is not dependent on their order of entry into the analysis. However, the amount of variance explained by each of these sets, unless they are independent, depends on the order of entry. One is thus determining the effect of the second set, controlling for the effect of the first set, and so on. The multiple regression analyses not only make it possible to identify statistically significant correlations between antecedent and outcome variables, but also to determine whether an apparently meaningful influence of an antecedent variable is genuine, or only the result of its correlation with other significant factors.

Our quantitative studies have also utilized the recently developed set correlation method (Cohen, 1982), which is a multivariate generalization of multiple regression/correlation (MRC). It is possible, in MRC analysis, to represent information on virtually any kind of independent variables. However, in MRC there is one dependent variable in an analysis. Set correlation makes it possible to create sets of dependent variables and relate them in one analysis to sets of independent variables. Any coding of information possible on the right hand side of the equation in MRC is possible on both sides of the equation in set correlation, making it possible to partial out one set of dependent variables from each other, as well as partialling out independent variables.

LIMITATIONS OF QUANTITATIVE METHODS

Quantitative analyses are the product of routine methods involving a minimum of judgment and evaluation. Judgment is involved in the development of categories and the establishment of scoring criteria and procedures. Once these are established, however, quantitative methods must of necessity be routine. The demand for reliability in scoring also limits the possibility of the full utilization of the available data.

The rigors of quantitative methods of data treatment, therefore, may preclude the identification of meaningful subtleties in the developmental course of individual subjects. For example, one mother reported an extraordinary level of persistence in her young son, but only in selective activities which had engaged his interest. Forcible interruption of such an activity before he himself was ready to terminate it usually resulted in a prolonged tantrum. For example, at 18 months he began to learn to tie shoelaces, and for several days spent most of his waking hours tying and retying his brother's and father's shoelaces, as well as his own. This activity was observed one evening by our interviewer, just as his mother had described it. Finally, when she insisted he stop because it was bedtime, he responded with a loud tantrum. This selective persistence, with intense and sometimes explosive reactions if frustrated in carrying through such activities, played a highly significant role in this boy's developmental course throughout childhood. Yet, because the areas of such marked persistence were few in number at any one time, his overall quantitative item scoring for persistence, while high, in no way revealed the full significance of this special behavioral characteristic.

Interactionist theory postulates that behavioral characteristics can change at any age-period, even qualitatively, if a significant change in organism or environment alters the dynamics of the developmental process. Such change may take many different directions and forms in different individuals. These idiosyncratic developmental patterns cannot be adequately captured by quantitative group methods, but require qualitative studies. As Rutter has put it, the importance of interaction effects makes it "evident that, as a consequence, it is difficult to make valid, broad, sweeping generalizations about human behavior. Attention must be paid to the specifications of person-situation interactions. . . . it may be suggested that it is preferable to take an idiographic approach which explicitly focuses on the individuality of human beings—not just in the degree to which they show particular traits or even in terms of the traits which are relevant to them, but more generally in terms of the idiosyncrasies which make each person uniquely different from all others" (1980, p. 5).

HOW RIGOROUS ARE STATISTICAL METHODS?

The mathematical precision of statistical methods in behavioral studies all too often confers an aura of authority and certainty on the results of the analyses which may be misleading. As Kraemer has put it, "The common statistical analytic techniques used in the vast majority of psychiatric research reports (t-tests, analysis of variance, linear regression and correlation approaches, their multivariate extensions and their variations) are all based on assumptions that data are normally distributed, that variances in subgroups are equal, that associations between variables are linear, and that effects are additive. The fact is that data are almost never normally distributed, and other assumptions fail too often to be taken for granted" (1981, p. 310).

The assumptions underlying various statistical methods may be necessary, but they make for fallibility. Hence, the arguments that proliferate as to the superiority of one analytic technique over another, as well as to the interpretation of findings. Spearman could argue from his principal component factor analytic approach that there was a single *g* factor which measured innate general intelligence. Thurstone, with his simple structure solutions, considered that Spearman's *g* was a meaningless average of an arbitrary battery of tests, devoid of psychological significance (Gould, 1981). "The principal component and simple structure solutions are mathematically equivalent; neither is 'better.' Information is neither gained nor lost by rotating axes; it is merely redistributed. Preferences depend on the meaning assigned to factor axes" (Gould, 1981, p. 301).

RELIABILITY, VALIDITY, AND RELEVANCE

The importance of reliable measures and ratings cannot be overestimated. However, the concern for reliability must be balanced with an equal concern for meaning, relevance, and validity. "To the statistician's dictum that whatever exists can be measured, the factorist has added the assumption that whatever can be 'measured' must exist. But the relationship may not be reversible, and the assumption may be false" (Tuddenham, 1962, p. 516).

It is all too easy for the behavioral researcher to slip into the "ivory tower" attitude which cherishes the "good" measure of reliability above the "right" measure of validity (Kraemer, 1981). "When the right thing can only be measured poorly, it tends to cause the wrong thing to be measured, only because it can be measured well. And it is often much worse to have good measurement of the wrong thing—especially when, as is so often the case, the wrong thing will in fact be used as an indicator of the right thing—than to have poor measurements of the right thing" (Tukey, 1979, p. 486).

The key issue of relevance is posed by McCall in his critique of developmental psychologists who treasure experimental methods with high levels of reliability. "The experimental method now dictates rather than serves the research questions we value, fund and pursue; as a result the process of development as it naturally transpires in children growing up in actual life circumstances has been largely ignored. Do we not want to understand naturalistic development? Should this not be at least one of the major goals of our science? What value is our knowledge if it is not relevant to real children growing up in real families and in real neighborhoods?" (1977, p. 334).

It may seem a truism to state that statistical methods and the computer should be the servant and not the master of the researcher. Yet, repeated experience with research reports in which tests of reliability and statistical significance were abundant, but in which data on relevance and validity were conspicuous by their absence, affirms the need to emphasize this issue. "It is the researcher who decides what data to collect and how, what analytic techniques to use, how to enter the data into the analysis, how to interpret the results, who is right or wrong" (Kraemer, 1981, p. 316).

To conclude, it is our conviction from our experience with the NYLS that quantitative methods are essential for an adequate analysis of the behavioral development of any study sample. This may appear obvious to developmental psychiatrists, but is by no means so to most psychiatrists. On the other hand, a complete reliance on quantitative methods may serve to limit the scope of such an investigation and to ignore the richness of findings which can emerge from the qualitative analysis of the developmental course of individual subjects. This may appear obvious to developmental psychiatrists, but it is by no means so to many developmental psychologists. As a result, the optimal treatment of a body of longitudinal behavioral data necessitates the integrated combination of both quantitative and qualitative methods.

CHAPTER 7

Multiple Regression Analyses: Correlations Between Three-Year Ratings and Early Adult Adaptation

For these analyses, the ratings at Year 3 were chosen as the independent variables because the data for that year include temperament, adjustment scores, and maternal attitudes and practices ratings. These variables include:

1. Temperament — 9 attributes.
2. Difficult-easy temperament. Two ratings were utilized: a) the criterion for difficult being at least 4 of the 5 categories comprising this constellation above the median cutoff (irregularity, withdrawal, low adaptability, negative mood, high intensity), but always including high intensity, to distinguish this pattern from the slow-to-warm-up constellation. The criterion for easy temperament was similar, and included at least 4 of the 5 categories below the median cut-off, but always including low or moderate intensity. Subjects neither difficult nor easy were coded as 0. This gave a variable with 2 attributes. In the tables below, this rating is labelled DIFFICULT/ EASY; b) Difficult-easy as one continuous score developed by a summation of the weighted scores for the 5 categories. All subjects were scored on this continuum, and this gave a variable with one attribute. In the tables below, this variable is labelled DIFF CHILD SCORE.
3. Subject's home adjustment — 12 attributes (sleep, feeding, discipline, etc.).
4. Subject's global home adjustment score — 1 attribute (Adj. Global Score).
5. Maternal attitudes and practices — 9 attributes (disapproval, conflict, permissiveness, etc.).

These 5 variables actually represent 3 sets utilized as independent variables: 2 for temperament (the 9 attributes and difficult-easy temperament), 2 for 3-year adjustment (the 12 attributes and the global adjustment score), and one for maternal attitudes and practices.

The outcome dependent variables in early adult life were:

1. Global adjustment rating, converted into a bootstrap score, and the average of the scores of the 3 raters became the dependent variable. In the tables the acronym AVOWN (average of the raters' *own* bootstrap scores) is used as the label for this variable.
2. Difficult-easy temperament. As with this variable at 3 years, a continuous score derived from the summation of the 5 categories making up this constellation was used. Two ratings were used: a) the average of the 3 raters' scores from the interview data; and b) the scores from the early adult temperament questionnaires. (Note: the criteria and methods of scoring for these variables are detailed in Chapter 4.)

In the multiple regression analyses, several orders of entry of the 3 sets of independent variables (temperament, adjustment and maternal attitudes) were explored. With an interactional developmental model, the order of entry of the variables is not guided by a specific theory. None of the variables is viewed as primary, secondary or tertiary. Thus, inasmuch as they are mutually interactive for each dependent outcome variable, in one analysis adjustment was entered first; in another, temperament was first; and in still another, maternal attitudes was first. This approach was utilized to obtain a maximum view of the pattern of relationships between the earlier characteristics of the child and parents and the adult adjustment and temperament outcomes. In essence, we have explored the effect of certain predictor sets when the child was 3 years old on specific early adult ratings.

A summmary of these multiple regression analyses is presented in Tables 1, 2 and 3. Table 1 details the relationship of the childhood variables to adult adjustment, Table 2 of these variables to adult difficult-easy temperament from the pooled interviewer ratings, and Table 3 to adult difficult-easy temperament from the questionnaire. In each analysis, the relationships are determined with different order of entry of the 3 childhood variable sets.

To spell out the meanings of the numbers and statistically significant correlations in these tables, Table 1 will be utilized as the model example. In the columns ORDER OF ENTRY (First, Second, and Third) the numbers in parentheses, e.g. (.33) — the first such number in the first column — represents R, the Pearson product-moment correlation. The number to the left, not in

TABLE 1
Effect of Age 3 Predictor Sets on Adult Adjustment (AVOWN); Hierarchical Multiple Regression Analysis

ORDER OF ENTRY:

First-	Second-	Third-	
ADJUSTMENT*	TEMPERAMENT	MATERNAL ATTITUDES*	ADJUSTED MULTIPLE R²
(12 attributes)	(9 attributes)	(9 attributes)	
—Discipline*		—Conflict*	
.1068 (.33)	.0020 (.04)	.0856 (.29)	.1944 (.44)
ADJUSTMENT	DIFF CHILD SCORE*	MATERNAL ATTITUDES*	
(12 attributes)	(1 attribute)	(9 attributes)	
—Discipline*	—Diff Child Sc*	—Conflict*	
.1068 (.33)	.0224 (.15)	.0689 (.26)	.1981 (.45)
ADJUSTMENT	MATERNAL ATTITUDES*	DIFF CHILD SCORE*	
(12 attributes)	(9 attributes)	(1 attribute)	
—Discipline*	—Conflict*	—Diff Child Sc*	
.1068 (.33)	.0639 (.25)	.0274 (.17)	.1981 (.45)
ADJUSTMENT	DIFFICULT/ EASY	MATERNAL ATTITUDES*	
(12 attributes)	(2 attributes)	(9 attributes)	
—Discipline*		—Conflict*	
.1068 (.33)	.0289 (.17)	.0762 (.28)	.2119 (.46)
ADJ-GLOBAL SCORE*	TEMPERAMENT	MATERNAL ATTITUDES*	
(1 attribute)	(9 attributes)	(9 attributes)	
—Adj-Global Score*		—Conflict* —No Factor*	
.0790 (.28)	0 (0)	.1338 (.37)	.1788 (.42)
ADJ-GLOBAL SCORE*	MATERNAL ATTITUDES*	DIFF CHILD SCORE*	
(1 attribute)	(9 attributes)	(1 attribute)	
—Adj-Global Score*	—Conflict* —No Factor*		
.0790 (.28)	.1056 (.32)	.0093 (.10)	.1939 (.44)
TEMPERAMENT	ADJUSTMENT*	MATERNAL ATTITUDES*	
(9 attributes)	(12 attributes) —Parents* —Discipline*	(9 attributes) —Conflict*	
.0160 (.13)	.0928 (.30)	.0856 (.29)	.1944 (.44)

TABLE 1 (continued)

TEMPERAMENT	MATERNAL ATTITUDES*	ADJUSTMENT	
(9 attributes)	(9 attributes) —Conflict* —No Factor*	(12 attributes)	
.0160 (.13)	.1549 (.39)	.0235 (.15)	.1944 (.44)
DIFF CHILD SCORE* (1 attribute) —Diff Child Sc*	ADJ-GLOBAL SCORE* (1 attribute) —Adj-Global Score*	MATERNAL ATTITUDES* (9 attributes) —Conflict* —No Factor*	
.0340 (.18)	.0477 (.22)	.1122 (.33)	.1939 (.44)
DIFFICULT/ EASY (2 attributes)	ADJ-GLOBAL SCORE* (1 attribute) —Adj-Global Score*	MATERNAL ATTITUDES* (9 attributes) —Conflict* —No Factor*	
.0257 (.16)	.0531 (.23)	.1292 (.36)	.2080 (.46)
MATERNAL ATTITUDES* (9 attributes) —Conflict*	ADJUSTMENT (12 attributes)	TEMPERAMENT (9 attributes)	
.1458 (.38)	.0248 (.16)	.0238 (.15)	.1944 (.44)
MATERNAL ATTITUDES* (9 attributes) —Conflict*	ADJ-GLOBAL SCORE* (1 attribute) —Adj-Global Score*	TEMPERAMENT (9 attributes)	
.1458 (.38)	.0388 (.20)	0 (0)	.1788 (.42)

*Variable set and particular attribute cited are statistically significantly related to the outcome variable ($p < .05$).

Number in parentheses following the Adjusted Multiple R^2 is the magnitude of the correlation associated with the value of the variance cited.

parentheses, in this case .1068, represents R^2, the amount of variance accounted for by the correlation.

In the last column, under the heading ADJUSTED MULTIPLE R^2, the number in parenthesis, e.g. (.44)—the first such number in the first line—represents the correlation between the 3 childhood variables as a group and the outcome variable, in this case AVOWN. The number to the left, not in parenthesis, in this example .1944, represents the square of this correlation, and signifies the amount of variance accounted for by the correlation.

The asterisks next to a number of the attributes or sets of attributes denotes those correlations which are statistically significant to at least the .05 level of confidence. Where a set is identified as statistically significant and then one or two subcategories are listed immediately below as showing a significant correlation, this indicates that when the set as a whole is entered in the multiple regression analysis, it is statistically significant. However, when the subcategory ratings are then entered separately, only those listed are significantly correlated with the outcome variable.

The three columns — first, second and third — provide a tabulation of the amount of variance accounted for by a predictive set or variable, depending on whether it is entered first, second or third in the multiple regression analysis. Thus, in Table 1, Adjustment, when entered first, accounts for .1068 of the variance. When entered second it accounts for either .0928 or .0248, depending on which other variable is entered first, and, when entered third, the amount of variance drops to .0235. The subcategory of conflict in the maternal attitude set, by contrast, shows a significant correlation when entered first, and also in all combinations when entered second or third.

CORRELATIONS OF 3-YEAR RATINGS WITH
ADULT ADJUSTMENT

One striking feature of Table 1 is that regardless of order of entry, maternal attitudes as a set of 9 attributes is always a statistically significant variable and that conflict and "no factor" within the nine attributes of maternal attitudes are the statistically significant components. Conflict is a cluster of items that includes both parental conflict in handling the child and the parents' general attitude toward one another. "No factor" represents those cases in which the 3-year parent interviews were not done. In a few instances this was because the parents were not available at that time for special reasons, such as prolonged absence from the New York area. Most of the "no factor" cases, however, comprise the youngest members of the sample, inasmuch as the resources for the parent attitudes interviews were exhausted before all the subjects reached 3-years of age. There were 26 "no factor" subjects out of the total sample of 133. The correlations for "no factor" are in a positive direction, i.e. with better adjustment.

When it is entered first, the adjusted SR^2 for maternal attitudes as a set is .1458 (corresponding to an adjusted $SR = .382$). The maternal attitudes set is clearly a significant predictor variable, alone or even controlling for the effects of our other third-year attributes. Another variable set that is almost always statistically significantly related to adult adjustment is adjustment at 3 years. When this variable set of 12 attributes is entered first, the adjusted

SR² is .1068 (adjusted SR = .327). Only when adjustment is entered *after* and thus controlling for maternal attributes does it fail to be statistically significantly related to adult adjustment. Within the subset of attributes that comprise adjustment at 3 years, discipline appears as a statistically significant component. When the summary score, global adjustment score, is substituted for the 12-item adjustment set, it, too, is statistically significantly related to adult adjustment. When this score is entered first the adjusted SR² is .0790 (adjusted SR = .281). The value of this summary score is that it is a *single* score and even when it is entered after parental attitudes it is statistically significantly related to adult adjustment. This was not true for the adjustment set as a whole.

Temperament as a 9-attribute set at 3 years, on the other hand, is not significantly related to adult adjustment in any of the combinations of variables we employed in the multiple regression analysis. When it is entered first, temperament yields an adjusted SR² of only .0160 (adjusted SR = .126). However, the difficult-easy child score is statistically significantly related to adult adjustment in all of the analyses in which it was employed, in combination with adjustment at 3 years and parental attitudes. When entered first, the difficult-easy child score yields an adjusted SR² of .0340 (adjusted SR = .184). The use of the dichotomous score difficult/easy temperament is not as valuable as the continuous difficult-easy child score; in none of the analyses in which the former was employed was it statistically significantly related to adult adjustment, even when entered first.

Given the various sets of three predictor variables at 3 years and adult adjustment as the outcome, the cumulative adjusted SR² ranged from .2119 (cum. adjusted SR = .460) to .1788 (cum. adjusted SR = .423). At age 3 adjustment by itself accounts for about 11 percent of the variance. But when the maternal attitudes set is controlled, adjustment accounts for only about 2 percent of the variance, and in the latter instance is not statistically significantly related to the outcome variable of adult adjustment.

On the other hand, the maternal attitudes set at age 3 accounts for about 15 percent of the variance, and when adjustment at age 3 is controlled, maternal attitudes still account for 6 percent of the variance and is still significantly related to the outcome variable. In fact, regardless of the other age-3 variable sets that are controlled, maternal attitudes never account for less than 6 percent of the variance. None of the other age-3 variables or variable sets are as significantly related.

Temperament as a set of 9 attributes accounts for only about 1.5 percent of the variance, and when this variable set is controlled it has no significant effect on the relationship between adjustment or maternal attitude and adult adjustment.

CORRELATIONS OF 3-YEAR RATINGS WITH ADULT
DIFFICULT-EASY TEMPERAMENT FROM INTERVIEW

Table 2 summarizes the assessment of the relationships between the same sets of characteristics of the children at age 3 years and their difficult-easy adult temperament scores derived from pooled interview raters. The latter served as the dependent variable and the sets of characteristics previously used served as the independent variables.

As can be seen from Table 2, the set of the nine temperament attributes at age 3 were significantly related to difficult adult when these were entered first; the adjusted SR^2 was .0847 (the magnitude of the associated correlation is .29). The temperament set was significantly related even as the third set of variables entered after (and thus controlled for) the maternal attitude set and either the adjustment set or the global adjustment score. The adjusted SR^2s were, respectively .0891 (.30) and .0736 (.27). In these analyses the associated variances remained fairly constant. However, when the temperament set is entered second after the adjustment set, the variance is reduced to about 6 percent, and temperament is not statistically significantly related to the difficult-easy adult outcome. This is also true when temperament is assessed controlling for the age-3 global adjustment score; the variance drops to less than 4 percent.

Thus, the relationship between temperament as a set of attributes and the difficult-easy adult outcome is affected by the particular pattern of other age 3 variables that are controlled for. However, in the main, we can conclude that it is a significant predictor variable. When the temperament set is statistically significantly related to difficult-easy adult temperament in those analyses, the specific component that is by itself also significantly related is adaptability; in one instance, mood is also significantly related. Both of these temperament categories are also components of the difficult-easy child and difficult-easy adult scores.

On the other hand, in none of the combinations of sets of age 3 variables is the adjustment set of 12 attributes significantly related to the difficult-easy adult outcome. When it is entered first, the adjusted R^2 is .0310 (.18) and the variance it accounts for never exceeds 3 percent, regardless of the order of entry.

The set of maternal attitudes (9 attributes) at age 3 is significantly related to the difficult-easy score when it is entered first (adjusted R^2 is .0871; $R = .30$) with conflict and no factor as the significant specific components. It is interesting to note that the maternal attitude set remains statistically significantly related to the difficult adult temperament outcome when the adjustment and temperament sets are both controlled for, but is not significantly related when

TABLE 2

Effect of Age 3 Predictor Sets on Difficult Adult Temperament (Interview);
Hierarchical Multiple Regression Analysis

ORDER OF ENTRY:

First-	Second-	Third-	
ADJUSTMENT	TEMPERAMENT	MATERNAL ATTITUDES*	ADJUSTED MULTIPLE R²
(12 attributes)	(9 attributes)	(9 attributes) —No Factor*	
.0310 (.18)	.0613 (.25)	.0784 (.28)	.1707 (.41)
ADJUSTMENT	DIFF CHILD SCORE*	MATERNAL ATTITUDES	
(12 attributes)	(1 attribute) —Diff Child Sc*	(9 attributes)	
.0310 (.18)	.0736 (.27)	.0598 (.24)	.1644 (.41)
ADJUSTMENT	MATERNAL ATTITUDES	DIFF CHILD SCORE*	
(12 attributes)	(9 attributes)	(1 attribute) —Diff Child Sc*	
.0310 (.18)	.0507 (.23)	.0827 (.29)	.1644 (.41)
ADJUSTMENT	DIFFICULT/ EASY	MATERNAL ATTITUDES	
(12 attributes)	(2 attributes)	(9 attributes)	
.0310 (.18)	.0258 (.16)	.0748 (.27)	.1316 (.36)
ADJ-GLOBAL SCORE*	TEMPERAMENT	MATERNAL ATTITUDES*	
(1 attribute) —Adj-Global Score*	(9 attributes)	(9 attributes) —Conflict* —No Factor*	
.0418 (.20)	.0387 (.20)	.0957 (.31)	.1762 (.42)
ADJ-GLOBAL SCORE*	MATERNAL ATTITUDES	DIFF CHILD SCORE*	
(1 attribute) —Adj-Global Score*	(9 attributes)	(1 attribute) —Diff Child Sc*	
.0418 (.20)	.0608 (.25)	.0597 (.24)	.1623 (.40)
TEMPERAMENT*	ADJUSTMENT	MATERNAL ATTITUDES*	
(9 attributes) —Adaptability*	(12 attributes)	(9 attributes) —No Factor*	
.0847 (.29)	.0077 (.09)	.0784 (.28)	.1708 (.41)

(continued)

TABLE 2 (continued)
*Effect of Age 3 Predictor Sets on Difficult Adult Temperament (Interview);
Hierarchical Multiple Regression Analysis*

TEMPERAMENT		MATERNAL ATTITUDES*		ADJUSTMENT		
(9 attributes) —Adaptability*		(9 attributes) —Conflict* —No Factor*		(12 attributes)		
.0847 (.29)		.0990 (.31)		0　(0)		.1708 (.41)
DIFF CHILD SCORE* —Diff Child Score*		ADJ-GLOBAL SCORE (1 attribute)		MATERNAL ATTITUDES* (9 attributes) —Conflict* —No Factor*		
.0863 (.29)		.0056 (.07)		.0704 (.26)		.1623 (.40)
DIFFICULT/ EASY* (2 attributes) Diff/Dum*		ADJ-GLOBAL SCORE (1 attribute)		MATERNAL ATTITUDES* (9 attributes) —Conflict* —No Factor*		
.0470 (.22)		.0166 (.13)		.0889 (.30)		.1525 (.39)
MATERNAL ATTITUDES* (9 attributes) —Conflict* —No Factor*		ADJUSTMENT (12 attributes)		TEMPERAMENT* (9 attributes) —Adaptability*		
.0871 (.30)		0　(0)		.0891 (.30)		.1709 (.41)
MATERNAL ATTITUDES* (9 attributes) —Conflict* —No Factor*		ADJ-GLOBAL SCORE (1 attribute)		TEMPERAMENT* (9 attributes) —Adaptability* —Mood*		
.0871 (.30)		.0155 (.12)		.0736 (.27)		.1762 (.42)

*Variable set and particular attribute cited are statistically significantly related to the outcome variable ($p < .05$).

Number in parentheses following the Adjusted Multiple R^2 is the magnitude of the correlation associated with the value of the variance cited.

only the adjustment set is controlled. (In the former instance the adjusted SR^2 is .0784 (.28) and in the latter it is .0507 (.23). The components of maternal attitudes that are statistically significant are conflict and no factor.

When the difficult-easy child score is used in the analyses, rather than the temperament set, it is always significantly related to difficult-easy adult outcome, regardless of the other variables controlled. When it is entered first, the adjusted R^2 is .0863 (.29) and remains at about this level when controlling for adjustment and maternal attitudes.

RELATIONSHIPS BETWEEN 3-YEAR RATINGS AND ADULT DIFFICULT-EASY TEMPERAMENT FROM QUESTIONNAIRE

An analysis similar to the preceding one was performed with the adult difficult-easy temperament score from the questionnaire instead of from the interview as the dependent variable. A summary of this analysis is presented in Table 3.

As can be seen from Table 3, the results of the analysis involving difficult-easy adult temperament derived from the questionnaire are strikingly different from the two outcome variables previously discussed. In the temperament questionnaire analysis, of the 12 combinations, each involving 3 predictor variable sets, only 5 have a variable set that is statistically significantly related to this outcome. Thus, of 36 tests of significance, only 5 are statistically significant; in the analysis involving adult adjustment as the outcome, 24 of the 36 were statistically significant, and when difficult-easy adult temperament derived from the interview raters was the outcome variable, 19 of the 36 were significant. While N for this adult questionnaire analysis is substantially less than for the adult interview analysis (70 as compared to 132), the lack of significance is not solely due to the lack of power; the adjusted R^2 and SR^2 are distinctly smaller throughout.

When entered first, only difficult-easy child at 3 and global adjustment are statistically significantly related to the questionnaire outcome variable; the adjusted SR^2 for the former is .0546 (.23) and for the latter it is .0452 (.21). None of the other four age-3 variables are found to be statistically significant in the arrays of age 3 variables except the temperament set. When this variable is entered first, the adjusted SR^2 is .0899 (.30), but it is not statistically significantly related to the outcome variable. However, when the temperament set is entered third, controlling for the parental attitude set and either the adjustment set or the global adjustment score, the temperament set is statistically significantly related to difficult adult questionnaire. The respective adjusted SR^2s are .1789 (.42) and .1544 (.39). In other words, the temperament set alone accounts for about 9 percent of the variance, but when the other two variables are controlled for, temperament accounts for approximately 15 percent and 18 percent of the variance. The component of temperament that is significantly related is mood.

TABLE 3

*Effect of Age 3 Predictor Sets on Difficult Adult Temperament (Quest.);
Hierarchical Multiple Regression Analysis*

ORDER OF ENTRY:

First-	Second-	Third-	
ADJUSTMENT	TEMPERAMENT	MATERNAL ATTITUDES	MULTIPLE R²
(12 attributes)	(9 attributes)	(9 attributes)	(3 sets)
.0770 (.28)	.0451 (.21)	.0359 (.19)	.1580 (.40)
ADJUSTMENT	DIFF CHILD SCORE	MATERNAL ATTITUDES	
(12 attributes)	(1 attribute)	(9 attributes)	
.0770 (.28)	.0317 (.18)	0 (0)	.0614 (.25)
ADJUSTMENT	MATERNAL ATTITUDES	DIFF CHILD SCORE*	
(12 attributes)	(9 attributes)	(1 attribute) —Diff Child Score*	
.0770 (.28)	0 (0)	.0822 (.29)	.0614 (.25)
ADJUSTMENT	DIFFICULT/ EASY	MATERNAL ATTITUDES	
(12 attributes)	(2 attributes)	(9 attributes)	
.0770 (.28)	0 (0)	0 (0)	0 (0)
ADJ-GLOBAL SCORE* (1 attribute) —Adj-Global Score*	TEMPERAMENT (9 attributes)	MATERNAL ATTITUDES (9 attributes)	
.0452 (.21)	.0390 (.20)	.0275 (.17)	.1117 (.33)
ADJ-GLOBAL SCORE* (1 attribute) —Adj-Global Score*	MATERNAL ATTITUDES (9 attributes)	DIFF CHILD SCORE (1 attribute)	
.0452 (.21)	0 (0)	.0497 (.22)	.0070 (.08)
TEMPERAMENT	ADJUSTMENT	MATERNAL ATTITUDES	
(9 attributes)	(12 attributes)	(9 attributes)	
.0899 (.30)	.0322 (.18)	.0359 (.19)	.1580 (.40)
TEMPERAMENT	MATERNAL ATTITUDES	ADJUSTMENT	
(9 attributes)	(9 attributes)	(12 attributes)	
.0899 (.30)	.0362 (.19)	.0320 (.18)	.1581 (.40)

TABLE 3 (continued)

DIFF CHILD SCORE* (1 attribute) —Diff Child Score*	ADJ-GLOBAL SCORE (1 attribute)	MATERNAL ATTITUDES (9 attributes)	
.0546 (.23)	.0141 (.12)	0 (0)	.0070 (.08)
DIFFICULT/ EASY (2 attributes)	ADJ-GLOBAL SCORE (1 attribute)	MATERNAL ATTITUDES (9 attributes)	
0 (0)	.0421 (.21)	0 (0)	0 (0)
MATERNAL ATTITUDES (9 attributes)	ADJUSTMENT (12 attributes)	TEMPERAMENT* (9 attributes) —Mood*	
0 (0)	.0295 (.17)	.1789 (.42)	.1580 (.40)
MATERNAL ATTITUDES (9 attributes)	ADJ-GLOBAL SCORE (1 attribute)	TEMPERAMENT* (9 attributes) —Mood*	
0 (0)	.0077 (.09)	.1544 (.39)	.1117 (.33)

*Variable set and particular attribute cited are statistically significantly related to the outcome variable (P < .05).

Number in parentheses following the Adjusted Multiple R^2 is the magnitude of the correlation associated with the value of the variance cited.

"NO FACTOR" SUBJECTS

As reported earlier in this chapter, the 26 subjects without the 3-year interview for maternal attitudes and practices showed a statistically significant positive correlation with the early adult adjustment scores. These "no factor" subjects were mostly the youngest members of the sample. Possible explanations for this finding were explored.

There was a slight sex difference in the no factor subjects, 11 males versus 15 females. Only 8, or 31 percent, were firstborn, as compared with 59 percent of the remainder of the sample (63 out of 107). Of the 26 no factor subjects, 17, or 65 percent, had at least one older sib in the study, while this was true of only 25, or 23 percent, of the remainder of the sample. Only 3 of the no factor subjects, or 11 percent, were identified as a clinical case at any age-period, as contrasted with 54, or 53 percent, of the remainder of the sample. These differences in birth order, presence of an older sib in the study, and incidence of clinical cases were all statistically significant at the .01 level of confidence. The no factor subjects were significantly correlated with early adult easy temperament, but there was no correlation with difficult-easy temperament at age 3.

Two possibilities come to mind to explain the correlation of the "no factor" subjects with better early adjustment. Inasmuch as these were mostly younger children, the parents may have been more relaxed and assured out of the experience gained with their firstborns. Or, the informal and, in some cases, formal counseling and reassurance many of the parents received from the research staff with their first child in the study may have had beneficial effects on their handling of their younger child or children in the study. Our data are not sufficient to test the validity of either or both of these possibilities.

CHAPTER 8

Set Correlation Analyses: Correlations Between Childhood and Early Adult Ratings

As indicated in Chapter 6, the set correlation method makes it possible to create sets of dependent variables and relate them in one analysis to sets of independent variables (Cohen, 1982). With this technique, the variables in a set of dependent variables can be partialled out from each other, in the same way as a set of independent variables.

In a multiple regression correlation, the R^2 statistic is a measure of the association between the independent and dependent variables. R^2 indicates the proportion of the variance in the dependent variable explained by the set of independent variables. There is an analagous statistic in set correlation called the multivariate R^2 (MVR^2), which estimates the proportion of the generalized variance of the set of dependent variables explained by the set of independent variables.

As in the R^2 multiple regression correlations, the multivariate R^2 is an inflated estimate of the size of the association in the given sample. The unbiased MVR^2 takes into account the number of variables in the sets and the number of subjects in the sample.

In the set correlation analyses, the following sets of variables were used:

Independent Variable Sets

CHR (childhood ratings) = GS 3 (Global adjustment score, age 3), GS 5, 1 (Global adjustment score, age 5 from parent), GS 5, 2 (Global adjustment score, age 5 from teacher), DIFCHILD 3 (difficult-easy temperament, age 3), DIFCHILD 5 (difficult-easy temperament, age 5).

CHE (childhood environment) = CONFL (parental conflict, age 3), ECON (parental living standards, age 3), SEPDIV (separation or divorce of parents at any age), DEATH (death of parents at any age).

CLC (clinical cases) = CLIN 1 (clinical diagnosis before age 6 versus diagnosis before age 12), CLIN 2 (clinical diagnosis anytime before age 12 versus no childhood clinical diagnosis.

Age 3 = GS 3; DIFCHILD 3
Age 5 = GS 5, 1; GS 5, 2; DIFCHILD 5
GLO (Global Score) = GS 3; GS 5, 1; GS 5, 2
DCB (Difficult-easy both 3 and 5) = DIFCHILD 3; DIFCHILD 5

In the childhood ratings (CHR), the global scores were used, inasmuch as the multiple regression correlations had shown the 3-year global score, rather than the 12 individual ratings, to be significant. For the same reason, difficult-easy temperament was used, rather than the 9 individual categories, and maternal conflict alone of the various maternal attitudes and child-care practices. The rating for parental living standards at age 3 (ECON) was included because of suggestive though not significant findings from the multiple regression correlations. This rating is derived from a set of items that concerns the relative living standards of the family: presence of financial stress, amount of paid household help, and degree of crowding of home, as well as overt living standards. However, it must be pointed out that these items are rated within the context of the middle- and upper middle-class socioeconomic level of the NYLS families.

Dependent Variable Sets

AVOWN (Average interviewers' Bootstrap Adjustment Score), DIFADULT (difficult-easy adult temperament from pooled interviewers' ratings), CLINADULT (clinical diagnosis in early adult life).

In the set correlation analyses, various combinations of the independent variable sets were utilized. After the effects of the independent set or sets were examined, the effects of those same sets partialling for the effect of other independent variable sets were examined.

When a set or partialled set was identified as a significant predictor of adult outcome, the relationships between the variables of the set and the adult dependent variables both as a set and individually were also examined.

Five set correlation analyses were done. In each analysis the dependent variable set was the same (AVOWN, DIFADULT, and CLINADULT) but a different combination of the independent variable sets was utilized.

As can be seen from Table 1, the set of 11 variables representing childhood adjustment, difficult-easy temperament, childhood environment, and presence of a clinical diagnosis (CHR, CHE, CLC) accounts for .429 of the generalized variance of the adult attribute set. (This is reduced to .341 in the unbiased estimate of MVR^2). The set (CHR, CHE) accounts for .374 of the generalized variance of the adult set (or .294 in the unbiased estimate). Adding the clinical child variables (CLC) to the predictor set, the amount of generalized variance explained in the adult set is increased by only .055.

The set of 9 variables representing childhood adjustment and degree of difficulty and childhood environment (CHR, CHE) accounts for .374 of the generalized variance of the adult attribute set. The set of 2 clinical variables (CLC) accounts for .168 of the generalized variance of the adult attribute set. Of the two clinical variables, CLIN 2 has much more effect than CLIN 1. CLIN 2 is a dichotomous variable, differentiating between those children with or without a preadolescent clinical diagnosis, and has an R^2 at .135 with the set of adult variables, affecting all 3 — AVOWN, DIFADULT, and CLINADULT. CLIN 1 differentiating between an early childhood clinical diagno-

TABLE 1

Set Correlation Analysis (A)

Independent Variable Set	Multivar. R^2 (MVR^2)	Unbiased Estimate of MVR^2	Signif. Indep. Var.	R^{2a}	Dep. Variables Signif. Affected by Indep. Var.
CHR, CHE, CLC	.429**	.341	CONFL	.120	AVOWN, DIFADULT
			DIFCHILD 3	.106	DIFADULT
			CLIN 1	.135	DIFADULT
CHR-CHE	.374**	.294	CONFL	.120	AVOWN, DIFADULT
			DIFCHILD 3	.106	DIFADULT
CLC	.168**	.141	CLIN 1	.059	CLINADULT
			CLIN 2	.135	all 3
CLC-CHR	.104*	.074	CLIN 1-CHR	.039	CLINADULT
			CLIN 2-CHR	.075	all 3
CLC-CHR, CHE	.076^{ns}	.044			

*p<.05 **p<.001 ns not significant

a) R^2 is the multiple correlation of the significant independent variable (immediately to the left) with the 3 variable adult set.

Note: In this Table, and in all the subsequent Tables in this chapter, the abbreviations and acronyms used for the variables are spelled out on pages 1 and 2 of the chapter.

sis (before age 6), and a late childhood clinical diagnosis (before age 12) is significantly related only to CLINADULT, and has an R^2 of .059 with the adult attribute set.

CLC-CHR is the clinical variable set (CLC), partialling out the effect of the childhood rating set (CHR). The multivariate R^2 .104 (significant at the .05 level) of CLC-CHR with the set of adult attributes indicates the effect of childhood clinical status, over and above the effect of the childhood adjustment and difficulty ratings. CLC-CHR, CHE is the clinical variable set, partialling out the effect of both the childhood rating and childhood trauma sets. The effect of the clinical variables, over and above the effect of the other childhood variables, is measured by a multivariate R^2 of .076, which is not statistically significant. Thus, childhood clinical status does not significantly predict adult status, once the childhood adjustment, difficult temperament, and environmental variables have been included in the analysis.

Only three of the individual independent variables have significant multiple R^2s with the adult set. CONFL is a significant predictor of AVOWN ($\beta = .287$), and DIFADULT ($\beta = .230$). DIFCHILD 3 is a significant predictor of DIFADULT ($\beta = .257$). CLIN 2 (having a clinical diagnosis before age 12) is a significant predictor of DIFADULT ($\beta = .238$). (The Beta number reflects the magnitude and direction of relationship among the variables.)

The two variables, GS3 and DIFCHILD 3 in the set called Age 3, account for .174 (significant at the .001 level) of the generalized variance of the adult

TABLE 2
Set Correlation Analysis (B)

Independent Variable Set	Multivar. R^2 (MVR^2)	Unbiased Estimate of MVR^2	Signif. Indep. Var.	R^2	Dep. Variables Signif. Affected by Indep. Var.
Age 3	.174**	.147	GS3	.093	AVOWN, CLINADULT
			DIFCHILD 3	.106	DIFADULT
Age 5	.122ns	.079	none	—	AVOWN
Age 3-Age 5	.134*	.106	GS3-Age 5	.043	AVOWN, CLINADULT
			DIFCHILD 3-Age 5	.099	DIFADULT

Age 3 = GS3, DIFCHILD 3
Age 5 = GS51, GS52, DIFCHILD 5
**p < .001   *p < .01   ns not significant

attribute set. GS3 has an R^2 of .093 with the adult attribute set. GS3 is significantly related to AVOWN and CLINADULT, but not to DIFADULT. DIFCHILD 3 has an R^2 of .106 with the adult attribute set, but is significantly related only to DIFADULT.

The set called Age 5, consisting of three variables, GS51, GS52, and DIFCHILD 5, accounts for only .122 of the generalized variance of the adult attribute set. Age 5 is not a significant predictor of the adult attribute set as a whole, being significantly related only to AVOWN.

The partialled set, Age 3-Age 5 explains .134 of the generalized variance of the adult attribute set. The size of the relationship of Age 3-Age 5 to the adult set indicates the effect of the age 3 variables over and above the effect of the age 5 variables. The partialled age 3 variables, GS3-Age 5 and DIFCHILD 3-Age 5 are significantly related to the same adult variables as their unpartialled counterparts. The size of the MVR^2 between the partialled age 3 variables is reduced because some of the effect of the age 3 variables is shared with the age 5 variables.

The three global adjustment scores, GS3, GS51, and GS52, comprising the set called GLO, are significantly related to the adult attribute set, explaining .143 ($p < .05$) of the generalized variance of that set. GS3 is the only significant member of GLO, explaining .093 of the variance in the adult set. Although GS3 is significantly related to all 3 members of the adult set, its relationship to AVOWN is much stronger than its relationship to the other two adult variables.

The two difficult-easy child variables comprising the set called DCB explain .148 ($p < .01$) of the generalized variance of the adult set. DIFCHILD 3 is significantly related to both AVOWN and DIFADULT. DIFCHILD 5 is a weaker variable than DIFCHILD 3, explaining half as much of the variance in the adult set ($R = .053$) as does DIFCHILD 3 ($R = .106$). DIFCHILD 5 is significantly related to both AVOWN and CLINADULT, although the set DCB containing both difficult child variables is not significantly related to CLINADULT.

When the effect of GLO is partialled from the effect of DCB, the amount of generalized variance explained in the adult set is reduced to .114 ($p < .05$). The DIFCHILD 3 variable explains .067 of the variance of the adult set, over and above the effect of the global adjustment ratings.

When the effects of the difficult child variables are partialled from the effects of the childhood global adjustment ratings (GLO-DCB), we see that the childhood adjustment ratings have no significant effect on the adult set, over and above the effect of the difficult-easy child set.

The childhood environment set, CHE, is significantly related to adult at-

TABLE 3
Set Correlation Analysis (C)

Independent Variable Set	Multivar. R^2 (MVR^2)	Unbiased Estimate of MVR^2	Signif. Indep. Var.	R^2	Dep. Variables Signif. Affected by Indep. Var.
GLO	.143*	.102	GS3	.093	all 3 (mostly AVOWN)
DCB	.148**	.121	DIFCHILD 3	.106	AVOWN, DIFADULT
			DIFCHILD 5	.053	AVOWN, (CLINADULT)[a]
DCB-GLO	.114*	.085	DIFCHILD 3-GLO	.067	DIFADULT
GLO-DCB	.106[ns]	.062			

GLO = GS3, GS51, GS52
DCB = DIFCHILD 3, DIFCHILD 5
*p < .05   **p < .01   ns not significant
a) CLINADULT is significantly affected by DIFCHILD 5, but not by the set DCB as a whole.

tribute set, explaining .213 of the generalized variance (p < .01) of the set comprised of the variables AVOWN, DIFADULT and CLINADULT. CONFL is the strongest variable in the environment set, being significantly related to all 3 adult variables, and explaining .120 of the variance in the adult set. ECON is significantly related only to DIFADULT ($R^2 = .031$ between ECON and the adult set as a whole). Death has an R^2 of only .015 with the adult set, with a weak relationship with AVOWN and DIFADULT. The variable SEPDIV, indicating the separation or divorce of parents, is not a significant predictor of adult status in this or any of the other set correlation analyses.

TABLE 4
Set Correlation Analysis (D)

Independent Variable Set	Multivar. R^2 (MVR^2)	Unbiased Estimate of MVR^2	Signif. Indep. Var.	R^2	Dep. Variables Signif. Affected by Indep. Var.
CHE	.213**	.165	CONFL	.120	all 3
			ECON	.031	DIFADULT
			DEATH	.015	AVOWN, DIFADULT
CHE-CHR	.148*	.093	CONFL-CHR	.081	AVOWN, DIFADULT
CHE-CHR, CLC	.120[ns]	.063			

*p < .05   **p < .01   ns not significant

When the effect of the childhood rating set is partialled from the effect of the childhood environment set, the generalized variance of the adult attribute set explained by the partialled set CHE-CHR is .148 ($p < .05$). The only variable in the environment set with a significant effect on the adult set, over and above the effect of the childhood rating set, is CONFL, which has an R^2 of .081 with the adult set. CONFL-CHR significantly predicts AVOWN and DIFADULT, but not CLINADULT.

When the childhood environment set is examined, partialling out both CHR and CLC, the resulting set explains .120 of the generalized variance of the adult set, which is not statistically significant.

The childhood rating set CHR, consisting of the 3 global adjustment scores and the 2 difficult child scores, explain .244 of the generalized variance of the adult attribute set. Two of the five variables in the set CHR are significantly related to the adult attribute set. GS52 has an R^2 of .063 with the adult attribute set, and is a significant predictor of AVOWN. DIFCHILD 3 has an R^2 of .106 with the adult set as a whole, but is a significant predictor only of DIFADULT. The childhood rating set as a whole does not significantly predict CLINADULT. However, one member of CHR, GS3, is a significant predictor of CLINADULT. (GS3 has an R^2 of .093 with the adult set as a whole).

When the effect of the clinical child set is partialled from the effect of the childhood rating set, the resulting set CHR-CLC explains .184 ($p < .05$) of

TABLE 5
Set Correlation Analysis (E)

Independent Variable Set	Multivar. R^2 (MVR^2)	Unbiased Estimate of MVR^2	Signif. Indep. Var.	R^{2a}	Dep. Variables Signif. Affected by Indep. Var.
CHR	.244**	.188	GS3	.093	CLINADULT[b]
			GS52	.063	AVOWN
			DIFCHILD 3	.106	DIFADULT
CHR-CLC	.184*	.123	DIFCHILD 3-CLC	.099	DIFADULT[c]
CHR-CLC, CHE	.155[ns]	.089			

*$p < .05$ **$p < .01$ ns not significant
a) R^2 is the multiple correlation of the significant independent variable (immediately to the left) with the 3-variable adult set
b) CLINADULT is significantly predicted by GS3, but not by the set CHR as a whole
c) AVOWN is significantly predicted by the set CHR-CLC, but no member of the set is individually significant

the generalized variance of the adult attribute set. The only variable in the childhood rating set which individually has a significant effect on the adult set, over and above the effect of childhood clinical status, is DIFCHILD 3, which has an R^2 of .099 with the adult set, and is a significant predictor of DIFADULT. (AVOWN is significantly predicted by the set CHR-CLC, but not by any individual member of that partialled set.)

When both the clinical child set and the childhood environment set are partialled from the childhood rating set, the resulting set, CHR-CLC, CHE explains .155[ns] of the generalized variance of the adult set. Thus, the childhood rating set is not a significant predictor, over and above the effects of childhood environment and clinical status combined, of the adult attribute set.

CHAPTER 9

Sex

Differences

There are many reasons for examining attributes of our study group separately for girls and boys. In the years up to adolescence, girls are developmentally more mature than boys. This is not a global effect – the genes exert their influence at different times and there must be many functions of differential development of the sexes as a group that are yet to be identified. Yet we do know some of these parameters. Girls as a group are linguistically faster developmentally than boys. Their neurologic integration is ahead in infancy and early childhood. Height and weight curves move toward adult status at a faster pace and sexual maturity, both physically and socially, begins at earlier ages. It is for such reasons that many studies decide to use boys only (or girls only) as subjects. Thus they avoid the confounding possibility that disparate trends may wash out important effects. Such studies are left, however, with two choices, each of which is to be found in various reports: 1) to assume that trends can be applied to the opposite sex even though minor details may differ; or 2) duplicate the study using subjects of the opposite sex – hoping that changing environmental features will not have altered the essential nature of the antecedent variables.

In the New York Longitudinal Study a third option was chosen. A sample of sufficient size was gathered, with equal distribution of males and females, so that it became possible to identify sex differences in the various variables of functional significance with which we were concerned.

Seventy-nine comparisons between the means for males and female were done, using T-tests.

1. *Age 3 Attributes*

   Adjustment. There was no difference between males and females in the global score. In the individual adjustment categories, there was one significant difference. Boys had more eating problems than girls.

   Temperament. There was no difference between males and females in the continuous easy-difficult child variable. There were 3 significant differences in individual temperamental attributes. Girls had higher scores on activity level and sensory threshold and lower scores on persistence.

   Maternal Attitude Factors. Boys received higher scores than girls on the factor called maternal concern.

2. *Age 5 Attributes*

   Adjustment. There were no differences between males and females in the adjustment scores from the parent interview. However, there were differences in the scores from the teacher interview. The boys had higher scores (poorer adjustment) in the global adjustment rating from the teacher interview. Boys were rated by teachers as having more motor problems and coping problems than girls.

3. *Temperament*, Ages 1, 2, 4

   There was no difference, at any age, in score on easy-difficult temperament between boys and girls. However, in year 1, girls had higher activity levels than boys. In year 2, boys were more adaptable than girls. In year 4, boys again had higher scores than girls on adaptability and girls had higher threshold levels than boys.

4. *Adult Attributes*

   Adjustments. There was no difference between men and women in the bootstrapped global score (AVOWN). However, there were significant differences in 4 of the 13 categories of adjustment. Women had higher scores (better adjustment) in social relationships, person orientation, communication and emotional expressiveness.

   Temperament. Men did not differ significantly from women on the continuous easy-difficult variable. However, women were significantly higher than men in activity level, rhythmicity and intensity, as derived from the interviews. It should be noted that there were no differences in temperament between men and women as ascertained from the temperament questionnaire. However, the questionnaire sample was substantially smaller (n = 70) than the interview sample (n = 132).

These sex differences are not striking. The 19 significant correlations are scattered throughout the different ratings. The only consistent significant finding was higher activity level for females, found in years 1 and 3, and in early adult life.

The previous two chapters have detailed the specific statistically significant correlations between sets of childhood variables and adult outcome measures.

The question of whether there were sex differences in the relationship between childhood predictors and adult outcomes was explored in three multiple regression analyses. In each analysis the same independent childhood sets were used: CHR (childhood global adjustment scores at age 3 from the parent interviews and at age 5 from the parent and teacher interviews, and easy-difficult temperament at 3 and 5 years); CHE (childhood environment scores, which included parental conflict, separation-divorce and death, and the relative living standard of the home at age 3); and CLC (clinical diagnosis in childhood). In the first analysis the dependent variable was AVOWN (bootstrap adult adjustment score), in the second it was early adult easy-difficult temperament, and in the third analysis it was a clinical psychiatric diagnosis. In each analysis the question posed was whether the interaction set, that is sex in interaction with each of the independent variables, added significantly to the level of correlation produced by the independent and sex variables separately.

The three multiple regression analyses revealed only weak evidence for sex differences in the relationships between childhood predictors and adult outcome. For the childhood rating set (CHR), the interaction set was not significant, over and above the CHR set itself, in predicting any of the three adult outcome variables. The interaction set was barely significant (.05 level), over and above the childhood environment set (CHE), in predicting the adult variables. However, a different member of the interaction set was significantly related to each adult variable, making for an inconsistent pattern of relationship. The interaction set was significant, over and above the childhood clinical set (CLC), only in the prediction of the adult adjustment score (AVOWN). Thus, sex differences did not appear to influence the relationship between childhood predictor sets and adult outcomes in the majority of the analyses. Further, where there was a significant relationship, it tended to be weak and inconsistent.

CLINICAL CASES

In the childhood period 25 boys and 20 girls received a clinical diagnosis of a behavior disorder. In the adolescent period there were 12 new cases, 6 boys and 6 girls. This sex distribution corresponds to the usual clinical findings, with a preponderance of males over females in the childhood period, and an equalization in adolescence. However, other clinical studies generally report a percentage of males in the childhood cases greater than our finding of 56 percent. As discussed in Chapter 5 above, the relatively large number of childhood behavior disorder cases in our NYLS sample, as compared to some other reports, may be due, at least in part, to the possibility that some of the cases might have recovered spontaneously and not come to clinical attention had they not been subjects in the longitudinal study. It may be that this was true more for the girls than the boys, i.e. that childhood behavior disorders in girls with spontaneous recovery are more likely, as compared to boys, to be overlooked in other studies. However, our data do not offer any information with which to test this possibility.

OTHER NYLS SEX DIFFERENCES ANALYSES

The above analyses reported the influence of sex differences on the relationships between single antecedent variables or sets of variables, (such as CHR, the childhood adjustment, and easy-difficult temperament rating scores) and single outcome measures, using multiple regression analyses. A large number of comparisons between the means for males and females were also done, using T-tests. The results of these analyses were not at all impressive with regard to the influence of sex differences.

Two other approaches to the NYLS data with regard to the influence of sex differences have been explored. Cameron (1977, 1978), rather than analyzing the influence of sex differences on the relationships between single independent variables or sets of variables and outcome variables, has explored the possible effect of sex differences in the NYLS sample on the interrelationship between a pair of risk domains (children's temperament and parental behaviors) and the incidence of behavior disorder. This approach is consistent with our goodness of fit model (see Chapter 2). In this model, healthy development results not from the child's temperament alone, or from parental and other environmental expectations alone, but from a goodness of fit expectations.

Cameron utilized a "parental pathology" score, computed by summing the scores on the three parental dimensions of parental conflict, maternal rejection, and inconsistent parental discipline, taken from the 3-year parental attitudes and child-care practices interviews. His high risk temperament score comprised a summation of high persistence, withdrawal, low adaptability, and negative mood — corresponding in the main to our difficult child constellation, plus high persistence. He found that "with the focus on *prediction* of subsequent behavioral problems, first-year temperament scores were found to be predictive of mild cases of either sex. Prediction of moderate-to-severe cases, however, could not be achieved on the basis of temperament data alone, but could be achieved for girls' cases by resorting to a global parental pathology score . . . moderate-to-severe male clinical cases were harder to predict" (1978, p. 146). Cameron emphasizes, as we have done, that it appears "insufficient for predictive clinical purposes to determine *only* the child's initial temperament. By the same token, measurement of parental responses to the child, in and of themselves, are not enough" (1978, p. 147). This caveat, while applicable to predictive studies in general, may be especially important for the investigation of the influence of sex differences on behavioral development.

CONTINUITY/DISCONTINUITY IN TEMPERAMENT

As indicated earlier in this chapter, there were no striking sex differences in temperament in the preschool or the early adult years. A recent study by Korn (in press) has focused on the issue of continuity in easy-difficult temperament from infancy to early adult life from the NYLS data. Overall, as was to be expected from our own findings, there was little difference in predictability between boys and girls when the sample as a whole was examined, in this case using a quartile analysis. However, differences did appear when the extreme quartiles were examined. Girls in the extreme quartile for *easy* temperament showed greater continuity from early childhood into early adulthood than did the boys. By contrast, the boys in the extreme quartile for *difficult* temperament showed greater continuity than did the girls.

These findings suggest an interpretation based on the temperament-environment interactional model. Some parents, teachers and peers, at least, might have subscribed to conventional stereotypes of masculinity and femininity. According to these standards, the temperamentally difficult boy with his intense reactions and insistence on his own positions (slow adaptability) may be considered masculine and be tolerated or even approved (one of our fathers cheerfully approved of his very difficult young son, who was indeed difficult to raise, as "lusty"). By contrast, similar behavior in a young girl might easily be labeled as "unfeminine." On the other hand, the quiet responses and easy adaptability of the easy child could easily conform to a stereotype of "femininity." As such, it could be encouraged in a girl and discouraged in a boy. Thus, any stereotyping of a child's behavior along these lines could lead to the reinforcement and increased continuity over time in at least some temperamentally difficult boys and temperamentally easy girls.

OTHER STUDIES OF SEX DIFFERENCES IN TEMPERAMENT

Several studies from widely distinct national groups on sex differences in temperament have been reported. Persson-Blennow and McNeil (1981), in a demographically representative sample of 160 Swedish children longitudinally studied at 6 months, 1 and 2 years of age, found only a few scattered significant sex differences. Males were significantly more adaptive both at 6 months and 1 year. At 6 months males were also more active and less distractible than females.

Hsu and his co-workers (1981) reported a study of a group of 349 4–8 month-old Chinese infants in Taiwan, using the Carey temperament questionnaire. Out of the 9 categories, only approach/withdrawal showed a significant difference, with males being more willing to approach the new than females. Furthermore, there were no sex differences in the 5 subcategories on the Carey scale (difficult, slow to warm up, intermediate high, intermediate low, and easy).

Finally, Maziade and his associates (1984) assessed a total of 335 4-month infants in Quebec, also utilizing the Carey questionnaire, and retested at 8 months the same sample plus an additional 384 infants. At 4 months significant differences between boys and girls were found in approach/withdrawal, adaptability, mood, persistence and distractibility. However, at 8 months only the difference in approach/withdrawal remained significant (girls were higher approachers).

DISCUSSION

Overall, the findings from the NYLS and from other centers abroad are consistent in the absence of striking sex differences in temperament. These findings lend support to the hypothesis of a biological basis for temperament which is not sex-linked, but by no means imply that temperament is immutable. The number of studies showing the significant levels of discontinuity of temperament over time (Thomas and Chess, 1977; Carey and McDevitt, 1978; Korn, 1984) indicate that the temperament, like any other psychological characteristic, is not immutable, and is subject to the influence of the constantly evolving process of organism-environment interaction.

A major concern of the voluminous literature on sex differences revolves around the questions of identifying even complex cognitive functions and personality traits which show differences between the sexes, and the determination of whether these differences are entirely biological in origin, entirely the result of social experience, or some combination of the two (Maccoby and Jacklin, 1974; Birns, 1976; Burstein et al., 1980; Tieger, 1980; Gilligan, 1982). While our review of this complex subject has not touched upon a large number of the variables considered in the literature, several points can be made. For temperament, the various crosscultural studies suggest a biological basis which is not sex-linked. Environmental influences do modify the expression of temperament, but a sex-linkage to this modification is clearly evident thus far only in the report by Korn (1984), cited above in this chapter. Furthermore, although our various quantitative childhood ratings and environmental variables do show significant relationships with early adult life outcome, the evidence for sex differences in the level of these relationships is at best weak.

This does not mean a conclusion that the differences in social environmental influences experienced by our NYLS subjects as they grew up were negligible in their effects. In individual subjects the effects were sometimes substantial and even dramatic, as will be indicated in various of the case vignettes in later chapters.

CHAPTER 10

Summary and Overview of the Quantitative Analyses

The previous three chapters have detailed our major quantitative analyses of the NYLS data, using multiple regression and set correlation techniques. These studies have focused on three issues: 1) the relationship between preschool and adult temperament; 2) the relationship between various characteristics of the childhood period and the level of young adult behavioral functioning, including the presence or absence of a behavior disorder; and 3) the identification of any significant sex differences in our various childhood and early adult life ratings.

The consideration of the adolescent ratings was not included in these analyses. Their inclusion would have enhanced the scope of the quantitative studies, but would also have considerably increased the complexity of the analyses. Limitation of resources did not make such an extension of the study possible. However, the adolescent data have been used extensively in our qualitative analyses, as will be evident in subsequent chapters.

The salient significant findings in these quantitative analyses will now be summarized.

TEMPERAMENT

Early adult temperament, as a dependent variable, is encapsulated in the continuous score "difficulty-easy adult," derived from the summation of the 5 temperament categories which make up this constellation. For year 3, the difficult-easy temperament rating was calculated both as a similar continuous score, and as a dichotomous score. This latter rating identified children as having difficult temperament who scored above the median cutoff in 4 out of 5 categories, but always including high intensity, and as having easy temperament if they met the same criteria, but below the median cutoff.

The continuous difficult-easy temperament score of the sample at age 3 is significantly related to the adult score derived from interviewer ratings in both the multiple regression and set correlation analyses. In the former, the relationship remains significant even when adjustment at Year 3 and parent attitudes at Year 3 are controlled for. In the set correlation analyses, the significant relationship between difficult-easy temperament scores in Year 3 and early adult is repeatedly confirmed. Two other measures of temperament in Year 3 are also significantly related to difficult-easy adult, namely overall temperament including all 9 categories, as well as the difficult/easy temperament dichotomous score. However, neither of these remains significantly related to difficult-easy adult when adjustment at Year 3 is controlled for. Thus, the most salient relationship between pre-school (Year 3) and young adult temperament we find in these two sets of analyses is the correlation between the difficult-easy temperament scores in the two age groups.

When the difficult-easy temperament score in the young adults is based on the questionnaire, rather than on interviewer ratings, we again find that only the difficult-easy temperament score at Year 3 is significantly related. In this set of analyses, overall temperament or the difficult/easy dichotomy at Year 3 are not significantly correlated with the young adult questionnaire difficult-easy score.

The greater predictive value of the childhood continuous difficult-easy score, as compared to the dichotomous rating, most likely stems from the fact that the former rating incorporates all the 5 temperament scores making up this constellation in all the subjects, which is not true of the dichotomous rating. Also, a multiple item index can be expected to show greater reliability than a single item index.

PREDICTION OF ADULT ADJUSTMENT

Adult adjustment as an outcome variable in the multiple regression and set correlation analyses was included both as the bootstrapped adjustment score (AVOWN) and as a dichotomous, clinical/non clinical diagnosis. A wide range of independent variables was included in the two sets of analyses. In the multiple regression analyses, adjustment in the young adult was significantly correlated with parental attitudes in Year 3 — with parental conflict a significant component. The parental attitudes set was significantly related with young adult adjustment even when controlling for age 3 adjustment, adjustment *and* temperament, and adjustment *and* difficult-easy temperament. The components of parental attitudes, conflict, and no factor were thus particularly striking, especially since the significant relationship between parental conflict (Year 3) and adult adjustment was also confirmed in the set correlation analyses.

The set correlation analysis confirmed the predictive significance of early parental conflict with adult adjustment, and in addition showed a significant correlation between the early relative living standards of the family and adult adjustment. These analyses also showed a significant correlation between early parental conflict and adult clinical status.

The difficult-easy temperament score in Year 3 was also significantly correlated with adult adjustment. This was shown in the multiple regression analyses, even when controlling for adjustment, as well as for adjustment *and* parent attitudes. It was also confirmed in the set correlation analyses. The latter analyses also showed a correlation between difficult temperament at age 5, but not at age 3, and early adult clinical status.

The level of the children's adjustment in the pre-school period is significantly related to adult adjustment. In the multiple regression analysis the Year 3 adjustment set was significantly related with adult adjustment, but not significant when controlling for parent attitudes in the same age period. However, in the set correlation analyses we find that adult adjustment is significantly correlated with the global adjustment score at Year 3 and the global adjustment score at school at Year 5. The global adjustment score at Year 3 is also significantly related to the clinical/non clinical assessment in the young adult.

What seems to be an even more striking precursor of adult adjustment is the presence or absence of a clinical diagnosis in childhood. This is significantly correlated with adult adjustment even when the childhood ratings of global adjustment *and* difficult-easy temperament are partialled out. The clinical/nonclinical childhood attributes are also significantly related to the adult clinical/nonclinical assessment.

We were also interested in the relatedness of certain special childhood events to later adjustment. Separation or divorce, and death of a parent were considered, and these two factors were included in the set correlation analyses as parts of the variable CHE (childhood environment). Death of a parent has a weak, but insignificant relationship with young adult adjustment, while separation or divorce is not a significant predictor of adult status in any of the set correlation analyses. Parental conflict at age 3 and later parental separation or divorce showed a correlation of .28, significant beyond the .01 level.

SEX DIFFERENCES

Sex differences were not striking, whether in temperament in the first 5 years and early adult life, or adjustment scores at 3 years, 5 years, and early adulthood, or maternal measures at 3 years. The evidence for sex differences in the relationships between childhood predictor variables and adult outcome was also weak. There were more boys than girls among the clinical cases in childhood, and an equal number in the new cases in adolescence. An analysis of the extreme quartiles for early childhood easy and difficult temperament did show greater continuity to early adulthood for easy temperament in girls, and for difficult temperament in boys.

OVERVIEW

The results of these quantitative analyses confirm and expand on the previous more limited NYLS data analyses which indicated significant relationships between early childhood temperamental characteristics and parental attitudes and the development of behavior disorders (Thomas, Chess and Birch, 1968; Cameron, 1977; Cameron, 1978; Terestman, 1980).

Outstanding in the high-risk factors in childhood for a relatively poor overall adjustment and/or the presence of a psychiatric disorder in early adult life were difficult temperament, parental conflict, the presence of a behavior disorder, and the global adjustment score at age 3 years.

In the set correlations, these early childhood variables account for 34 percent of the variance for early adult functioning, which is indeed impressive considering the 15-year age span involved, and the tremendous physical and psychological changes and social expectations in the transitions from childhood to adolescence to early adulthood. At the same time, this still leaves over 60 percent of the variance unaccounted for. This could possibly reflect in part methodological weaknesses in our rating systems or the failure to identify additional functionally significant variables. However, an interactionist viewpoint would predict that quantitative group measures could not capture the many special features of the child's behavior and the environmental influences which could affect the sequences of psychological development differently in different youngsters.

Not all children with difficult temperament develop behavior disorders. Some children with easy temperament do develop a behavior disorder. Some youngsters are able to cope successfully with a home atmosphere rife with parental conflict. Most children who show behavior disorder do recover by early adulthood.

For the exploration of the dynamics of individual developmental patterns which do not conform to group trends, as well as the identification of specific significant variables and their interaction in single individuals or small groups with special features of interest, qualitative analyses are necessary. Our approach to such analyses and the findings are detailed in the chapters to follow.

PART III

Qualitative Analysis

CHAPTER 11

Approach to Qualitative Data Analysis

Dr. Jacob Cohen, our consultant for quantitative methods of data analysis, has always quipped, "The statistician wants as few variables as possible, and as large a series of cases as possible. The clinician wants as many variables as possible, and is satisfied with a small series of cases." Dr. Cohen was in no way facetious in propounding this epigram. He demanded rigor and mathematical sophistication in our use of quantitative methods, and took a dim view of statistical methods which relied on small samples with multiple variables. On the other hand he had the greatest respect for our efforts, as clinicians, to gather as much information as we could from as many sources as we could, to make possible the qualitative analysis of special small subgroups of our NYLS sample. Always, before deciding how to lay out a sophisticated and even complex statistical strategy aimed at identifying the relationships between different variables and ratings, he would ask us, as the clinicians: What questions do you want these analyses to answer? What issues are important to you? Only then would he make a judgment as to whether a statistical analysis could answer our questions, and, if so, which statistical approach was most appropriate. We can still hear his caution to us, repeated over the many years: "The quantitative methods are powerful analytic instruments, but never forget your clinical insights and studies. They are just as important."

What Dr. Cohen was communicating to us was that quantitative and qualitative approaches were not oppositional and adversarial. Rather, they were complementary, each with its own and different strengths and limitations, which, in combination, made for the most powerful approach to the analysis of a body of data. When viewed separately, these two approaches do appear contradictory. Methods of quantitative analysis appear neat, tidy and precise, with their specific objective criteria for reliability and tests of statistical significance, their quantitative rating schedules, and their utilization of the power of mathematical approaches and computer programs. Methods of qualitative analysis, by contrast, appear crude, untidy, subjective, and lacking the precision provided by mathematics and the computer.

Yet quantitative analyses have their limitations. A correlation of .50, with a p value of .001, is impressive, but it still accounts for only 25 percent of the variance, leaving 75 percent of the significant relationships still unidentified. Qualitative analyses have their own types of limitations, whether it is the clinician's assertion that his "clinical experience" is a sufficient validation of his hypothesis, or whether it is the accumulation of a mass of naturalistic descriptions, which are indigestible and unanalyzable because they are not sharply focused and not precisely relevant to the hypothesis of the particular investigation. This problem has especially plagued a number of longitudinal behavioral studies, which have made the futile attempt to guard against the danger of overlooking the data which would later prove to be highly important but too late to retrieve — a risk which is inherent in any long-term longitudinal study. In attempting to hedge against this risk, these investigators have tried to gather information to cover all behavioral contingencies, a truly impossible task. The result, instead, has been that "in the absence of specific questions to be asked of the data all kinds of information that could be obtained about the subjects of the study have at times been unselectively accumulated. When the data were subsequently analyzed and reported, much of the available information held but little interest to the investigation, with files upon files of developmental data still gathering dust in many places" (Escalona and Leitsch, 1952, p. 25).

We have tried to utilize the power of quantitative methods of analysis as fully as possible, as indicated in the previous chapters. But we have at all times kept in mind that the hypotheses which motivated the development of the NYLS came from the clinical data we gathered in our day-to-day professional work. Furthermore, the 9 categories of temperament and the 3 constellations of the easy, difficult and slow-to-warm-up child were formulated through the separate qualitative analyses conducted by Dr. Birch and ourselves. When the computer verified one or another of our categories, as when the factor analysis also showed the easy-difficult temperament constellations, this was all well and good. When the factor analysis, however, did not identify the combination of categories typical of the slow-to-warm-up child, this did not induce us to eliminate this constellation from our findings. Factor analyses are fallible, and we had no reason to believe that this negative finding proved that our clinical identification of the slow-to-warm-up constellation represented poor judgment on our part.

On the other hand, when we judged clinically that divorce or separation of the parents had a negative influence on the subject's later overall adjustment, the statistically powerful regression multiple analysis showed that this relationship was spurious, and that it was parental conflict (which correlated with divorce) which was the significant predictive variable (Chess, Thomas, Korn et al., 1983). As another example, it was our hypothesis that difficult temperament in the young child would be correlated with poorer adjustment in the childhood years, but that this relationship would have disappeared by early adult life. However, the multiple regression analyses (see Chapter 10) showed a significant predictive value for early childhood temperament for both the childhood years and early adult life.

Yet, qualitative analysis can be a most powerful instrument in studies of normal and deviant psychological development, as well as in many other scientific fields. Piaget, Vygotsky and Freud, as well as a host of other investigators who have made significant contributions to developmental psychology and psychiatry, relied entirely on this analytic approach. The same holds true for the identification and categorization of the major psychopathological syndromes, whether it be autism, the developmental dysphasias, or other child and adult psychiatric disorders.

A key strategy in qualitative analyses is the accumulation of banks of naturalistic descriptive data, on which the reexamination of established theories, the formulation of new hypotheses, and the verification or rejection of new concepts can be based. The developmental psychologist, McCall, puts this issue clearly, in his concern at the disdain of so many psychologists for such descriptive data. "Historically, description is not one of the psychologist's delights—it is a second-class method of study to be used by default, not by choice" (1977, p. 334). As he emphasizes, "Developmental psychologists should accord description the esteem other disciplines do because much has been learned at its hand; consider the theory of evolution, the plate theory of continental drift, and our knowledge of the early evolution of *Homo Sapiens*. . . . we might look into our own backyard at Jean Piaget to observe the impact detailed naturalistic description can have on a discipline even when the maximum number of subjects is only three" (McCall, 1977, p. 337).

REQUIREMENTS FOR QUALITATIVE ANALYSIS

Qualitative analysis makes many demands upon the investigator. Judgment is required in the selection of the character and scope of the descriptive information to be collected. Judgment is also required in the formulation of data-gathering strategies which will be adequate to the task of obtaining a sufficiency of relevant and analyzable information. For example, the data required for the identification and categorization of temperamental characteristics must include descriptions of behavior in a number of situations, and also behavioral sequences over time. Information on behavioral characteristics in one setting and over a short period of time may be valuable for a number of purposes. But such data cannot suffice to determine whether the one slice of behavior is typical for the individual or is distorted by some adventitious influence, and typicality is a key issue for the categorization of temperamental individuality.

Judgment is also required in the rejection of parental or observer statements which purport to be objective descriptions of behavior, when actually they are subjective, biased reports. Thus, one mother stated that her 3-month old boy was jealous and cried if she talked to someone else while holding him. The "jealousy" was presented as a description, when, in fact, it was an interpretation. The "crying" was an objective description, which might have had several alternative explanations. Perhaps, the mother raised her voice in talking to someone across the room as compared to the softness of voice in talking to her infant son, and he was reacting to the loudness, perhaps because he had a low sensory threshold for sound. As another instance, one of our interviewers in the young adult follow-up reported one young man as "depressed." For this judgment there was no objective behavioral evidence or subjective report of such by the subject. But this was the interviewer's judgment; he must be depressed because of the many truly tragic experiences in his life.

Finally, judgment is required so that the pertinent data scattered through a mass of narrative and observational data can be identified, extracted, and organized into a coherent scheme for purposes of classification, rating, and conceptualization. Mendeleev is said to have kept with him at all times a set of index cards, with each element and its known properties tabulated on a single card. He kept arranging and rearranging the cards, to the amusement of his friends. But, finally, after innumerable such rearrangements, he emerged with the fundamental concept of the Periodic Table of Elements. There are no simple blueprints or mathematical procedures which will automatically lead the investigator to a coherent, conceptually logical order of a mass of qualitative data. One thing is certain. The task cannot be turned over to the computer. "The infallibility of the computer confers no infallibility on the researcher. The computer simply performs the task more efficiently and more cheaply, even if the task performed is the wrong one" (Kraemer, 1981, p. 317).

THE VERIFICATION OF A QUALITATIVE ANALYSIS

One of us (S.C.), after interviewing a number of our NYLS parents and obtaining detailed descriptive accounts of their infants' behavior in the routines of daily living, became aware that there was a consistent patterning that she could identify as she listened to the parents' accounts. One group of parents, a small minority, reported graphically the difficulties they were having. Their baby cried loud and often, sometimes without apparent cause, reacted negatively and vigorously to new foods or most other new experiences, and then adapted only slowly. Sleep and hunger cycles were irregular, further increasing the difficulties of child care for the parents. Other parents, a larger number, described the exactly opposite kind of baby. The parents did not give these descriptions in any systematic organized fashion, but as items interspersed among other specific reports of their infant's behavior, which related to other characteristics of the child. However, the pertinent items were striking enough, had a sort of logical unity, and were duplicated by the accounts of some, but by no means all parents. From this qualitative analysis of the parental interviews came our formulation of the "difficult child" and "the easy child," and the concepts that these were temperamental intrinsic characteristics of the child and not the consequence of parental management, and, further, that these characteristics might have a significant influence on the child's developmental course.

How could we "prove" these formulations. No quantitative experimental test could be devised for this purpose. A factor analysis which showed a clustering of most, but not all of the characteristics of the easy versus difficult child was helpful, but not conclusive (Thomas, Chess and Birch, 1968). The strong predictive value of the difficult child rating for later behavior disorder development, not only in the NYLS but in our mentally retarded and congenital rubella samples, as well as reports along the same direction by other investigators (Graham et al., 1973), gave strong confirmation to the hypothesis. Further support came from numerous vignettes reported to us from a number of sources (Thomas, Mittelman et al., 1982). Putting these all together, the evidence in favor of our concept of the easy-difficult child is substantial, but not sufficient to convince some skeptics (Vaughn et al., 1981; Bates, 1980). But the kind of experimental proof that we expect in the more exact physical sciences is just not possible in behavioral studies — even leaving aside the ethical restrictions imposed in any investigations involving human subjects. Rather, we should accept McCall's advice to "marshall evidence from as many . . . strategies as possible, realizing that each is deficient in itself . . . Each approach is inadequate by itself, but each makes a vital contribution to the conclusion" (McCall, 1977, p. 335).

PITFALLS OF QUALITATIVE ANALYSES

The meaningful utilization of qualitative data depends on the flexibility and judgment of approach of the researcher. The danger lies in justifying looseness as flexibility and in offering one's personal judgment as "proof" of an hypothesis or categorization. The clinical researcher who rests on the infallibility of his "clinical experience" is in the same boat as the quantitative analyst who rests on the infallibility of his computer and his mathematical formulas. The first is content without concern for form and structure; the other is form and structure without concern for content.

It is the responsibility of the clinical researcher to separate data from hypothesis, to formulate alternate explanations to his or her own favored one, and to develop strategies for obtaining the objective descriptive information which is relevant to the determination of the validity of the different hypotheses. Otherwise, hypothesis and data are confounded, and we are presented with statements that this child is in "the Oedipal Stage," or that this other child is in "the latency period," as if these are descriptive data rather than interpretations based on one conceptual framework. Or assumptions are made as to underlying psychodynamic mechanisms, and a subject is reported to be "anxious" or "hostile" or "depressed" when there is no objective evidence for the judgment.

Another pitfall results from an investigator's fear of the necessity for selectivity in data collection and analysis, that is, for the requirement to select the items from a mass of qualitative data that are relevant to the goals of his or her research aims, and to be ready to discard or file away the remaining data as irrelevant. There is then the hope that an audiotape or videotape recording will provide a full record of an interview or observation and eliminate the necessity for such selectivity. Or, if the judgment involved in the selection process turns out to be faulty, hopefully one can return to the tapes. But this is a false hope. In John Le Carré's novel, *The Little Drummer Girl*, a young woman, Charley, is interrogated exhaustively while someone takes notes. At one point, the note-taker asks her to wait, while he catches up with his notes. Charley asks, in exasperation, "Why don't you dash out and buy a bloody tape recorder?" Her interrogater replies calmly, "Because we don't have a week set aside for reading transcripts . . . The car selects, you see, dear. Machines don't. Machines are uneconomical" (1983, p. 125). Tape recordings can be very useful for many purposes, but they cannot relieve the investigator of the necessity for being selective. If he listens to an audiotape, his ear has to be selective, and if he watches a videotape, his eye has to be selective.

THE INTEGRATION OF QUALITATIVE AND QUANTITATIVE ANALYSES

Fortunately, one does not have to choose between a commitment to either qualitative or quantitative analytic methods. Quite the contrary. The two methods should proceed in a coordinated integrated fashion. The qualitative approach can be considered the "cutting edge" (to use our colleague Sam Korn's phrase) which takes a body of data, or even scattered bits of information, and categorizes them, structures them, organizes them, and draws hypotheses from them. Quantitative methods then quantify the categories and structures, and test the hypotheses with the rigors of appropriate mathematical methods. The results of the quantitative analyses can then be scrutinized anew qualitatively for their implications, for the identification of connections not explicated in the results of the quantitative findings, and for the formulation of modified or new hypotheses.

We have attempted to achieve this integration of the qualitative and the quantitative in our analysis of the NYLS data, as presented in this volume. Previous chapters have detailed our formulations of behavioral characteristics in subject and parent through qualitative inductive analysis, and our transformation of these characteristics into qualitative ratings which could then be subjected to statistical analysis. In subsequent chapters, these quantitative findings will be used as a basis for further qualitative studies, as in the high-risk versus low-risk groups. These, as well as other qualitative investigations, such as the clinical course of the various types of behavior disorder, will use statistical techniques where relevant, to identify significant relationships among variables. Finally, the theoretical and practical implications of both the qualitative and quantitative findings will be explored.

CHAPTER 12

High- and Low-Risk Subjects at Three Years and Early Adult Outcome

The qualitative analysis of the developmental course of our subjects' lives from infancy to early adulthood leads to the idiographic examination of the longitudinal records of specific individuals. If, however, such an approach were to consist of anecdotal reports of arbitrarily selected cases in a serendipitous search for meaningful relationships and sequences, it would run the risk of providing interesting idiosyncratic information with little or no general applicability.

To avoid such an anecdotal approach in our idiographic analyses, we have utilized a number of strategies for identifying the specific subjects to be studied, and the specific issues to be explored. In this chapter we have taken the predictive findings from 3 years to early adult life established by the multiple regression and set correlation analyses to identify those subjects who at 3 years were at high risk, intermediate high risk, and low risk for unfavorable early adult outcome. We have then chosen for detailed study the records of several subjects whose lives have gone counter to the general group prediction, with the aim of identifying those factors which may have influenced such an outcome.

As summarized in Chapter 10, both the multiple regression and the set correlation analyses identified difficult-easy temperament at age 3 and parental conflict at age 3 as significantly correlated with early adult adjustment. With these findings, the 3-year-olds with both difficult temperament and marked parental conflict should be at high risk for unfavorable outcome in early adulthood. Conversely, the 3-year-olds with easy temperament and low parental conflict should be at low risk for unfavorable outcome in the early adult period.

Four groups of subjects at age 3 were identified: 1. the extreme quartiles for both difficult temperament and severity of parental conflict (n = 5); 2. the extreme quartiles for both easy temperament and low parental conflict (n = 8); 3. the extreme quartiles for easy temperament and for severe parental conflict (n = 6); and 4. the extreme quartiles for difficult temperament and for low parental conflict (n = 3). The first group should be at highest risk, the second at lowest risk, and the third and fourth groups should be at intermediate/high risk.

For each group, a tabulation of the individual subjects was made, with outcome charted in terms of the early adult adjustment score and the presence or absence of a behavior disorder, including age of onset, diagnosis, and outcome in adolescence and early adult life. The bootstrap score was utilized for the adult adjustment rating (see Chapter 5 for a description of the rationale for this scoring technique). Although the interviewers' global adult adjustment ratings were on a scale ranging from 1 to 9, the calculation of the bootstrap score expanded the range of scores in both directions, from 0 to 10. The tabulations also included sex, 3-year IQ, and 3-year global adjustment score.

These tabulations are presented in Tables 1, 2, 3, and 4.

Before proceeding to the detailed consideration of individual subjects, a comparison of the 4 groups reveals a number of points of interest.

DIFFERENCES IN ADULT ADJUSTMENT

As was to be expected from the quantitative analyses, the high- and low-risk groups (Tables 1 and 2) differ in the outcome measures of early adult adjustment score and the presence or absence of a behavior disorder.

The mean adult adjustment score for the high-risk subjects was 4.92, and for the low-risk group was 6.78. This difference is statistically significant at the .05 level (one-tailed t-test, t = 2.13). The median score for the total NYLS sample was 6.01, so that the mean for the high-risk group was over one rating point below, and that for the low-risk subjects almost one rating point above this median. Thus, the combination of difficult temperament and parental conflict in a preschool child does create a higher risk for poorer than average functioning in early adult life, at least for a population with the sociocultural characteristics of the NYLS.

However, the difference in adult adjustment score between the two groups was not ubiquitous. Two of the 5 high-risk subjects had outcome scores above

TABLE 1

Difficult Temperament and Severe Parental Conflict, Age 3 and Outcome

Subject Code #	Sex	IQ Age 3	Adult Adj. Score	Age 3 Adj. Score	Age, Onset Beh. Disorder	Diagnosis	Status in Adolescence	Status in Early Adulthood
005	M	104	3.43	1.61	4	Adj. Dis., Moderate	Recovered	Recovered
231	F	Not Obtained	3.66	1.73	3	Adj. Dis., Moderate	Recovered	Recovered
052	M	122	4.01	1.77	6	Adj. Dis., Mild	Recovered	Recovered
026	M	127	6.21	1.44	4	Adj. Dis., Moderate	Worse, Avoid-ant Dis. of Adolescence	Recovered
049	M	110	7.31	2.02	No Behavior Disorder		—	—
		116*	4.92*	1.71*				

*Mean Score

Note: The tabulations for the adult and age 3 adjustment scores are in opposite directions. A *higher* adult score signifies better adjustment, whereas a *lower* age-3 score signifies better adjustment.

TABLE 2

Easy Temperament and Low Parental Conflict, Age 3 and Outcome

Subject Code #	Sex	IQ Age 3	Adult Adj. Score	Age 3 Adj. Score	Age, Onset Beh. Disorder	Diagnosis	Status in Adolescence	Status in Early Adulthood
235	F	123	4.71	1.39	13	Antisocial Personality Dis. Severe	Onset	Recovered
009	M	Not Obtained	5.81	1.18	No Behavior Disorder		—	—
204	F	139	6.29	1.20	6	Adj. Disorder, Moderate	Recovered	Recovered
211	F	116	6.48	1.14	No Behavior Disorder		—	—
045	M	120	6.86	1.16	No Behavior Disorder		—	—
054	M	118	7.17	1.38	4	Adj. Disorder, Mild	Recovered	Recovered
042	M	110	8.22	1.21	6	Adj. Disorder, Mild	Recovered	Recovered
203	F	131	8.69	1.00	No Behavior Disorder		—	—
		122*	6.78*	1.10*				

*Mean Score

the NYLS median (6.21 and 7.31), and 2 of the 8 low-risk youngsters had outcome scores below this median (4.71 and 5.81).

Again, as expected from the quantitative analyses, for the intermediate high-risk groups (Tables 3 and 4) the mean adult adjustment scores were intermediate between the low-risk and high-risk groups, and the same, 6.43, for both. However, the group with easy temperament and severe parental conflict does include one subject with the second highest adult adjustment score (9.49) in the entire NYLS sample. And the group with difficult temperament and low parental conflict includes one subject with a superior adult adjustment score (7.91).

RISK LEVEL AND BEHAVIOR DISORDER

For the NYLS sample as a whole, 57 subjects, or 43 percent, developed a behavior disorder in childhood or adolescence, with average age of onset at 7 years. As expected, the high-risk subjects showed a substantially higher incidence of disorder, 4 out of 5, or 80 percent. They also had, on the average, an earlier age of onset, 4 years as compared to 7 years. As to severity, almost half the behavior problems in the total sample were mild adjustment disorders (26 out of 57), while only one of the high-risk cases was in this category, the other 3 being adjustment disorders of moderate severity. However, the high-risk cases did not include any of the 5 cases of severe adjustment disorders or 2 cases of conduct disorder from the total sample.

By contrast, only 4 of the 8 low-risk subjects, or 50 percent, developed a behavior disorder. Age of onset was also later, averaging 7 years, with one of the cases with onset in adolescence. Of the 3 cases with onset in childhood, 2 out of 3 were mild, and only one a moderately severe adjustment disorder. However, when compared to the total NYLS sample, the incidence of behavior disorder of the low-risk subjects was slightly higher, 50 percent as compared to 43 percent. Average age of onset was identical, namely 7 years.

Of special interest is the finding that, in both the high-risk and low-risk groups, all the behavior disorder cases arising in either childhood or adolescence were evaluated as recovered in early adult life. This was also true of the intermediate group with difficult temperament and low parental conflicts (Table 4). Only for the intermediate group with easy temperament and severe parental conflict (Table 3), did 2 out of 3 clinical cases continue to show a psychiatric disorder in early adulthood. This is in contrast to the finding from the quantitative analyses (see summary in Chapter 10) that the presence of a clinical diagnosis in childhood is statistically significantly related to the assessment of a clinical disorder in early adult life. Furthermore, the set correlation analyses had shown a significant correlation between parental conflict at age 3 and the presence of a psychiatric disorder in early adulthood. This relationship is not evident in the high risk group, but is in the intermediate group with easy temperament and severe parental conflict. This apparent opposition to the findings from the quantitative analyses will be examined in Chapter 17, which deals with the reasons for differential outcome of the childhood and adolescent behavior disorders in early adult life.

IQ SCORES

Mean IQ scores at age 3 corresponded to the mean for the sample as a whole for the low-risk group, and were lower than this NYLS mean for the high- and intermediate-risk groups. The means were lowest for the two groups (2 and 4) which included severe parental conflict.

3-YEAR ADJUSTMENT SCORES

In contrast to the schedule for the adult adjustment score, for the 3-year adjustment ratings the lower the score the better the adjustment, with 1.0 being the best rating and 5 being the most severely disturbed. For the NYLS sample as a whole, the mean 3-year score was 1.37, with a S.D. of .21. As was to be expected, the low-risk group had a favorable mean score of 1.10, with no subject being more than .02 points above the total sample mean. The high risk group, by contrast, had a mean score of 1.71, with all subjects being above the total sample mean. The two intermediate groups showed mean scores very close to the total sample mean.

SEX DIFFERENCES

In the high risk group (Table 1), 4 of the 5 subjects are male, whereas in the low-risk group (Table 2) sex distribution is equal — 4 girls and 4 boys. In the overall NYLS sample there were no significant sex differences found for either difficult temperament or parental conflict. This was also true for the extreme quartiles for these two variables at age 3 for the total NYLS sample.

This overall lack of sex differences in the total sample makes the finding of sex differences in the high-risk group especially striking. The sample size is small (5) and the finding by itself might be considered accidental. However, if we turn to the two intermediate high-risk groups (Tables 3 and 4), we find the same striking sex difference in the group with easy temperament and severe parental conflict — 5 boys and one girl. There are only 3 subjects in the

TABLE 3

Easy Temperament and Severe Parental Conflict, Age 3 and Outcome

Subject Code #	Sex	IQ Age 3	Adult Adj. Score	Age 3 Adj. Score	Age, Onset Beh. Disorder	Diagnosis	Status in Adolescence	Status in Early Adulthood
032	M	132	3.37	1.63	2	Adj. Disorder, Mild	Worse, Depressive Neurosis, Mod.	Worse, Narcissistic Personality Disorder
006	M	124	3.54	1.09	5	Adj. Disorder, Severe	Worse, Narcissistic Personality Disorder	Improved, Depressive Neurosis, Moderate
048	M	97	3.67	1.36	No Behavior Disorder	No Behavior Disorder	—	—
033	M	91	3.87	1.33	16	Antisocial Personality Disorder, Mod.	Onset	Recovered
034	M	94	6.58	1.20	No Behavior Disorder	No Behavior Disorder	—	—
236	F	137	9.49	1.42	No Behavior Disorder	No Behavior Disorder	—	—
		113*	6.43*	1.34*				

*Mean Score

116

TABLE 4
Difficult Temperament and Low Parental Conflict, Age 3 and Outcome

Subject Code #	Sex	IQ Age 3	Adult Adj. Score	Age 3 Adj. Score	Age, Onset Beh. Disorder	Diagnosis	Status in Adolescence	Status in Early Adulthood
012	M	133	5.59	1.16	6	Adj. Disorder, Mild	Recovered	Recovered
218	F	117	5.79	1.14	No Behavior Disorder		—	Recovered
201	F	107	7.91	1.63	7	Adj. Disorder, Mild	Worse, Adj. Disorder Moderate	
		119*	6.43*	1.31*				

*Mean Score

117

group with difficult temperament and low parental conflict, but in any case the sex distribution is not remarkable.

If we combine the two high conflict groups, we find that they include 9 males and 2 females. The two low conflict groups by contrast, include 5 males and 6 females. The numbers are small, but this difference in sex distribution of the two groups is statistically significant at less than the .10 level (Fisher's exact test).

Thus, it would appear that boys are more vulnerable to parental conflict in their early years, and that this vulnerability is evident with either extreme of difficult or easy temperament. In this regard, a study by Wolkind and DeSalis (1982) is of interest. They obtained interview-based measures of temperament on a sample of 4-month-old infants from lower-class London families, from which they constructed a difficult-easy scale. When evaluated at 42 months, the temperamentally difficult children had more behavior problems, as did the children of the depressed mothers in the sample. Maternal depression, however, was associated with child behavior problems only if the child had been in either the extreme difficult or extreme easy quartile temperamentally, but not if he had been in one of the middle quartiles.

There are a number of substantial differences between Wolkind and DeSalis' data and ours — age of temperament and outcome ratings, social class of the samples, criteria for the rating of difficult-easy temperament. Also, their data do not include an analysis of sex differences. However, what is of interest is that in their study, as in ours, an undesirable parental environment — in their case, maternal depression, in ours parental conflict — was associated with unfavorable outcomes for children with either extreme difficult or extreme easy temperament. Wolkind and DeSalis suggest that different mechanisms may be operating with the two types of children. Our own tentative explanation is along similar lines. The temperamentally difficult child requires a patient and consistent parental approach for optimal development to occur (Thomas, Chess and Birch, 1968), an approach which is not likely with parents in severe conflict over child-rearing methods and other issues. The temperamentally easy children tend to develop behavior problems when the parents' system of values, practices or demands on the child are idiosyncratic and contradictory to what the child meets in the outside world in the peer group. The child has adapted easily at home, in line with his temperamental style, but then comes into conflict with the outer world. Such idiosyncratic or ambiguous parental values and practices may very well be more frequent if the parents are in severe conflict or if the mother is depressed. This hypothesis remains to be tested.

In our NYLS sample, this vulnerability to severe parental conflict appears to be true for boys but not girls. It is of interest that clinical studies of the incidence of behavior disorders in childhood consistently report a significantly higher rate among boys, though no clear data exist as to the source of this greater vulnerability. Our findings do not explain the source of this apparent vulnerability of boys to parental conflict, but they do suggest that some part of the greater incidence of behavior disorders among boys may be linked to this specific vulnerability.

INDIVIDUAL SUBJECT ANALYSES

We now turn to the heart of this predictive analysis from 3 years to early adulthood, namely the idiographic study of the anterospective records of selected subjects. The criterion for the choice of subjects for this analysis is a simple one—namely, those individuals whose early adulthood outcome was substantially in an opposite direction to their group trend, as predicted by the multiple regression and set correlation analyses, and as evident in the tabulations of Tables 1–4 of this chapter. This criterion makes possible a focused rather than a purely anecdotal exploration of the longitudinal records, by structuring the study to investigate the reasons for the unpredicted early adult outcome in these subjects.

HIGH-RISK SUBJECTS WITH SUPERIOR ADULT ADJUSTMENT

The high-risk youngster, Michael, with a 6.21 adult outcome score, had the onset of a behavior disorder at age 4 years. The major symptom was a failure to participate in nursery school activities. Qualitative evaluation of his behavioral records from the parent and teacher interviews, as well as his behavior when brought for psychometric testing at age 3, and for clinical evaluation at age 4, indicated a typical slow-to-warm-up temperamental pattern. There were a number of reports in the parental interviews of intense reactions, such as "jumped up and down with pleasure" or "cried loudly," sufficient to give Michael a relatively high intensity rating on the quantitative scoring, and, together with the withdrawal and slow adaptability tendencies, to place him on the difficult side of the difficult-easy temperament spectrum. The rating of severe parental conflict at age 3 made by the independent interviews was confirmed in his statements when interviewed at age 22. His parents' relationship, he said, "had always seemed volatile," his father "seemed to be very critical," and "there is a lot of parrying between them." He started nursery school at age 3, had an initial reaction of crying and clinging to his mother, but then adapted gradually with considerable quiet participation.

The following year at nursery school started with the same gradual warm up. Then, in November, before he had had the time he required to develop a firm positive adaptation, he developed an upper respiratory infection which kept him out of school for a week. On his return to school, his initial withdrawal response was again evidenced, followed by the beginning of active involvement, but then interrupted again by a recurrence of his respiratory infection. For the next half year this pattern of brief periods at school interrupted by upper respiratory illnesses continued, and his lack of participation on each return to school evoked greater teacher concern. Clinical evaluation revealed this same slow-to-warm-up pattern in the playroom session, but no evidence of insecurity, anxiety, or other psychopathology. A favorable prognosis was given, and this was confirmed in the subsequent years. At the beginning of each school year Michael showed a similar withdrawal tendency, followed by gradual positive adaptation. There were no breaks in attendance due to illness, in contrast to his second nursery school year experience. As a result, his favorable course in school was sustained, and the initial withdrawal tendency became less and less evident with each succeeding school year. The parental conflict did not appear to be a direct factor in the development of his behavior problem at age 4, though it is possible that it may have intensified his difficulties with adaptation to new situations.

Throughout his middle childhood years Michael functioned well, without evidence of any psychopathology. However, in adolescence he began to experiment with drugs, and said he was "at the tail end of the counterculture." By age 16, he was into a number of drugs, including marijuana, cocaine and LSD. His school grades suffered and his relationship with his parents deteriorated. When evaluated clinically again at that time, the negative reactions to new situations and demands were again quite evident, and the diagnosis of avoidant disorder of adolescence was made.

Michael's adolescent disorder appeared to be a new and different episode of psychopathology, rather than a recurrence of his earlier childhood difficulties. His father was highly successful and respected in his profession, and Michael's older brother and sister were high achievers academically. He characterized himself as the "baby" of the family, and felt strongly alienated from his parents, whom he described as "two generations" away from him. His response to this family constellation was one of withdrawal and passive rebellion, which was consistent with his temperamental characteristics.

When seen for his interview at 22 years, Michael showed a dramatic change from his stormy adolescent period. He was relaxed, self assured, saying, with a smile, "I like myself." He was a serious student of music, enrolled in a conservatory, and was busy composing as well as performing. His interest in music began when he was 9, but he did not pursue it consistently until he graduated from high school. He was now seriously committed, and had two years to graduate with a degree. He smoked marijuana only occasionally, drank very little, and had given up all other drugs. His social life was active and enjoyable, and he described his heterosexual functioning as fulfilling and pleasurable. He had also held a number of part-time jobs, though his parents were paying for his schooling. He still had stress reactions in some new situations, especially in performing before new and strange groups. Once he habituated, however, the tension diminished and left. Overall, he commented that it still took him "a considerable amount of time to adapt to a new situation."

Michael's positive change from adolescence can be attributed to the flowering of his musical talent and commitment, which gave him an independent direction and goal in life, separate from the academic careers of his father, brother and sister, yet one respected in its own right. Also helpful has been his charming manner and social grace, which were much in evidence in the interview.

The other high-risk youngster, Stanley, with a superior adult adjustment score (7.31), had never shown symptoms of a behavior disorder throughout childhood and adolescence. But his favorable development was achieved not only in spite of difficult temperament and a rating of severe parental conflict at age 3, but with clear evidence that this conflict continued throughout his boyhood and adolescence. Moreover, his mother was compulsively intrusive and controlling, and his father passive and aloof. Here are some of Stanley's statements from his adolescent interview. "Parents argue a great deal, usually started by mother . . . They don't understand one another and, although my father tries to settle arguments, my mother remains mad . . . Mother has a peculiar habit which bothers me of asking personal questions about my father and brother." And from his interview at age 20: Father is "quiet, very hardworking . . . We're not the most close-knit family . . . Mother is bright, interested in many things, compulsive and very impatient . . . She's also sarcastic and cynical." His brother, Roy, 3 years older, also an NYLS subject, told the interviewer at 16 years that his mother tells him he's wrong 24 hours a day. "We're at one another's throats all the time." At his 23-year-old interview he described his father as a quiet background figure and not especially close to anyone in the family and his mother as controlling, nagging and intrusive.

The brother Roy did develop a behavior disorder in childhood, and when a clinical evaluation was done at 6 years by one of us (S.C.) it was very evident that the mother was indeed compulsive, pressuring, intrusive and controlling, while the father was a passive figure who dealt with his wife's battles with Roy by avoidance.

Given this family environment, it is not surprising that the older brother did develop a behavior problem; but how did Stanley escape? Actually, the two phenomena were related. Roy was temperamentally very distractible and this led typically to "forgetfulness" in finishing a task or meeting a time deadline. He would start an activity with every intention of completing it and then be distracted by some adventitious stimulus. To the mother, Roy's failure to carry through her requests and instructions meant only that he was challenging and opposing her. She put it that "he does everything he can to make my life miserable," and that "all he has to know is that I want him to do something for him to do the opposite," and she could only focus on her demand that he do her bidding on her terms. Repeated discussions with her in which the many instances of similar behavior on Roy's part with his friends, in which he would "forget" a pleasurable date he himself had made, were of no avail. The battle with Roy continued unabated into his adolescence, as he himself described it in his adolescent interview.

By contrast to Roy, the mother viewed Stanley as a model son. Even though of difficult temperament, Stanley was not distractible and "forgetful." The mother's constant refrain was "Stanley does what I ask him, why can't Roy." Our staff interviewer's comment was that the mother "has always described Stanley very positively, speaks about him with warmth."

Given this attitude on his mother's part, Stanley was not caught up in any destructive struggle with her, and could view her with objectivity and even affection. His critical comments on her, quoted above, were interlarded with positive observations, "She's very talented in many things, interested in many things. . . . She's bright, so's my father. . . . We get along fine." His positive relationship with the father has involved specific activities, such as tennis. He has kept emotionally aloof from both parents, doesn't discuss problems with them, though he feels he would get a positive response from them if he did. He describes his relationship with his older brother Roy as friendly but not at all close.

It is of interest that this objectivity and emotional detachment from his parents have not prevented Stanley from developing an active social and sexual life and communicating freely with his friends on a level appropriate to a 20-year-old young man.

LOW-RISK SUBJECTS WITH LOW ADULT ADJUSTMENT SCORES

The girl, Bernice, with easy temperament and low parental conflict at age 3, but with an adult adjustment score of 4.71, showed a positive development throughout her early and middle childhood years. In spite of her overall relatively mild intensity rating on the item scoring, she did show intense reactions in selected situations which engaged her interest. In addition, she had a high activity level. This combination made for occasional quick intense and even impulsive behavior with resulting mild difficulties. On each such occasion, the parents joined in setting limits firmly and consistently but quietly and supportively, and the problem behavior quickly disappeared. The disturbances were never sufficiently prolonged or severe to warrant a clinical diagnosis.

At age 13, behavioral difficulties again appeared in relationship to increased academic demands, the onset of puberty, and the complexities of adolescent peer interactions. Within a few months, her father, who had been a stabilizing authoritative (but not authoritarian) figure in the family, died suddenly and unexpectedly. The same advice for quiet consistent limit setting had again been recommended, but this time the mother could not follow our advice. Bereft of her husband and his influence, stretched to her limits physically by having to return full-time to a demanding and difficult job, she was unable emotionally to cope with her daughter's crises and outbursts, in addition to attending to the needs of her other three young daughters. The girl's problems escalated, her interaction with her mother and sisters became increasingly hostile and disruptive, and she developed a severe sociopathic behavior disorder, including truancy, sexual promiscuity, stealing and lying.

Psychotherapy was arranged several times during this period by her mother, but failed each time because of Bernice's lack of commitment. It appeared clear that if her father had lived, he and her mother, working together as they had in the girl's earlier years, would probably have prevented this highly unfavorable adolescent development.

The story does not end there. Bernice had refused to be interviewed at age 16, but did agree to an interview at age 22. She gave a cheery greeting with a bright smile and made a charming appearance. With each question she launched into an animated discussion with a great deal of introspection and relevant spontaneous elaboration. She spoke freely of her adolescent antisocial behavior. "I was the one who would run out of the house at 4 A.M., steal $20.00 from my mother's purse, cut classes. I did a lot of bad things then, but I was ready to blame others. Now I take all the responsibility on myself."

Bernice was now self-supporting, self-reliant, and launched on her own merits on a career which absorbed her. Her social relationships were active and positive. Her relationships with her mother and sisters, however, were distant, though superficially friendly. All this was confirmed by her mother in a separate interview.

When asked directly in the interview how she explained this dramatic positive change from adolescence, Bernice gave first emphasis to her mother's announcement that when she was 18 she would have to be on her own, that her mother would no longer be legally responsible for her. "It was brutal, but it worked." Her mother had consulted one of us (A.T.) frequently during Bernice's adolescence for help in controlling her behavior. These discussions were supportive and helpful to a limited extent, but did not effect any significant change, either in Bernice's behavior or her mother's helplessness and hopelessness. The mother became progressively demoralized, and especially could not cope with Bernice's violent tantrums when confronted with a new misdeed. Beyond this, her other 3 daughters each complained, and legitimately, that Bernice's violent antics created such turmoil at home that they could not study or relax, and were even afraid to invite their friends to the home. They could only look forward to the time when they themselves could leave home, a view they communicated openly to their mother. This only increased her despair at the threatened destruction of the close, affectionate family she and her husband had worked so hard to build over the years. Finally, it was pointed out to the mother that she could order Bernice out of the house when she was 18, and, given their complete alienation from each other, this might be the only solution, however regrettable it might be. With this perspective, the mother achieved a degree of patience and hopefulness, as she waited for this fateful birthday.

Bernice added that she always had a sense "in my own brain" of facing situations and coping with them when she had to. "I think I was born with this capacity." She also felt that several teachers in her last two years of high school had influenced her positively. As to why she had her adolescent difficulties, she emphasized the effect of her father's death. She was sure she would have rebelled, anyway, as a teenager, but knew her father, if he were alive, would have set limits effectively. "I probably idolize my father because he's not here, but I think of him all the time." She remembered many incidents of things they did together. She and her father were remarkably similar temperamentally.

When forced to leave home at 18, "I went down a little, floundered for 2 years, worked in this bar." Then she mobilized herself, drew on her artistic interests and talents, and applied for professional training to a top institute. Turned down because of poor high school grades, she went to a less demanding school, got all A's, reapplied to the first school, was accepted, and went through her training successfully. She then proceeded to obtain work in her highly competitive field. She is clearly talented in her chosen field, but there was an element of luck in her success in obtaining her first job. This was achieved through a friend of her father's, whom she met by chance and who offered her a position on a low rung of the career ladder. However, it was by her own merit and determination that she not only succeeded in this job, but seized the opportunity to train herself further and gain a promotion.

It is of interest that her chosen field was in a professional area similar to, though not identical with her father's. She herself offered the comment in the interview that she had perhaps picked it "maybe perhaps of my father. Seemed exciting, glamorous."

The advice to her mother to order Bernice out of the house at 18 had been given with trepidation. It was a gamble, which hopefully would make this youngster, with her many assets and positive childhood development, face the consequences of her behavior as an independent adult. But there was the risk that she would not be able to cope with such a sudden severe demand, and that her antisocial behavior would only intensify and lead to some disastrous outcome. However, nothing else had helped, and there were her mother and three sisters to be considered, whose lives at home were being perpetually disrupted by Bernice.

Beyond her mother's "brutal" insistence that she be independent, and the influence of her high school teachers, the decisive element in Bernice's dramatic change appears to have been the motivation for her career, which has been intense and persistent. Fortunately, this motivation was combined with superior intelligence and talent in her chosen field. It is of interest that in the interview Bernice commented spontaneously on her high activity level and intensity of reactions, both of which had been prominent since early childhood. "I'm very intensely expressive." Some people have advised her to be "low-keyed, I can't be that way. I'm going faster than that."

But Bernice was by no means entirely out of the psychological woods, even if clearly on her way, when we interviewed her at 22 years. Her self-image was quite ambivalent. She spoke positively of her talents, of "feeling on top of everything" when working, and had a sense of her capacity to face situations and cope with them. On the other hand, she emphasized her "insecurity" when not working, and still "disliked" herself at times. She had a number of heterosexual experiences, without any sexual problems as such, and lived with a young man from 18–21. This relationship was close and positive at first, then gradually deteriorated until they both broke it off. She feels on guard: "don't want to be out of control, don't want the heartaches of a relationship now."

It is our impression that Bernice, now at age 22, is psychologically prepared to take advantage and prosper if she is fortunate in her career opportunities and in the positive attributes of her next heterosexual relationship. If, however, she meets with serious difficulties in her work or with the next man to whom she becomes attached, it appears a toss-up as to whether she could cope successfully and productively with such a stressful situation. Psychotherapy at this time appeared desirable, and this was suggested to her.

Jim, the other low-risk subject with an adult adjustment score below the total sample median, actually scored very close to the median — 5.81 as compared to 6.01. His development, family environment and functioning can all be characterized as average, with one major exception. His father deserted his mother before he was born, and he was raised as an only child by his mother and grandmother. He has not to this point shown any overt evidence of disturbance at the lack of a father figure in his life. Jim was included in the group with low parental conflict, because this was objectively true, and also because there was little conflict between mother and grandmother. Jim was brought up in a family with modest resources and modest but definite expectations and demands, and he himself, at age 22, was functioning with modest talents, goals and ambitions, but without overt problems or psychopathology. An IQ score was not obtained at 3 years; at 6 years it was 119, in the bright normal range, just below superior. Overall, his functioning could be characterized as positive, but average for the total NYLS sample.

EASY TEMPERAMENT AND SEVERE PARENTAL CONFLICT, AND SUPERIOR EARLY ADULT OUTCOME

Kathy was next to the highest early adult adjustment score in the total NYLS sample, has had a positive healthy developmental course from infancy onward, in spite of a rating of severe parental conflict at 3 years. Her 3- and 5-year home adjustment scores were lower than the mean for the high adult adjustment group (see Table 1, Chapter 13), but there were no indications of deviant behavior that were even suggestive of the possibility of a behavior disorder. Her 5-year school adjustment score was favorable. Teacher reports, from nursery school through second grade, were uniformly favorable, with comments on her remarkable intellectual level, her maturity, sociability, and readiness to help other children.

This highly positive developmental course continued smoothly through childhood and adolescence; at her early adult interview at age 20 she was pleasant, friendly and cooperative, talked openly and at ease on all subjects, and elaborated spontaneously and appropriately in her answers. She was functioning at a high level in all areas, and communicated a superior self-image which appeared appropriate. A follow-up interview with her parents 3 years later confirmed the continuation of this developmental pattern, with Kathy at that point doing well in a demanding graduate professional training curriculum.

In their early adult interviews, both Kathy and her sister (also a NYLS subject) separately gave similar descriptions of their parents. Their parents were markedly different in personality characteristics and in child care practices. "My mother was the disciplinarian, my father wanted to be the good guy." Undoubtedly, these were the issues identified in the 3-year parental child care and attitudes interview, which made for the rating of severe parental conflict. However, Kathy maintained a positive relationship with each, could discuss problems with each one separately or jointly. "They respect what I have to say." At the same time Kathy was able to maintain a degree of emotional distance which undoubtedly served to minimize the impact of their different views, behavior, and attitudes. "I was never into doing things with my family. Never saw my family as my friends. I wanted to do things with my friends, not with them on weekends, or holidays. I found it dull."

SUMMARY AND OVERVIEW

The group tabulations emphasize the high risk potential of difficult temperament in early childhood. This has been confirmed in a number of studies (Graham, Rutter and George, 1973; Thomas and Chess, 1977; Wolkind and DeSalis, 1982), and reflects the special child-rearing demands such children impose on their parents, the guilt feelings, hostility and insecurity the youngsters stimulate in many parents, and the stress of adaptation to new peer groups and school situations which is temperamentally typical for such children.

Parental conflict appears to be even more significant as a high-risk factor than difficult temperament. Thus, if we compare the two intermediate high-risk groups (Tables 3 and 4), while both had the same mean outcome adult scores, there was a marked difference in the outcome of the childhood and adolescent clinical cases in early adult life. The 2 cases in the difficult temperament and low parental conflict group had recovered by early adulthood, while of the 3 cases in the easy temperament and severe parental conflict group, 2 were still psychiatrically disturbed in early adult life. All of the parents with behaviorally disturbed children had been offered parent guidance and counseling by us, and with a few exceptions accepted this. This procedure was effective with most cases involving children with difficult temperament (Thomas, Chess and Birch, 1968), if the parents could follow the therapeutic strategy consistently and cooperatively. However, this was less likely in families with severe parental conflict, a situation which mitigated against a joint cooperative approach to the child's problem.

It is probable that our interview data did not catch all the cases of parental conflict, or the degree of severity when conflict was identified. This was one area which at least some of our NYLS parents were reluctant to expose to our interviewers, no matter how cooperative and open they were otherwise. Thus, for example, one set of parents came for clinical consultation when their son developed a mild adjustment disorder at 5 years, 8 months. On the 3-year interview for parental practices and attitudes, they had scored at the median point for the sample as a whole for parental conflict. They then told one of us (S.C.) that they were in severe conflict with each other (actually, this led to divorce some years later). They stated that they had concealed this fact from our interviewers, but now that their son had a behavior problem they considered it necessary and important to report this fact.

The finding that all the clinical cases in the high-risk group had recovered by early adult life is not consistent with the results of the quantitative analyses. There is no obvious explanation for this contradiction from the tabular data, and the issue will be pursued further in Chapter 17.

An unexpected finding was the striking difference in vulnerability to parental conflict among boys compared to girls, whether for those with the extreme of difficult or easy temperament. This finding merits further research, in view of the evidence from a number of studies that the incidence of behavior disorders for boys is significantly higher than for girls.

In the individual subject analyses, we have been strongly impressed by the positive value of a firm commitment to a career direction in influencing the recovery from a behavior disorder. This was evident with Michael and Bernice. The question may be raised whether such a commitment was the cause or effect of the improved functioning. However, in neither case could we find indication of any life events or other factors which might have first produced the recovery from the behavior disorder antecedent to this work commitment. Our finding is consistent with the report by Vaillant and Vaillant (1981) on a sample of 456 inner city men followed from age 14 to 47. They found that the rating at age 14 of capacity to work surpassed all other variables, including social class and multiproblem-family membership, in predicting adult mental health and capacity for interpersonal relationships. Such a work commitment also appears relevant to our concept of task mastery as one of the primary goals of human behavior (See Chapter 2).

As to the factors that led to serious work commitment in these subjects, they are undoubtedly multiple—talent, acceptance of their families' standards and values, some degree at least of self-confidence, opportunity and even luck, and the knowledge that their parents would support them in specific career-directed training programs.

The individual life histories also highlight the fact that any temperamental characteristic or constellation can be involved in behavior disorder development—Michael with his slow-to-warm-up pattern, Roy with his distractibility, Bernice with her high activity and intensity, others with easy temperament. And even though children with difficult temperament are at higher risk for behavior disorder development, this is by no means inevitable, as the life history of Stanley documents. It is not temperament as such, or parental or other environmental factors as such, which determine the child's psychological course, but the goodness or poorness of fit between the environmental expectations and demands and the child's temperamental style and capacities.

It is also evident from the tabulations that, even if a child is at high risk in early childhood for less than optimal psychological development and for the onset of a behavior disorder in the childhood years, this does not necessarily predict the continuation of the psychopathology into adolescence or early adult life. Symptoms of deviant behavior in early childhood are not to be disregarded as trivial and unimportant. They may be the harbingers of significant degrees of psychiatric disorders in subsequent years. On the other hand, they should not be assumed to foretell the inevitability of an ominous future which could be alleviated only by intensive and extensive psychiatric treatment. The high-risk young child with a behavior disorder is not at all doomed to an unhealthy psychological future.

CHAPTER 13

Childhood Antecedents
of Early Adult Adjustment

In the preceding chapter, subjects who, at 3 years of age, were at high and low risk for subsequent unfavorable psychological functioning were identified, and their developmental course to early adult life studied. To complement that predictive analysis, this chapter will undertake a postdictive study, by identifying subjects with either very high or very low early adult adjustment scores and exploring the patterns and significance of their earlier childhood functioning.

The 13 subjects with early adult adjustment scores of 8 or higher were selected, and an equal number of those with the lowest adult scores (0.78 to 3.42). Tabulations were made of: IQ scores at 3, 6, and 9 years; adjustment scores at 3 and 5 years from the parental interviews, and at 5 years from the teacher interview; age of onset of a behavior disorder, if present; and outcome of such or disorders in early adulthood.

A number of comparisons can be made from Tables 1 and 2.

Sex distribution is equal in the high-score group, but the low-score group shows a higher percentage of males.

The high-score group shows a higher mean IQ score at 3, 6, and 9 years with the difference most marked at 3 years. This difference is statistically significant at the .05 level at 3 years, but not at 6 or 9 years, using the 2-tailed pooled variance t-test.

Mean adjustment scores at 3 and 5 years were also all more positive for the high-scoring adult group (in our 3- and 5-year ratings, a lower score represents a more positive adjustment level). This difference is statistically signifi-

TABLE 1

High Adult Adjustment Score

Subject Code #	Sex	Adult Adjustment Score	IQ 3 yrs	IQ 6 yrs	IQ 9 yrs	Adj. Score 3 yrs (Home)	Adj. 5 yrs (Home)	Adj. 5 yrs (School)	Age Onset Beh. Disorder	Outcome, Beh. Dis., Early Adult Life
212	F	9.77	164	148	132	1.01	1.15	1.00	—	—
236	F	9.49	137	130	—	1.42	1.23	1.07	—	—
267	F	9.31	151	—	—	1.29	1.12	1.13	—	—
063	M	8.96	—	—	—	1.31	—	—	—	—
014	M	8.92	143	150	—	1.10	1.15	1.14	—	—
203	F	8.69	131	148	—	1.00	1.02	1.00	—	—
215	F	8.56	140	144	136	1.18	1.21	1.00	—	—
041	M	8.49	142	136	—	1.46	1.07	1.10	—	—
250	F	8.43	147	127	—	1.09	1.05	1.16	—	—
067	M	8.39	123	120	—	—	1.03	1.11	—	—
210	F	8.33	141	128	—	1.20	1.71	1.00	—	—
042	M	8.22	110	112	100	1.26	—	—	5	—
053	M	8.05	135	147	138	1.59	1.33	1.05	—	Rec.
7F 6M			Mean 139	Mean 135	Mean 127	Mean 1.24	Mean 1.19	Mean 1.07		

131

TABLE 2
Low Adult Adjustment Score

Subject Code #	Sex	Adult Adjustment Score	IQ 3 yrs	IQ 6 yrs	IQ 9 yrs	Adj. Score 3 yrs (Home)	Adj. 5 yrs (Home)	Adj. 5 yrs (School)	Age Onset Beh. Disorder	Outcome, Beh. Dis., Early Adult Life
038	M	0.78	118	121	117	1.46	1.40	1.25	7	Worse
229	F	1.49	135	127	—	1.33	1.50	1.17	15	Worse
039	M	2.06	126	131	112	1.73	1.76	1.48	16	Unchanged
022	M	2.18	—	133	124	1.19	1.13	1.07	7	Worse
208	F	2.19	100	106	99	1.94	1.80	—	2	Worse*
016	M	2.77	116	144	—	1.26	1.16	1.28	5	Worse
237	F	2.78	120	133	—	1.60	1.84	1.57	4	Worse*
043	M	3.01	131	130	129	1.23	1.48	1.51	16	Improved
056	M	3.07	109	123	—	1.55	1.41	1.29	—	—
214	F	3.31	105	108	103	1.36	1.34	1.31	3	Worse*
032	M	3.37	132	140	128	1.63	1.40	1.18	2	Worse
209	F	3.41	—	115	—	1.21	1.19	1.00	13	Worse
002	M	3.42	168	150	128	2.10	1.53	1.13	3	Worse
	5 F, 8 M		Mean 124	Mean 128	Mean 118	Mean 1.43	Mean 1.46	Mean 1.27		

*Worse by adolescence, then somewhat improved in early adulthood

132

cant at the .05 level for the 3-year home adjustment rating, at the .01 level for the 5-year home adjustment, and almost reaches the .05 level for the 5-year school rating, using the same t-test.

Only one of the 13 subjects in the high scoring adult group developed a behavior disorder. This one case was a mild brief adjustment disorder, with onset at age 5 and recovery by 7 years. By contrast, all but one of the low adult score group developed a behavior disorder in childhood or adolescence, with persistence into early adult life. In addition, of the 8 cases with onset of behavior disorder in childhood, the average age of onset of symptoms was 4.1 years, as compared to 7 years for the NYLS sample as a whole. The 4 cases with behavior disorder onset in adolescence showed essentially similar childhood adjustment ratings and IQ scores as the low adult adjustment group as a whole, except for a somewhat higher mean IQ score at 3 years.

The presence of a psychiatric disorder in early adult life in all but one of the low score group was to be expected, given the criteria for rating early adult adjustment (see Appendix C). What is noteworthy is the finding that in 8 of the 12 cases the onset of disorder was in childhood, and in 5 of these cases onset was before the age of 5.

HIGH OUTCOME SCORE WITH CHILDHOOD BEHAVIOR DISORDER

By contrast, in the high outcome group, not only were there none with a behavior disorder in adolescence or early adult life, but only one in childhood. This was a boy, Ralph, with a marked slow-to-warm-up temperament, whose 3-year IQ score could be obtained only after several attempts because of his initial, quiet refusal to participate. At 5 years, when he started school, he went for one day and then refused to attend. There had been no evidence of problem behavior at home. Clinical evaluation was done at this time, with negative findings except for the prolonged period required for him to be at ease in the playroom. Once involved, he became absorbed in imaginative and complex block building, was responsive, but only communicative nonverbally. The diagnosis was mild adjustment disorder, and the parents were advised as to the necessity for quiet patient handling with any demanding new situation, with the expectation that Ralph would require a prolonged period to make a positive adaptation.

Ralph started first grade the following year. As the teacher reported in the springtime, "In the beginning he was very apprehensive, gradually accepted routines and participated. With change in routines becomes apprehensive for a while." The next winter the family moved from the city to a suburb with a more demanding curriculum and academic expectations. Because of this, and with the fact that Ralph would be one of the youngest second-graders (because of his December birthdate), and with the knowledge that at best he would find this change stressful because of his temperamental pattern, it was decided to start him in the new school in the first grade. This worked out successfully. At the end of the school year, the teacher reported that Ralph was "sweet, shy, quiet. After 2 weeks he began raising his hand for help when he needed it." At first he was behind in reading, but with help from the teacher and his mother he improved. "Likes to complete his work . . . is liked by the other children. Not verbal." His adjustment to the new home and community had also become positive, and it was judged that he was now, at age 7, recovered from this adjustment disorder.

This evaluation was confirmed in subsequent years. His second-grade teacher called him "an extremely quiet boy. It took him 2–3 months to settle down. Follows routines. If routine is changed, Ralph holds back until sure, then does. Excels in math and will occasionally help another child. Other children like him, he plays actively with the other boys." And his third-grade teacher reported that "at first he was inattentive, but recently (December) there has been steady improvement in work level and participation."

In subsequent years, Ralph's positive adaptation to school came quickly each year, he did well academically, was active in sports, and made friends easily. His developmental course through adolescence was smooth and uneventful.

When interviewed at age 20, Ralph immediately made a positive impression. He had a pleasant smile, was animated, and answered all questions promptly, energetically, and with much relevant spontaneous elaboration. He described a growing sense of self-confidence, initiative, and independence from his family since going away to college two years previously. He was doing well academically, was clear as to his interests and goals, and was pursuing them systematically. He also spoke of his expanded ability to socialize easily since starting college, and had made a close relationship with a young woman for the first time in the past year. There were evident conflicts between some of his beliefs and attitudes and his religious teachings, and Ralph discussed these clearly and thoughtfully. His coping mechanisms were direct and successful. He commented that in the past any new experience tended to make him anxious, but that this was no longer true.

It appears that Ralph had been able to master successfully the successive demands for adaptation to the new, which his slow-to-warm-up temperament made stressful and difficult. Without the constructive support of his parents, once they were clear as to the issue, and without favorable school settings, the story might have been different. As it was, Ralph's successive positive experiences in mastering the stresses of new situations gave him a basis for the progressive development of a healthy sense of self-confidence and self-esteem. The multiplicity of new demands then involved in going away to college became a challenge rather than a threat, and became an opportunity for rapid psychological maturation.

LOW ADULT SCORE WITHOUT BEHAVIOR DISORDER

The one subject in the low adult adjustment score without a clinical diagnosis, Barry, was interviewed at age 19 years. He was tall, overweight and walked slowly. His voice and expression were bland, even apathetic at times, with an occasional brief appropriate smile. Responses to questions were brief and generally pertinent, but with many noncommittal and vague answers, and with no spontaneous elaboration. School performance was mediocre, and his social and sexual life appeared routine. He had no serious interests or goals, and his one hobby was betting on horse racing. He had never worked during summers or after school. He had some interest in active athletics. His use of alcohol and marijuana was moderate to moderately heavy, according to his account, and he was currently experimenting with cocaine. However, there was no indication of a true addictive pattern. Overall, he appeared lacking in energy, interests and goals, but there was insufficient psychopathology to warrant a clinical diagnosis. These data from the interview with Barry were confirmed in an interview with his mother a year later. She emphasized that he had no goals, "he'd like to do nothing and be rich."

Barry's childhood temperament scores were not remarkable and did not appear to enter significantly into any excessively stressful interactional pattern with environmental demands and expectations. His 3- and 5-year adjustment ratings were less than average, but there were no indications from the sequential parent and teacher reports, or from his behavior during IQ testing, of significantly deviant psychological functioning throughout childhood. The parental conflict score at age 3 was moderately severe, in the third quartile, and his parents divorced when he was 12. He stated, at 19, that the divorce came as a surprise, that he was not aware of conflict, had no idea of what was wrong, and never discussed the issue with his parents. He lived for 1½ years with his mother after the divorce, then moved in with his father because of friction with his mother. His father died of a heart attack when he was 17, and this precipitated a period of mild depression for some months. Following his father's death, he returned to living with his mother, but had some continued friction. He described his father in more strongly positive terms than his mother, whom he called "tough and self-centered."

Of special interest in his family history was the extraordinary extent to which his parents alienated and antagonized successive teachers of both Barry and his older brother by their continual complaints about the inadequacies of the school and the teachers. The parents were as one in refusing to consider that the teachers had any right to make demands on their sons, and rather insisted that it was the teachers' responsibility to stimulate the boys' interest in learning. Both boys went to good schools with excellent teachers, but this did not deter the parents from their repeated carping and their refusal to make demands on Barry for academic performance.

From the data, it was possible to evaluate Barry's level of functioning at age 19 as highly unsatisfactory, given his intellectual and physical health assets, the opportunities provided by his parents' upper middle-class status, and the excellent elementary and high schools he had attended. But whether his marginal and indifferent involvement in the early adult interview represented a defensive avoidance of any meaningful expression of psychological distress, or whether it was one more typical manifestation of a life style, could not be determined. The reasons for his low level of functioning were also not entirely clear. His parents' extreme assertion of teacher responsibility versus his lack of responsibility may have crystallized in Barry a passive receptive attitude toward life's opportunities and challenges. His own rather remarkable expression of indifference to his parents' conflict and divorce may have been genuine or may have concealed a deeply traumatic effect of this stressful life experience.

As much as it may be difficult to try to predict the future of many of our young adult NYLS subjects, this is especially so in Barry's case. Will he develop progressive evidence of a substantial psychiatric disorder? Will he drift through life on some marginal level of functioning? Will he make a dramatic change, become seriously committed to some meaningful life goal, and become a responsible respected adult? At this point we can only fall back on the cliché, "Time alone will tell."

LOW VERSUS HIGH RISK

The two adult groups were also compared as to the frequency of the extreme quartiles for difficult versus easy temperament at 3 years, and for severe versus low parental conflict at age 3. This comparison is presented in Table 3.

On the basis of chance alone, approximately 3 subjects (¼ of 13) should fall within each of the extreme quartile distributions. The noteworthy findings from Table 3, therefore, are the relatively high occurrence of easy temperament and low occurrence of difficult temperament in the high adult adjust-

TABLE 3

High vs. Low Adult Scores and 3-Year Difficult-Easy Temperament and Parental Conflict

Adult Adj. Score	Dif. Temp.	Easy Temp.	Severe Conflict	Low Conflict
High	1 (Female)	5 (4 F., 1 M.)	2 (1 M., 1 F.)*	4 (1 F., 3 M.)
Low	2 (1 F., 1 M.)	3 (1 F., 2 M.)	6 (4 M., 2 F.)	0

*The N for this cell is 10, as the special parental interviews were not done for 3 subjects. All the other N's in this table are for the entire sample of 13 in each group.

ment group, and the high rate of severe conflict subjects and absence of any with low conflict in the low adult adjustment group. The N's are small, but the findings suggest that in this sample the young adults with the highest level of functioning were more likely to have had easy rather than difficult temperament at 3 years, and that the young adults with the lowest level of functioning were more likely to have parents in severe conflict with each other at age 3.

With regard to the 3-year low-risk combination of extreme qualities of easy temperament and low parental conflict, only one of the high adult adjustment group showed this combination. None showed the 3-year high-risk pattern of difficult temperament and severe parental conflict. This high-risk combination was not found in any of the low adult adjustment group, though one girl with severe parental conflict was in the extreme fourth quartile for difficult temperament at age 3, and had a parental conflict rating in the third quartile (moderately severe).

"NO FACTOR" SUBJECTS

Finally, the two adult groups were compared as to the number of "No Factor" subjects, i.e. the absence of the parental interviews for child-care practices and attitudes at 3 years. As detailed in Chapter 7, the no factor subjects showed a statistically significant positive correlation with the early adult adjustment scores. These youngsters were mostly the youngest members of the NYLS sample, and 65 percent had at least one older sib in the study, as compared to 23 percent in the remainder of the sample.

There were 3 out of 13, or 23 percent no factor subjects in the high adult adjustment group, compared to 21 percent for the remainder of the NYLS sample. For the low adult adjustment group, however, there were no subjects in the no factor subgroup. This finding suggests that ordinal position and the presence or absence of an older sib in the study did not significantly affect early adult outcome with regard to high level of functioning, but did affect outcome with regard to low level of functioning.

EARLY SCHOOL FUNCTIONING

As indicated earlier in this chapter, the mean 5-year school quantitative adjustment scores were more positive for the high outcome adult groups, and the difference from the low outcome group almost reached the .05 level of significance. In addition, qualitative cullings of the teacher interviews from nursery school through the first grade for the high and low outcome groups were compared.

The subjects with the high young adult adjustment scores were consistently reported by successive teachers, with a few exceptions, as having many interests, an orientation to learning and learning easily and quickly, and being industrious; in some cases they were even described as having a "passion" for work. They were attentive, cooperative, often were rated as outstanding in their contribution to the class, and had positive social relationships with their classmates. Some evoked enthusiastic comments such as, "She is one of the most perfect children I've seen."

There were a few exceptions. The boy, Ralph, whose case vignette was given earlier in this chapter, consistently evoked cautious and even critical evaluations from his early grade teachers at the beginning of each school year because of his slow-to-warm-up temperament and consequent gradual involvement in the academic and social activities of the class. By springtime, the teachers had become positive in their judgments, though they did not consider Ralph as outstanding. One boy, socially highly competent and a good learner, early showed unusually aggressive tendencies. In nursery school the teacher commented that "somehow he manages to get into aggressive situations," and his first-grade teacher described him as "socially charming, loving and giving and manipulative, shrewd and aggressive . . . but the other children like him." As a young adult he was strikingly charming, manipulative, interested in aggressive sports, but functioning at a high level in all areas.

This is not to say that this high outcome group had similar personality characteristics. Not at all. They were different temperamentally: some were assertive and expressive, while others were quiet and reserved; some were very gregarious, others were on the shy side, though they did make good friendships; some were active class "leaders" who took the initiative in helping, others were not in the forefront in their class activities. This differentiation was even more evident in the early adult interviews. They were all functioning at high levels, had positive and healthy self-images, but varied tremendously in their temperament, goals, interests, and the types of relationships they made with the interviewers.

In contrast to the high outcome group, teacher reports in the early grades for most of the low adult outcome group described behavioral difficulties of varying types and severity. This was to be expected, inasmuch as 8 of the 13 subjects in this group had developed a behavior disorder by the age of 7 years. The teacher reports reflected these problems quite accurately and consistently from one grade to another. Even those in the group who did not develop a clinical behavior disorder until adolescence, as well as the one subject without such a diagnosis, had at best average social and academic functioning in the early school years. The exception was a girl, Sylvia, who had consistent superior teacher reports, and whose overall functioning, in and out of school, was indeed on a high level until adolescence. She then developed a major depression, with recurrent episodes into adult life. (Her case history is detailed in the next chapter as Case 2).

THE HIGHEST AND THE LOWEST

It is of interest to compare the developmental course of the young woman, Barbara, who had the highest young adult adjustment score (9.77) with that of the young man, Bruce with the lowest score (0.78).

When interviewed at age 22, Barbara made an immediate strongly positive impression. She was attractive, neatly and casually dressed, alert, quickly responsive to all questions and comments, and quite animated with graceful gestures and easy, frequent and appropriate laughter. Her answers and comments were to the point, with a great deal of thoughtful spontaneous elaboration. She discussed issues objectively, but also described her feelings and emotional reactions easily. Her comments on the various important people in her life were detailed, thoughtful, and differentiated, so that each emerged as a distinct personality. Her self-image was highly positive and clearly described, "I have come to recognize and accept that now and for at least the last 6 years I have been in a period of almost continuous change, a sense of temporary quality to my decisions, a sense of changing wishes and goals. But my values have stayed the same." This variability did not bother her, "I can accept it."

Barbara was in the final year of her professional training, which she will complete 2-3 years ahead of the average student. Her life goals were clear, she had many interests, made friends easily, and always had a few intimates. She has had two successive love relationships which were emotionally close and sexually fulfilling. She expected that there would be other loving, sustained, long-range relationships, but the question of marriage or children at this point did not seem important to her. She has worked regularly during summers since adolescence, and said she always performed well. There was no history of substance abuse.

Barbara's parents were divorced when she was 2 years old, and both subsequently remarried. She has lived with her mother and stepfather, though she has also maintained a continuous and active relationship with her father and stepmother. She detailed the positive values and problems for her in each of these relationships. She had clearly been able to use four parents, instead of two, as sources of strength and support, and to identify and compare differing styles of coping in the two households, taking what was best from each. Her relationships with her two older brothers were also warm and friendly. Her mother went back to full-time work when Barbara was 1½ years old. The family had a full-time housekeeper, who was now retired, though Barbara has maintained active personal contact with her.

Her IQ score at 3 years was in the very superior range, 164, though not the highest in the NYLS sample. (The highest 3-year IQ score, 168, was achieved by a boy who had a behavior disorder starting at age 3, which became gradually worse over the years, so that in early adulthood he was in the low adjustment group.) Her IQ dropped on subsequent testing, but remained in the very superior group. She scored consistently in the extreme quartile for easy temperament in each of the first five years of life, and again when this was rated at ages 16 and 22. (She was not included in the low risk group in the previous chapter, inasmuch as the parental conflict score was in the second, and not the lowest quartile.)

Her 3- and 5-year adjustment scores at home were positive and her 5-year school adjustment score was the most strongly positive possible (1.00). This latter rating was most impressively confirmed by successive teacher comments. At age 5, "Ready to try everything, persists until finished, does not ask for praise. Has one special friend but is friendly with all, and other children like her. Usually happy, smiling, can become angry (legitimately). A pleasure to have her in the group." At age 6, "One of the first scholastically, works quickly, grasps concepts quickly, nice attention span, will play with children or alone, was voted class president. A well adjusted, happy child." And at age 7, "Good attention span, works quickly. With adults is warm, natural, spontaneous. She is a leader, other children ask her for help, which she gives. Interested in both things and people. An outstanding, superior type, no flaws in her personality."

This highly positive functioning socially and academically continued smoothly throughout childhood. In adolescence the data from the interviews with her mother and herself gave her the highest adjustment rating on our scale.

In a follow-up telephone interview when she was 24, her mother reported that Barbara was successfully launched on her career, and had made a new love relationship with a young man in the same profession.

The NYLS subject, Bruce, with the lowest early adult adjustment score, was interviewed when he was 20. His dress was neat and casual, and his manner friendly and cooperative. He spoke in a low, even voice and smiled appropriately. His responses to all questions were highly elaborated intellectual generalizations with many literary allusions, with small nuggets of factual data embedded in the stream of verbalization. The interview extended over a 3-hour period, but the actual factual material obtained was relatively sparse. It was possible to determine that his social and school functioning was poor, and that he did not pursue his expressed interests in any organized systematic fashion. He had not had any actual sexual experience, said he did not masturbate, but did have considerable sexual fantasy and imagery. No substantial emotional relatedness to any other person was evident.

There was considerable defensive denial, elaborated at length in obsessive intellectualizations. In a variety of ways he expressed the idea of constructing an ideal fantasy world, with the real world as secondary, and hopefully not a problem. When asked about self-image, he sighed, "nothing but problems," and then launched into a long discussion of various writers. To take one fragment, "in Walker Percy there is a character in one story about an aunt who tries to stimulate her nephew to remembrance of former enthusiasms. This is comparable to my mother who tried to remind me of my former excitement about the character Jean Christophe. But my romantic idealizations and enthusiasms are gone for everyone not just to my mother".

No overt thought disorder was elicited in the interview. Because of this, the clinical diagnosis was obsessive character neurosis, severe, rather than a schizophrenic disorder. However, the latter diagnosis could not be ruled out.

The interview with his father (the parents were divorced) essentially confirmed the information and impressions obtained from Bruce. The father made such comments as "I'm worried about him . . . I don't know why he doesn't have girl friends . . . He's imaginative, bright and inventive. Has such a sense of alienation." The mother stated that Bruce has had a "sick and up-and-down life. I'm very fearful about his ability to survive."

In a follow-up telephone interview with him, when he was 24, Bruce reported that he was teaching music at a private school. The school was closing at the end of the year because of lack of funds, and he expected to be out of work. He had also enrolled again at college, his third different institution, and said he hoped to go on to a degree in musicology. He had had previous training in a technical field, which he then gave up. His work record was sporadic, and he has also lived off a family trust fund. The obsessive verbalizations were hardly in evidence in this telephone interview, and, again, no thought disorder was evident.

Bruce's temperament scores put him in the second quartile for difficult temperament at one year, in the third quartile at 2 and 3 years, and in the fourth quartile at 4 and 5 years, and again in adolescence and early adulthood. In other words, from a first year rating of relatively easy temperament this changed progressively and quickly within 2 years to extreme difficult temperament, and remained there.

The degree of open parental conflict and dissension was extreme, even extraordinary. This was evident not just in that the 3-year parental score was in the extreme quartile for severe conflict, but even more so in the many interviews and discussions with them over the years. A typical statement by the father (when Bruce was 8 years old) accused the mother, "He needs a different kind of attention that you are not willing to give or capable of giving. It requires a sensitivity. Had you allowed your own ambitions to be thwarted, something could be done." (The father's reference to his wife's "ambitions" referred to her work commitment outside the house.) The mother insisted she worked only part time, and that her schedule was flexible and did not encroach on the children's needs. She complained that if she were 5 minutes late coming home her husband considered this "poor interest and negligence." She felt constantly criticized by her husband and was appalled at the extent that her actions were determined not merely by what she "thinks is correct to do but also to try to avoid being censured by my husband." She was highly emotional in her accounts of how they disagreed about all kinds of childcare issues from the time Bruce was an infant. In general, the father felt they should respond to all of Bruce's demands and the mother wanted to set limits. Thus, Bruce cried a lot at night, the father thought he should be picked up each time until he stopped crying, but the mother felt they should let the child cry it out, and the father then called her "a cruel and unnatural mother." So this went, with feeding routines, discipline, etc., etc. Our own judgment was that the mother tended to make and push confrontations in a histrionic fashion, the father tended to underplay, to minimize, to make up.

Beyond these violent disagreements over childcare practices, the parents were in sharp conflict with each other over many other issues. Their marital relationship deteriorated progressively, they began to talk openly of divorce by the time Bruce was 8, the father left home a number of times for brief periods, and they were finally permanently separated and then divorced when Bruce was an adolescent.

In nursery school, kindergarten, and first grade, Bruce adapted fairly well and had friends, though there were comments by the teachers that he "overreacts to little things," "tangential involvement with activities," "often mind is wandering." By the second grade, the teacher, though saying that he had "knowledge and depth and tremendous creativity, not apparent on surface," reported that he "seems isolated from the children . . . tends to change direction to suit himself . . . during a discussion, he may appear to be listening, but when questioned, it seems that he has not been listening . . . when he is in trouble will sit and dawdle or decorate his papers. Will not come for help." The third-grade teacher called Bruce "very much of an isolate," and this was reaffirmed by the fourth-grade teacher, who felt it had become worse. "Bruce is intent, intelligent and has a one-track mind. He is scatterbrained and about five jumps behind. He never knows what's going on. This is true in almost everything. Bruce is oblivious to what is expected of him at the moment. If the group is playing a game, he is still playing it after it is over."

When Bruce was just 8 years of age, his mother requested a clinical evaluation with one of us (S. C.) because of symptoms she had begun to notice some 4 months previously. (This was at the time when his teachers had begun to report significantly deviant behavior.) The mother came alone, the father refusing to do so because he did not believe there was a psychiatric issue. He sent along a note which in essence blamed the mother for any problems. She detailed a host of symptoms: overreaction, easily upset by things not going as he wished, disorganized in approach to activities, dawdling, immature and silly behavior, poor peer relations, unwillingness to shift from ongoing activity, facial tic, and minor reversals in writing. The mother asked whether Bruce could be brain-injured or dyslexic because he was one of a pair of twins, the more fragile one, and had letter reversals. In the clinical interview, Bruce was clear, in very good contact, and his thinking was relevant and connected. Aspects of difficult temperament were in evidence. Also clear, from the mother's statements and Bruce's comments, was that a negative pathogenic interaction had developed between his mother and himself. Diagnosis was adjustment disorder, moderately severe. There was no evidence of brain damage or dyslexia and this was confirmed by the 6-year psychometric testing and the subsequent 9-year testing.

Parent guidance was attempted, but was a complete failure. The father came only a few times, and his basic attitude remained that his son had no psychiatric disorder, that it was his wife who was the problem. The mother came frequently and eagerly, and appeared each time to understand the logic and necessity for a patient, consistent and calm approach to Bruce, especially in view of his difficult temperament. But then she would report elaborately and melodramatically on the problems with both her twin sons in the interim, describe her insistent, intrusive and confrontational response, and the frequent, but erratic culmination in a blow-up on both her part and the boy's, even at times to the point of physical assault on him. She would agree that this was bad, and resolve to do better; but there was little change. She could not consider seriously the possibility of psychotherapy for herself. Bruce for his part refused to consider direct psychotherapy for himself, echoing his father's position that his mother was making up the problem.

The father consented to a joint follow-up discussion when Bruce was 13, when a permanent parental separation appeared inevitable. However, no consensus could be reached as to the best way to deal with this issue with the boys. The two parents did agree in describing Bruce as "explosive." When crossed he would blow up, bang doors, "use baby language and spit on the floor." On the positive side, his school progress had been good and he was in a special progress class because of his superior intelligence, though his academic functioning was quite uneven. He was a competent violinist and played in the school orchestra. The parents' impression was that socially he was doing better.

At 16 years, in the routine follow-up interview, the parents reported further improvement in Bruce's school and social functioning. They also stated that his earlier childhood symptoms were now minimal. In the interview with Bruce himself, no clear cut evidence of psychopathology could be elicited, either through Bruce's description of himself and his functioning, or in the interviewer's observations of his verbalizations and behavior. We, therefore, made the judgment of recovery from his childhood adjustment disorder.

However, with the continuation of the pathogenic family environment, we wondered whether this recovery would be stable or transient, or whether, indeed, both Bruce and his parents were covering up the indications of a continuing behavior disorder in the 16-year interviews. And, indeed, in the 20-year interview, as detailed above, a full-blown psychiatric disorder was strikingly in evidence, even though there had been no traumatic life experiences in the previous 4 years. Whether the apparent improvement which was evident in the 24-year telephone interview was substantial, or at best tenuous and temporary as was the 16-year improvement, will be evaluated at subsequent follow-ups.

Bruce's pathological developmental course can be viewed as the outcome of the interaction between his difficult temperamental pattern and a family environment of most severe parental strife, tension, and conflict over childcare practices. It is of interest that Bruce's identical twin had the same quartile scores for difficult temperament from early infancy to early adulthood, except for the second year. This twin was not identified as a clinical case until age 16, when the diagnosis of schizoid personality, moderately severe, was made. At the 20-year evaluation he was considered to be clinically unchanged, and his adult adjustment score was 2.06, placing him third from the bottom for this rating in the total NYLS sample.

SUMMARY AND OVERVIEW

This postdictive analysis shows in general the correlations established for the NYLS sample as a whole by the multiple regression and set correlation analyses. There are some exceptions, such as the lack of correlation of low parental conflict at age 3 with the high adult score group, and of 3-year difficult temperament with the low adult score groups, reflecting, again, as was evident in the predictive analysis in the previous chapter, individual variations within the group trends.

Perhaps the most striking finding was the total absence of a behavior disorder at any time in the high adult score group, with one minor exception. It is true that many of the NYLS subjects with behavior disorders in childhood or adolescence recovered and went on to a good and even high level of functioning by early adulthood. However, none of this latter group, with the one exception, had reached a superior level by early adult life. It would appear that, at least for our NYLS population, it required a consistent healthy and productive developmental course from early childhood onward to attain a superior level of functioning in early adulthood. (It should be emphasized that the adult ratings were made on an individual basis and not by any rank ordering scheme.) The presence of a childhood or adolescent behavior disorder signalled the occurrence of a period of excessive stress and difficult adaptation, which prevented such a consistent positive psychological evolution. However, it appears reasonable to predict that at least some of the subjects whose recovery from a childhood or adolescent disorder has been followed by a healthy developmental course will attain a superior functional level by their mid or late twenties or early thirties.

This correlation between childhood disorder and early adult outcome might appear to give credence to the theoretical positions which emphasize the special and even determinant importance of early childhood experiences for subsequent psychological development. But we and others (Clarke and Clarke, 1976; Kagan et al., 1978; Thomas and Chess, 1977) have identified too many exceptions to such formulations to make it a tenable hypothesis. (In Chapter 18 we will cite some of the instances of dramatic changes from childhood to early adult life).

What has been the case with these young adults with superior adaptations and functioning and strongly positive self-images in early adult life is that they have had everything going for them, not only in early childhood, but in later childhood, in adolescence, and in early adulthood. They were predominantly of easy temperament and persistent in task mastery and learning, and, with one exception, of superior intelligence. Their parents, even when in conflict with each other, were consistent in emphasizing standards and goals of excellence and work commitment, and were able to give their children and did give them all the support necessary to pursue these goals. Even the young woman who decided after a brilliant college record to take a routine office job and make her prime commitment to marriage and motherhood, much to her father's disappointment, still retained his affection and respect.

These youngsters all went to good schools and lived in stable neighborhoods with peer and adult groups with the same value systems as their parents. Temperamentally and intellectually, they were able to take advantage of the opportunities presented to them at sequential age-periods. It was not that their early life made them invulnerable and insulated them from destructive effects of later traumatic experiences. Rather, they received consistent approval from their parents, teachers, and peers for their abilities and accomplishments, and what followed was a flowering of a positive self-image from this acceptance and from the knowledge of their successes at social functioning and task mastery. It was this consistent positive reinforcement from themselves and others in a favorable environment which made for the superior developmental courses in these youngsters. As we have put it elsewhere, development is "a fluid, dynamic process which continually possesses the possibility of modification and change of pre-existing psychological patterns. At the same time, the potential for reinforcement of the old exists with the same or even greater strength as does the possibility for change. Continuity over time does not imply that a reified structure insulated from change exists intrapsychically. Such continuity can better be conceptualized as the result of consistency in the organism-environment interaction" (Thomas and Chess, 1977, pp. 193–194).

The similarity in the dynamics of psychological development in this superior group in no way resulted in personality characteristics that were carbon copies of each other. They were all friendly, cooperative and at ease in an interview setting. But some were very expressive with a wide range of appropriate emotional display; others were somewhat reticent and even-tempered. Some had great charm, others were quiet and self-contained. Some were gregarious with many friends that they made easily; others had a few friends, and were even shy, though in no case was there any real problem of socialization. Their interests, goals and life styles also showed great variability. One might even speculate that it is in such a superior group that personality differences may even be most evident, as each youngster develops to the fullest extent the potential of his temperamental traits, his abilities and interests, and takes advantage in his or her own individual way of the specific opportunities offered by the environment.

The low adult score group offered striking contrasts to the superior group in their life histories and developmental courses. These issues will be examined in Chapters 16 and 17, which deal with the origins and evolution of behavior disorders.

CHAPTER 14

Six Cases of Depression in Childhood and Adolescence

Depression in childhood and adolescence, previously considered rare (Kanner, 1957; Slater and Roth, 1969), has in recent years been recognized as an important clinical syndrome which is by no means uncommon (Carlson and Cantwell, 1980; Cytryn et al., 1980; Kashini et al.,1981). In addition, there is a consensus, as reflected in DSM-III (1980) that depression in childhood does not differ clinically in any basic aspect from adult depression and that the same diagnostic criteria used for adult affective disorders are to be employed for children as well. Increasing skepticism has also developed regarding the usefulness of the concept "masked depression" in children, which enjoyed considerable favor 10–15 years ago (Cytryn and McKnew, 1974; Glaser, 1967). In this formulation, depression is not overtly manifested, but is inferred from the presence of a variety of disturbed behavior, such as aggressiveness, hyperactivity, delinquency, and psychosomatic symptoms. With such an approach, the concept of depression was stretched and diffused to the point where it lost its nosological and clinical significance, and there is currently a wide agreement that the term "masked depression" should be abandoned (Kovacs and Beck, 1977; Carlson and Cantwell, 1980; Cytryn et al., 1980).

As to etiology, Kashani and co-workers (1981) have very recently provided a systematic and comprehensive survey of the literature. They detail the seven main conceptual models in the adult literature — biochemical, genetic, learned helplessness, life stress, behavioral reinforcement or interpersonal disturbance, cognitive distortion, and sociological — and review the applications that have been made of each of these models to childhood depression. They conclude that the groundwork has been set to explore childhood depression from various theoretical and methodological approaches, but that "the research on children is still at the preliminary stages of mostly descriptive study" (p. 151). Other authors have emphasized the need for prospective follow-up projects (Cantwell and Carlson, 1979) and for studies of children without gross environmental deprivation (Gittelman-Klein, 1977).

Six cases of depression arising either in childhood or adolescence have been identified in the NYLS population. The data in these cases are prospective, and in addition the subjects have not suffered the environmental deprivation which might in itself be an etiological factor (Gittelman-Klein, 1977). It, therefore, appears desirable to detail the developmental and clinical features of each case. The data are sufficient for the exploration of a number of questions: Is the clinical syndrome of childhood depression essentially similar to or different from adult depressive syndromes? If a major depressive episode occurs in childhood, is it a separate clinical entity, or can it represent the first episode of a recurrent depressive disorder which continues into adult life? Are there different etiological factors for a major depression and a dysthymic disorder (depressive neurosis), or are they distinguished only by criteria of severity and duration? What are the dynamic consequences of depressive symptomatology for a child or adolescent?

All diagnoses were converted to DSM-III categories. The data from the clinical evaluations and follow-ups made this conversion possible without difficulty in all cases. Information on mood for all subjects was especially available from all interview and observation protocols. This resulted from the fact that our temperamental categories include a rating for *quality of mood,* so that one objective of all inquiries of subjects, parents and teachers, as well as of all subject observations, was the gathering of detailed reports of unhappy, depressed or irritable mood, as well as the frequency of cheerful, happy periods. Routine questions in parent and subject interviews as to sleep patterns, level of physical activity, school and social functioning, special interests, frequency of crying episodes, and response to praise covered most of the additional DSM-III criteria for major depression (DSM-III, pp. 213-215). The clinical evaluations also covered these items in greater detail, as well as exploring the subject's self-concept and self-evaluation, attitudes toward the future, and thoughts of death or suicide.

Two of the cases meet the DSM-III criteria for recurrent major depression, 3 fit the category of dysthymic disorder (or depressive neurosis) and one fits the category of adjustment disorder with depressed mood. Psychotic features were not present in any of the cases at any time.

CASE REPORTS

Case 1. Recurrent Major Depression,
First Evident at 8 Years

When Harold was 8 years of age, his mother requested a clinical evaluation because of behavioral difficulties of one year's duration. He disliked
school, was very shy, and had few friends. He also feared new situations, and
was frequently stiff, moody, and quiet. In addition, his mother had a period
of severe depression, culminating in a two-week hospitalization, with electro-
shock treatment.

There was a very strong maternal history of depression. His mother's maternal grandfather and granduncle committed suicide, his mother has had periodic depression, one aunt and one uncle committed suicide, and his sister had
periodic depressions since adolescence.

In the clinical evaluation, he showed a moderate depressive behavioral pattern. In addition, his drawings were of monsters and weird creatures with violent or dark heavy colors. Because of the severe family disturbances in the
preceding three years, it was not possible to identify the depressive episode
clearly as either primary or secondary.

In the succeeding few years there was significant improvement in social
functioning and school achievement, though Harold continued to dislike
school. At age 12, however, he was again depressed, and dislike of school
was intense. Duration of the acute symptoms could not be pinpointed from
Harold or his mother, but probably did not exceed several months. This was
succeeded by a chronic low-grade and variable depressed mood with the major expressions being dislike of school and social difficulties. At the 17-year
routine follow-up interview, Harold was well-mannered, direct, shy, and rarely smiled. He stated he could slip into an unhappy mood for no apparent reason, at which times he would be irritable and fatigued, and would avoid people. His mother agreed with this description, saying, "He's not happy, but
he is easy to live with." His recollections of school were entirely negative. He
was deeply interested in music and had taught himself piano, banjo, and
guitar. Several months after this interview he developed an acute severe depression which lasted two weeks. He was treated with imipramine and niacin,
with apparent improvement, and the medication was continued for two years.

When interviewed at 22 years of age, he again appeared quiet, serious and
thoughtful. He described recurrent depressions, giving ages 9, 15, 17, 18 and
19 as the times of occurrence. Each lasted months, although medication "took
the edge off." He considered himself very vulnerable to stresses and conflicts

in social relationships, especially with women, was unsure sexually, and had had three disappointing love affairs. He protected himself by withdrawing to music. He had moved to his own apartment and earned some money in a job mopping floors, but was basically supported by his mother. He practiced music most of the day. He summarized his existence as going from slow deadness to acute crises. At one point he did wish to die, slept most of the time, stayed apart from everyone. Yet he had cultivated a "personality act" which he could use when needed, especially for public musical performances (non-paying). He could be his "real self" only with his mother, sister, and one or two friends. With all other people he used his intellect to "read them." Shortly after this interview he began active psychotherapy.

Outside of his first depression at age 7-8, there has been no evidence that the subsequent episodes were precipitated by any specific situational stresses. He has met the DSM-III criteria for major depression, showing dysphoria, loss of interest in usual activities, fatigue, feelings of worthlessness, and diminished ability to think and concentrate.

Case 2. Recurrent Major Depression, First Symptoms at 13 Years

Sylvia did not come to clinical attention until age 21 years. Her childhood development was smooth, with no special environmental stresses or evidence of unusual deviant behavior. There were reports throughout childhood of short periods of moodiness, stubbornness and anger, but not greater than in many other youngsters. School and social functioning appeared excellent throughout childhood. At the 17-year interview she was pleasant and friendly, described herself as happy, with "wonderful" parents and an active social life with several close friends. This same report was given by her parents. She did report that she blew up on occasion at home, with yelling and slamming of doors. Her only self-critical statement was, "I'm too sensitive sometimes. I get insulted without necessary provocation."

The clinical consultation at age 21 was requested by the mother, because of Sylvia's intense obsessive preoccupation with the condition of her hair and skin. She kept insisting that they were terribly ugly, which in fact was not true. This had been going on for months, with Sylvia demanding to see one doctor after another, all of whom made benign evaluations. She had shifted colleges twice, though because of superior grades she had in the past year been accepted by, and was attending, a top-level college. She was now threatening to drop out of this school. Her mood was depressed and she kept repeating that she didn't want to live unless her skin and hair were "cured." There was a history of one love affair at 17–18, which the young man broke off to her distress.

Hospitalization was arranged because of the severity of the symptoms. No evidence of thought disorder was found. Projective testing indicated a pattern of marked emotional detachment from people and avoidance of intimacy.

She was discharged slightly improved and was followed thereafter by one of us (A. T.). For almost a year her course was stormy, with many suicidal threats and several wrist-cutting acts. These acts appeared to have a large manipulative element, specifically, attempts to pressure her mother to accede to various unreasonable demands. There was then gradual improvement, she returned to college, and graduated a year later Phi Beta Kappa. During this period her mood was generally pleasant, at times even gay, but interspersed with short periods of depression. These periods responded moderately to medication with amitryptiline. Neurotic features were strongly evident throughout. She could not communicate easily even with her good friends, social relationships were mainly superficial, and her academic and other work showed obsessive perfectionist trends. Her preoccupation with her skin and hair subsided, but this was replaced by a pattern of blaming her parents and others for her problems and difficulties. This did not, however, develop into paranoid thinking.

In her therapeutic sessions, Sylvia kept insisting that she had always been depressed, at least as far back as age 13, and perhaps to age 8, and had always covered it up by a facade of cheerfulness and friendliness. She remembered much preoccupation with thoughts of death and her own unworthiness. It appeared at first that these memories might represent retrospective falsification, until Sylvia brought in a number of poems written between ages 12 and 15, and these were indeed suffused with melancholy and hopelessness. However, neither in her recollections nor in our own anterospective records could we find any significant situational stresses which could be identified as a cause for this depressed mood in childhood and adolescence. Sylvia did report that her father had had several severe depressions in adult life, and that both grandfathers had been depressed, and two uncles had had severe mental disturbances. This family history was confirmed by her mother.

One judgment was that Sylvia was suffering from a chronic recurrent major depression, with onset in middle childhood. She had reacted to this depression and the negative self-image it has produced with the elaboration of extensive neurotic defense mechanisms of denial and projection. The consequences of her neurotic behavior in turn intensified her depression, with recurring periods of escalated symptoms as a result.

In the year following her college graduation, Sylvia's course was again stormy. She had several periods of acute depression, alternating with relatively benign periods. She had several jobs, did well in each at first, and then, when depressed again, made unreasonable demands and quit in anger. Conflict with her parents continued, essentially as in the past, with excessive and unrealistic expectations on her part which they could not meet; these ended in mutual reproaches and blow-ups. One short period of hospitalization was required because of the severity of one of the depressed moods.

Finally, the following year, when Sylvia was 24, a remarkable and dramatic positive change occurred. She became alert, poised, and animated, with a bright, engaging smile, and talked with self-assurance about herself and her plans. She was enrolled in graduate courses and had been accepted for a doctoral program with full tuition scholarship in a prestigious university. She was working part-time supporting herself, had many friends, was getting along well with her parents, and had not felt this well for years. And she was no longer concerned about the condition of her hair or skin, which now were at most minor problems. As to her long periods of disturbance, she remembered them as times of "low self-esteem." In addition, in this depression-free period she reaffirmed her recollections of unhappiness and morbid preoccupation with death in her late childhood and adolescent years. Her parents confirmed Sylvia's report, emphasizing that she seemed "very pleased with herself and self-assured." Neither from Sylvia nor her parents could any environmental change be elicited which might have influenced such a remarkable psychological turnabout. Actually, she had an unhappy brief sexual affair with a manipulative arrogant young man during that year, but this did not produce any significant negative effect on her affect or behavior.

In discussion with her, Sylvia was fully receptive to the formulation that she had suffered from episodes of depression, with secondary neurotic defensive reactions. She expressed confidence that if the depression recurred, she would be able to cope with it more effectively than in the past.

Sylvia did start her graduate studies the following year, at age 25. In the first semester, she did outstanding work, obtained a research assistantship, made a number of new friends, socialized easily, and felt strongly that she was now clear as to her goals in life. She did have a frustrating experience with a young man, a graduate student in another department. They became friendly, Sylvia wanted to carry it further, but the young man refused. This distressed her, she felt that she must have a substantial psychological problem in the area of heterosexual relationships, and psychotherapeutic discussions of this issue were initiated, again with one of us (A.T.). However, no evidence of depression was elicited, either objectively or subjectively, or of interference with her academic work.

However, early in the spring semester, Sylvia began to experience difficulty in concentration, her academic work slipped, and she became increasingly detached socially. By the beginning of March a severe recurrence of her depression was evident. She put it that, "I am so deeply troubled. I don't know that I can make it from week to week. I'm so tired. I feel so indifferent to everything, like I just don't care, even though I know this is the right life for me, in academia. I feel like nothing matters. It is so hard for me to work; I work so slowly and so poorly. This is my life and if I can't make it then I will have to die." She also became very anxious, with apprehension that she was ruining her career and life.

In the first contact with her, after recurrence of symptoms, anxiety was a predominant feature and she was started on diazepam. This had no therapeutic effect. The symptoms of depression quickly became predominant, both subjectively and objectively. She was switched to ludiomil, with a quick, positive effect. Her depression diminished substantially, and even though she still thought and worked slowly, her hopelessness disappeared, and she was able to catch up with her academic work. Mild symptoms persisted, however, and became moderately worse over the summer. Her medication was switched to desyrel, with a quick favorable response.

Sylvia began the next academic year in high spirits. Her work went well, she passed her qualifying examination, and started a love affair which was satisfying both emotionally and sexually. She tried reducing her medication but then began to feel "melancholy." She increased the dosage but after a month (by November) began to have side reactions. Though these were minor, she used them as an excuse for irregular use of her medication.

Simultaneously, her love affair began to deteriorate. According to her account, which appeared to have at least some truth to it, her lover was inconsiderate and inconsistent. He would expound how much he loved her, wanted to be with her, yet on many occasions would change his plans and not be with her when she expected him, and do this without notifying her. Sylvia did not make this an issue with him, for fear of losing him, but did press him to spend more time with her. When this was unsuccessful she became increasingly agitated, and resorted to suicidal threats, which only alienated him. She also reported deterioration in her academic performance and research activity.

By February Sylvia's depression began to lift, but her agitated neurotic behavior continued, with defensive avoidance of self-examination by claiming hopelessness and helplessness. However, by the beginning of May her symptoms began to improve — whether spontaneously, or because of psychotherapy, or, most probably, a combination of both. Her work and social functioning improved and she was able to challenge her lover directly with regard to his conflicts and ambivalence. Also, for the first time ever, she began to be analytically introspective in a productive way in her psychotherapeutic sessions, without becoming defensively hopeless in discussions of her neurotic behavior patterns. Her basic neurotic problem crystallized as a deep feeling of psychological inferiority, undoubtedly at first the effect of her teen-age depressive period, with a system of defenses to keep others from knowing how terrible a person she was. With this, she had tried to maintain a facade of normalcy by denial of intrapsychic problems, and when this mechanism boomeranged, to resort to the opposite defense of hopelessness and helplessness.

Over the next few months, to the time of this report, her improvement continued. Her prime psychological problem is no longer the episodes of depression, which are effectively controlled thus far by medication. Rather, it is the neurotic character structure and defensive strategies which originally resulted from the impact on her of the depressive episodes as a teenager, but then developed a life of its own. With the control of the depressive illness by medication, the extent and specific characteristics of her neurosis have become evident. The prognosis now appears favorable, with her beginning ability to examine her neurotic functioning objectively, together with a recognition that she may not be the hopelessly inferior person she had assumed herself to be.

Sylvia has met the DSM-III criteria for recurrent major depression, with the recurrent episodes of depressed mood, low energy level, self-depreciation, decreased effectiveness at school, decreased ability to think clearly, social withdrawal, and pessimistic attitude toward the future.

In the following 3 cases, the diagnosis of dysthymic disorder, or depressive neurosis, was based on the DSM-III criteria of a chronic depressed mood and associated symptoms, but not of sufficient severity and duration to meet the criteria for a major depressive syndrome (*DSM-III*, pp. 220–223).

Case 3. Dysthymic Disorder, With Onset of Behavior Disorder at 5 Years, and First Appearance of Depressive Symptoms at 10 Years

Richard, an extremely persistent child temperamentally, had severe tantrums in nursery school and first grade when ongoing activities in which he was absorbed were abruptly interrupted by his teachers. Mood quality was positive throughout the first five years of life. Family history was not significant for mental illness. Clinical diagnosis was adjustment disorder, severe, onset at 5 years.

The tantrums were alleviated by transfer to another school in which his persistent intensive interest in academic work was not only permitted, but encouraged. However, beginning in the fourth grade, a number of episodes recurred in which, as in the first grade, his selective intense persistence was frustrated in a number of situations, with explosive, violent outbursts on the boy's part. By age 10, he showed helplessness and hopelessness as soon as he was pressed to face a problem. By this time Richard had accepted the repeated expressions of disapproval and condemnation by teachers, parents and peers of his explosive tantrums as valid, and had begun to think of himself as a "bad boy," doomed to repeat his irrational explosions and to suffer the consequences. At this time, a significant depressive element had emerged in his symptomatology, and the diagnosis of depressive neurosis appeared warranted. A course of psychotherapy was instituted and led to a marked improvement.

He did well for the next few years, except for occasional moodiness and crying episodes. However, his father, to whom he had been quite close, had a fatal heart attack when Richard was 11. Also, he became entangled in severe conflict with one of his teachers, his school work and behavior deteriorated, and by age 14 the school judged him to be depressed. The diagnosis of depressive neurosis was reaffirmed. His next few years were uneven, though he attained a respectable academic average. At the 17-year interview he indicated satisfaction with himself and did not appear depressed. His mother, however, judged him to be insecure, intolerant of frustration, and timid. His relationship with his mother was characterized by frequent hostile outbursts on his part. Episodes of oppositional behavior were also evident in school. With his symptomatology, and the lack of evidence for depressive symptoms, the diagnosis of an oppositional disorder was made. He continued through college with improvement in his oppositional behavior, and by age 22 he had been admitted to graduate school.

At the 22-year interview Richard was cooperative, but spoke in a low voice, giving the briefest of replies with only occasional animation. He belittled both his graduate work and competence in job interviews. Although reporting highly successful work in his core interest — with adequate documentation — as well as in a group of other interests, Richard downgraded himself as deadline-oriented and dilettantish. All his school memories were bad, and he recalled only his tantrums and blow-ups and poor high school and college performances. Despite his marked persistence and recognition of his positive qualities, Richard flatly stated that he was pessimistic about control of his life, and that most interactions came out wrong. Socially, he considered himself dull, and indicated that if some one was nice to him on first meeting, he wondered what their problem was. One such person was a girl whom he subsequently married, and this appeared to be the one action of which he approved. His wife was the only one he felt he could communicate with emotionally, although not totally. He stated that his work improved after they began living together. He had had several courses of psychotherapy through older childhood, adolescence, and now in early adult life. Depressive symptoms were most in evidence at this time, with no indication of oppositional behavior, and the earlier childhood diagnosis of depressive neurosis, somewhat improved, was reaffirmed.

It appears that by age 10 Richard's earlier severe adjustment disorder had evolved into a dysthymic disorder, or depressive neurosis. Subsequent positive influences, whether through psychotherapy or his own successful achievements, had temporary ameliorative effects, but did not serve to resolve his psychopathology decisively.

Case 4. Dysthymic Disorder, With Onset of
Behavior Disorder at 30 Months, and First Appearance
of Depressive Symptoms at 17 Years

Norman had always been a temperamentally distractible child with a short attention span. Family history was not significant for mental illness. Intelligent and pleasant, the youngest in his class throughout his early school years due to birth date, he started his academic career with good mastery. Though his attention span was short, he concentrated well and learned easily and quickly, even if in short spurts. Teacher reports in his early school years were uniformly positive with regard to academic progress and social behavior, and gave no indication of the symptoms of an attention deficit disorder. This negative finding was confirmed in the various clinical evaluations done from 56 months onward.

However, his parents were impatient and critical of him because, at home, he showed quick shifts of attention, dawdling at bedtime, and apparent "forgetfulness." At 56 months a clinical evaluation was done because of various reactive symptoms such as sleeping difficulties, nocturnal enuresis, poor eating habits and nail tearing, and a diagnosis of mild adjustment disorder starting at 30 months was made. Year by year his symptoms grew worse, and his academic standing slipped. His father, a hard driving, very persistent professional man, became increasingly hypercritical and derogatory of Norman. The father equated the boy's short attention span and distractibility with irresponsibility, and a lack of character and willpower. He used these terms openly to the boy and stated that he "disliked" his son. The mother grew to understand the issue, but no discussion with the father as to the normalcy of his son's temperament and the impossibility of the boy's living up to his standards of concentrated hard work succeeded in altering the father's attitude. He remained convinced that Norman had an irresponsible character and was headed for future failure — indeed these provided the seeds of a self-fulfilling prophecy. There were several times when the boy tried to comply with his father's standards and made himself sit still with his homework for long periods of time. This only resulted in generalized tension and multiple tics, and Norman could not sustain this effort so dissonant with his temperament — another proof to himself and his father of his failure. The clinical diagnosis made during this childhood period was an adjustment disorder of increasing severity. Direct psychotherapy was arranged in early adolescence, but Norman entered this with a passive, defeated attitude and the effort was unsuccessful.

When seen at age 17, he had already dropped out of two colleges in one year. He was dejected and depressed, extraordinarily self-derogatory, said he could not finish anything he started, was lazy, and did not know what he wanted to do. Subjective symptoms and objective evidence of depression dominated the clinical picture at this age-period, and the diagnosis of depressive neurosis was made.

At age 18, with a catastrophic work-study foreign program behind him, and hostile family relationships, Norman stated he wished psychiatric help. It was arranged and he successfully sabotaged it.

At age 20 there was a hypomanic episode — diagnosed in emergency consultation with an outside psychiatrist and confirmed by one of us (S.C.). He responded to lithium, which he then refused to take because it destroyed his good mood. The hypomanic behavior gradually diminished over several months. Whether this single episode was drug related is unclear, as Norman declared that he took no drugs whatever except marijuana; however, his father reported him to be highly involved in many drugs at the time. Now, at age 24, there has been no recurrence.

When interviewed at age 22, Norman was essentially nonfunctional, living at home, sleeping most of the day away, and holding an occasional brief job. A denial defense mechanism was very much in evidence, with the repeated assertion that he was fine and getting along well with his parents, and that he knew his career as a musician and song composer would blossom in the near future. He requested psychotherapy again. This was instituted but failed because of frequent missed and late appointments, and his depressed, lethargic and parasitic life-style continued as before. Symptoms of manipulativeness, exploitation of family and friends, and self-absorption were now dominant, and the diagnosis of narcissistic personality disorder, severe, was made.

Case 5. Dysthymic Disorder, With Onset of
Behavior Disorder at 13 Years, and First Appearance of
Depressive Symptoms at 16 Years

Olga was a temperamentally difficult child whose early developmental course was relatively smooth. No family history of mental illness was elicited. Parental attention was focused on her older sister, Nancy, who also had difficult temperament. The father made unrealistic demands on the older girl, the mother was uncertain and inconsistent, and with this pattern of parent-child interaction Nancy developed a severe behavior disorder in her early school years. The parental preoccupation with Nancy's behavior and problems left them less demanding and more patient with Olga's negative reactions to many new situations, and with her slow adaptability and intense responses. However, when Nancy blossomed out with dramatic and musical talent at 9 years of age, parental attitudes toward her were transformed from critical and derogatory judgments to positive and supportive ones. Olga then became the family "scapegoat," and her life became filled with increasing stress and turmoil as her parents responded to her as they had earlier to her older sister. Symptoms of explosive anger outbursts, insomnia, and overeating appeared, and by age 13 had become severe enough to warrant the diagnosis of conduct disorder. By age 16 Olga was a drug abuser, using mostly barbiturates, and severe depressive symptoms had developed. She was self-derogatory, felt socially isolated, described herself as depressed much of the time, and commented that "I've managed to mutilate my life." Diagnosis at this time was depressive neurosis, severe.

However, within the year, Olga went through a sudden dramatic religious conversion experience with no apparent precipitating event or influences. Following this, progressive improvement in symptoms and functioning developed, and when interviewed at age 20 only mild residual symptoms remained. Diagnosis at this time was depressive neurosis, recovered. Follow-up inquiry two years later confirmed the continuation of positive functioning.

Case 6. Adjustment Disorder with Depressed Mood,
With Onset of Behavior Disorder at 13 Years, and
First Appearance of Depressive Symptoms at 13 Years

Brad's childhood development was outwardly benign throughout childhood. Like Olga, Brad was a temperamentally difficult child, but, also like her, parental attitudes were sufficiently patient and flexible throughout his childhood so that a pathogenic child-parent interaction did not develop. Family history was negative for mental illness. At age 12 his parents divorced, which was acutely traumatic to the youngster. He remained with his father of his own choice, though there were frequent conflicts and verbal fights between them. His relationship with his mother became hostile and distant. At the same period he became aware that his sexual orientation was crystallizing as homosexual. With these temperamental characteristics of negative reaction to new and slow adaptability to change, this quick sequence of stressful experiences and adaptational demands proved too difficult for him to master. Brad began to be depressed and by age 13 this was clinically evident. He had trouble getting up in the morning, did poorly at school, could not make friends, and began to be a heavy abuser of marijuana. At age 15, he also began to be an alcohol abuser. Two attempts at psychotherapy were unsuccessful because of his resistance. Diagnosis was a depressive disorder, starting at age 13, which met the criteria for an adjustment disorder with depressed mood (*DSM-III*, pp. 299–301).

At age 15 Brad went to a special boarding school where all of the students were in Gestalt therapy. At first his adjustment there was precarious, mainly because of his drug abuse. But gradually his functioning improved, both socially and academically, and his alcohol and drug use diminished. His sexual orientation did not change. When interviewed at age 18, he showed no signs of depression, but sufficient disturbance in functioning remained to warrant the diagnosis of narcissistic personality disorder.

DISCUSSION

The prospective data in these 6 cases and their comparison with the other subjects in the NYLS permit at least tentative answers to the questions raised in the introductory section of this chapter.

Episodes of major depression do occur in children and adolescents, and the symptoms appear to be continuous in character and with the symptoms in early adult life. There was no evidence for a separate clinical entity of depression for the childhood period. The findings in our two cases of major depression are consonant with the emphasis in the current adult literature on the importance of genetic and biochemical factors in the etiology of major affective disorders (Allen et al., 1974; Schildkraut et al., 1978; Gershon, 1979).

As to the differences between a major depression and a dysthymic disorder, DSM-III distinguishes between the two categories only quantitatively, the dysthymic symptoms being "not of sufficient severity and duration to meet the criteria for a major depressive episode" (p. 221). However, in the cases reported here there were also striking qualitative differences between the two groups. Cases 1 and 2, with the diagnosis of recurrent major depression, had strong family histories of depressive illness, and the depressed episodes did not appear to have been precipitated by situational stress or a pathogenic parent-child interaction. Cases 3, 4, and 5, with the diagnosis of dysthymic disorder or depressive neurosis, had negative family histories and marked chronic stressful life situations and experiences antedating the onset of depression. Only with the category of adjustment disorders with depressed mood does DSM-III give the criterion of a maladaptive reaction to an identifiable psychosocial stress, but it also stipulates a time-limited disturbance (pp. 300–301). This latter criterion applies to our case 6, but not to cases 3, 4, and 5, which rather correspond to DSM-III's criterion for a neurosis, as showing a disturbance which "is relatively enduring or recurrent without treatment and is not limited to a transitory reaction to stressors" (p. 10).

Although our case sample is small and permits of only tentative generalization, these qualitative differences between the cases of major depression and those with either a dysthymic disorder or an adjustment disorder with depressed mood correspond to the traditional clinical distinction between a primary and secondary depression. It is true that the symptoms of depression as such and the dynamic consequences of the depressions were not qualitatively different in the two types of cases (cases 1 and 2 versus cases 3, 4, 5 and 6), and by themselves would not have distinguished the primary from the secondary syndromes.

However, the differentiation of primary from secondary depression does have important therapeutic implications. Psychotherapy and parent guidance can be useful in both types, but the kind of insight to be achieved and the dynamic issues to be defined will be different in a primary as contrasted to secondary depression. With a primary depression, the emphasis to the parents and the child or adolescent patient has to be on the biological basis of the illness, its amelioration with medication where possible, and the attempt to prevent or minimize recurrences by avoiding excessive environmental stress of various kinds. With a secondary depression, the prime focus has to be on identifying the specific pattern of "poorness of fit," as we have called it (Thomas and Chess, 1977), that is, the dissonance between the demands and expectations of the environment and the child's capacities, motivations and behavioral style which is producing the child's psychopathology. Treatment, whether by parent guidance or psychotherapy, or both, can then focus on the alteration of this poorness of fit, so that the child can cope effectively with environmental demands. Medication may, of course, also be useful at times as an additional therapeutic agent in cases of secondary depression.

As Case 2 (Sylvia) illustrates, youngsters with the primary depression syndrome may develop extensive defense mechanisms in response to their affective and cognitive distress, and the behavioral, emotional, and ideational consequences of the defense mechanisms may dominate the clinical picture. Treatment may have to be directed at first to these secondary symptoms, but this does not change the nature of the long-term goals of treatment.

We have reviewed our prospective data for the age-periods preceding the onset of depression in these 6 cases in the attempt to identify some significant predictive factors. The temperamental scores for negative mood for each of the first 5 years of life were tabulated for each case. This score rates the child on the proportion of items of positive mood expression (smiling, laughing) as compared to negative mood (fussing, whining, crying) in the parent interview protocols. The hypothesis to be tested was that children who develop a depressive syndrome are predisposed by an earlier temperamental tendency to negative mood quality. The scores were compared with those of the NYLS sample as a whole in terms of a quartile categorization. This tabulation is shown in Table 1.

As can be seen from Table 1, this hypothesis of antecedent temperamental negative mood is supported for the primary depression cases for case 1, but not for case 2. For the secondary depression cases, two showed preponderance of positive mood in all of the first 5 years of life, and two a mild tendency to negative mood. Overall, therefore, the cases with depressive syndrome did not consistently show an earlier life tendency to negative mood temperamentally.

As to other temperamental traits in childhood, the 2 cases of major depression did not show any anterospective longitudinal data indicating that either child's temperamental characteristics played a significant role in the genesis or evaluation of the depressive disorder.

TABLE 1

Quality of Mood for Each of the 6 Cases for the First Five Years of Life as Compared to the Total NYLS Sample. Quartile 1 is Most Strongly Positive Mood, Quartile 4 the Most Strongly Negative Mood.

Year	Case 1	Case 2	Case 3	Case 4	Case 5	Case 6
1	4	1	1	2	3	2
2	4	2	1	1	2	3
3	4	4	2	1	at median	3
4	4	1	2	2	3	insuf. data
5	3	2	1	1	3	insuf. data

By contrast, each of the 4 cases of depressive neurosis (cases 3–6) or adjustment disorder with depressed mood showed one extreme or another for a particular temperamental trait or constellation. For case 3, it was extreme persistence, for case 4 marked distractibility and short attention span, and for cases 5 and 6 it was the difficult temperament pattern. And in each case the particular temperamental characteristic did play a significant role, in interaction with excessive parental or other environmental expectations and demands, in the genesis of the depressive disorder.

These findings suggest tentatively that the biological factors which may be significant etiological factors in the development of a major depression are not strongly related to temperament. On the other hand, if we postulate that the depressive neuroses and adjustment disorders with depressed mood are secondary depressions, i.e., the result primarily of a pathological course of psychological development, then it is consistent to find that temperament plays a significant etiological role, as it does in many other types of adjustment and personality disorders (Thomas, Chess and Birch, 1968; Chess et al., 1983).

However, in these cases (cases 3–6), the influential significant temperamental factor was different in 3 out of the 4 cases. Furthermore, other children in the NYLS with similar temperamental traits and with pathological developmental courses showed a host of symptom patterns in which depressed mood was at most a minor component. We have been unable to identify any significant differences in the clinical cases with depressive syndromes as contrasted to the other cases of behavior disorder, whether it be their behavioral characteristics prior to the onset of symptoms, their patterns of social functioning, or the type of pathogenic parent-child interaction. This negative finding has also been true of 2 other cases with early onset of behavior disorder, one at 4 years, the other at 5 years, with worsening in adolescence, and the appearance of depressive symptoms in early adult life.

It should be emphasized that the depressive symptoms in the 6 cases we have presented were major findings both on subjective report and objective clinical evaluation, and contributed strongly to the disturbances in functioning which each youngster suffered. This was in marked contrast to the negligible or at most very modest evidence, either subjectively or objectively, of depressed mood in the NYLS subjects with other types of behavior problems or those without any psychiatric disorder.

In other words, our data suggest that the reason for depression as a major symptom choice in an evolving behavior disorder is not likely to be found in the child's temperamental characteristics, the pattern of parental functioning, or the nature of the environmental stresses. The predisposing cause may rather be biological, though data are not as yet available to test this hypothesis.

CHAPTER 15

Three Cases of Brain Damage

In three of the NYLS subjects, significant signs of neurological dysfunctions were identified in early childhood. A number of features of their development course have been of special interest, and have been previously reported through the childhood period and into adolescence (Birch, Thomas and Chess, 1964; Thomas and Chess, 1975). These three cases have now been followed into early adult life, and the findings bear on several issues of theoretical and practical significance: Are there specific behavioral symptoms or symptom complexes that result from brain damage in early life? What special features characterize the developmental course of such youngsters? What evidence, if any, is there to support the concept of "minimal brain dysfunction" (MBD)? What are the special stresses suffered by brain-damaged children and what are the parental and teacher approaches that are necessary to ameliorate the harmful effects of such special stresses? Our data, however, do not permit us to consider the influence of physiological factors, namely the type, size and locus of the brain lesion, the exact time of life at which the nervous system was damaged, and the character of the neuropathological process.

This term "brain damage" as applied to these three cases is open to criticism because of the absence of direct evidence of structural damage to the brain. On the other hand, the other popular term "minimal brain dysfunction" is unsatisfactory because the brain dysfunction in these three subjects is much more than minimal. Other terms that attempt to avoid these objections have been suggested by various workers, but have not achieved broad acceptance.

Therefore, as in our earlier reports, we have continued to use the label of brain damage for these three cases.

The case histories will first be detailed, and the implications of the data then discussed.

REPORT OF CASES

Case 1

Bert was born prematurely, one month prior to term, and had a birth weight of 2.1 kg (4 lb, 12 oz). His neonatal course was stormy with respiratory distress accompanied by periods of apnea and dyspnea. Respiration improved by the third day of life and supplemental oxygen was discontinued. Bert's development during the first two years of life was substantially retarded. He did not sit without support until 11 months and did not walk until 22 months of age. Swallowing, particularly of a spontaneous and nonnutritive type, was inefficient. Adaptive motor functioning, such as reaching and grasping and object manipulation, was grossly clumsy and uncoordinated; transfer of objects from hand to hand was poor, even at 18 months of age.

On neurological examination at age 5 years 4 months, Bert was noted to be grossly awkward with poor gross motor coordination and inability to climb and to skip. Fine coordination, however, was at an age appropriate level. A repeat examination at age 6 years confirmed the findings.

Bert's expressive language development lagged substantially behind age expectation, although his comprehension appeared to be good. He did not use single words consistently until 39 months of age, and expressive language improved gradually thereafter. At 4 years, the range of his expressive language was almost age-appropriate, but his speech was grossly dysarthric, contained much slurring and stuttering, and was largely incomprehensible, even to his parents. Although there was some improvement in enunciation by age 5, his speech continued to be characterized by poor rhythmicity, excessive rate, slurring, and a high-pitched tone containing little or no variation. On the basis of a formal speech evaluation at age 5 years 2 months, speech therapy was recommended and initiated. Psychometric testing was done at 4 years 1 month and Bert achieved a Stanford-Binet IQ score of 110. This was considered minimal because of the examiner's difficulty in understanding his speech. Repeat testing at 6 years 2 months resulted in an IQ of 112, with a ceiling performance at 10 years and wide scatter among age levels. Again, the IQ was estimated to be minimal, this time because of the child's distractibility and slowness in working.

Bert's early school progress was excellent except for a tendency to reverse letters and numbers, which interfered with correct written arithmetic. His oral arithmetic was at a superior level.

From early infancy onward, Bert showed the typical pattern of easy temperament, with positive approach responses to most new situations, biological regularity, quick adaptability, and predominant positive mood of mild to moderate intensity. He was also motorically active, but showed no evidence of hyperkinesis. Although he was somewhat distractible, he had good persistence and would, from infancy, sustain his orientation in goal-directed activities.

Bert retained these characteristics of temperament through childhood and into adolescence. When misunderstood in his efforts at verbal communication, he would patiently and persistently repeat his statements until they were understood. In the early school years, when other children teased him about his peculiar speech, he would work conscientiously to improve his enunciation. Bert's parents combined a generally permissive approach to child care with demands for and expectations of high intellectual achievement. As a consequence, they were most attentive to the details of his developmental course, and each lag evoked requests for consultation from the study team. In particular, his delayed language development and cluttered speech aroused noticeable parental anxiety because they feared the possibility of intellectual subnormality. It was not until psychometric evaluation demonstrated his general intellectual intactness and his superior receptive language function that they were reassured as to his intellectual competence.

In contrast to their demands for intellectual achievement, both parents were substantially permissive in connection with the immediate requirements of daily living. They did not demand compliance with their requests and frequently failed to establish clearly defined limits. In a few areas, however, the father in particular made extremely clear-cut demands, which were both peremptory and, in part, unreasonable. These included his insistence on instantaneous and invariable compliance with certain safety rules and the recognition of the inviolability of parental possessions. When management problems deriving from lack of clear parental structuring became genuinely irksome to the parents at various times, they requested guidance from the study psychiatrist. On these occasions, the parents were advised to clearly define their demands on the youngster and to make no modification in a demand until they were certain that Bert understood what was expected of him. In addition, the parents were reassured that Bert's difficulties in adaptation were to a considerable degree normal for his age and not always evidence of neurological or psychological disorder.

In this preschool and early middle childhood period, both parents were able to modify their practices in accordance with these suggestions and provided Bert with a clearer definition of their requirements for social behavior. In accordance with his general temperamental pattern, Bert responded positively and quickly to the setting of limits. Several psychiatric evaluations through the age of 8 consistently failed to disclose any evidence of substantial behavioral disturbance.

During the ninth year of life, however, Bert developed impairment of school functioning associated with difficulty in reading and arithmetic, which included letter and number reversals. Avoidance reactions to reading occurred and he began to fuss and cry over homework. In addition, he began to have social difficulties with other children for the first time. He became the scapegoat of his class and his friends began to avoid him. On clinical interview at 8 years 9 months, Bert showed some residual speech difficulty. Noticeable left-right confusion was present. He frequently did not listen to what the examiner was saying. No other pathological findings were noted. The diagnosis was brain damage with primary perceptual difficulties and mild reactive behavior disorder.

Beyond his problems with school and peer group activities, the major source of stress for Bert revolved around his relationships with his father. The mother responded to his fussing and crying and his defensive avoidance of school work with supportive encouragement and help, but, as in his earlier childhood, she tended to be inconsistent and insufficiently firm in setting limits. Again, however, she was responsive to parent guidance discussions and able to modify her approach in a desirable direction. The father, on the other hand, became increasingly critical of Bert's behavior and academic difficulties. Beyond this, the father, whose own speech was highly articulate and carefully enunciated, was constantly irritated by Bert's persistently eccentric speech pattern, even though much improved from earlier childhood. He would correct Bert's speech in a loud voice and, at times, would shout until the boy was reduced to tears. In the parent guidance discussions with the father, he accepted the formulation that Bert's difficulties had an organic basis and in no way represented laziness, carelessness or a hostile, negativistic response to the standards of his parents and teachers. However, in practice, the father was unable to modify substantially his rigid, critical and overly demanding approach to his son. The stress this imposed on Bert, combined with his already existing difficulties with his speech, reading, and written arithmetic, was sufficient to impair his social functioning with his peer group. However, even in this situation of multiple stresses, his temperamental characteristic of noticeable adaptability was still in evidence, and the behavior problem that developed was only of mild degree.

During the next year, Burt showed some progress in his schoolwork.

However, he continued to have little social involvement with peers. A discussion with the parents when Bert was 10 years 7 months disclosed their concern that he whined when requested to do something, cried easily, showed immature, silly behavior, tried to show his superiority when others made mistakes, and was once again speaking in a sloppy fashion. All these behaviors evoked repeated parental reproval and nagging, especially by the father, with frequent crying responses by Bert. At this time it was believed that Bert's behavioral disturbances were primarily reactive and defensive in character. In addition to his long struggle to master his many handicaps and the stress resulting from his father's attitudes and behavior toward him, he was now also faced with the competitive challenge of his intellectually and socially successful younger sister. On the basis of this evaluation, the parents were advised to plan situations in which he would not have to compete with his sister's greater competence. It was also recommended that they avoid public criticism of Bert and insist on the completion of limited tasks firmly but patiently. The parents followed these recommendations in the main, and Bert began to carry out assigned responsibilities and developed some good friendships. His father, though, continued to express dissatisfaction with Bert's behavior. A growing negative interaction between father and son was clearly developing and the youngster's demoralization over his academic handicaps, while improved, was still present.

Further therapeutic intervention became necessary. It was decided that direct individual psychotherapy for Bert, supplemented by tutoring and frequent discussions with the parents, would be more effective than family therapy. At this point Bert was 13 years old. This program was accepted by the parents and carried through for the next 18 months. During this period Bert showed good progress, began doing his homework promptly and well, and became much more relaxed and sociable. Therapy was discontinued at this time, both because of his improvement and his increasing reluctance to continue.

At the age-16 interview, Bert was in his junior year in a demanding private high school and doing adequate work. He had learned to respond to his father's pressures by gestures of acquiescence. For example, his father was an expert sailor and Bert pretended to greater enthusiasm for sailing than he in fact had, explaining, "It makes him happy and I don't mind." He was persistent and hardworking, a very friendly youngster, and had finally made two friendships, though he continued to have difficulty with casual social relationships. He was beginning to show a single-minded concentration on areas of his own interests, which were primarily in the direction of useful community and civic projects. For example, he had just organized a number of his schoolmates to clean up an abandoned lot and convert it into an attractive play area. His organizational ability and persistence in such endeavors was indeed impressive. However, this same single-minded focus made him oblivious to the shifting relationships and attitudes of others. In addition, he was beginning to exhibit not only a desirable persistence but an irritating perseveration. This was evident in his repetitiveness in the interview, and was also reported as an increasing irritant to the parents, especially the father. The diagnosis at this time was organic personality syndrome, mild.

It was clear that Bert's future friendships would be based oń mutual involvement in an engrossing occupation. Hopefully, as an adult, if he found an area of functioning congenial to his interests and with an opportunity to work in such an area, his good intellect, persistence, and organizational talents might lead him to a successful and constructive career.

Bert had further therapy during his high school years, which focused primarily on his academic difficulties. His parents felt the treatment was successful in training him to concentrate.

After completing high school, Bert went to an out-of-town college, in which he enrolled in a complicated and demanding science curriculum to prepare himself for a career in environmental issues. He found this very difficult, but plugged away doggedly and achieved marginal passing grades. When interviewed again at 22 years, he was again pleasant, friendly and mild-mannered. He had a number of buttons pinned to his shirt and jacket, with slogans against cigarettes and violence. He was voluble, with rapid speech, though with only a slight residue of his childhood speech abnormalities. He was focused on political and social issues and detailed his activities and beliefs at length, with much repetitiveness. There was marked inhibition in social and sexual areas, though he denied any problems, and used his absorption in his studies and causes as a rationalization. Bert was completely task-oriented; friendships had no emotional content, but were related to his political-social activities. He described his father as self-righteous and opinionated, saying, "He always thinks I'm wrong." They had many arguments, which his mother tried to mediate. The diagnosis of organic personality syndrome was reaffirmed.

The interview with his parents confirmed the judgment of social isolation, as well as a marked tendency to perseveration. He had no friends and never dated, and always ended up by antagonizing his roommates at college by insisting on their participation in one social cause or another. Similar issues arose at home. For example, he got very angry at his mother because she wiped up spilled tomato juice with a newspaper, telling her she should have used a sponge because a newspaper could be recycled. But he was often helpful around the house, and performed conscientiously on part-time summer jobs. Both parents praised his determination, persistence, and concern for humanity. The father stated that his relationship with Bert was a positive one and that he respected his many admirable qualities, but he was clearly very critical of his son's speech, sloppy habits at home, and especially of his rigidity and perseverativeness. Both parents still found it most difficult to grasp the concept that Bert's behavior problems were primarily the result of organic brain dysfunction, in spite of the innumerable discussions with them to this effect over the many years.

Follow-up at age 24 showed Bert to be a rather handsome young man. His voice was masculine with appropriate inflection, and no remnant of his earlier high-pitched tone. His manner was pleasant, even gracious, and he chatted easily, informally and appropriately on a number of topics, such as the art work in the office, his hi-fi set, etc. He was in the sixth and final year of his academic studies, and expecting both a B.S. degree in Environmental Sciences and an M.A. in public administration and planning. He failed several courses the first time, but repeated them with final passing grades. He had never dropped a course. He has been active in many community activities, and enumerated 10 of them - running a bloodmobile, teaching cardiopulmonary resuscitation, first aid, and swimming, sitting on several student committees, testifying at state and city hearings on air and water pollution, etc. The previous summer he had worked for the city inspector supervising the construction of a sewage treatment plant. His social life was as before, with his friendships deriving from his various activities. As to young women, he had no girl friend and never had — "not enough time." He reported that he has not masturbated, and that sexual feelings did not bother him, saying that he was "too busy and too tired." On principle, he avoided completely liquor, tobacco, caffeine drinks, marijuana and any stimulant or depressant drugs. He stated that his relationship with his father was more peaceful, with occasional arguments; with his mother he felt closest, and with his sister he was friendly though distant. At the end of the interview, he chatted amiably, ignored the interviewer's goodby, and literally had to be given his coat and ushered into the hallway, still talking.

Two years later, Bert called one of us and asked to come in to discuss his problems. It was then 6 months following his graduation from college; he had been unable to find a job in his own field, and was living at home and doing part-time work in a family business. In the interview Bert launched into a recital of grievances against his father, who objected to his life style of sleeping late and staying up late, his manner of dress, and his reluctance to take a full-time job outside his own field. His father was also insisting that he now pay rent for living at home, which Bert felt was very unfair. He was distressed that his mother tended to side with his father, or at best stay neutral, instead of defending him. It was clear that he was looking to us to be his advocate and intervene on his behalf with his parents, and would be quite content to continue his present pattern of life. Psychotherapy was indicated to define the issues of independent mature functioning, as well as to explore his social problems. He accepted this recommendation, and at this writing therapy has just been initiated.

Case 2

Barbara was the product of a full-term pregnancy and normal spontaneous delivery, with a birth weight of 3.6 kg (7 lb 15 oz). Her neonatal course was uneventful. At 7 weeks of age, hemangioma of the chest wall and inversion of the feet were noted by the pediatrician, who treated the latter condition with Denis Browne splints. The achievement of motor and language landmarks was well within normal age ranges. However, as language developed during her second year, she showed a noticeable tendency to be querulous, repetitious, and echolalic. Her play, though age and sex appropriate in its initiation, tended to be disjointed and ill-directed.

Although Barbara's motor landmarks were normal, her coordinated motor functioning was noticeably inadequate. Clumsiness and gross uncoordination, accompanied by much tripping and falling, were noted throughout the first four years of life. Repeated neurologic examinations from age 4 years on resulted in findings of alternating hyperphoria of the adducting eye in lateral gaze, jerky movements of the trunk when sitting, choreiform movements of the arms and body when the arms were maintained in extension, clumsiness of gait, generally diminished muscular tone, and brisk deep tendon reflexes. The general diagnostic impression was that of mild dyskinesia accompanied by hyperactivity.

Intellectual testing was conducted at 3 and 6 years with the Stanford-Binet, and at 6 years 9 months with the WISC. Her IQs ranged from 91 to 106, with the highest score attained at age 6. Wide scatter was shown in both verbal and performance scales, with poorest achievement in comprehension and best on picture completion. During testing she was both distractible and perseverative. Perceptual and perceptual motor testing at 6 years resulted in performances that were substantially below her intellectual level and age expectancy.

In her temperamental characteristics, Barbara was highly active, irregular, very nonadaptive, and had a tendency to withdraw from new stimuli and social situations. Her threshold of responsiveness was relatively low and she tended to respond intensely even to weak stimuli. Her mood was predominantly negative, her distractibility high, and her persistence very low. This difficult temperament pattern persisted, and she was rated in either the third or fourth extreme quartile for this constellation all throughout early childhood, and again in adolescence and early adult life. The high activity level, high distractibility and low persistence also remained characteristic of her behavioral functioning.

As Barbara grew older, she gradually elaborated a pattern of hyperkinesis, restlessness, arrhythmicity, deviance in language usage, ritualistic behavior, tendency toward tantrums, destructiveness in play, ready distractibility, and poor motor coordination manifested in clumsiness, tripping, and frequent falling.

During her infancy, Barbara's parents attempted to be "permissive" and to organize their relations to her in terms of a child-centered self-demand approach. Such practices had disastrous consequences for this irregular, nonadaptive child who elaborated many routines into complex rituals. Many procedures of childhandling — bedtime, dressing, feeding, play, bathing, toileting — became characterized by fixed rituals. When the parents then tried to reduce these by the introduction of structure, Barbara tended to respond by disorganization, characterized by wild screaming, running around, and tantrums. In turn, the parents responded to the child's initial reaction to change by quickly reverting to the old routines. This inconsistency was accompanied by noticeable fluctuation in parental attitudes and behavior. At times they showed tenderness, at other times they were highly punitive to the point of beating and incarceration, despite Barbara's extreme panic when she was locked up or hit. Such punitive practices were primarily carried out by the father, with the mother continuing to remain relatively consistent in her display of positive feelings. Despite these real and continuing difficulties in management, the parents, during the infancy and preschool years, persisted in minimizing the pathologic character and inappropriateness of Barbara's behavior. Under most circumstances they tended to interpret her impulsiveness as spontaneity, and her hyperactivity and compulsive intrusion into other people's affairs as desirable curiosity and interest. Only when such behaviors began to result in the disruption of normal social functioning did they acknowledge them as signs of abnormality and agree to a psychiatric consultation.

A clinical evaluation was then done, at age 49 months, with the findings of neurologic dysfunction enumerated above. The diagnosis of organic personality syndrome with severe adjustment disorder was made, with age of onset placed at 24 months. The parents were not receptive to the possibility of direct treatment for Barbara, and parent guidance sessions were ineffective in changing the father's approach.

By age 6, Barbara's social relations with her peers had become highly negative. She was friendless, incapable of remaining in a normal school situation, dangerous to herself and to other members of the household, destructive, perseverative, and impulse-ridden. These behaviors resulted in her being placed in a residential institution for training and care at 6 years 11 months of age. This treatment was in another city to which the family had moved. It was one of the leading treatment and training child psychiatry centers of the area, with a highly competent and experienced professional staff. One of us (S.C.) visited the center after Barbara's admission to review her case with the staff. The psychiatrists there had made a diagnosis of childhood schizophrenia based on Barbara's behavior and the extreme concreteness manifest in her thinking. On a phenomenological level, the diagnosis appeared fully warranted.

Barbara was returned home almost one year later on a trial basis, but her behavior deteriorated steadily and after two months she was placed in another residential school. During her stay there, her behavior improved, her symptoms ameliorated, and she made educational advances. At the end of about 2½ years, she was again returned to her home. Once more there was regression, not only within the family but also in her peer relationships at the public school in which she was enrolled. Barbara became subject to physical aggression; she was hit and threatened with group violence because the other children were angered by her behavior.

The following year, at age 12½, she was enrolled in a private therapeutic day school and placed under the care of a psychiatrist. This situation lasted for two years until the family moved back to the New York area. Barbara's psychiatrist then recommended a residential school that would emphasize a structured therapeutic milieu. When the family returned to the New York area, psychometric testing was done by our research staff psychologist. Barbara achieved a full-scale WISC score of 99 (performance score, 87; verbal score, 110). Her functioning was variable and spotty, with considerable intrascale variability. Barbara was entered at a residential school at that time, when she was almost 15 years of age, and remained there until graduation at 18. She did fairly well academically, taking the usual high school subjects. She had a summer job as a clerk typist between the tenth and eleventh grades, managed commuting easily, and pleased her employer by her work. She also began to make a few friends at school, though there was difficulty in maintaining consistent relationships.

Her visits home, however, during these high school years were full of turmoil. She would explode with rage over even the most minimal criticism by her father, with violent verbal attacks against both parents. Her mother's statement was that "Life is hell every time Barbara comes home" and Barbara agreed that she was largely responsible for the altercations, but explained that "I have to prove to my father that I'm not afraid of him."

Barbara was reevaluated clinically at age 17 by one of us (S.C.). Her affect and visual contact were appropriate, her use of language was clear, connected, relevant, and age-appropriate. There was some clumsiness to her walk and other movements. Perseverative behavior and speech were still evident. There was no evidence for the diagnosis of schizophrenia, and the diagnosis of organic personality syndrome with adjustment disorder was reaffirmed.

After graduation from high school, Barbara moved to a youth residence hotel, went to business school for a year, and learned shorthand and typing. Her life since then has been one of turmoil, with the most extreme fluctuations in mood, behavior, and functional levels. She has held a number of office jobs, at which she impressed her supervisors by her competence, and became skilled at more complex tasks, such as statistical typing and the use of a word processor. With each job, however, she becomes anxious over any new stress or demand, stays home for a day or several days, and eventually quits or is fired. She has her own apartment, but her parents help her financially at times, and her mother has to come in on occasion to clean it up.

She has been sexually active since 19, and claims no problems in this area. She was married at 22 to an obviously disturbed young man, they quarreled constantly and violently, and divorced after 2 years. Barbara now, at 26, has a boyfriend, but comments that, as usual, she has picked someone with many problems, probably more than she has. Her weight fluctuates greatly, but overall she remains on the obese side. Her mother says, "she can be sweet, tender, helpful, thoughtful as long as it doesn't inconvenience her," but if she finds herself in a new situation that's frightening or challenging, she "gets furious, shouts, cries, walks away." Barbara confirms this judgment, and says she is afraid to be a mother for fear she would, in a rage, batter her child. On one occasion when violently angry, she put her hand through a windowpane; on other occasions she has cut her wrists and fingers superficially. She is able to make friends, but does not appear able to have a sustained relationship, or one with any depth. A recent course of psychotherapy, during her marriage, was not helpful.

At her most recent follow-up, at age 26, Barbara again made a positive and friendly affective contact. She showed some awkwardness of gait. She felt that at times she had perceptual difficulties at work, such as with spacing and lining up typed material to be parallel, although her boss tells her he is satisfied. She openly mourned her inability to control her moods, and felt a sense of helplessness over the course of her life. The same diagnosis was made, and a course of treatment with another psychiatrist arranged. As of this writing, 6 months after starting treatment, she has established a positive relationship with her therapist and is working, but her basic life style has not changed significantly.

Case 3

Kevin was the result of his mother's first complete pregnancy following 13 years of marriage. Problems of infertility and spontaneous abortion had existed previously, but this pregnancy was uneventful and the delivery uncomplicated. Kevin weighed 3.6 kg (8 lb 1 oz) at birth.

His neonatal course was stormy, with poor feeding and frequent vomiting. During the first two months of life, he sweated excessively and had pylorospasm with propulsive vomiting after each feeding. There were repeated respiratory infections during the first months of life; one episode at 4 months of age was sufficiently severe to require brief hospitalization. The development of both motor functioning and language was substantially delayed. Kevin did not sit without support until 11 months, and did not stand without support until 21 months. On examination at 21 months he was found to have noticeable pronation of the feet and substantially reduced muscle tone. His behavioral organization was appropriate for a child 15 months of age. Neurological examination at 3 years 8 months disclosed severe disturbance of gait, deep tendon reflexes that were excessively brisk in the lower extremities, and unsustained bilateral clonus. Language development at that time was at least 9 months behind age expectation. Speech evaluation at 5 years 4 months of age showed dysarthria, abnormal sound substitutes and distortions, and elements of echolalia and perseveration.

The first formal psychometric evaluation was carried out when Kevin was 4 years 3 months of age. He was friendly and cheerful, but readily distractible and restless. His speech was sparse and frequently incomprehensible. Testing was incomplete because he tired quickly, but a basal age on the Stanford-Binet of 2 years 6 months was established, with some successes at the 4-year level. Repeat testing at 5 years 1 month resulted in an uneven test performance. He was hyperactive and readily distractible to all stimuli, tended to be imitative and perseverative, to have poor manual coordination, and to show a high degree of randomly associative behavior. He attained a basal age of 2 years 6 months, a mental age of 3 years 8 months, and an IQ of 72.

Despite his mildly subnormal intelligence, occasional hyperactivity, and prominent motor and speech disorder, Kevin was not an excessively difficult child to manage. Although he was moderately active and irregular as an infant, he tended to approach new situations and express a positive mood. His thresholds of arousal were fairly high and he was moderately nonadaptive. An early easy distractibility coupled with a high level of persistence in the first year was replaced after the second year by moderate distractibility but continued high level of persistence. Perhaps most importantly, from the early months of life onward, he was a child whose responses were characterized by a low level of intensity. Thus, even abnormal behaviors were mildly expressed.

From the sixth month of life onward, when they first became convinced of abnormality in his development, Kevin's parents accepted the fact that his difficulties in learning and his developmental delays derived from primary neurologic damage. However, they were reluctant to accept the possibility that his intellectual retardation might be permanent. Within this framework, they were highly accepting and very fond of the boy. Their demands were appropriate to the level of his intellectual and physical capacities, and their efforts at training him were consistent and patient. Social contact with other children was encouraged and planned, and the parents placed him in a normal nursery school for children one year his junior, with the hope that he would be able to go on to a normal elementary school. However, on psychometric testing at the age of 6 years 2 months, Kevin obtained an IQ of 76. He was distractible and perseverative and his speech was still unclear. The parents refused to consider school placement on the basis of mental retardation but accepted referral to a special school for brain-injured children.

In this school his placement was at age level. The intellectual levels of the other children were at or closer to the normal level than Kevin's. He required intensive tutoring and, even with this, his learning progress was slow. His parents consistently explained away his low academic achievement scores with the statement, "He doesn't take tests well." Reports to our longitudinal study staff from the school personnel did indicate no major behavior problems other than those involving the modifications of management necessary because of his intellectual and physical limitations.

It was clear that Kevin's mild hyperactivity was not producing any important behavior difficulties nor contributing to his slow academic progress. The latter, while retarded, was consistent with his intellectual level. Amphetamine medication was therefore not considered appropriate and was not prescribed.

A psychiatric reevaluation by the study psychiatrist was done with Kevin at 14 years of age. He looked his stated age but showed no facial expression and had his mouth constantly open. His attention wandered constantly and he repeatedly squirmed in his chair, played with any object within reach, and wandered about the room. His mother stated that his behavior in this session was typical of his reactions to new people in new situations — that is, he was more distractible than at other times, more active, and less able to produce what he knew. On psychological testing at about this time he had a full-scale Wechsler Intelligence Scale for Children (WISC) score of 59. Projective tests did not show sufficient psychopathology to warrant a diagnosis of behavior disorder. The psychologist did report similar avoidance reactions to the test situation, as observed by the psychiatrist in the clinical examination session.

His parents continued to minimize his intellectual defect and exaggerate his academic progress. They insisted he had no behavior problems and reported his social relations to peers and teachers as amiable. They clearly maintained their patient, positive, and supportive approach.

Kevin's behavioral response to the clinical examination and to psychological testing at 14 years suggested that he might be developing a reactive defensive pattern of stress and demand. However, the data were insufficient for a diagnosis of behavior disorder. The hyperactivity and distractibility were also still mild and there was no evidence that they were producing substantial problems in functioning. On the other hand, it was our judgment at that time that "the stresses and new demands that adolescence may bring may lead to intensification of his defensive reactions and the development of a behavior disorder" (Thomas and Chess, 1975, p. 460).

A follow-up interview was obtained with the parents when Kevin was 21 years of age. They described him as having the same "good natured" disposition as always. He had graduated from a course in special education 6 months previously, and since then was working in a sheltered workshop for retarded citizens. He belonged to several clubs for young adults with similar handicaps, but had made no individual friends. The parents described Kevin as self-sufficient around the house and helpful with domestic chores; but at the same time he had difficulty with personal hygiene and had to be reminded to change his clothes. He also shaved the same side of face twice without looking into the mirror and failed to do the other side. The parents stated he had no fears, but he did prefer to stay in the house playing the radio, TV or records; if a stranger came in he left the room. His speech was largely unintelligible.

Having been thus warned that a direct interview with him was impossible, a telephone call was made to him when he was alone in the house. After about 15 rings Kevin picked up the phone and made a muffled unidentifiable sound. To the routine questions, "Is that you, Kevin?", "Is your mother or father home?", "When will they be home?", he responded with unintelligible explosive barks.

It was evident that the defensive avoidance pattern noticed at the 14-year evaluation had intensified over the subsequent years so that at age 21 he was socially isolated and withdrawn. His club attendances were undoubtedly pro forma exercises arranged by his parents, but without any positive socializing effect as yet. The difficulties in functioning now warranted the clinical diagnosis of organic personality disorder, mental retardation, moderate, with adjustment disorder, and the onset judged to be at about 15 years.

DISCUSSION

The original reports on the behavioral consequences of brain damage tended to consider the "brain-damaged child" as a single syndrome characterized by hyperkinesis, distractibility, perseveration, perceptual disturbance, emotional lability, atypical cognitive functioning, and disturbances in impulse control (Goldstein, 1936; Strauss and Werner, 1943; Bradley, 1957). Subsequent studies, however, reported that while this syndrome does occur in some children as a consequence of central nervous dysfunction, the behavioral sequelae of brain damage in children can be very diverse both in severity and type of behavioral, intellectual, and perceptual disturbance (Laufer and Denhoff, 1957; Birch, 1964, pp. 3–12; Eisenberg, 1964, pp. 61–77; Chess, 1969, pp. 126–137). Most recently, in an extensive survey of this issue, Rutter (1981) has concluded that "there appear to be rather few specific cognitive or behavioral sequelae of brain injury (in children). The association between brain damage and social disinhibition provides one of the few exceptions" (p. 1542). The children who showed social disinhibition Rutter described as being markedly outspoken and showing "a general lack of regard for social convention. Frequently they made very personal remarks or asked embarrassing questions, and sometimes they undressed in social situations in which this would ordinarily be regarded as unacceptable behavior. Some of these disinhibited patterns also included forgetfulness, overtalkativeness, carelessness in personal hygiene and dress, and impulsiveness" (1981, p. 1541).

Of our 3 cases of brain damage, only Case 2, Barbara, fit the original descriptions of the hyperkinetic brain-damaged child. Again, only Barbara, of the 3 cases, showed a number of the symptoms corresponding to Rutter's description of social disinhibition.

We, ourselves, have been impressed with the finding of perseveration in brain-damaged children, both because of its frequency and its functional significance. Perseverative speech and behavior were present in our 3 cases, and in cases 1 and 2, Bert and Barbara, contributed significantly to their disturbances in psychological development. In Bert's case, perseveration had not been a significant factor in his childhood problems, which revolved primarily around his difficulties with speech, reading, and written arithmetic. However, by adolescence his repetitiveness in speech and behavior became a source of irritation to his parents and peers, and contributed significantly to his increasing social isolation through adolescence and into early adulthood. His perseverative tendencies have thus far not interfered with his work functioning. However, his jobs have been either temporary or part-time, and he has not as yet been put to the test of a substained full-time work demand.

In Barbara's case, repetitive speech was evident as it developed in the second year, and perseveration was noticeable in both the 3- and 6-year IQ testing. The elaboration of perseverative behavior into fixed and complex rituals was a major symptomatic development in childhood, with violent screaming and tantrums at any attempt to change them. The problem of ritualistic behavior was ameliorated with her residential psychiatric treatment, but what has remained is a marked anxiety reaction, at times to the point of behavioral disorganization, to demands to change her routinized, repetitive way of functioning. This has been especially noticeable in her job difficulties, but has also affected her social relationships.

Beyond these 3 cases, a sample of 88 cases of neurologically damaged children evaluated by one of us (S.C.) in a consultation practice was compared with a matched group of 88 children without evidence of brain damage and also brought for psychiatric consultation because of behavioral difficulties (Chess, 1972). The two groups were compared for the symptoms of hyperactivity, short attention span, distractibility, mood oscillation, high impulsivity and perseveration. Perseveration was the sole symptom statistically more characteristic of the brain-damaged youngsters. As to the other symptoms, only when compared in clusters of 3 or more were they significantly related to neurological damage.

This study was flawed in that the effect of mental retardation in the neurologically damaged group was not partialled out. However, in our 2 cases in which perseveration was a functionally significant factor in their developmental course, both Bert and Barbara were of normal intelligence. We have made this same observation time and time again over the years, in clinical practice, with brain-damaged children of normal intelligence whose parents have sought psychiatric help. The same was also true of the parents of our mentally retarded and congenital rubella longitudinal samples, whose children were also brain-damaged. Whatever their other concerns over their child's problems, these parents have consistently echoed each other with the same complaint. "With the other children, I expect them to say, 'Why can't I' and repeat this a few times, but I know it will pass. But with Joey, it is clear it will go on forever. No matter how patient we try to be, we get fed up." "This repeating over and over again drives us all up a wall". "It simply does not seem fair to the other children. They bring their friends home less and less, and tell me they are embarrassed by how Peggy keeps bothering their friends with these same questions and stories time after time." And when forced to put a stop to such a youngster's perseverative question or act, if the parents had to get moving to some other activity, they could predict the storm and even violence that could result.

Whether perseveration is a statistically significant behavioral consequence of brain damage in children of normal intelligence is a question of interest. However, there can be no doubt that when it does occur in such youngsters, it requires high priority in parent and teacher guidance and in direct treatment, because of the serious effect it can have on social relationships, learning, and school adjustment, and the danger of its potentiation of other symptoms and disabilities. An analogy can be drawn with the occurrence of a significant degree of arteriosclerosis in diabetes. This may occur in only a small proportion of those suffering from diabetes, but when it shows itself, arteriosclerosis is a potentially ominous finding, which may jeopardize the health and even the life of a diabetic whose illness is otherwise well controlled.

Second to perseveration in the problems of management of a brain-damaged child is the presence of impulsivity, especially when it contains an aggressive component. Impulsivity, as we have seen it clinically, appears to be related to Rutter's (1981) description of the syndrome of "social disinhibition." The inability to predict and hence to stave off undesirable impulsive acts can be very troublesome and disruptive to family life. Parents can also find themselves constantly tense and on the alert, for fear of the safety hazards created by such behavior.

Our earlier report (Thomas and Chess, 1975) on these 3 brain-damaged cases emphasized the role of temperamental factors in their behavioral development throughout childhood. Bert was a youngster with easy temperament in childhood, adolescence and early adulthood, and, in spite of his academic difficulties, perseverativeness, and the unrealistic and rigid expectations of his father, was able to adapt positively to most situations, master a demanding academic curriculum, and maintain a pleasant, friendly demeanor. It is only now, in adult life, that the cumulative stresses and limitations in social functioning and independent living have emerged as major psychological problems. Kevin also was characterized by easy temperament, except for moderate nonadaptability, and the behavioral difficulties occasioned by his neurological dysfunction and mental retardation were easily managed by his parents within a sheltered environment.

Barbara, by contrast, was in the third or fourth extreme quartile for difficult temperament in childhood, adolescence and early adulthood. This high risk factor was further complicated by high activity and marked distractibility, and a pathogenic family environment, and Barbara sustained severe symptoms and evidence of serious psychopathology from early childhood onward. It is of interest that her younger sister, also an NYLS subject but without Barbara's difficult temperament and neurological dysfunction, has also described consistent traumatic experiences with her rigid punitive father, but has remained free of behavior disorder.

Barbara's case history suggests that difficult temperament when combined with brain damage becomes an even greater risk factor for behavior disorder development than in normal children. In similar fashion, a study of 52 mildly retarded children (Chess and Korn, 1970) indicated that retarded children with even mild manifestations of the difficult temperament constellation are especially vulnerable to the development of a behavior disorder. And a study of a population of congenital rubella children with various combinations of physical handicaps (Chess, Korn and Fernandez, 1971, pp. 128–130) showed a similar vulnerability of a combination of difficult temperament and physical handicap as with the mentally retarded children.

It is, of course, not temperament alone, nor brain damage or other handicap alone, or excessive and inappropriate environmental demands alone which determines the genesis or evaluation of a behavior disorder. It is rather the continuous interactional process among these influential factors which shapes the developmental course of handicapped children, or, for that matter, of children without handicaps.

It is clear that we do not consider that temperamental characteristics such as high activity, irregularity in biological functioning, withdrawal reaction to new situations, negative responses to new situations, intensity of reactions, distractibility, or persistence to be the consequence of brain dysfunction. Rather, these characteristics are at one extreme of the normal distribution curve of individuality in behavior style. They should not be confused with such pathological behavioral characteristics as hyperactivity, rigidity of behavior, negativism, hyperdistractibility, or perseveration. The necessity of this caveat is indicated by the discussion of our reports on temperament in Wender's (1971) influential volume on minimal brain dysfunction (MBD). Wender believes that several of our temperamental attributes are relevant to the MBD syndrome (1971, pp. 57–58). In addition, he judges that 13 of our first 42 children with behavior disorders "were fairly typical instances of the MBD syndrome" (1971, pp. 43–44). However, outside of the 3 cases detailed in this chapter, none of the other clinical cases in the NYLS sample showed any significant evidence of neurological dysfunction on clinical and psychometric study or on long-term follow-up evaluations. Actually, in recent years, increasing doubts have been raised by a number of investigators and clinicians as to the validity and usefulness of the MBD concept (Carey and McDevitt, 1980). To quote from Rutter's (1982) very recent comprehensive survey of this question, "So far as the . . . qualitatively distinct type of minimal brain dysfunction concept is concerned, we need to have recourse to the Scottish-type verdict of 'not proven.' Undoubtedly, claims regarding this type of minimal brain dysfunction have far outrun the empirical findings that could justify it" (p. 31).

A final point of theoretical interest is raised by the history of the second case, Barbara. Was the diagnosis of childhood schizophrenia, made when her pathological behavior had reached psychotic proportions, an error? Or is the behavioral syndrome we designate as schizophrenia a final common behavioral pathway that may have many different causes? This is not to suggest that childhood psychosis is a direct relation of neurological dysfunction alone. As in the case of Barbara, the psychotic syndrome may be the result of the interaction of a number of pathogenic factors, which may very well be different in different children.

CHAPTER 16

Origins of Behavior Disorders

A major goal of the NYLS has been the earliest possible identification of those subjects who developed a behavior disorder at any age-period from infancy onward. With the scope of the anterospective data both preceding the onset of the disturbance and concurrent with its beginning, and with the detailed clinical evaluation of each case as it came to our attention, we had a special opportunity to explore the factors involved in the origins of behavior disorders. Any such exploration must rest on some theoretical framework. In our case we have been firmly committed from the beginning to an interactionist viewpoint, as defined in Chapter 2. By now, this viewpoint has gained the acceptance of the great majority of developmental psychiatrists and psychologists, but this was far from the case when we started the NYLS in 1956.

DIVERSITY

Within this interactionist framework, our qualitative analysis of the origins and evolution of behavior disorders required a consideration in each case of: 1. the youngster's own characteristics — temperament, abilities, motivations and goals; 2. intrafamilial characteristics — parental attitudes, childcare practices, aspirations, personality attributes, ethical standards, sociocultural values, sib influences; and 3. extrafamilial factors — peer group standards, school expectations and demands, community value systems and opportunities.

As we culled and evaluated the pertinent data from each subject's anterospective record, we were quickly and deeply impressed by the diversity so evident in the developmental course of individual children. So many person and situation variables were influential in the developmental process, so many different outcomes were possible, so many different traits were the significant ones for different individuals, so much differentiation and so many roles were evident, and differently from one individual to another—both for healthy as for pathological outcomes—that the search for simple formulas and categorizations appeared to be totally unrealistic. Yet, we found that, with few exceptions, the developmental studies of the 1950s and 1960s were straitjacketed by formulations that could not do justice to the scope and significance of such human diversity. Instinctual drive reduction theories, stimulus-response models, concepts of linear continuity in development, an insistence on the all-importance of early life experience, formulations of invariant development stage sequences, or an emphasis on personality traits as fixed or global—all such concepts failed to provide us with a model that could encompass the subtleties, complexities and richness of the life histories of our NYLS subjects.

THE GOODNESS OF FIT MODEL

The interactionist view provided us with a general theoretical framework for determining the kinds of data to be collected and culled in the NYLS, as well as in our other longitudinal studies. But by itself it was not an adequate conceptual model for identifying the *specific* factors that were influential in the development and evolution of a behavior disorder in any individual subject. Nor was it a sufficient basis by itself for structuring strategies of early intervention and treatment in individual cases. This requirement for a suitable specific application of the interactionist viewpoint led us to the formulation of the goodness of fit model, as we have defined it in Chapter 2. This model makes it possible to scrutinize the assessments of the behaviorally disturbed individual's motivations, abilities and temperament, as well as his behavioral patterns and their consequences, to identify the expectations, demands and limitations of the environment, and then to define the factors responsible for the pathogenic developmental course. Thus, for example, if consultation is requested for a girl who stands passively at the periphery of a group, and if assessment reveals a slow-to-warm-up temperamental pattern, then attention can be focused on whether the parents and teachers are making a demand for quick, active group involvement. If a boy disrupts his class with bizarre behavior, the clinical evaluation may show a severe reading disability which has been overlooked, with defensive avoidance behavior. If we know that the handicapped youngster may have special difficulties in mastering new complex demands and expectations in adolescence, this can provide a guide to ensure continued goodness of fit.

As these examples indicate, the significant factors involved in the development of a poorness of fit with consequent emergence of a behavior disorder may vary from case to case. No hierarchy of importance can be established in which any single variable is presumed to be the decisive factor in all instances of deviant behavior — whether it be the child's own characteristics, parental attitudes and practices, the dynamics of the family system, early life experience, or the stresses imposed by the school or community. Otherwise, we would be repeating a frequent approach in psychiatry which, over the years, has been beset by general theories of behavior based upon fragments rather than upon the totality of influencing mechanisms.

Furthermore, a poorness of fit cannot be identified by a consideration of the child's characteristics alone, or of environmental influences alone. The issue is always that of the interactional process between child and environment, though the significant factors in both child and environment, as well as in the dynamics of the interactional process, may vary from individual to individual. There are a few exceptions to this general formulation. A pervasive developmental disorder such as infantile autism may be decisively determined by the child's characteristics, and environmental influences may at most mitigate or exacerbate the disorder. Or an overwhelming environmental stress may be pathogenic for individuals with widely varying personality structures (K. Erikson, 1976; Terr, 1981), though the severity and the specific symptoms may vary from person to person.

In recent years, developmental research has emphasized increasingly the complexity and diversity of human psychological functioning, and the richness and variability of the interplay among the many influential factors that are evident from person to person (Rutter, 1980; Thomas and Chess, 1980). The developmental psychologist, Mischel, has summed up nicely our present state of knowledge, noting that recent research gives us a view of "the person as so complex and multifaceted as to defy easy classification and comparisons on any single or simple common dimension, as multiply influenced by a host of interacting determinants, as uniquely organized on the basis of prior experiences and future experiences, and yet as rule-guided in systematic, potentially comprehensible ways that are open to study by the methods of science" (Mischel, 1977, p. 253).

It is just such a view of the human being as multifaceted, complex, and uniquely organized and yet "rule-guided in systematic, potentially comprehensible ways" that makes our goodness of fit model an appropriate framework for the consideration of the origins and evolution of behavior disorders.

VARIETIES OF POORNESS OF FIT

The case vignettes in Chapters 12 through 15 illustrate some of the factors and the variations in their dynamic interplay that can make for a goodness of fit or a poorness of fit and a favorable versus an unhealthy developmental course in individual youngsters. From our culling and qualitative analyses of the behavior disorder cases in the NYLS sample, a number of general observations can be made regarding the functional significance of different influential variables.

TEMPERAMENT

Temperamental categories or constellations, even at the extreme ranges, were not by themselves the causes of behavior disorder development. And in some, though not many cases, temperament did not play a significant role in the development of a behavior problem. Also, although children with certain temperamental characteristics were more vulnerable to behavior disorder, disturbed development did occur with any temperamental pattern. In effect, no temperamental characteristic conferred an immunity to behavior disorder development, and neither was it fated to create psychopathology. Thus, in no way do we advocate a temperament theory of personality or psychopathology.

Difficult Temperament

The difficult temperament constellation clearly placed a child at greater risk for behavior disorder development than did any other set of temperamental characteristics. This was evident in our quantitative correlations between the 3-year ratings and early adult outcome, as summarized in Chapter 10. This extends our early observations on the vulnerability of the temperamentally difficult child for behavior disorder development in the childhood years (Thomas, Chess and Birch, 1968), a finding confirmed by reports from other centers (Graham et al., 1973; Maurer et al., 1980; Wolkind and De Salis, 1982).

A temperamentally difficult child presents a difficult management issue for most mothers, starting in early infancy. The baby who tends to cry loudly with new foods, new people and new places, and then adapts slowly, and whose hunger, sleep and elimination patterns tend to be irregular, does not quickly develop regular feeding and sleep schedules and is not easily toilet trained. The first experiences of such a child with peer play groups, birthday parties, a new school, or new visitors to the home will all too often be occasions of much fussing and even turmoil.

Parents respond to the difficulties and demands of such a child in various ways, depending on their own personalities, attitudes and expectations. They may become hostile, guilty, overdemanding or appeasing, helpless, confused and inconsistent, or get embroiled in a struggle with the child for control and domination. Any of these responses, or combination of them, only makes it more difficult for the child to adapt positively, and leads to an escalating poorness of fit and the likelihood of a behavior disorder development.

The potential for a poorness of fit for the temperamentally difficult child is thus present from early infancy onward. Where a behavior disorder developed, it was likely to have an early childhood onset. Thus, in our NYLS clinical sample, the age of onset for the childhood cases with difficult temperament were all by age 7 years. Of the 12 cases with onset in adolescence, only 2 had difficult temperament. In one of these, the girl Olga described in Chapter 14, the youngster did not become the subject of parental disapproval and excessive demands until her middle childhood years. The other case was a boy, the twin brother of Bruce (Chapter 13), whose parents did not respond unfavorably to his temperamental characteristics. However, there was severe parental conflict and discord which kept increasing over time. It would have been stressful for almost any child to cope with this family environment, but especially so for an intensely reactive and slowly adaptive youngster, as in this case. The stress created by the parental discord increased as this friction became more open and more bitter, and symptoms of a schizoid personality disorder appeared at age 16 and grew worse into early adult life.

In the parent interviews in the childhood years, we asked for overall general comments on the child, though these were not used in the temperament item scoring. These comments were reviewed in the children with difficult temperament. In the first year, most of these parents gave positive, even glowing judgments of their babies, even as they reported discrete items of difficult behavior. By the second year, and even more in the third year, these positive statements diminished to be replaced by such comments as, "He's so miserable to take care of, you never know what's wrong with him." This sequence indicates that, in the cases of poorness of fit between early childhood difficult temperament and dissonant parental handling, the temperamental characteristics preceded the negative parental attitudes. Furthermore, there was no consistent parental pattern that could be identified in these cases. Parental attitudes ranged from blaming the child to blaming themselves, from vacillation to extreme rigidity, and from excessive demands to appeasement. Also, most of these parents functioned quite differently with their other children who did not show this difficult temperamental constellation.

Some parents were able to cope in a benign positive fashion with their youngster's difficult temperament, and in these instances the child's developmental course, if not always smooth and easy, was basically healthy. A striking example was Carl, a boy who scored as one of the most difficult children in the entire NYLS sample for each of the first three years of life. Whether it was the first bath or the first solid foods in infancy, the beginning of nursery and elementary school, or the first birthday parties or shopping trips, each experience evoked stormy responses, with loud crying and struggling to get away. This was his parents' first child and the mother was shaken by this behavior and worried that there must be something wrong with herself as a mother. The father, however, was self-assured and relaxed, and even took satisfaction in his young son's vigorous reactions, which he characterized as "lusty." Interestingly enough, the father was of opposite temperament, with quiet positive mood much in evidence. He was actively involved in caring for Carl, and very soon, without any orientation from our staff interviewer, came to realize that if the youngster's initial intense negative reactions were treated quietly and patiently, he would adapt gradually. "He's always like that with anything new, but he always gets over it," was his judgment, accurate enough because of the positive parental handling. Furthermore, once adapted, Carl's intensity of responses gave him a zestful enthusiastic involvement, just as it gave his initial negative reactions a loud and stormy character. With the reassurance and support she received from her husband, and with the repeated evidence of Carl's eventual healthy functioning, the mother also finally relaxed and gained confidence in her maternal role. With this goodness of fit, Carl did not become a behavior problem. There was a temporary period of stress and turmoil when he had to meet a number of new situations and demands simultaneously on entering college away from home, but he coped successfully on his own, and the disturbance was transient.

It must be emphasized that the temperamental constellation we label as difficult is difficult in those cultures such as ours in which demands are made on the young child for the early establishment of regular sleep and feeding schedules, for quick adaptation to new situations and new people, and for cheerful acceptance of the rules and routines of the family. In different cultures, with different types of demands and expectations of the young child, difficult temperament may not impose the same stresses, or have the same high risk potential for behavior disorder development. Substantial evidence in this direction has already been provided by Super and Harkness (1981) in a study of a rural farming community in Kenya. From maternal interviews, cross-validated with naturalistic observations of the child's daily behavior, Super and Harkness identified a group of infants with biological irregularity, intense negative reactions and slow adaptability, corresponding indeed to the difficult temperament constellation. However, for the Kenyan mothers, these babies were not difficult to manage. Irregularity in sleep or feeding rhythms was no problem, since the infant was always with the mother or an older sib, slept beside the mother and was nursed whenever he or she awoke during the night. Fussing and slow adaptability were not issues of concern, because these parents, unlike so many American parents, did not view such behavior as alarming signals of a beginning behavior problem. Rather, their common statement was that "one cannot know about personality until the child is old enough, about 6 or 7 years, to take responsibility in household economic chores" (p. 82). Within this context, it was easy for these fussy, irregular and nonadaptive Kenyan babies to experience a goodness of fit with their environment.

Easy Temperament

The temperamentally easy children, at the opposite end of the temperamental spectrum from the difficult youngsters, were by contrast to this latter group at low risk for behavior disorder development. This was evident in the quantitative analyses, and also by qualitative evaluation. Thus, from our qualitative ratings, about 10 percent of the total NYLS sample showed difficult temperament. Of these 14 youngsters, 10, or 71 percent, had behavior problems, and in each case temperament played a significant role in the origin of the disorder. By contrast, in the much larger group of easy children (40 percent), there were only 4 cases of behavior disorder in which this temperamental constellation was influential in the development of problem behavior. There were also several other behavior disorder cases in temperamentally easy children in which temperament did not play a significant etiological role.

As a further contrast, the clinical cases with difficult temperament showed a wide variety of types of poorness of fit between their characteristics and environmental demands. The 4 cases with easy temperament, on the other hand, showed only one type of poorness of fit. Put very simply, the child learned something very well at home which then did not fit in the "outside" world.

In all 4 youngsters, the parents imposed a set of idiosyncratic standards and rules of behavior which the child accepted quickly and firmly, given the temperamental characteristics of positive reactions to the new, with positive mood and easy adaptability. But then the idiosyncratic pattern proved maladaptive with peers or school, or both. There was a goodness of fit at home, but a poorness of fit outside the home which then produced excessive stress and behavior disorder symptoms.

One boy was taught formal polite manners at home, appropriate for an adult, but not for a 3-year-old in our culture. His pedantic formalistic behavior made him an immediate scapegoat with his peer group, resulting in the development of a number of fears. Another boy was encouraged by his mother's amusement at his "cute" remarks in public as well as at home, and went on as he came to school age to elaborate increasingly embarrassing and obnoxious comments about adults and other children in a loud and attention-getting voice. Not surprisingly, he turned from an "enfant terrible" to a disruptive influence in school, with academic underachievement and increasingly poor peer relationships. One girl with high intelligence learned poorly in the first grade, had few friends, and disregarded classroom instructions and the rules of games. Her parents had put great store on the expression of "individuality" and encouraged her "creative impulses." This made for highly enjoyable interchanges with her lively imaginative parents, but in no way prepared her for the necessities of learning and following rules and procedures, either in school or in play with her peers. Another girl's mother was concerned that her daughter not be "pressured" for academic achievement as she herself had been in her own childhood. To prevent this outcome, the mother discouraged all her daughter's task mastery activities and emphasized instead the importance of social graces. At her 3-year IQ testing session, the girl turned the occasion into a social situation but her test performance was uneven and inferior. This pattern came to characterize her school functioning, in which she was socially charming but had an increasingly severe learning problem.

It is true that many children are able to learn one set of rules within the family, and shift gears in the outside world to a different set of expectations. It is our impression that these 4 youngsters could not make such a shift because with their easy temperaments they learned easily and solidly, and what they learned at home was so rigidly fixed that, even with their easy temperament, they could not adapt differently in the outside world. What they had learned all too well at home was then so maladaptive outside the home that a pathogenic poorness of fit developed very quickly.

Slow-to-warm-up Temperament

These children were also at higher than average risk for behavior disorder development, with approximately 50 percent becoming clinical cases, as compared to 71 percent for the difficult temperament youngsters. In contrast to the latter group, the slow-to-warm-up children typically did not present substantial difficulties at home in the early years. They did not have the biological irregularity of the difficult children, and the mildness with which their negative reactions were displayed made it possible for their parents to be patient and understanding. Problems usually developed in the school setting and with peer groups, in which they were often expected to participate actively and quickly in new settings. The case vignettes of Michael in Chapter 12 and Ralph in Chapter 13 illustrate this sequence. In some cases, overprotective parents tried to insulate their shy children from disturbing new situations, which only served to inhibit the achievement of social competence and task mastery. In one such case, a boy's IQ score at 6 years dropped sharply from his 3-year level, he began to avoid challenging demands, and persisted in requesting servicing from his mother which was no longer appropriate for his age.

Other Temperamental Characteristics

In this middle-class group, the parents attached great importance to educational achievement and to success in professional careers or business. For both these goals, persistence was considered desirable and even essential. The youngsters who were highly distractible and nonpersistent were likely to evoke strong criticism from their parents who demanded persistence at task activities which they could not meet. The pathogenic consequences of this type of poorness of fit are illustrated in the case vignette of Norman in Chapter 14. Another highly distractible child who was always "forgetting" to fulfill to the end his parents' requests and demands was sometimes considered to be willfully disobedient, with unhappy consequences for both child and parent (Roy, Chapter 12).

High persistence, though usually greatly valued by parents and teachers, was in some cases a mixed blessing. This was especially true if the child's persistence was extreme and if his response to a premature termination of his activity by a teacher or other outsider was a loud and disruptive tantrum. The consequences of repeated episodes of this kind are illustrated in the case vignette of Richard, in Chapter 14.

High activity did not create problems for this sample, whose families could provide adequate safe play space and facilities to meet the motoric needs of such youngsters. In a few cases, low activity was interpreted by parents and teachers as mental sluggishness and contributed to a negative interactional process with a behavior disorder outcome.

Sensory threshold characteristics did not play a significant role in the origin of any of the clinical cases. Carey (1974) has reported an association between frequent night wakening in infancy and low sensory threshold.

TEMPERAMENT MATCH

If parent and child are similar in their temperamental characteristics, does this favor a goodness of fit? If they are dissimilar, does this promote a poorness of fit and behavior disorder development?

We do not have the systematic temperament ratings on the NYLS parents required for a quantitative study of this issue of temperament match. From a number of our qualitative judgments of parental temperament, however, it is clear that there is no simple linear relationship between parent-child temperament match and the developmental outcome in the child.

Thus, in the case of Carl cited above in this chapter, the father's optimal approach to the boy's difficult temperament was enhanced by his own opposite characteristics of quiet positive mood and easy adaptability. By contrast, the mother of another temperamentally difficult girl herself reacted quickly, negatively and loudly to irritating situations. The result was a series of yelling matches and blow-ups between mother and daughter, which contributed to the development of a behavior disorder in the child.

In one family, highly and intensely expressive parents were confused and antagonized by their young daughter's tendency to mild negative mood reactions. In another case, a mother recognized the nature of her daughter's easy temperament, identified it with her own childhood behavioral pattern, but considered this an undesirable characteristic.

Basically, the issue of goodness or poorness of fit between parent and child is not one of temperament match or mismatch. It is rather the issue of goodness of fit between parental expectations and demands and the child's capacities and characteristics. These expectations and demands may or may not be influenced by the parent's own temperament. The parent's temperament again may or may not affect the response to the child's temperament. And when the parent's temperament does influence his or her behavior and demands with the child, the direction of this influence can vary from family to family, depending on a host of factors which have shaped the parent's attitudes, goals and standards.

OTHER CHILD CHARACTERISTICS

A wide variety of characteristics, other than temperament, may influence the child-environment interactional process to produce a poorness of fit and a behavior disorder.

In our NYLS sample, a number of such influential factors have been evident. In the two cases of recurrent major depression detailed in Chapter 14,

Harold and Sylvia, the evidence indicates that these illnesses were biologically determined. This corresponds to the consensus among researchers in this field as to the etiology of this type of depressive illness. The symptoms of depression not only affected significantly the level of psychological functioning in both youngsters, but in Sylvia's case they also stimulated the development of a system of psychodynamic defense mechanisms which further complicated her adaptive possibilities.

Brain damage, as it was evident in the three cases described in Chapter 15, also had serious and even profound effect on each youngster's ability to achieve and sustain satisfactory levels of social competence and task mastery. In each case, perseverativeness, a direct symptomatic behavioral expression of the brain damage, was a prominent factor in producing a pathogenic poorness of fit. Beyond this, the final developmental pathway of these three youngsters was determined not only by the direct consequences of the brain damage, but also by the influence of their temperamental patterns, and by the response of the parents to their behavioral characteristics. In Barbara's case, the manifestations of her difficult temperament exaggerated the deviant aspects of her behavior, made her management extremely demanding, and brought to the fore the hostile tendencies of her father. The consequence was a stormy and severely disturbed developmental course, with many symptoms and even periods of behavioral disorganization.

In Bert's case, his easy temperament served to mitigate the stressful consequences of his brain damage — the speech difficulty, the dyslexia, the perseveration — as well as the impact of his father's critical and highly pressuring demands. As a result, his developmental course showed none of the turmoil, overt tension and behavioral disruption that characterized Barbara's history, and he reached adult life as a cheerful, friendly and cooperative young man. The consequences of his brain damage were in this sense masked, but still profound in his academic difficulties, social isolation, sexual inhibition, and work problems.

The third brain-damaged youngster, Kevin, presented a typical clinical picture of neurological impairment with mild mental retardation. His level of functioning would have inevitably been limited because of these handicaps, but his problem was compounded by his parents' attempts to minimize the extent of his intellectual deficit. By trying to maintain him in schools and social activities with intellectually normal children, they succeeded only in subjecting him to social and intellectual demands and expectations beyond his adaptive capacities. A defensive avoidance pattern leading to social isolation was the end result.

There have been no cases of autism or other types of pervasive developmental disorders, attention deficit disorder, or pure developmental language disorders in the NYLS sample. There have also been no behavior disorders which could be judged as originating from a maladaptive conditioned reflex pattern.

For this population, academic achievement was highly prized by parents and community. An IQ score below 120 was considered to be "below normal." One set of parents consulted us about their teenage son who was showing a great deal of school difficulty, with poor achievement and negativistic attitudes regarding school attendance and homework. He was not actually one of our study sample, but his three older brothers were, and we had accumulated a good deal of information about this youngest son and the family over the years. From these data, there was no evidence of psychopathology, and this was confirmed in a direct interview with the youngster. Psychiatric testing gave an IQ score of 105. When this test result was communicated to the parents, they took this information as a calamity. "He's retarded, we can't believe it." It became clear that the parents had been making demands for academic achievement much beyond their son's capacities and he had responded to this poorness of fit with defensive negativism and avoidance.

Physical characteristics of the child can also play a significant role in the development of a goodness or poorness of fit. The reaction of others to the degree of physical attractiveness (Sorell and Nowak, 1981) or to the presence of a physical disfigurement (Richardson et al., 1961) can heighten, mitigate, or distort the impact of the physical asset or handicap on the youngster and affect his self-image and level of functioning. In the handicapped subjects of our congenital rubella sample, this interactional process between handicap and environmental response and its consequences has been strikingly evident in a number of cases (Chess, Fernandez and Korn, 1980). In the NYLS group, one girl (Diana, Chapter 18) was born with a tight anal sphincter. This resulted in infrequent, painful and constipated bowel movements, alternating with large and painful evacuations. Various medical procedures, such as sphincter dilation and medication, gave partial relief. The problem was not aggravated initially by the child's response to her symptoms, inasmuch as she had the positive mood and quickly adaptive characteristics of the easy temperament pattern. Her mother's reaction was another story, with marked and frequent shifts in approach, which ranged from permissiveness to pressure, from reassurance to anger. The youngster could not cope with this combination of bowel symptoms and inappropriate maternal handling, and by age 3 years developed a defensive coping mechanism of avoidance, hiding in corners or behind the furniture when she moved her bowels.

PARENTAL CHARACTERISTICS

Parental characteristics played a highly significant role in the origins of behavior disorders in their children. In most cases this resulted from the attempt to impose demands and expectations which were inappropriate and excessive for the particular child's temperament or abilities. The many ways in which such poorness of fit developed have been illustrated in the various case vignettes in preceding chapters and in the preceding section of this chapter. In some cases such unrealistic demands reflected rigidly set attitudes on the parent's part, as in the case of Norman's father, (Chapter 14), or Roy's mother (Chapter 12). More often, however, the unrealistic demands and goals were set by well-intentioned parents who were ignorant of the inappropriateness of these pressures for their particular child's temperament, or who did not realize the consequences for the child with his peer group or in school. In such cases, most parents were quickly responsive to counseling and guidance.

We have indicated above that the child's temperament by itself did not produce a behavior disorder. This is implicit in the definition of temperament as a normal behavioral attribute. By contrast, in some 6 cases parental dysfunction as such was sufficiently extreme to become the decisive and even exclusive element in a child's behavior disorder development. In 2 cases, that of Bruce (Chapter 13) and his twin brother, the etiological factor was extreme open parental discord. Both youngsters did have relatively difficult temperament, but this appeared to play only a secondary pathogenic role. In one boy's case, there was not only severe parental conflict resulting in the father's leaving the house in the child's early years, but the mother's functioning was chaotic, disorganized, and unpredictable. Even with an easy temperament and good intelligence, the son could not cope successfully with this truly malignant home environment.

Another boy's parents were also in constant conflict, with the mother taking an intrusive aggressive role in which she actively derogated the rather passive father to the son. Still another boy suffered a somewhat similar parental environment, but the parents did combine to manufacture an image of their son as possessed of unusual intellectual and creative abilities (which was not true). When teachers in succeeding grades reported that the boy was deficient in completing assignments, not only did the parents refuse to make demands on him, but they complained loudly and insistently to teachers, other parents, and their son that it was all the teachers' fault. "The trouble is they don't know how to stimulate him." Their fantasy vision almost had the character of a *folie à deux*. The son himself was gradually transformed from a cheerful ac-

tive young child into a self-centered, apathetic, drug-abusing young man with
no meaningful interests or goals.

One girl, Olivia, also suffered from a family environment of parental conflict and bickering. The mother, a successful professional, constantly belittled
the father, who had a modest education and a job with low social prestige.
He responded by withdrawal into alcoholism and frequent flights from the
household, eventually returning home with passive resignation to his fate. The
mother, also intrusive into her two children's lives, kept appealing to them
for sympathy for her "plight." The son, not in our study, left home as soon
as he could be independent. The daughter by age 16 developed a severe personality disorder.

SIB RELATIONSHIPS

The most frequent statement of the subjects in the early adult interviews
regarding their sib relationships was that they quarreled and fought a great
deal as children, but that as they grew older this diminished and was replaced
by increasingly warm and even close friendships. In one case, an only child,
a boy, had a father who left home and broke off all contact with the family
when he was a young child, and a mother who became chronically ill and died
when he was a teenager. The psychological support he received from his older
half-brothers contributed strongly to his ability to master these highly stressful
life events.

In other instances, sib relationships were distant and even antagonistic into early adult life. This was most evident when one or the other or both sibs
evidenced some type of behavior disorder.

In a few instances, the dynamics of the pattern of sib relationships within
the larger context of the family system were significant factors in the development of a behavior disorder. One boy with a slow-to-warm-up temperament
had an older brother and younger sister who were active, approaching and
articulate youngsters. They were quick to bring their interests and activities
to the parents' attention, and their slowly responsive brother was gradually
pushed out to the periphery of the family group. He responded by further
withdrawal and by age 4 years had a mild adjustment disorder, with symptoms of fearfulness with new people, clinging to his mother, and social isolation at nursery school.

One girl was characterized temperamentally by mild expressiveness, slow
movement, and relatively frequent negative mood. Her parents, both highly
verbal and communicative individuals, could not appreciate and respond to
her positive interests because of her deadpan expression. Beyond this, her

younger sister was quick-moving, assertive and even impulsive, and moved into action immediately and positively, to her parents' delight, leaving her older sister to plod along behind her. By her fifth year the older girl's negative reactions had escalated into pathological negativism and quarrelsomeness.

Another girl, Olga (Chapter 14), had a benign relationship with her parents and a positive early childhood development. Even though of difficult temperament and with a demanding, rigid father, she escaped a poorness of fit because his pressures and unrealistic expectations were focused on her older sister, also of difficult temperament, with highly unfavorable consequences to the latter. When the older girl blossomed forth with artistic talents in middle childhood, she reaped highly salutary approval from parents and community, and Olga now became the family scapegoat, with pathological consequences. (We are not at all convinced that this family "required" a scapegoat. We rather suppose that if both daughters had shown easy temperament and other characteristics consonant with their parents' standards, both would have had a smooth developmental course.)

By contrast, Stanley (Chapter 12), was saved from a pathological behavioral course, even though of difficult temperament and having a controlling mother with unreasonable expectations and a passive detached father. The mother locked herself into a battle with the older son who manifested frequent forgetfulness and other annoying behavior. Although this behavior was due to marked temperamental distractibility the mother interpreted it as deliberate disobedience and provocation. Stanley, by contrast, was not forgetful, late or untidy, and his mother regarded him as a model son.

In a number of instances, the youngster with less than optimal functioning due to a behavior disorder had one or more sibs who were functioning well. The differential reactions of parents, peers and teachers to such contrasting behavioral levels served to increase, even if they did not cause, the severity of the behavior disorder.

PEER GROUP INFLUENCES

The development of peer relationships usually represented the first major social demand on the younger child after the mastery of the processes of early socialization within the nuclear family situation. Whether these peer interactions occurred primarily in informal settings with relatives or neighbors, or in more structured nursery schools or child-care centers, they represented for most preschool children a qualitatively new situation and experience to master.

In contrast to the earlier infancy period, the preschool child brought to the new issue of peer relationships not only his temperamental traits but also the more complex behavioral patterns he had already begun to develop. Parental expectations and goals for the child's peer group adaptation were also not infrequently different than for the development of regular feeding and sleep schedules and toilet training. The peer group might also expect standards of behavior at variance from those of the parents. Finally, the child for the first time had to cope with a new and demanding life situation without the continuous presence and assistance provided by the parents in the earlier adaptational issues within the family.

Many children, of course, mastered the social and task demands of peer group relationships successfully, whether smoothly or with some turmoil. For others, however, these new demands either initiated a poorness of fit and behavior disorder or intensified and extended the already existing maladaptive behavioral patterns. The clinical vignettes in preceding chapters illustrate some of the types of pathogenic interactional processes that resulted from the new expectations involved in peer relationships.

These new demands and expectations were especially stressful for the temperamentally difficult and slow-to-warm-up children, with their negative reactions to new situations and slow adaptability. If, however, the parents had previously handled such a child's responses to the new with quiet, patient consistency, then they were likely to maintain the same approach with the youngster's initial difficulties in peer adaptation. As an example, in one such family the parents enrolled the child in nursery school. After a few weeks the teacher advised the parents to withdraw him because his behavior indicated he was not "ready for nursery school." The parents responded that he was "never ready" at the beginning, and to be patient. By the end of the school year the teacher was enthusiastically rating the child as her best pupil.

By contrast, for the temperamentally easy child the development of peer relations usually took the same positive, uneventful course as had the child-environment interaction in the family. The exceptions, as indicated above in this chapter, occurred in those cases in which there were sharp contradictions and conflicts between the family standards and values, which the child had learned easily and firmly, and the expectations and judgments of the peer group.

The reverse situation tended to be typical of the highly distractible child. Such a youngster often met increasing parental annoyance as he "forgot" to come to meals when called, neglected to put his toys or playthings away, or took excessive time to get dressed while everyone waited impatiently. While some of these similar issues arose in peer group activities, the positive aspects of his temperamental trait were often more in evidence here than in the home situation. The distractible youngster, with his quick and expressive awareness of new stimuli, often became a welcome member or even a leader in a social group because of his sensitive responsiveness to the feelings and desires of others.

SCHOOL DEMANDS

The beginning of formal education in the school setting made a number of new demands on the child, separately and in combination. These included the mastery of increasingly complex cognitive tasks and the simultaneous requirements to adapt to a new geographic setting, to strange adults in unfamiliar roles, and to a host of new rules and regulations. Peer group activities became more elaborate and challenging, even to the child with previous nursery school experience.

Thus, of the 13 clinical cases with onset of symptoms in middle childhood, between 6–12 years of age, the poorness of fit and behavior disorder development was related primarily to school demands in 6 instances, and partially in 2 others. The nature of the poorness of fit varied greatly from case to case. The girl with easy temperament, noted above in this chapter, whose parents had taught her to develop her "individuality" and "creativity," was as a result resistant to the necessities of school learning and to following the rules and procedures required in this setting. In the case of Bruce (Chapter 13) the consequences of extreme and open parental conflict were first manifested clinically in problems of school adaptation.

In Bert's case (Chapter 15), the father's insistent demand for excessively high standards of behavior in personal manners did not initiate the development of a behavior disorder in the early childhood years. However, similar paternal expectations for superior academic functioning became entirely inappropriate and highly stressful in view of the boy's dyslexia. Symptoms consequent to this poorness of fit began at age 8 years. Kevin (Chapter 13), the brain-damaged youngster with mild mental retardation, suffered from his parents' attempt to minimize the extent of his intellectual deficit. This led them to enroll and keep him as long as they could in schools and social groups with intellectually normal children. The consequences of this poorness of fit were slowly cumulative and were sufficiently evident by age 15 years to warrant a clinical diagnosis.

In a number of other youngsters with onset of a behavior disorder in the preschool years, the same pattern of poorness of fit carried over into the school setting, with problems of school adjustment and learning added to their previous symptoms in the home and/or with peer relations. This was especially true with some of the temperamentally difficult and slow-to-warm-up children, where a pathological adaptational pattern developed in relationship to inappropriate parental management and was carried over into the school situation. In the case of Norman (Chapter 14), his father's demands for persistent task performance which this distractible and non-persistent youngster could not meet started with various activities in the home. Once Norman started grade school the father's major focus shifted to the insistent expectation that his son sit and concentrate on his homework without a break, no matter how long this took. This clearly contributed to a progressive deterioration in Norman's level of academic achievement.

By contrast, in some of the behavior disorder cases whose onset related to excessively stressful home situations, school functioning was not impaired. In several instances, the child's involvement in school activities actually served as a healthy counterforce to the pathological home environment. Thus, in one case a boy suffered from the consequences of severe parental conflict, which was markedly exacerbated by the inconsistent, contradictory, and even disorganized handling by a seriously disturbed mother. He was finally sent to a boarding school, where his symptoms disappeared quickly. Another boy with a mild adjustment disorder resulting from parental conflict and a pressuring mother finally began by age 12 to literally shut his parents out by retreating to his room. School was a haven in which he could function well and also distance himself further from his parents. Aided by his coping mechanism and by supportive psychotherapy, his symptoms disappeared by early adult life. (By contrast, Bruce [Chapter 13] could not achieve such distancing, probably because of the extraordinary degree of open conflict and the intrusiveness of his mother.) Another girl, with marked intensity and persistence, developed symptoms by 6 years when her parents responded to her immediate reactions by confrontations which escalated into turmoil and disorder. By contrast, in school, her teachers were quiet and patient, though firm, and her intensity and persistence became assets in that setting.

ADOLESCENT ISSUES

The effects of the "sexual revolution" are apparent in the NYLS sample. None of the 12 cases of behavior disorder originating in adolescence showed a disturbance of sexual functioning as a primary symptom. One girl, Bernice (Chapter 12), was sexually promiscuous, but this was only one of a number of her problems with impulse control. Another girl was promiscuous, both heterosexually and homosexually, but again this was only one of a number of symptoms expressive of an adolescent rebellion against a domineering and intrusive mother. Still another adolescent girl was sexually inhibited, but this again was one manifestation of severe social inhibition with both sexes. Two boys with increasingly serious behavior disorders starting in childhood had by adolescence significant disturbances of functioning in many areas, including sexual impotence.

Temperamental characteristics were much less involved in the pathogenesis of a behavior disorder in adolescence as compared to the childhood years. One girl, Olga (Chapter 14), with difficult temperament escaped a pathogenic interaction with her parents in childhood because her father's rigid and punitive demands were focused on her older sister, also of difficult temperament. When this older sister blossomed forth with artistic talents which met with her parents' and community approval, the father's attention was transferred to Olga, who now in adolescence became the family scapegoat. Another girl with a marked slow-to-warm-up pattern had difficulty in her initial nursery school adaptation, though not sufficiently to warrant a clinical diagnosis. Her middle childhood years went rather smoothly, though she remained a shy youngster who was frequently timid in new settings. With this behavioral pattern and with a markedly overprotective mother, her positive self-image was quite fragile. In adolescence she had a delayed puberty and became increasingly self-conscious about her body image and her social competence with her peers. These problems came to a head when she went off to college, where a severe anxiety state with multiple symptoms quickly developed.

There were several cases of adolescent rebellion, one the girl mentioned above with hetero- and homosexual promiscuity, another a boy who rebelled against his father's rigid moralistic standards, and a third, a boy who resented his mother's remarriage after his father's death. Another boy, Michael (Chapter 12), developed an adjustment disorder at 4 years which resolved completely in the next few years. In adolescence he gradually felt inferior to and alienated from his professionally successful father and his academically highly achieving older brother and sister. Rebellion took the form of multiple drug abuse and deterioration in school functioning.

There were two cases of depressive illness with onset in adolescence. One, Sylvia (Chapter 14), showed a recurrent major depression; the other, Bert (Chapter 14), developed an adjustment disorder with depressed mood in reaction to his parents' divorce, his ambivalent relationship with each parent, and his awareness that his sexual orientation was crystallizing as homosexual.

One girl, Lily, whose family had moved frequently because of her father's work assignments, lacked the environmental stability and continuity to ameliorate her difficulties with impulse control. Abetted by a choice of friends with antisocial tendencies, she became involved in a number of thoughtless but not serious delinquent acts. The parents set firm rules, the family living situation was stabilized, and the girl recovered quickly.

SOCIOCULTURAL INFLUENCES

Sociocultural influences on the child's development are pervasive and profoundly important from birth onward (Thomas and Chess, 1980). Prenatal development may be seriously affected by the mother's nutritional state or her addiction to alcohol or other drugs, conditions which are significantly correlated with social class status.

Parental attitudes, practices, expectations and demands reflect the values and standards of their community. And where parental standards are idiosyncratic, the child who learns them is exposed to conflict and stress when he encounters the antagonistic reactions of his peer group. The expectations of the peer group, the school, and the community at large, as well as those of the parents, are shaped by sociocultural values and judgments. These values and judgments, therefore, always enter into the child-environment interactional process and the development of a goodness or poorness of fit. The choice of symptoms where a behavior disorder develops is also shaped by social class factors and by cultural values which influence the functional areas in which demands for adaptation and mastery are made on the child (see discussion in Chapter 18).

These comments are not intended as a recommendation that parents should indoctrinate their children to conform to all the conventional standards of the outside world. However, even parents who pride themselves on their commitment to one or another type of "counterculture" should be aware that much of what they transmit to and expect from their children is influenced by the standards of the dominant culture. Parents may be legitimately concerned in teaching their children attitudes and values which are at odds with those of their community, such as with regard to racial and sex equality. If they do so, however, they should be aware of the conflict and stress the child will then encounter with his peer group, and make sure that they as parents give their child the special support he or she may need to cope with such a conflict.

CHAPTER 17

Evolution of
Behavior Disorders

In the preceding chapter, the factors involved in the origins of behavior disorders in the NYLS sample from infancy through adolescence have been examined. In the present chapter, the follow-up data on the clinical course of these cases will be evaluated. The basic question at issue here is the identification in the individual cases of the dynamic forces responsible for the change of a poorness of fit to a goodness of fit and consequent improvement or recovery from the disorder, or for a continuation of the poorness of fit with lack of improvement or worsening of the clinical problem.

PREDICTION FROM INITIAL CLINICAL DIAGNOSIS

For the 41 cases of adjustment disorder diagnosed in childhood, a tabulation was made with regard to early adult outcome according to sex and severity at initial diagnosis.

As can be seen from Table 1, female cases showed a higher percentage of recovery by early adulthood and a smaller percentage unchanged or with worsening than did males. The numbers, however, are small, and the findings can only be considered suggestive. As regards the prediction from initial severity of symptoms, the mild cases showed the highest percentage of recovery by early adulthood and the smallest percentage unchanged or worse, with the moderate cases next, and the severe cases with the highest percentage unchanged or with worsening. Again, the numbers are small and the findings only suggest a trend. For both males and females, and for both the mild and

TABLE 1

Outcome Childhood Adjustment Disorder Cases in Early Adult Life

Sex	Recovered	Improved	Unchanged-Worse
Male	16 (64%)	4 (16%)	5 (20%)
Female	13 (81%)	1 (6%)	2 (13%)
Severity of Symptoms			
Mild	20 (77%)	3 (11.5%)	3 (11.5%)
Moderate	7 (70%)	1 (10%)	2 (20%)
Severe	2 (40%)	1 (20%)	2 (40%)

moderate cases, the great majority were evaluated as recovered in early adult life.

No trend as to predictability was evident in the childhood adjustment disorder cases with regard to age of onset of symptoms or type of symptomatology. The numbers for the other childhood cases (conduct disorder and organic personality syndrome) are too small to attempt to define any trend.

The 12 new cases that appeared in adolescence presented as a group more severe symptoms than did those arising in childhood. The diagnoses were varied, with 4 adjustment disorders, and with no more than 2 cases in any of the other diagnostic categories — major depression, depressive neurosis, antisocial personality disorder, schizoid personality disorder, borderline personality disorder, generalized anxiety disorder, and organic personality syndrome. Of the 12 cases, 6 were considered as recovered in early adult life, 2 improved, 2 unchanged, and 2 as worsened. Of the 4 cases with the least severe diagnosis, i.e., adjustment disorder, 2 were recovered and 2 improved. Thus, the development of a behavior disorder in adolescence did not necessarily predict an unfavorable outcome into early adult life.

DIFFICULT TEMPERAMENT AND PARENTAL CONFLICT

The previous chapter reported the importance of childhood difficult temperament and severe parental conflict as pathogenic influences in the development of a behavior disorder. Similarly, the quantitative analyses, as summarized in Chapter 10, identified these two variables at age 3 years as significantly correlated with unfavorable early adult adjustment. There have been, however, individual subjects with either difficult temperament (Carl, Chapter 16) or severe parental conflict (Kathy, Chapter 12) who maintained a healthy developmental course throughout childhood and adolescence and into early adult life.

As reported in Chapter 12, the 5 high-risk subjects, those in the extreme quartiles for both difficult temperament and parental conflict at 3 years, showed an especially high incidence of behavior disorders (4 out of 5), which were also on the average of greater severity than for the clinical sample as a whole. Unexpectedly, the 4 behavior disorder cases in this high-risk group were all evaluated as recovered in early adulthood, an outcome opposite to the quantitative analytic findings for the NYLS sample as a whole. The longitudinal records of these 4 high-risk subjects with behavior disorder onset in childhood and recovery in early adult life were examined in detail to identify the factors which appeared responsible for this outcome.

For 3 of the 4 cases, the key finding in each subject appeared to be the development of emotional distancing from the parents, starting in middle childhood and progressing through adolescence into early adulthood. With this distancing, the youngster was able to disentangle him/herself from the tensions and conflicts produced by the severe parental conflict, and go on to develop positive peer relationships and good levels of school and work achievement.

One of these 3 cases was Roy (Chapter 12) who was in constant conflict with a compulsive, pressuring and controlling mother. His father was a passive figure who dealt with his wife's battles with their son by avoidance. The boy's conflict with his mother did not derive from his difficult temperament pattern, but rather from his high distractibility. This led typically to "forgetfulness" in finishing a task or meeting a time deadline. To the mother, Roy's failure to carry through her requests and demands only meant that he was challenging and opposing her. Her interpretation was that "he does everything he can to make my life miserable," and this to her justified her demands that he do her bidding on her terms. (Her reports of frequent intense negative reactions and slow adaptability on Roy's part may have been factually correct and responsible for his extreme quartile difficult temperament score. However, these behavioral characteristics were probably as much, if not more, the result of his battles with his mother than they were the expression of an intrinsic temperamental pattern).

With this severe conflict with his mother, Roy developed a number of tics and adjustment difficulties in his first school years. A number of discussions with the mother failed to alter in the least her subjective judgments of her son's behavior, or to alter her intrusive controlling demands. However, as he grew older, Roy learned on his own to limit his conflicts with her. This he did primarily by not communicating his plans and activities to her, and in effect progressively freezing her out of his life. As an example, his mother phoned one of us when he was a high school senior complaining that Roy refused to inform her of his college application activities, which he was handling entirely on his own. She asked us to intervene and make him confide in her, which, of course, we politely but firmly refused to do. With this effective localization of the stress and tension in his life, Roy's symptoms gradually improved in middle childhood and disappeared in adolescence, and his peer relationships and school activities became competent and sources of positive feedback. When interviewed at age 22, he was friendly and cooperative and answered questions thoughtfully and with much relevant elaboration. His professional goals were clear and he was pursuing them in an organized committed fashion. He made friends easily, though he indicated that he was overconcerned with and oversensitive to the reactions of friends and co-workers. He described the battles with his mother as continuing through his adolescence. He sought psychotherapeutic help because of this, said it helped a little, but most helpful were his peers who gave him "affirmation." Once he left home to go to college, the frequency of contentious issues dropped off sharply. He did resist his mother's demands that he call home frequently. "I had to show them they were not the first in my thoughts." On the other hand, he was now able to be more objective about his mother, realizing that she had psychological problems of her own, which were unrelated to him, and that perhaps they could get to accept each other.

Another youngster, Lori, with difficult temperament, was truly bedevilled by a psychotic father. In her early childhood, before the parents separated, the father had frequent rages, choked her mother in her presence, constantly undermined the mother, and wanted her to "change places with my own mother" so she would die in his mother's place. By age 3 years, Lori developed multiple symptoms, with sleep disturbance, tantrums, vomiting and avoidance of new situations. The diagnosis was adjustment disorder, moderately severe.

When she was 5, the mother picked herself up, moved with the children to another city, and got a job. The father followed and continued to harass her, though she was able to keep him from returning to live with her. The household then became relatively peaceful, and as Lori went on in elementary school, and then high school, she learned to model her behavior on other children's, picked up their independence, learned social graces, and gradually assumed increasing responsibility for her younger brother in the after-school hours until the mother came home from work. By early adolescence her childhood symptoms had disappeared and she was considered to have recovered from her behavior disorder. In adolescence she did develop a hair-pulling tic, but we did not consider this sufficient in itself to warrant a clinical diagnosis.

In the early adult interview, at age 22, she made a pleasant, attractive appearance, although she was moderately overweight. She answered all questions with thoughtful and relevant elaboration. She was graduating from college, was clear as to her main area of interest, but not sure as to the specific career direction to pursue. She had a number of hobbies and sociopolitical commitments, had friends of both sexes, and did not appear sexually inhibited. She was almost entirely self-supporting financially, through scholarships, loans, and jobs. Her hair-pulling tic was still a problem. When it came to a discussion of her parents, her answers were sparse, without the elaboration so evident in other areas of her life. As to her mother, her comment was, "Don't talk to her too much. I like her as a person but we don't have a confiding, close relationship. I don't allow her to hover, I rarely go home." As to her father, "I hardly talk to him, have little contact of any kind. He would like it but I wouldn't." Lori was critical of her mother for allowing any contact with her father, but "I never talk to her about it, just ignore it." As to her self-image, Lori stated, "I like the things I've done". But she was self-critical for not always living up to her own standards.

Overall, Lori had come a long way in establishing her independence, self-sufficiency and self-assurance, given the extraordinary turmoil of the family in her early years, combined with her own difficult temperament. Her mother's separation from the psychotic father was undoubtedly crucial, enabling Lori to distance herself from her parents and proceed to cope effectively with the social and academic demands of the outside world. Her hair-pulling tic and her excessively self-critical judgments appeared to reflect the psychological price she has had to pay for her struggles, but they were not sufficient to justify a clinical diagnosis at that age.

A third subject with difficult temperament and parental conflict ratings was Michael, the high-risk youngster with superior adult adjustment described in Chapter 12. Clinically, he conformed to the slow-to-warm-up constellation, though there were sufficient parental reports of high intensity behavioral items which, combined with his withdrawal, slow adaptability, and negative mood responses, were sufficient to also give him a difficult temperament rating from the quantitative item scoring. Severe parental conflict, though present, was muted in the children's presence, so that Michael, at age 22, could describe their clashes in relatively benign terms, as "volatile," with "a lot of parrying between them." His parents were responsive to counseling, and Michael's childhood behavior problem resolved quickly. His middle childhood years were uneventful. However, in adolescence he did develop a more severe behavior problem, characterized by symptoms of rebellion against his parents' standards, from which he felt strongly alienated. He also felt competitively inferior to his highly achieving older brother and sister. With a geographic and emotional distancing from his family and the development of his independent talents and goals, his symptoms dwindled and had disappeared by his 22-year-old evaluation.

The fourth youngster in this group, Nicky, developed a mild adjustment disorder with nocturnal enuresis, teasing, and tantrums by 6 years. Parental handling was in conflict, and the mother herself was very inconsistent, vacillating, and punitive with the boy. Though most parents with severe conflict were not amenable to effective parent guidance, in Nicky's case the parents were able to put aside their problems with each other, accept our advice, and change their approach to Nicky for the better. With this, his symptoms disappeared in the next few years.

It was by no means true that all the youngsters with difficult temperament and severe parental conflicts eventually showed a resolution of their behavior disorders. A contrasting group was typified by Ronald, who was rated in the extreme quartile for difficult temperament and his parents in the third quartile for conflict at age 3 years. Parental conflict escalated and became increasingly overt as the years went by, culminating in a separation and bitter divorce battle in Ronald's middle childhood. By age 3, Ronald had developed symptoms of a severe adjustment disorder, which grew worse by adolescence, with a diagnosis of severe narcissistic personality disorder. This disorder continued into early adult life, with serious impairment of academic, social, and sexual functioning.

Ronald was never able to distance himself from his parents, especially his mother. Like Roy's mother, described above in this chapter, Ronald's was intrusive, pressuring and controlling. But Ronald's response was quite different from Roy's. Roy reacted with passive resistance and focused successfully as he grew older on limiting the conflicts with his mother by shutting her out of his life. Ronald, by contrast, by age 3, was engaged in active oppositional behavior and one-upmanship tactics. With his superior intelligence, he was able to devise ingenious tactics which effectively baited his mother, keeping them tightly involved with each other in active combat throughout his childhood and into adolescence and early adulthood.

What made for this qualitative difference in Roy and Ronald's coping mechanisms is not obvious from our data. There did not appear to be any clearly influential difference in their relationship with their fathers. No significant differences in other environmental factors could be identified. There was, however, a definite difference between the two mothers which may very well have been important. Ronald's mother could be charming and ingratiating and also commanded respect for her professional accomplishments. Roy's mother, by contrast, showed evidence of psychological disturbance in her everyday life, and could boast of no special achievements. This difference could very well have made it easy for Roy to distance himself from his mother, and difficult for Ronald to do so.

DISTANCING FROM THE PARENTS

We are in no way suggesting that a close parent-child relationship was necessarily an unfavorable developmental influence. Many of the NYLS subjects without behavior problems, or with disorders that did not involve conflict with the parents, had strong positive ties with one or both parents, and this clearly constituted an important asset for the youngster. On the other hand, such a positive relationship did not necessarily immunize the youngster against the possibility of developing a behavior disorder. This is evident in the cases of children with easy temperament who became clinical cases, as detailed in the previous chapter.

Where child-parent conflict was a significant factor in the origin of a behavior disorder, however, the youngster's ability or lack of ability to distance himself psychologically from his parents and develop his own independent existence outside the home appeared important and even decisive in determining the course of the disorder. This was evident in the cases of Roy and Ronald, as well as in a number of other subjects. One striking case history in this regard can be cited. Olivia (mentioned briefly in the preceding chapter) suffered from a family environment of severe parental conflict and bickering. The mother had a successful professional career and the father had only a modest education and a job with low social prestige. The mother constantly derogated the father, and did so openly in front of their two children. He reacted by withdrawal into alcoholism and frequent flight from the household, after which he would return home with passive resignation to his fate. As to her children's lives, the mother was intrusive and controlling, and kept appealing to them for sympathy for her "plight." The son, not in our study, left home as soon as he could.

Olivia herself began to feel and act socially isolated in middle childhood. At age 11, she went to sleep-away camp, "that changed me." This was her first time away from her parents, she found that her peers wanted to be with her, and she made a number of friends. Her parents, however, disapproved of the camp and withdrew her abruptly. They had to literally take her home by force. She did keep a number of the friendships, no longer felt a loner, and made friends in school.

The home situation, however, continued to deteriorate. Her father's drinking increased and Olivia's mother was always in turmoil. Her brother, with

whom she had been very close, had moved away by this time and she missed
the support he had given her. "I couldn't relate to either my father or mother,
went to my room and retreated into my fantasies." Multiple symptoms began
to develop and by age 16 she had chronic school lateness with poor achievement in spite of superior intelligence, both homo and heterosexual promiscuity, heavy drug use, insomnia, and severe asthma. The diagnosis was borderline personality disorder, severe.

At this time, when Olivia was 16, her mother discovered her homosexual
activity, went into a panic, and insisted that the girl have psychotherapy. This
was arranged with an excellent psychiatrist, but Olivia was completely resistant, feeling that her mother had forced her into it, and the treatment was
abandoned after 6 months as completely unsuccessful.

We did not see Olivia again until she was 22, when she came for the regularly scheduled early adult interview. Given the severity of her disorder in adolescence, the degree of impairment of functioning at that time, and the continuation of the pathogenic family atmosphere, it was predictable that we would
find her still seriously disturbed as a young adult. But the opposite was true.
Olivia was literally transformed. She had just finished college with good
grades, and was clear as to her academic interests and professional goals. She
had worked summers and after school, and her lateness was under control.
She said she used to blame her mother for this problem, "she was always being late," but now accepted this issue as her own responsibility, "I'm not making excuses for it."

She was no longer sexually promiscuous, had given up her homosexual activity, and was living with a young man to whom she was exclusively committed. She had many friends and made new ones easily. Her drug use had
almost completely disappeared and her asthma and insomnia were markedly improved. As to her self-image, she described herself as "very stubborn,
but I think I'm reasonable. Basically, I like myself, not uncomfortable with
myself." As to her father, she had a lot of trouble relating to him at all. "He's
so disillusioned with himself and the world, blaming everybody for it." She
remembered the resentment and fights with her mother in the past and felt
her mother was trying to control her and was "rigid and domineering." Once
Olivia had moved away from home after starting college and came home very
infrequently, her relationship with her mother improved. She was no longer
angry with her, but "can't be supportive and close because of all the past re-
sentments." Her mother appeals to her for help and support about the father's
problems, but Olivia kept repeating she did not know what to do to help, and
in any case she had to keep her distance from her mother. As to her brother,
he was in the merchant marine and she rarely saw him.

Olivia did have a special positive relationship with a female professor in her own field, who was about her mother's age. This professor became her mentor, encouraged her academic interests, and had taken her on a summer field trip to South America two years previously. "It was a completely new experience for me, I awoke again, like with summer camp."

Three years after her early adult interview, Olivia requested a consultation with one of us (A. T.). Two years previously she had married the young man with whom she was living, even though she knew they had personality differences. She felt, however, that their strong mutual sexual attraction and the important positive role he had played in her development as a young adult would ensure a successful marriage. Instead, however, their relationship had deteriorated progressively and she was concerned over its outcome. Her husband said he "couldn't understand her," but did not think they needed help. He was, however, willing to participate in a treatment program.

Over the following year, weekly discussions were held with Olivia and her husband, separately and jointly. It became clear that they had widely disparate interests, and also that she was gregarious and he was not. She presented her ideas definitively and clearly, while he was often inarticulate and found it difficult to express himself. He was socially insensitive, not only to Olivia but to others, had grown up in a family with severe tensions and conflicts, and was still emotionally entangled with his parents. As the discussions progressed, he became able to talk freely and to accept the evidence that he had substantial psychological problems. Both he and Olivia made serious efforts to accommodate to each other's idiosyncracies, but it became evident that their marriage had reached a point of no return, and after a year they separated.

During this year of treatment, it was possible to evaluate Olivia's psychological status in depth. No evidence of significant psychopathology could be found. She was working full-time on an office managerial level, had started graduate school, had an active social life, and was taking the major responsibility for their household. All these functions she carried through competently and quietly. When asked how she explained the marked change since adolescence, "You were a mess then," she was surprised at the question, said she remembered her adolescence vaguely, and that she was such a different person now. She did say she "had gotten a focus in life, several of them. School, my relationship with Kevin (her husband), my music and other interests."

There appears no doubt that Olivia achieved a dramatic transformation psychologically from adolescence to early adult life on her own. Her relationship with the female professor and the positive influence of her relationship with Kevin in its first few years were undoubtedly important factors. But what appeared most significant was her ability to distance herself from her parents once she was able to leave home. It was within this context that she was able to profit from her relationship with the professor and with Kevin.

By contrast, Norman, whose case history is detailed in Chapter 14, was never able to distance himself from his parents, and especially from his father. His high distractibility and short attention span brought criticism and impatience from his parents, even in his early years, because of his quick shifts of attention, dawdling at bedtime, and apparent "forgetfulness." This escalated, as he grew older, into increasingly hypercritical and derogatory judgments by his father, himself a hard driving very persistent professional man. Norman accepted his father's standards as valid, tried to comply with them, which was impossible given his temperamental characteristics, and finally said of his father's pronouncements that Norman lacked character and will-power, "Let's face it, my father is right." No amount of discussion could alter the father's viewpoint or Norman's, and he came to early adult life with a severe psychiatric disorder and a pessimistic prognosis for the future.

IDIOSYNCRATIC FACTORS

In a number of cases, idiosyncratic factors influenced substantially, and sometimes even decisively, the course of a behavior disorder. Such unpredictable variables derived either from special life events and experiences, or from unanticipated psychological changes within the youngster.

Unpredictable Events or Changes in Life Situation

The case history of Bernice (Chapter 12) illustrates this issue. The sudden death of her father when she was beginning to have problems of impulse control in early adolescence was followed by the development of a severe sociopathic behavior disorder. In childhood she had also had several periods of behavioral difficulties because of her quick intense reactions, but these disappeared with quiet, firm and consistent limit setting by her parents. When this pattern reappeared in a more exaggerated and complex form in adolescence, it is likely that if the father, a stabilizing and authoritative (though not authoritarian) figure in the family, had lived, he and her mother, working together as they had in the girl's earlier years, would probably have prevented this highly unfavorable adolescent development. However, bereft of her husband and his influence, and stretched to her limits physically and emotionally by having to return to a full-time demanding and difficult job, the mother was overwhelmed by her daughter's outbursts and crises. Her own outraged explosions and ineffectual attempts to punish Bernice's delinquent behavior then only served to produce defiance and alienation in the youngster, with progressive escalation of pathological functioning.

One young man, Nelson, with a smooth development course through childhood, started experimenting with drugs at 14 years, with moderate use of marijuana and less frequent use of cocaine, LSD, and mescaline. A year later he became a follower of an Indian guru who came to the United States at that time. He quickly became deeply involved, "completely monopolized my whole life." Within a few months he had given up all drug use. His parents, though unhappy with their son's absorption in this Indian philosophy, with its hours of daily meditation, did not oppose it, because of their great relief at his renunciation of drug use. The involvement with the guru continued until he was 23, at which time he went through an intense period of conflict with his goals and personal commitments. Nelson became quite depressed, finally decided to break with the guru, and formed a close relationship with a young woman. Within a year his depression had lifted, he plunged into his work in the computer field with quick success, and his relationship with the young woman appeared stable and strongly positive.

It is possible to visualize other types of special life events as having a significant influence on the course of a behavior disorder. On the negative side, these could include crippling accidents or disabling illnesses, loss of a highly important supportive figure, or some highly traumatic experience. On the positive side, these could include the cure of a disabling illness or the development of a meaningful relationship to a healthy supportive individual previously missing from the youngster's life. The experience of Olivia (noted above, in this chapter) with the professor who became her mentor illustrates this latter possibility.

Unpredictable Changes in the Individual

Nancy (cited briefly in Chapter 14) was a difficult child temperamentally from early infancy onward. The parents responded to her intensity of reactions, biological irregularity, negative mood and slow adaptability in a way that produced extreme stress and disturbed development in the youngster. The father was highly critical of her behavior, rigid in his expectations for quick positive adaptation, and punitive when Nancy did not respond to his demands. The mother was intimidated by both husband and daughter, and vacillating and anxious in her handling of her child. By the age of 6 years Nancy had developed explosive anger outbursts, fear of the dark, thumb-sucking, hair pulling, and poor peer group relationships. Her symptoms and clinical findings were marked enough to warrant the diagnosis of conduct disorder, moderately severe.

Psychotherapy was instituted, with modest improvement. But an unexpected change occurred when in the fourth and fifth grades Nancy showed evidence of musical and dramatic talent. This brought increasingly favorable attention and praise from teachers and other parents. Fortunately for Nancy, these talents also ranked high in her parents' own hierarchy of desirable attributes. Her father now began to see his daughter's intense and explosive personality, not as a sign of "a rotten kid," his previous label, but as evidence of a budding artist. She was now a child he could be proud of, and he easily made allowances for her "artistic temperament." With this view of Nancy, the mother was also able to relax and relate to her positively. In the next few years Nancy's symptoms melted away and she was considered as recovered. When seen in the routinely scheduled adolescent interview at age 17, she was bright, alert and lively. She was involved in a number of activities that interested her, reported an active social life, good school functioning, and a pleasant relationship with her parents. There were no symptoms of psychological disturbances. Her report was confirmed in the separate interview with her parents, who described her as "hot-headed," but did not consider this a problem.

When seen again in the routinely scheduled early adult interview at age 22, the adolescent report of positive functioning was reaffirmed. Nancy was a senior in a prestigious college and had clear-cut professional goals. She had experienced some tension in her first college year, but adapted successfully and thereafter enjoyed her academic work. Her heterosexual relationships also tended to have tempestuous beginnings, but then settled down positively. It was of interest that she recalled her childhood as having been a happy one, recalled the mutuality of interests with her father, and had no recollection of his hypercritical and punitive attitudes and behavior toward her in early childhood.

Because of our special interest in Nancy's dramatic developmental course, a follow-up interview was arranged with her two years later, at age 24. She was poised, relaxed and self-assured. She had started a professional career, was doing well at her job, but was concerned at its limited future, and debated whether to look elsewhere in the same field. She had a number of friends, but was not satisfied with the depth or permanence of her heterosexual relationships. She expressed a desire for professional counseling for these problems of living, and she was referred to an experienced psychotherapist. After seeing her for a year the therapist reported that Nancy's problems with her career and with men had merited professional help, but that they were not extreme, and did not reflect any significant degree of psychopathology.

The two cases of major depression (Harold and Sylvia, Chapter 14) represent biologically based unpredictable changes in the individual which were crucial in both the origin and evolution of a behavior disorder. In the 3 cases of brain damage (Chapter 15), the behavioral effects have been cumulative over time rather than unpredictable. Cases of other types of biologically based disorders which might not have been predictable in early childhood, such as attention deficit disorder or schizophrenia, have as yet not arisen in the NYLS sample.

It is not always possible to identify the origins and dynamics of an unexpected idiosyncratic change in a youngster with a behavior disorder. A case in point is Olga (Chapter 14), a girl with a severe disturbance beginning in early adolescence who, at age 16, underwent a sudden dramatic religious conversion experience, following which her symptoms improved progressively. The girl herself could offer no explanation for this conversion experience and we ourselves could find none after an extended interview at age 20. Some might consider that this religious change represented an aggressive, hostile act against her parents; others might believe that it was perhaps the expression of a defense mechanism of sublimation. On the other hand, it could be that her new religious faith, whatever its cause, gave her a basis for new goals and patterns of adaptive coping, which led to a mastery of the life situations and expectations which previously were threatening and overwhelming. The data presently at hand are not sufficient to choose among these alternative explanations, but Olga's future developmental course should provide the answer.

EFFECTS OF TREATMENT

In a number of cases, the evolution of the behavior disorder was significantly influenced by the therapeutic procedure of parent guidance. This was especially true in the adjustment disorder cases. Where the parents were jointly able to alter their demands and expectations of the child so that a poorness of fit could be changed to a goodness of fit, improvement and recovery from the behavior disorder usually followed quickly. Where the parents did not carry through the recommendations offered to them, the outcome was unfavorable. The rationale for parent guidance, the specific procedures utilized, and the differential outcome with different families are detailed in Chapter 19.

Psychotherapy was instituted for a number of the behavior disorder cases in childhood, adolescence, or early adulthood. In some instances, this was arranged at the parents' initiative. In others it was the result of our recommendation, usually when parent guidance had proven ineffective.

The effectiveness of treatment varied widely from case to case. In some instances it proved ineffective, most usually if the youngster was resistant, as with Olivia in adolescence (this chapter), or if the parent-child interaction was so malignant that both parent guidance and psychotherapy could not ameliorate the pathological developmental process, as in Norman's case (this chapter). In other youngsters, psychotherapy was either partially or markedly effective, and influenced in a positive way the course of the behavior disorder.

The psychotherapuetic approach, the frequency of sessions, the length of treatment, the age period at which therapy was initiated, and the nature and dynamics of the problem all varied from case to case. With this multitude of variables, it was not possible to draw any inferences as to the factors responsible for successful psychotherapy.

Pharmacological treatment in the two cases of recurrent major depression has been helpful, as has been remedial education and tutoring in the youngsters with problems of learning.

OVERVIEW

Our follow-up data are in accord with other reports on the favorable outcome of many, if not most behavior disorders originating in childhood. However, a significant number did not improve or even grew worse in adolescence and early adult life, and it was not always possible to predict the developmental course of the disorder in the early period after its identification. Hence, we would suggest active appropriate therapeutic intervention in all cases.

The previous chapter emphasized the diversity so evident in the developmental course of individual children. This was especially evident in tracing the factors involved in the origin of behavior disorders. So many person and situation variables were influential in the development of a behavior disorder that the search for simple formulas and categorizations was totally unrealistic.

In tracing the course of the behavior disorders in individual subjects, the same diversity has been strikingly evident, which again defies explanation by any simplistic unidimensional theoretical model. The case histories cited in this chapter bear witness to this conclusion.

In some instances, striking consistency in the course of a behavior disorder was evident from childhood into early adult life, as in the cases of Ronald and Norman. This did not appear to result from the persistence of some psychological attribute buried in "the unconscious" and invulnerable to environmental influences. Rather, it seemed to result in continuity over time of the individual-environmental interactional process, a concept emphasized by other developmental researchers as well as ourselves (Sameroff, 1975; Vaillant, 1977).

In many other instances, change in the severity and symptomatology of a behavior disorder over time was strikingly evident, as illustrated in a number of cases cited in this chapter. The factors involved in such change have been diverse and usually unpredictable ahead of time. Two influential factors can be emphasized from our data. One was the responsiveness of the parents to the therapeutic procedure of parent guidance. This will be discussed in detail in Chapter 20. The other was the ability of the youngster with a behavior problem to distance himself psychologically from his parents, and in so doing attenuate and neutralize their pathogenic influence on his development.

This psychological distancing from the parents should not be equated with the healthy process of separation and the growth of an independent capacity for functioning which is a hallmark of normal development from childhood through adolescence into adult life. This healthy process of individuation, which was clearly evident in our subjects without behavior problems, does not necessarily involve psychological distancing from the parents. Quite the contrary, in many cases the parents actively supported and encouraged their youngster's striving for independent functioning, and with this the relationship between parent and child flourished and grew closer rather than distant. The distancing utilized by some of the behavior problem cases rather represented a defensive coping mechanism in the face of an unhealthy child-parent interaction, a defensive mechanism to be regretted, but at the same time essential for the youngster's recovery from his behavior disorder.

CHAPTER 18

Symptom Choice

It is the symptom or symptoms which motivates the individual or the child's parents to seek professional help. It is also the symptom which challenges the researcher or clinician to call on his conceptual framework to explain its origin and evolution. As a result, the range of positions that have been advanced to account for the origin, selection, and development of symptom varies widely, and includes constitutionalist, motivational-psychodynamic, learning theory, and sociocultural concepts.

In tracing the ontogenesis and vicissitudes of symptoms over time, it is not sufficient to assert that they have antecedents in the individual's life history. Such a statement merely argues that behaviors have causes. What is required for an understanding of symptom formation and evolution is a consideration of the dynamics of the individual-organism interaction over time, as well as the influence of the psychological developmental changes at sequential age-periods. Thus, symptoms in the young child represent primarily abnormalities of overt behavior. As the child grows older, more complex mechanisms of behavioral mediation are developed progressively. These include an increasingly expanded subjective life characterized by ideation, abstraction, and symbolic representation. These developmental changes with age are reflected in the nature of the child's psychological functioning, which becomes increasingly ideational and less dominated by immediate influences and by direct expression in action. These changes have two major consequences for symptom evolution. One is the alteration in the manifestations of disturbance. The other is an increasing influence of ideas, attitudes, and values on behavior,

218

so that a behavior disorder often comes to be expressed more indirectly and to involve a variety of substitutes for action, in the form of disturbing feeling-states and distorted attitudes and cognitive characteristics. Further, the child becomes increasingly aware of and responsive to the behavior, attitudes, values, and ideas communicated by significant adults and peers as he grows older.

These changes in the child's psychological organization over time result in a developmental progression of symptoms. Failure to recognize such a developmental course may result either in the erroneous attribution of complex psychological mechanisms to the young child or in the assumption that similarity in the overt expression of a symptom in the young child and the adult justifies the assumption of similar meaning and dynamic consequences to the symptom over this wide time-span. The first of these tendencies has been most evident in many psychoanalytic formulations, and is well described by Anna Freud: "Some psychoanalysts credit the newborn already with complex mental processes, with a variety of affects which accompany the action of the various drives and, moreover, with complex reactions to these drives and affects, such as for instance guilt feelings" (1953, p. 12).

The second tendency can be frequently found in behaviorist theories, which assume that the same simple conditioned reflex pattern serves to determine exclusively the structure of a phobia or other psychological symptom years after its onset, as it did in the original development of the symptom (Eysenck, 1963).

In addition, psychoanalysts have tended to utilize two related formulations to explain symptom choice. One is the judgment that the symptom constitutes a symbolic representation of an internalized conflict, or a repression of or reaction formation against an unacceptable, presumable instinctual drive. The other is that the symptom is the result of a motivational drive, but expressed in a displaced or symbolic form. Thus, gastric disturbances became the expression of conflict over oral dependency drives, ulcerative colitis the result of "repressed destructive impulses and disturbances in or loss of a key relationship, accompanied by a feeling of hopelessness or despair," and neurodermatitis the expression of a "conspicuous longing for physical contact that had been frustrated by undemonstrative parents" (Alexander and Selesnick, 1966, pp. 393-395).

It is undoubtedly true that in some cases symptoms may express symbolically an unresolved conflict, or a strategy to resolve such a conflict, or an attempt to achieve some specific goal. Thus, a child with an unrecognized reading disability, and fearful of having his deficiency exposed in school, may engage in disruptive clowning behavior to conceal his problem when called upon by the teacher. Another child for whom school represents a threatening situation, for whatever the reason, may develop gastric distress and even vomiting on school mornings due to anxiety, and then utilize these symptoms as an avoidance strategy. Or an adult may deal with potential or actual anxiety by one or another defense mechanism which leads to specific types of symptomatology.

However, all too often, the evidence for such psychodynamic interpretations is questionable, frequently consisting of the assumption that if the symptom can be explained psychodynamically, this is *ipso facto* proof of the validity of the interpretation. What is ignored is the crucial issue that alternative formulations are also possible and that additional independent data are required to test the validity of the various possibilities.

With the above considerations in mind, our longitudinal data have been analyzed qualitatively in terms of the following questions:

1. Given an individual-environment that is excessively stressful, what factors determine the specific symptoms that appear?
2. Once a symptom appears, how do its consequences affect the ontogenesis and evolution of the symptom?
3. What consequences for symptom characteristics occur as a result of development of sequential new age-stage levels of functioning?

ORIGIN OF SYMPTOM CHOICE IN CHILDHOOD

The development of a behavior disorder in the young child, as was also true at later age-periods (Thomas and Chess, 1980), derived from a poorness of fit between the goals, abilities and temperament of the child, and the expectations and demands of the environment. The type of symptom, on the other hand, resulted in the main from the specific areas in which excessive demands were made by parents, teachers or peers. Temperamental characteristics also played a part in shaping the manifestations of symptoms.

Sociocultural Influences

A tabulation has been made of the types of symptoms manifested by the NYLS subjects with behavior symptoms in the first 9 years of life (Thomas, Chess and Birch, 1968). There were only two cases with symptoms referable to feeding difficulties. Moreover, in these two instances, the feeding problem did not represent the major source of parental concern over the child's behavior. Elimination difficulties were also infrequent, with two cases of bowel problems and only one of enuresis. Masturbation, though frequently reported, was rarely characterized by the parents as a problem. By contrast, symptoms in the areas of sleep, discipline, speech, peer relationships, and learning, were prominent in both the expressions of parental and teacher concern and in their effects on the child's overall behavioral functioning.

These variations in frequency of different types of symptoms paralleled very closely the child-care practices and expressed standards and attitudes of this middle-class NYLS parent group, including those without, as well as those with, problem children. Irregularity of feeding, for example, was frequently reported by the parents in the routine interviews, but with the statements that they realized this was "not important," the child's "health was not suffering," it was "so easy and inexpensive" to prepare the child's meal that it did not matter if he was "picky and choosy" with his food, etc. These attitudes went along with a tolerant non-pressuring approach to feeding, with little or no attempt to change a child's limited and idiosyncratic diet.

A similar permissive attitude and child-care practice was expressed toward toilet training. If anything, early training, even if not forcibly imposed, was considered undesirable and even psychologically dangerous. Masturbation was observed and reported by many parents in their young children, but again with the statement that since they knew it was "harmless and normal" they did not try to stop it. It was the impression of the staff interviewers that a number of parents were not really comfortable with this stated permissive attitude, and that they might have intervened forcibly to try to stop their child's masturbation were it not for the weight of the dominant professional authority of the time (Spock, 1957).

By contrast, the parents as a group were not as ready to be tolerant of deviant or inconvenient behavior in the areas of sleep, discipline, speech, peer relationships, and learning. The parents were willing and even eager to devote their time and energies to the young child in the early evening hours. But this was coupled with the expectation that, once the child's bedtime hour arrived, they expected to spend the remaining hours before their own bedtime pursuing their own interests and activities. Furthermore, frequent interruption of nighttime sleep did impair the efficiency of the parents' work functioning the following day. As a result, the tolerance and permissiveness shown toward irregularities and difficulties with feeding and toilet training were here conspicuously absent. Firm and even rigid demands for regular bedtime schedules and annoyance at frequent night-awakening were instead the rule.

Similarly, a young child who learned the rules of safety and of social living in the family slowly and incompletely could also be objectively a problem for the parents. This was stated openly by many of the parents, was implied by others, and was clearly reflected in the demands and expectations of the child in these areas.

The relatively large number of cases with symptoms of mood disturbance, difficulties in peer relationships, speech problems, and learning deficiencies in the early school grades closely paralleled the parents' hierarchies of goals and values for their children's optimal developmental course. As a group, these parents were attuned to the pronouncements of the presumably authoritative professional child-care experts of the time, who, almost without exception, proclaimed the ominous prognosis for the future of any early emotional or social difficulties. The parents gave high importance to intellectual achievement, and early problems with speech or learning were viewed with great concern. As a result, emotionality, peer relations, speech development, and learning were areas of active and high parental expectation.

Idiosyncratic environmental factors were also influential in a number of cases in determining the functional areas in which symptoms appeared. For example, in one family, a mother had great difficulty in adapting her child-care practices for effective handling of an extremely temperamentally difficult daughter. She was vacillating and inconsistent, and also intimidated by her husband's rigid and punitive attitudes toward the child. However, she was clear on the necessity of her young daughter's learning rules of safety, and in this area she was consistent and quietly persistent in her demands. As a result, the youngster developed severe symptoms in a number of areas, but none with regard to learning and following rules of safety. In another case a father had unrealistic expectations that his son, who was temperamentally distractible with low persistence, should be able to sit quietly and persistently for hours at a time when doing his homework. When the boy tried to meet his father's demands and sat with his homework evening after evening without a break, he ended by developing multiple tics.

Specific extrafamilial factors were also influential. This was especially evident in the young children with easy temperaments who adapted easily to behavioral patterns expected by their parents, which then came into sharp conflict with peer standards outside the home. For example, one set of parents set high store in formalistic standards of politeness. Their highly adaptable son learned these rules easily and quickly and by age 3 years this bright, otherwise well-functioning youngster was parroting the formal gestures and phrases of politeness appropriate to an adult, but conspicuously out of place in the current suburban children's world. As a result, he found himself the butt of ridicule and teasing by his agemates, and developed severe apprehension in the area of peer social relationships.

The relationship between symptom choice and parental sociocultural values and expectations was highlighted in a comparison of the middle-class NYLS clinical cases with those in the working-class Puerto Rican (WCPR) sample (Thomas, Chess, Sillen et al., 1974). By contrast with the NYLS parents, the WCPR parents did not demand a regular bedtime and sleeping routine from their preschool children. It was no issue if the child stayed up until the parents went to sleep themselves, and if he slept very late in the morning. With this approach, only one of the WCPR children showed a sleep problem in the preschool years. However when the children reached 5–6 years and began attending school, the situation changed significantly. They now had to get up early and regularly, which required the imposition of a regular and early bedtime. Five of the children now developed sleep problems, usually a resistance to going to bed, with accompanying temper tantrums.

The story was different with regard to disturbances in the area of motor activity. Half of the WCPR clinical cases under 9 years of age presented symptoms of excessive and uncontrollable motor activity, whereas only one NYLS youngster displayed this symptom (and this was a brain-damaged child). This marked difference in incidence appeared related to environmental circumstances. The WCPR families usually had a relatively large number of children and lived in small apartments with little space for constructive activity required by the temperamentally high-activity youngsters. Furthermore, these very children were even more likely to be cooped up at home for fear that if they ran around in the streets they would be in special danger of accidents. This was a realistic fear, given the nature of the street life in the East Harlem area of New York in which these families lived. Beyond this issue, safe playgrounds and recreational areas were not available as they were to the NYLS youngsters, who also lived in spacious apartments or private homes with backyards. In fact, one WCPR child who had been described by his teachers as "uncontrollably active" and by his parents as a "whirling dervish" became much more manageable when the family moved to a private house with a small yard.

The Influence of Temperament

As indicated above, environmental factors played a major, even decisive role in determining the functional areas in which symptoms developed, once a dissonant child-environment interactional process had set in. Beyond this, temperamental factors often influenced the form taken by the symptom of behavioral disturbance. Evidence for this judgment comes from several sources.

Cameron (1978) categorized the symptoms of the NYLS clinical cases in the childhood period under four headings: 1. *impositional*—symptoms representing excessive imposition of the child's own needs onto the ongoing situation; 2. *nonaccommodational*—a refusal to accommodate to change, instruction, or education; a negativistic, underadapting position; 3. *withdrawal*—a tendency to withdraw from situations or shut them out; and 4. *overadapting*—a tendency to overadapt to most situations, allowing others to dictate directions, abdicating preferences, and being generally overcompliant.

Cameron then compared first-year temperament scores for later emerging clinical cases displaying each of these four symptom forms with clinical cases without such symptoms. Cases with type 1 symptoms showed a preponderance of high persistence and negative mood scores in the first year; those with type 2 symptoms characteristically had low adaptability scores; and those with type 3 symptoms tended to have low persistence ratings, but unexpectedly were low rather than high in withdrawal scores. There were too few cases with type 4 symptoms to allow any statistical analysis of this category. Cameron concluded that, with the exception of temperamental withdrawal in type 3 cases, "the trends are in expectable directions; they suggest that if a child becomes a clinical case, the nature of that child's symptoms is, in part at least, a function of individual temperament style, as revealed during the first twelve months of life" (1978, p. 146).

Our own quantitative study of the relationships between temperament and the form of symptoms has been restricted to a comparison of our so-called *active* versus *passive* clinical cases (Thomas, Chess and Birch, 1968). The children we designated as having passive symptoms were essentially nonparticipators. They stood on the sidelines watching, taking no part in an ongoing activity. If other symptoms were also present, such as crying, active complaining, or the development of physical symptoms (such as nausea, stomachaches or dizziness) when pressured to participate, the child was considered to have active symptoms. All other symptoms other than passive, quiet nonparticipation were considered to be active. The youngsters with active symptoms made up 81 percent of the childhood clinical cases, and those with passive symptoms 19 percent. The small N for the passive cases limited the scope of the comparisons. The most significant finding was with regard to our Factor A, which comprised the easy-difficult temperamental constellation, with the omission of rhythmicity. The active cases, when compared with the nonclinical sample, showed a significant difference on Factor A toward difficult temperament direction at age 3, and an even more highly significant difference at ages 4 and 5. By comparison, the passive cases only showed a similar significant correlation with Factor A at ages 4 and 5, with a lesser level of correlation at age 4.

The qualitative study of the individual clinical cases reinforced and expanded the suggestion from the quantitative analyses of a relationship between temperament and symptom form. The difficult child commonly developed tantrum behavior, with screaming, kicking, throwing himself around, and throwing objects, in various combinations and for varying lengths of time. The persistent child with mild intensity whined and fussed for extended periods. The mild child with a low activity level typically showed quiet withdrawal, such as standing apart, sucking his fingers, and gazing into the distance. The slow-to-warm-up child also demonstrated similar quiet withdrawal responses. By contrast, intense children with high activity levels and approach responses typically had problems of overly quick and even impulsive behavior.

ADOLESCENT AND EARLY ADULT LIFE SYMPTOMS

The clinical cases with onset in adolescence also showed symptoms primarily in those functional areas which ranked high in the hierarchy of values of their families and peer group — school, social relationships, and antisocial behavior. Overt anxiety and depressive symptoms were also conspicuous in some cases. This probably reflected, at least in part, the ability of adolescents to verbalize and communicate their subjective mood-states, as compared to younger children. There was also much concern with questions of goals, identity and self-image among these youngsters with clinical problems, especially in the early adulthood period.

For those subjects whose psychiatric disorders persisted into early adult life, symptoms were similar to those in adolescence, with the addition in a number of cases of problems with work activities.

Of interest was the relatively minor part played by sexual issues in the symptomatology of the adolescents with psychiatric disorders, a trend which carried over into our early adult life follow-up. Traditionally, sex has been a major source of anxiety, conflict and confusion in adolescents and young adults. The "sexual revolution" of recent years is certainly reflected in the NYLS sample as a whole. In the adolescent and early adult interviews, as well as the more extensive and intensive clinical sessions, there was no mention of, much less preoccupation with, pregnancy, birth control, venereal disease, or masturbation. Heterosexual activity frequently began in early or midadolescence, and was reported to our interviewers without evident guilt, anxiety, or defensiveness.

With this overall trend, there were few symptoms reported by the subjects which related to sexual problems, such as impotence in the male or difficulty in achieving orgasm in the female, either in adolescence or early adulthood. And where such symptoms existed, they were invariably accompanied by conflicts and disturbances in other functional areas.

In this older age period, the relationship of symptom form to temperament was not as evident as in the childhood period. The progressive utilization and elaboration of defense mechanisms and the prominence of symbolism and language in coping strategies can serve to camouflage temperamental patterns of activity, adaptability, and emotional expression. It is our impression that temperament continues to play a significant role in many, if not most, cases in shaping the form taken by symptoms in adolescence and adult life, as well as in childhood. But with the increasing complexity of the individual-environment interactional process in these older age groups, teasing out the role of temperament in individual cases, as well as that of motivations and other psychological influences, becomes a demanding analytic challenge.

BIOLOGICAL FACTORS

In those clinical cases in which biological factors played a major or dominant etiological role, they also served to shape symptom choice and manifestation. This influence was clearly evident in our cases of brain damage in both the NYLS (see Chapter 15) and our congenital rubella sample (Chess, 1982). Prominent behavioral symptoms in the children with this diagnosis included perseveration, difficulty in shifting from one task to another, sudden shifts in mood or overreaction to minor stimuli, motility disturbances, and a high degree of distractibility. In addition, the motor and/or perceptual difficulties associated with the neurologic damage also created severe problems in some of the cases in coping with tasks, or in developing and maintaining satisfactory interpersonal relations.

In those cases of depressive syndromes in whom a biological etiological role is highly presumptive, the depressed mood and its consequences were also highly significant in influencing symptom choice and manifestation (see Chapter 14). Psychomotor retardation affected levels of adaptation in major functional areas, initiated various defense mechanisms with their consequences for symptom formation, and made it difficult, if not impossible, to develop healthy levels of self-esteem. With other severe biologically-determined psychiatric disorders, such as autism or developmental dysphasias, symptomatology is, of course, also the result of the biological disturbances and their psychological consequences.

SYMPTOM EVOLUTION

Piaget (1954, 1963) has pointed out that the child's level of cognitive functioning progresses developmentally. He has also defined and described the characteristics of sequential age-stage levels of cognitive development. Of interest here is his formulation, based on detailed and minute observations, that the infant and young child's cognitive capacities are primarily restricted to reflex-like and preoperational functioning, and that it is not until middle childhood that the intelligence of sensorimotor functioning begins to be transformed into advanced representational and operational thinking, with a shift still later to the development of the substantial capacity for symbolism and abstraction.

Our own data have confirmed in their own way this basic formulation of Piaget. Symptoms in the young child are shaped primarily by the concrete level of cognitive function, and subjective abstract operations are absent or minimal. With the development of more complex mechanisms of cognition, adaptation, and coping, achieved as the child grows older, earlier symptom expression and new symptoms take on characteristics which increasingly reflect subjective cognitive and emotional states, attitudes, goals, values, self-image, and psychodynamic patterns of defense. For example, one girl, Diana, in the NYLS sample, was first referred for psychiatric evaluation at the age of 43 months because of constipation, painful bowel movements, withholding of bowel movements, and refusal to use the toilet. Her problem had originated in early infancy as a physiological difficulty resulting from a tight anal sphincter. Dilation of the sphincter and various medications gave only temporary relief of symptoms of infrequent, large and painful evacuations.

Development was otherwise normal. The bowel problem, however, did not improve, and was instead aggravated by marked inconsistency in the mother's handling of the issue. She repeatedly shifted her approaches and ran the gamut from permissiveness to pressure, from reassurance to anger. By age 3, Diana had developed a defensive coping mechanism of avoidance, hiding in corners or behind the furniture when she moved her bowels.

Psychiatric evaluation at 43 months showed a charming and friendly youngster, without any evidence of psychopathology outside of the reactive response to the bowel problem. Parent guidance was attempted, but the mother could not sustain a patient, consistent, nonpunitive approach. Diana finally began to use the toilet when she was 4 years old, though recurrent episodes of severe constipation, withholding of bowel movements, and overflow incontinence and soiling continued to occur intermittently. As she grew into middle childhood, the early childhood defense of overt behavioral avoidance was replaced by a defensive denial on an ideational level. She would insist that she had not soiled herself, even when it was olfactorily evident that she had. No attempt at direct treatment was at first possible because of the child's persistent denial that any problem existed.

At age 9 years, however, the denial pattern was abruptly discarded and Diana requested help for her problems. This change came as a consequence of her being sent home from summer camp because her bunkmates could not tolerate the constant presence of a fecal odor. Also, a friend indicated that her problem was quite evident to others. The psychiatric discussions focused on her denial mechanism, resulting in quick insight and change on the girl's part. Together with this, she now cooperated in a schedule of nightly suppositories to help her develop a regular routine of bowel evacuation, a procedure she had previously resisted when denying the existence of any problem. In the following 6 months a regular pattern of bowel movements was established and the suppositories were discontinued. Follow-up showed no recurrence of the problem.

Of additional interest in this case was the personality evaluation at age 22 years. Diana was functioning well in all areas, had a positive self-image, appeared friendly and relaxed, and was symptom-free. Because of the linkage in traditional psychoanalytic theory of early difficulties and conflicts over toilet training with later personality traits of stinginess, excessive orderliness, preoccupation with cleanliness, and obsessive-compulsive tendencies—the so-called "anal personality"—this early adult interview probed specifically for any indications of these traits. None were found. Neither was she overly generous, untidy or disorderly, traits which might have been regarded by some as "reaction formations."

OVERVIEW

Our data on symptom formation and evolution are best conceptualized within our basic interactionist theoretical viewpoint. No simple rule could be formulated for any one-to-one linear relationship between early life experience or a specific defense mechanism and the character of the symptoms that emerged with the development of a behavior disorder. Similar causes could lead to different symptoms, and the same symptom could derive from difference causes. Any specific symptom could have varying significance in youngsters with different sociocultural backgrounds, temperaments, or developmental stage. The nature of the symptom does not provide a ready-made answer to the etiology and dynamics of the disorder through the application of one or another a priori formula. Rather, the symptom signals the presence of an unhealthy developmental course, whose nature can only be delineated by an identification of the relevant features of the individual's psychological organization and environmental influences, followed by an analysis of the interactional sequential course of these factors.

CHAPTER 19

Adolescent
Issues

Like infancy, adolescence constitutes an age period in which rapid biological change and maturation are coupled with qualitatively new environmental demands and expectations. As such, for the youngster with a healthy childhood development course, adolescence can be an expansive and stimulating period of psychological growth. For others, who have suffered from a behavior disorder in childhood, new coping potentials created by the maturational process and the changed environmental opportunities of adolescence may lead to a mastery of their psychological problems. For still others, however, the new demands of adolescence may prove excessively stressful, with the crystallization of a behavior problem or the exacerbation of a previously existing disorder.

The NYLS adolescent data provide specific examples of these different developmental courses in the passage through adolescence for a particular socioeconomic group at a particular historical period. The findings bear on a number of issues of theoretical and practical interest.

First, however, it is pertinent to report our survey of the sexual attitudes and behavior patterns of this group in response to the complex biopsychosocial expectations and opportunities created by sexual maturity in adolescence. A brief survey of substance abuse by the group will also be given.

SEXUAL ATTITUDES AND BEHAVIOR

In an earlier paper (Chess, Thomas and Cameron, 1976), we reported on the sexual data obtained from the subject and parent interviews in the adolescent period. (These data were derived from the 92 oldest subjects and their

229

parents from the total of 107 interviewed in adolescence.) Only one adolescent refused to answer questions relating to sex, though some others appeared uncomfortable, even if responsive.

This adolescent survey revealed a substantial degree of congruence between subject and parental reports regarding responses about friends of the same sex, opposite sex friendship, dating, steady dating, affairs, and casual sex. All three youngsters who reported affairs had this confirmed independently by the parent. In addition, three parents stated this when their son or daughter had not. In these latter instances, the parents had inferred that the youngster was or had been involved in an affair from the adolescent's behavior, rather than from any direct communication.

However, in spite of the changing sexual mores of recent years and the liberal attitudes which most of the parents and their youngsters espoused, there was apparently very little intergenerational discussion of actual sexual behavior. When a parent mentioned such discussion, it was most often as a result of some major conflict regarding the adolescent's behavior. In spite of this, the parents' general estimate of the extent of their youngster's sexual activity appeared in most cases to be correct. It was also evident that there was little discussion between most parents and their adolescent son or daughter about such matters as birth control, pregnancy, abortion, or venereal disease. Presumably, the youngsters obtained their information about the technical aspects of sex through the schools, libraries, family planning centers, or their peer group.

Therefore, our overall impression was that, by the time these subjects were sixteen, sex was a closed topic in most cases between themselves and their parents. The adolescents guarded their privacy quite carefully, and, for the most part, parents respected that privacy. This lack of intergenerational communication did not appear to extend beyond the family. Most of the youngsters and parents were quite comfortable and fairly open in talking about sex to our middle-aged interviewers. It is a reasonable supposition that the avoidance of discussion of sex by parents and youngsters was a manifestation of both the adolescent's drive to establish independence and a way of avoiding the family tensions and conflicts that such discussion might have provoked.

The inductive content analysis of the protocols suggested a developmental sequence in this adolescent population, which was true for both girls and boys. There appeared to be a progression from friends of the same sex, to mixed sex companionship, to dating, to desire for steady dating, to steady dating, and finally to actual sexual intercourse, either in the form of an affair or as casual sex. Individual youngsters reached different levels in this sequential progression by age 16–17 years. Also, this sequence was by no means fixed and invariant in all subjects. Some adolescents had always had friends of both sexes, and a few went directly from casual dating to sexual intercourse.

The "sexual revolution" of recent decades was reflected in our adolescent population in their patterns of behavior and in their open, guilt-free, and conflict-free attitudes about their sexual activity. There was also a notable absence of the concerns of earlier generations. There was no mention of, much less preoccupation with, masturbation, birth control, or the dangers of pregnancy or venereal disease in either the routine interviews or the clinical interviews and follow-ups. This clearly reflected a casual, matter-of-fact attitude toward these issues.

What did concern this adolescent group as a whole was the challenge of combining physical with emotional intimacy in a sexual relationship. Sex was not viewed with anxiety and conflict, but, with a few exceptions, neither was it embraced as a casual impersonal source of pleasure.

With this overall trend, as pointed out in Chapter 18, there were few symptoms relating to sexual problems (such as impotence in the male or difficulty in achieving orgasm in the female) reported by the subjects with behavior problems. And where such symptoms existed, they were invariably accompanied by conflicts and disturbances in other functional areas.

The early adult interviews provided another opportunity to survey the sexual attitudes and behavior patterns of the NYLS sample. Information was elicited as to the age of the first sexual intercourse and the nature of subsequent sexual activity. Even more so than in the adolescent interviews, the vast majority of the subjects responded to these questions promptly, calmly and without evasiveness or obvious defensiveness. A few showed some hesitation and one young man reacted with a nervous laugh and "now you're getting personal," but then answered directly. One young woman became obviously tense at the first question regarding sex and the topic was not pursued. Another indicated sex was a problem area, but would not elaborate. As with questions in other areas, some elaborated at some length in their responses and others gave brief specific answers.

The sexual data were tabulated as to age of first sexual intercourse, current sexual activities, sexual problems, and any special comments.

As can be seen from Table 1, by age 20 the great majority of the subjects had already had their first sexual experience. There was little difference as to the age of first sexual intercourse between males and females, except for a somewhat higher percentage for girls in the youngest group.

In the 12–15 year group, there was one who reported the first experience at 12 years; this was a girl with a severe behavior disorder beginning at 16

TABLE 1
Age First Sexual Intercourse

	12–15		16–18		19–20		None	
	M.	F.	M.	F.	M.	F.	M.	F.
% of sample	14%	21%	47%	43%	14%	12%	25%	24%

years, with recovery by early adulthood. Of the 4 subjects who reported their first sexual experience at age 13, two were boys, neither of whom was a clinical case, and 2 were girls, one of whom was a clinical case, the other not. For this earliest group as a whole, the percentage of clinical cases was very similar, 40 percent for the boys and 42 percent for the girls, and very similar to the 44 percent for the total NYLS sample.

At the other extreme, 25 percent of the males and 24 percent of the females had not had any sexual intercourse by the time of the early adult interview. Of these, this was judged by the interviewer to represent inhibition and a problem in the sexual area in 36 percent of the males and in the same percentage of the females. All the inhibited males were or had been clinical cases. This was also true of 60 percent of the inhibited females. Most of the others in this "none" category were young at the time of interview, 17–19 years, and appeared to have no problems with their dating patterns. For the older subjects in this group, the absence of sexual intercourse appeared to be primarily the result of religious scruples.

As to current sexual activity in those subjects who had already had their first sexual intercourse, 14 percent of the males and 13 percent of the females were rated as very active, and 78 percent of the males and 85 percent of the females as moderately or modestly active. Three young men and one young woman were currently not active. In only one, a socially inhibited young man, did this appear to have functional significance.

Seven males stated they had sexual problems or concerns. In three cases, this involved actual impotence, in the others anxiety and doubt about sexual capacity and performance. Five females reported difficulty in achieving orgasm or that sex was "not exciting." One young man of 20 would not discuss his sexual history, saying that he was "sexually inhibited." Two young women also refused to answer direct questions, indicating that sex was a problem area. A number of the subjects, while reporting that they had no difficulty with sexual functioning as such, stated directly or hinted that they were concerned with their difficulty as yet to achieve a sense of intimacy and closeness in their sexual relationships. This issue was more frequently expressed by the young women than by the young men. The great majority of the young adult subjects stated directly that they had no sexual problems. This report appeared fairly reliable in most cases, but probably reflected a denial response in some cases. Thus, one young woman who had denied any sexual problem in the routine interview, some months later requested an interview with one of us to discuss her concerns over her personal life situation. In this discussion she disclosed that she did have difficulty in achieving orgasm in her sexual relationships.

Experience with masturbation was reported by the great majority of the subjects, both male and female. Typically, it began in early adolescence and continued with variable frequency until early adulthood, when it dwindled or stopped altogether. In no case was there any evidence of preoccupation, anxiety, or guilt over masturbation, and in none of the clinical cases did excessive masturbation or disturbance over the act appear as a symptom.

In the early adult interviews, one young man of 18 and one young woman of 19 identified themselves as homosexual in their sexual orientation. The young man also had had several heterosexual experiences which he enjoyed, but much preferred his homosexual activity. The young woman had had two unsatisfying heterosexual experiences at age 16, but in the past year her relationships had been exclusively homosexual and satisfying. Two other young women, one 19, the other 21, had reported in their interviews active heterosexual functioning without problems, the first starting at 16, the other at 14. Several years later each informed their parents that they had become homosexually active and that this was now their clear sexual orientation. One other young man and three other young women reported one or more homosexual experiences in adolescence, but all were clear that their sexual orientation was now exclusively heterosexual. Though we have no specific data on this issue, it is our impression that the incidence of an occasional homosexual experience in adolescence was more frequent than was reported to us.

Finally, the correlations between the level of sexual functioning and the global adaptation score as rated from the early adult interviews was calculated. For males the correlation was .37 (p = .002), and for females, .48 (p = .0001). Inasmuch as the level of sexual functioning constituted one element in the raters' assessment of overall adaptation, a significant correlation was to be expected. The actual correlations are moderate, indicating that, for our ratings at least, the level of sexual functioning and overall adaptation in early adult life were by no means synonymous.

SUBSTANCE USE AND ABUSE

As a group, the NYLS subjects came into adolescence a few years after the peak in the late 1960s of drug experimentation and abuse among middle-class adolescents. Whether our data reflected this trend or whether other factors were also operating, overall this sample showed a modest use of alcohol, a preponderance of nonsmokers, and a small minority who had experimented with cocaine, LSD, and/or stimulants or depressive drugs. All denied the use of heroin. The majority of the group had tried marijuana, and a substantial number used it regularly, but only a few more than once a week.

The distribution of frequency and severity of alcohol and other substance use was heavily weighted toward the modest side. Approximately 75 percent of the group either denied any substance use or reported this as infrequent and confined to alcohol and/or marijuana. Among the moderate and heavy users, there were no cases of alcohol or other drug addiction. No psychotic reactions to LSD or the amphetamines had occurred, though several subjects reported "bad trips" with LSD. In one case (Norman, Chapter 14), a brief hypomanic episode may have been the result of a temporary period of heavy drug use. Norman himself asserted that he took no drugs except marijuana, whereas his father reported him to be highly involved in a number of drugs at the time.

It was clear that there was a definite tendency to underreporting by the subjects in their statements as to current substance use. This was to be expected in an area so heavily loaded with value judgment. Thus, a number of subjects in their early adult interviews reported a greater degree of substance use in their adolescent years than they had described in their adolescent interviews. These were subjects who in effect said, "Now that I'm no longer doing it, I can be honest about how much I did it in the past."

SMOOTH EXPANSIVE ADOLESCENCE

A number of the NYLS subjects confounded the stereotype of adolescent turmoil. The new demands of adolescence, whether social, sexual, academic, or work, were mastered constructively with expansion of their horizons, interests, and activities. Stress and tension may have accompanied their responses to these new challenges, but not excessive stress requiring evasions, retreats, or other defensive maneuvers. Symptoms of behavioral disturbance were conspicuous by their absence. The change in self-image and self-expectations stimulated by physical maturation and the knowledge that they were entering a transition period between childhood and adulthood were both sobering and exciting, but not threatening. By and large, these were the youngsters who had sailed through childhood in the same constructive fashion. On entering adolescence, they had a firm foundation of self-esteem, healthy behavioral patterns, positive relationships to family and peers, and effective coping mechanisms, which they then brought to bear on the challenges and demands of this new and more complex developmental stage.

Barbara (Chapter 13), with the highest early adult adaptation score, typifies this smooth expansive adolescent history most impressively. She made friends easily, including several intimate ones, did well academically and enjoyed school, worked summers in her teens and performed well, and had clear-cut career goals which she pursued effectively. Her first sexual experience was at 15 years, and she had continued sexually active since, without problems. She emphasized that, for her, sexual involvement required a feeling of emotional closeness to the young man, as well as a physical attraction. Her self-image was strongly positive.

Of special interest was the fact that her parents were divorced when she was two years old and both subsequently remarried. She lived with her mother, who worked full-time from the time Barbara was 18 months old. She described her parents and stepparents as different personalities, and her need to make a different relationship with each. Rather than this demand being a source of conflict and tension, or even anxiety and guilt, Barbara had clearly been able to use four parents, instead of two, as sources of strength and support. Her relationships with her two older brothers were warm and friendly.

Barbara did have an unusual array of resources, including highly superior intelligence, easy temperament, supportive parents, a charming manner, and physical attractiveness. But other youngsters for whom adolescence was a smooth expansive experience, even if on a more modest level than for Barbara, did not necessarily enjoy all these favorable influences. As an example, there is Mabel, the middle of three sisters. Her self-image was positive, but rather shaky, and she was concerned that her goals were unclear, though she was emphatic, at age 18, that she had serious purposes in life and wanted a useful career and meaningful emotional commitments. She made an immediate pleasant and cheerful impression, though she was not particularly physically attractive. Temperamentally, she had positive response to new situations, was easily adaptive, expressively intense, with both positive and negative mood components, and quite persistent. Her I.Q. scores were 135 at 3 years and 128 at 6 years.

Mabel's family was stable, though she felt her parents' relationship was not as close as it should be, and added, "Maybe that's why I don't want to get married." She respected her father deeply for his career success and personal qualities and felt close to him. As to her mother, she was ambivalent, both as to respect and closeness. She was highly competitive with her older sister,

"She always gets what she wants, knows how to play up. It kills me." However, she said that now that she is almost 19 and her sister 21, they are "very close." Her younger sister, 14, is very close to her, "I'm her big sister."

Her grammar and high school achievement levels were fairly high and she adjusted easily to the family's move to another state. Now in her second year of college, her grades are respectable, but not superior. She makes friends easily, both females and males. Her first and only sexual experience was at 17, and lasted a number of months. It took her a while to enjoy sex, and even then it was not very exciting. Now she wants to wait, "Maybe I'm picky." She worked as a salesperson the past summer (age 18) and did well. She is active in athletics, likes to read, and paints with oils a bit.

Mabel described infrequent periods of mild depression brought on by specific issues, but no other symptoms or difficulties in functioning. She had experimented with marijuana, had several bad reactions, and gave it up. She drinks occasionally, but never to excess, and denies any other drug use. She commented spontaneously that she herself "didn't go through teenage turmoil." This was confirmed in the separate parental interview, with her father's comment that Mabel did not have the stormy adolescence of her older sister. Overall, her parents described her as calm, dependable and responsible, and ". . . independent all the way. If she puts her mind to do something, like getting a job, she does it."

Like Barbara, Mabel's developmental course through childhood and adolescence has been characterized by smooth expansive functioning, with effective mastery of the demands of family, school, and peers. Her level of achievement in clarity of goals, academic success, and sexual functioning has not been as high as Barbara's, indeed a very high standard to match. But Mabel's long-range goals are healthy, her commitments are serious and determined, her self-confidence is basically substantial, and she has learned to master new demands and challenges directly without recourse to defensive maneuvers. It is reasonable to be optimistic about her further positive development with regard to both work achievement and the establishment of good intimate heterosexual relationships.

These two examples of smooth adolescent development are girls, but comparable vignettes could as easily be given from the male members of the NYLS sample.

TURBULENT BUT HEALTHY ADOLESCENCE

Other subjects mastered the demands and expectations of adolescence effectively, but in contrast to Barbara and Mabel, this healthy development was turbulent rather than smooth. A typical example was Danielle, Mabel's older sister.

Danielle's childhood development was uneventful, with easy adaptation to family expectations. Her IQ score at 3 years was 153, and at 6 years 141, placing her in the highly superior range. She did very well at school until age 12, and then her performance deteriorated. Her recollection of her high school years was that she hated school. "Everybody seemed bitchy and mean." She barely got by with mediocre grades. Her mother's comment was that she was "always on the phone, talking to her friends."

Danielle and her parents agreed in describing her adolescence as very stormy. There were many fights about her staying out very late. She labeled herself an "obnoxious brat" until 16, and her mother called her "self-centered, selfish, cared only about her own feelings. She drove me batty." The father, who was more detached, confirmed that Danielle "had difficult adolescence, got involved with dope for awhile, had us worried."

Her first sexual experience was at age 15, with a subsequent active sexual life. She denied any sexual problems. However, her heterosexual relationships have been intense and turbulent, especially with one young man with whom she was closely involved for three years, starting at age 15. He was a heavy drug user, and there was much conflict, "We fought like cats and dogs verbally." After their breakup by mutual consent, she was acutely upset for several months, cried a great deal, and withdrew socially. Then, coming out of it, she began to see her friends again, and a year later made a new active relationship with a stable, serious young man.

Danielle was a heavy user of marijuana from 15 to 18, coinciding with her affair with the drug-abusing young man. Following this, her use of marijuana diminished markedly. She denied any other substance abuse.

Danielle was interviewed at age 20, and presented herself as a friendly, cooperative, and highly expressive young woman. Her expressed self-esteem was high and appeared genuine. Her college grades were respectable, her social life active, and her relationships with the young man established the year before appeared relaxed and stable. She had a serious interest in art and painting and was considering going to graduate school in art history. Her mother now described her as "delightful, lot of fun, enjoy being with her. Concerned about people, a new development." The mother thinks this positive change was due to the family's move to another state outside the New York area two years before. Her father agreed that "She's great company, I enjoy her tremendously. She used to be hostile, hard to be with; she's growing into a real human being."

Danielle fits the stereotype of the rebellious, self-centered adolescent, with intense negativistic reactions to parental demands and rules. She was distinguished temperamentally by her intense emotionality, which was very evident in her parental reports as well as in her own interview. This made her adolescent challenge to family rules stormy, and her heterosexual affair with a drug-abuser turbulent and difficult. However, at no time during her adolescence did she get into social or legal difficulties, nor did she develop any evidence of psychopathology. We have to consider her adolescence, stormy as it was, as a positive and healthy developmental period, with continuity with both her earlier serene childhood and her emerging mature, self-confident adulthood.

CHILDHOOD DISORDER AND MASTERY IN ADOLESCENCE

For some of the NYLS subjects who suffered from a behavior disorder in childhood, the maturational process and the new environmental opportunities of adolescence provided the setting for mastery of their childhood problems. An example of this developmental sequence was Stuart, a temperamentally easy youngster with an IQ score of 122.

When Stuart was 8 years old, his mother was called to school by the teacher because of his disruptive behavior in the classroom. The teacher reported that the boy was in the habit of making loud personal remarks during class sessions or recreational periods. These comments were sometimes very perceptive and exposed a classmate's weak spots, or else, when directed to an adult, were highly inappropriate, though they might have been acceptable if addressed to a child. His remarks usually precipitated merriment and laughter among his classmates, but commonly this was in the middle of a lesson, making it difficult for the teacher to maintain discipline. The teacher noted that although Stuart made friends easily, these relationships were usually short-lived, due to his habit of making remarks which discomfited his playmates. His mother confirmed that she has noticed this same social problem.

A second difficulty was Stuart's failure to learn at a level consistent with his intellectual capacity. However, he did shine in learning situations which involved discussion. Here he had many good ideas that showed evidence of logical thinking, retentive memory, and good conceptualization. But, once left on his own to deal with subject matter in the absence of a social situation, he began to take shortcuts and skim through his lessons. In a sense, Stuart had to scintillate or bust. At this point the parents asked for a clinical consultation with us.

A scrutiny of the anterospective data, confirmed by an interview with the parents, revealed that they had looked upon Stuart as a delight from the time of his precocious speech development during his second year of life. His comments and questions in his penetrating little boy voice were so often incisive that family members and even strangers would stop to express their amusement. Indeed, even the target of his remarks was often greatly amused. With Stuart's easy adaptability, these responses proved strongly reinforcing and he took on the role of *enfant terrible*. Occasional remarks embarrassed his parents, for which he was scolded, but his overall behavior was encouraged and made for pleasant table conversation when guests were present. Thus, despite the fact that Stuart's parents did not themselves commit social gaucheries, they were quite inadvertently reinforcing the tendencies in their son's behavior which made him socially objectionable. His need to be clever and the center of attention also served to distort his motivation for school performance, with harmful consequences for his academic achievement.

A clinical evaluation showed no evidence of significant psychopathology beyond this obnoxious cleverness. A strategy of parent guidance was outlined which would transform the parents' positive reinforcement of Stuart's undesirable behavior to responses of discouragement of his undesirable cleverness. This was only partially successful, because his mother continued to find his behavior amusing and attractive. Though basically a serious person and highly successful in her own career, she had a lively and exuberant personality which resonated with Stuart's verbal pranks. Remedial tutoring was also arranged, but this was unproductive because of his lack of interest and attention.

Frequent follow-up discussions with the parents and with Stuart through middle childhood showed little change. As he entered adolescence, Stuart was a serious underachiever academically (he attended a prestigious private school with high standards). He had modified his verbal cleverness sufficiently so that he was no longer socially obnoxious. On the contrary, his ease in making friends and his charming manner made him immediately acceptable with peers and adults. He had become a good athlete and excelled at tennis. He discovered sex early, had his first experience at age 15, and began an active sex life with no difficulty in persuading a number of girls to go to bed with him. He discussed his sex life openly and often with his parents and older brother, clearly as a boastful expression of achievement and success.

Because of their continuing concern over Stuart's poor school performance and lack of seriousness, the parents arranged for family therapy with another therapist when he was 15, but without significant change. He was also seen by one of us at about the same time and his problems were reviewed with him. He was given his entire case history to read, and when he finished he commented cheerfully, "It said that I'm a loudmouth."

Stuart began smoking at 16, with consumption of one and a half packs of cigarettes a day. He began using marijuana at 16, but only occasionally. Alcohol use was erratic, with excessive use at weekend parties, and much less otherwise. There was no report of other substance abuse.

It would have been easy to predict at the time Stuart was 16 that he was headed for a lifetime career as a playboy who would utilize his social talents and charm to exploit his parents, friends, and especially women, a career in which he would be highly successful. And, indeed, this was the great concern of ourselves and his parents.

However, in the next few years Stuart made a truly remarkable turnabout. He began to apply himself seriously to his studies and his grades improved substantially. He explained this as "I realized I was going to college," and had to do better academically if he was to be accepted at a good college. He also took an unpaid job several summers teaching tennis to underprivileged children at public courts in the city. He was even made assistant director for the borough in this program.

Stuart's next follow-up was at 22 years, in the routinely scheduled early adult interview. He had just graduated with honors from a good college, in the top 10 percent of the class. He had found academic work interesting, had begun "to feel it was the real thing, leading to real work." He had been active in varsity sports, student government, and the college admissions office. He had worked each summer at various jobs, including one as an aide to a Congressman the previous summer. His career plans were definite, involving a career in business, and he was scheduled to start a graduate course in business administration in a leading university in a few months.

Stuart's social life was as easy and active as ever, with a number of close friends. He now had had a steady girl friend for the past 18 months and was thinking seriously of marriage. He reported some tendency to premature orgasm in the past few months, but did not appear anxious over this issue. However, he was concerned over his continued heavy smoking and his tendency "to drink to get drunk. I feel more at ease when I'm drinking, that bothers me, that I need it." He expressed satisfaction with himself, "I think well of myself, because I've achieved a lot of things that in the past I didn't know would excite me."

Overall in the interview Stuart was well-poised, made quick social contact, and showed a rather charming manner of which he was clearly aware. There was no evidence of overt anxiety or expressions of conflict or self-doubt, though his rather heavy smoking and drinking and recent orgastic prematurity may have reflected stress in the transition from early adolescent "playboy" to adult "career man."

Stuart's report was confirmed in the separate interview with his parents. The father put it that "He has matured fantastically, beautifully. Now he has proven to himself that he has an able mind, has worked like a dog. He is a nice human being, though he is still capable of being a nuisance and immature once in a while." The mother added, "The most different thing about Stuart now is motivation. He cares about succeeding, works to achieve and does." A follow-up report two years later from his parents revealed that Stuart had completed his graduate business course and obtained a promising position with a marketing firm.

How do we account for the dramatic change in Stuart, starting in mid-adolescence? The influence of his family group undoubtedly played a major role. Both parents had been high academic achievers and each had a separate successful career. The older brother was a serious, impressive student and one grandfather, an active member of the family, had had an eminent professional career. All of these—parents, brother, and grandfather—were respected by friends and community for their hard work and achievements. And it was evident to Stuart that his parents' work commitment had brought them very substantial social and financial rewards.

We can presume that this correlation of academic achievement and hard work with social and financial success in adult life had little meaning for Stuart in his childhood and early adolescent years. But when, at age 16, he began to face the fact that his college choice would depend on his school grades, and that this choice would influence his later options, this had a sobering influence. In his own words, "I realized I was going to college," and he determined to improve his academic record. Fortunately for him, with his superior intelligence and easy temperament, this shift in goals was easily attained and his success brought a progressive increase in his sense of self-esteem. With this, he was no longer the oddball playboy of the family, but a respected and fully accepted member. Also helpful was his discovery that while his verbal pranks were not as attractive to a sophisticated adolescent peer group, his social skills were so adequate that he did not require any special social acrobatics to make and sustain friendships.

Another pattern of childhood disorder with mastery in adolescence was evident in the case of Roy (see Chapter 17). This youngster was in constant conflict as a child with a compulsive, pressuring, and controlling mother, which led to a moderately severe adjustment disorder. Parent guidance was a complete failure. However, in middle childhood and adolescence, Roy was able to utilize the ever-increasing opportunities for activities outside the home to distance himself emotionally from his mother and, in effect, to progressively freeze her out of his life. With this, his symptoms disappeared and his peer relationships and school activities became competent and sources of positive feedback.

POORNESS OF FIT IN ADOLESCENCE

Finally, there were the youngsters for whom the new demands of adolescence proved excessively stressful, with the crystallization of a behavior problem or the exacerbation of a previously existing disorder. In other words, such an unfavorable adolescent developmental course reflected a poorness of fit between the individual's characteristics and capacities and the expectations of the environment.

As the adolescent begins to search for a sense of identity and position independent of his parents, the standards and values of the peer group assume a compelling influence. Where these values conflict with parental standards, a clash or series of clashes between parent and youngster inevitably results. In the NYLS group, such disputes arose over many issues — dress, hairstyle, curfew rules, tidiness in the home, manners, handling of money, school functioning, sexual behavior, and the use of alcohol or other drugs. In the great majority of cases, these conflicts were resolved without disruption of the basic stable positive relationship between youngster and parents. Often it was a matter of an agreement to disagree. This was the case even in some families where the intergenerational conflict was turbulent, as in the case of Danielle (this chapter, above).

In other cases, the clash between adolescent and parent occurred in the context of an unhealthy, stressful parent-child relationship. Where the youngster was able to distance himself or herself emotionally from the parent, such a conflict did not necessarily result in the development of a behavior disorder (see discussion of the issue of distancing from the parent in Chapter 17). In other instances, where the adolescent was unable to achieve this distancing, a pattern of adolescent rebellion was the typical outcome (see Chapter 16). One girl rebelled against an intrusive domineering mother, one boy rebelled against his father's rigid moralistic standards, another boy resented his mother's remarriage after his father's death, and another felt threatened by his professionally successful father and his academically achieving older brother and sister.

The demand on the adolescent for impulse control becomes more complex than in childhood because of the conflict in standards that may arise between adult values and those of the youngster's particular peer group. However, this did not become a source of significant behavioral deviance except in two girls, when the family environment lacked sufficient supportive stability (Bernice, Chapter 12; Lily, Chapter 16).

There were two cases of depression with onset in adolescence, one a major primary depression (Sylvia, Chapter 14), the other an adjustment disorder with depressed mood (Brad, Chapter 14).

Opposite to the pattern of adolescent rebellion against parental standards were the youngsters who were threatened by and retreated from the expectations of their peer group. An extreme example was a girl with a slow-to-warm-up temperament which had always made her socially shy. The increasingly complex social demands of adolescence, coupled with a delayed puberty and self-consciousness about her body image, led to progressive social inhibition and anxiety. She attempted to cope by clinging to her overprotective mother, but this did not serve her well, and she developed a severe anxiety state with multiple symptoms.

In those youngsters with childhood disorders in which poorness of fit continued to characterize their developmental course, the new demands of adolescence typically served to intensify their problems and magnify and increase their symptoms (e.g., Norman, Chapter 14; Ronald, Chapter 17).

ADOLESCENT TURMOIL

Traditionally, both in popular and professional writings, adolescence has been viewed as a period of marked emotional upheaval and turmoil arising from rapid physical changes, the onset of adult sexuality, and the expectation for increased responsibility within the family combined with beginning autonomy in functioning. This view was stated vividly by G. Stanley Hall in his classic volume on adolescence in 1904: "The teens are emotionally unstable and pathic. It is a natural impulse to experience hot and perfervid psychic states, and it is characterized by emotionalism" (1904, p. 74). This concept was further developed in the psychoanalytic literature, in which adolescence has been viewed as a period of emotional lability and instability, in which the upholding of a steady equilibrium would in itself be abnormal (Blos, 1979; Eissler, 1958; A. Freud, 1958). The psychoanalytic formulations have been summarized by the Offers. "Psychoanalytic theory describes adolescence as a time of psychologic imbalance, when the functioning of ego and superego are severely strained. Instinctual impulses disrupt the homeostatic arrangements achieved during latency, and inner turmoil results, manifesting itself by rebellious or deviant behavior, mood swings, or affective lability. Unresolved preoedipal or oedipal conflicts are revived; the repression characteristic of latency is no longer sufficient to restore a psychologic equilibrium. . . . The physical, muscular, and hormonal growth of the adolescent endows the rearoused drives with a potency denied to the former child and frightening to the developing adolescent" (Offer and Offer, 1975, p. 161).

The psychoanalytic view of adolescence as a period of turmoil was further extended by Erikson's influential concept of the "identity crisis" of adolescence. "In spite of the similarity of adolescent 'symptoms' and episodes to neurotic and psychotic symptoms and episodes, adolescence is not an affliction, but a normative crisis, i.e. a normal phase of increased conflict characterized by a seeming fluctuation in ego strength . . . what under prejudiced scrutiny may appear to be the onset of a neurosis often is but an aggravated crisis which might prove to be self-liquidating and, in fact, contributive to the process of identity formulation" (Erikson, 1959, p. 116).

These psychoanalytic formulations have been derived primarily from data obtained from adolescent or adult patients suffering from one or another psychopathological syndrome. Thus, the Offers point out that "Erikson does not present examples of healthy and adaptive adolescence. Surely, examples of true 'normative' crises ought to come from others than patients, exceptional individuals, and fictional or biographical profiles. These are the adolescents with whom Erikson has had contact, and they then circularly support the theory that he has spun based on his experience with them" (Offer and Offer, 1975, p. 163).

Indeed, the studies of unselected groups of adolescents do provide a different picture of this developmental stage. Coleman's survey of the literature found that the large scale empirical studies have concluded that "the teenage years are very much more stable and peaceful than had previously been concluded" (1978, p. 2). Rutter's comprehensive and systematic review of the pertinent literature came to a similar judgment. "It is also evident that normal adolescence is *not* characterized by storm, stress, and disturbance. Most young people go through their teenage years without significant emotional or behavioral problems. It is true that there are challenges to be met, adaptations to be made, and stresses to be coped with. However, these do not all arise at the same time and most adolescents deal with these issues without undue disturbance" (Rutter, 1979, p. 86). Our own data, as detailed above in this chapter, are fully in line with this judgment. Similarly, the Offers (1975), in a study of 73 middle-class, midwestern adolescent males, found that 23 percent were characterized by smooth continuous progression and 35 percent by alternating periods of spurts and leveling-off in their development, though functioning as adaptively as the continuous growth group. Only 21 percent of the group could be characterized as tumultuous, with substantial internal turmoil that manifested itself in overt behavioral conflicts at home and in school.

As to Erikson's concept of the "normative identity crisis" of adolescence, this categorization did not appear to apply to our NYLS population. Neither did it appear in the majority of the Offers' sample, nor did they "see evidence of superiority in development of those who do experience an Eriksonian-type identity crisis over those whose development is more marked by smoothness and ease of growth" (Offer and Offer, 1975, p. 163). We concur with Rutter's conclusion that "it seems misleading to view adolescence as a time of identity crisis. Of course, the development of a personal identity is a crucial part of growing up and much of importance in this connection happens during adolescence, but so also it does earlier in childhood and later in adult life" (Rutter, 1979, p. 87).

Overall, no a priori conclusion should be drawn as to the meaning of the presence or absence of adolescent turmoil in any specific individual. Each case should be evaluated on its own in the perspective of that youngster's overall behavior and functioning. The absence of turmoil may reflect smooth positive development. Turmoil may also be absent in adolescents with clinical behavior disorders characterized by inhibition and passivity in functioning. Adolescent turmoil, when present, may be a transient phenomenon in a healthy developmental course, may signal the onset of a clinical disorder, or may be one aspect of the adolescent symptomatology in a behavior disorder continuing from childhood.

OVERVIEW

The wide range of developmental paths into and through adolescence exhibited by our NYLS subjects emphasizes anew the fallacy of applying any unidimensional linear theoretical model to this or any other life-span period. The usefulness of the term "adolescent turmoil" is questionable, given its variable occurrence and meaning. The same is true of the concept of the adolescent "normative crises," given the smoothness with which so many youngsters achieve the passage through adolescence. As the Offers emphasize, their data, like ours, lead them "to hypothesize that adolescence, as a stage in life, is not a uniquely stressful period" (1975, p. 197).

We were also not impressed that the "generation gap" between parents and their adolescent sons and daughters merited the emphasis and concern expressed by so many mental health professionals and lay commentators. Those of our subjects with strong positive ties to their parents in childhood — indeed, a healthy majority of the total sample — maintained qualitatively similar relationships even as they strove in adolescence to develop their independence and freedom of functioning in the outside world. In a similar vein, Rutter concludes that "the evidence suggests that there has *not* been a widening of the supposed 'generation gap'" (1979, p. 143), and the Offers report that "in the social as well as the psychological realm, we have seen the continuity between generations . . . Most [adolescents] cherished the values of their elders (1975, p. 197).

Even some of those who agree that "the past portrayal of adolescence carried too heavy an emphasis on turmoil and maladaption" still view the adolescent process as "difficult" because this is "a period of extraordinary change, multiple conflicts, and marked societal demands upon the individual" (Fishman, 1982, p. 39). Yet early infancy is a period of even greater change and greater societal demands than is adolescence, and yet is not labelled a "difficult" period. The preschool years with its demands for peer play relationships and the early school years with their demands for formal learning are also periods of great change and new expectations. Yet we expect them to go smoothly for most youngsters. The childhood years may be especially stressful for some children, such as those with difficult temperament or learning problems, but we do not generalize from these particular cases and designate these periods as "stressful" for all.

What is different about adolescence is not the extent or uniqueness of change, but its quality and implications in our society. Parents take unqualified pleasure as they watch each new step in their child's physical and psychological development. But their reactions to the process of development in adolescence is likely to have some ambivalence. They may be pleased at their daughter's or son's sexual maturation, but worry at the same time whether the adolescent will use this new ability "wisely." They may be impressed by their teenage son's muscular development, but be concerned at the havoc he can now wreak if he gets angry or frustrated.

At the same time, the adolescent's assumption of more mature responsibilities and of an independent role in the family, as positive as this may be, is also coupled with the loss of the absolute parental and teacher control that existed in the childhood years. The adolescent now brings into his life from his peer group a new set of standards and values which may or may not conflict with the parents' value system. Even where the parents have adopted a permissive and flexible stance, as with sex education, and encouraged open communication on the subject, they may be disconcerted to discover that their adolescent son or daughter prefers to get his or her sexual education from the peer group rather than from them.

The adolescent encounters the ills and problems of the outside world, as well as its exciting opportunities, as he begins to move actively into this world on his own. His sharp responses, when they occur, may not reflect some inner identity crisis, but rather the characteristics of this world, characteristics to which most adults have become inured. It may be, in Anthony's phrase, that each "society gets the type of adolescent it expects and deserves" (Anthony, 1969, p. 65).

PART IV

Practical and Theoretical Implications

CHAPTER 20

Parent Guidance

Parent guidance represents a most valuable treatment strategy in child psychiatry. By this procedure, we mean the formulation of a program of altered functioning by the parents that could ameliorate excessive and harmful stress for the child. Whenever indicated, guidance of the parents can also include recommendations for other appropriate environmental changes that the parents can implement, such as a change in school placement or alteration of living arrangements for the child. Overall, this treatment procedure can be characterized by the title of a recent volume on the subject, *Helping Parents Help Their Children* (Arnold, 1978).

The basic emphasis in parent guidance is on the change in the parent's *behavior* and *overtly expressed* attitudes, and not on the definition or changes of underlying conflicts, anxieties, or defenses in the parent. The goal of parent guidance, in other words, is to change specific aspects of the parents' actual functioning with their child, but not to delineate or attempt to change directly any of their covert attitudes or defense mechanisms that, presumably, might be related to overt behavior and attitudes.

Such an approach assumes that a child's behavior problem does not necessarily reflect the existence of deep-seated anxieties, conflicts, or maladaptive conditioned reflex patterns which must be eliminated for treatment to be successful. Parent guidance may even be effective in ameliorating or resolving some of the parents' deep-seated anxieties and conflicts, either by itself or in combination with direct treatment of the child. When it comes to serious psychopathology in the child, such as autism, childhood schizophrenia or organic brain syndromes, the therapeutic role of parent guidance may be more modest.

Parent guidance procedures also assume that parental functioning which is detrimental to a child's psychological development does not necessarily reflect the presence of deep-seated anxieties, conflicts or pathological goals in the parent which must be changed before the child's symptoms can be ameliorated. It also assumes that if the parent does have some significant degree of psychopathology, this does not necessarily prevent her or him or both from making the changes in the specific behaviors that are proving detrimental to the child's psychological welfare. Anna Freud has put it well. She "refuse(s) to believe that mothers need to change their personalities before they can change the handling of their child" (1960, p. 37).

Parent guidance has the great virtue of enlisting the parents as direct allies in the therapeutic process, allies whose influence on the child is continuous and intimate from day to day. It is the very rare parent who does not really wish her child a healthy, happy and productive future, no matter whether her behavior is serving to promote or undermine this goal. It is the consonance of mental health professional and parent in their concern for the child's welfare that makes this therapeutic alliance possible. Parent guidance also involves advice couched in practical terms and spelled out with regard to the specific items of behavior to be changed. As such, the guidance recommendations are easily understood and make no demands that are beyond the capacities of the average parent. When effective, this approach avoids the necessity for long and expensive direct treatment of the child. In some cases, where direct psychotherapy of the child is required, simultaneous parent guidance may expedite significantly the course of the child's treatment. And finally, when effective, parent guidance also bypasses the alternative approach of an analysis of the parent's own psychopathological patterns, a procedure which is likely to be prolonged, arduous, and expensive.

GOODNESS OF FIT AND PARENT GUIDANCE

The goodness of fit conceptualization of the origins and evolution of behavior disorders in children, as we have detailed it in previous chapters, provides a useful theoretical guide for implementing a parent guidance procedure in individual cases. The diagnosis of a behavior disorder in a child is assumed to result from a poorness of fit between the child's capacities, motivations, and/or behavioral style and the expectations and demands of the environment. An analysis can then be made which identifies the specific features of child and environment which, in interaction with each other, are producing the poorness of fit and consequent psychopathological development. Once these specific features are identified, a program can then be formulated which will relieve the excessive stress the child is experiencing and ameliorate the symptoms of the behavior disorder. This program can be spelled out with the parents, and their understanding and implementation of the specific changes to be made can be monitored in follow-up sessions.

This strategy of parent guidance rests on the commitment to an *individualization* of the treatment strategy for any child and set of parents. With this commitment, counseling in general global terms is considered inadequate and even counterproductive. What is necessary, rather, is the identification of the specifics of the poorness of fit in each individual case, and this may vary qualitatively from one child to another.

PARENT GUIDANCE IN THE NYLS

As described in Chapter 3, our data-gathering procedures were geared to the early identification of any child showing evidence of a possible behavior disorder. In all such instances, this was followed quickly by a systematic clinical evaluation to substantiate or rule out the presence of a behavior disorder. In each case in which a clinical diagnosis was made, the anterospective records were culled to establish the specific pattern of goodness of fit in that individual child. Based on this analysis, parent guidance was offered to each set of parents.

In this manner, parent guidance was utilized in the early stages of a behavior disorder in almost every instance. In one case, the severity of the child's symptoms in school and with peers was such that psychotherapy was recommended concurrently with parent guidance. In another case, the parents decided to arrange for psychotherapy on their own, despite the recommendation that they give the guidance procedure further time.

The initial parent guidance session in each case started with our affirmation of a common concern with the parents for their child's welfare and a joint interest in eliminating the symptoms that were jeopardizing the youngster's happiness and functioning. We urged that both parents participate in the guidance discussions, and in most cases this was achieved. With both parents present, if conflict and disagreement between them became evident, the issue could be emphasized that they were still both committed to their child's interests and needs.

The rationale of the guidance program was then explained to the parents in terms of the concept of a goodness of fit between the child's characteristics and the parents' functioning as the essential basis for the youngster's healthy psychological development. The specific area or areas in which a poorness rather than a goodness of fit existed were then identified. This involved a description of the child's temperament, of any other child attributes that were pertinent, and of the particular parental behaviors and attitudes which, in interaction with the child's characteristics, were producing excessive stress. Other relevant factors where they existed, such as inappropriate school expectations, were also defined.

Throughout this discussion the parents were assured that the poorness of fit formulation in no way meant they were "bad parents," and that the same behavior on their part with a child with different attributes might have been positive rather than negative in its consequences. It was also emphasized that the child's disturbed responses to their well-meaning efforts did not mean that the youngster was "sick," "bad," or "willfully disobedient." This focus helped to clarify the basic thesis that the necessity for parental change in attitudes and behavior did not mean that they had wanted to harm the child. It was a question of lack of knowledge, misinformation, and confusion, rather than motivation, that had led to undesirable consequences for the child.

The parents were then offered specific suggestions and advice for changing the identified harmful attitudes and practices. Reference to concrete incidents in the child's life were made to illustrate each recommendation. For example, the initial intense negative responses to new situations and slow adaptability of a temperamentally difficult child were documented by details of the child's history with new foods, new people, new activities, new school situations, etc. These reactions were distinguished from anxiety or motivated negativism. The recommendations for parental change then followed logically, in terms of the goal of quiet, firm, and consistent handling, with patient expectation that positive adaptation would occur after a number of exposures to the particular new demand. It was also emphasized that whenever possible the youngster should be exposed to only one or two new situations at a time, so as not to overwhelm his capacity for adaptation. At the same time, shielding the child from *any* new demands and experiences to avoid the turmoil and tension these produced in child, parent and bystander was highly undesirable, for it left the youngster overprotected and unable to transform new stressful settings into habitual positive ones. A healthy self-system also could not develop without repeated experiences of successful mastery of the new.

The guidance formulation for a slow-to-warm-up child was essentially similar to that for the difficult child. Here, it was usually easier for the parents to carry through a quiet, patient regime, inasmuch as the youngster's withdrawal from the new did not produce the noisy embarrassing turmoil characteristic of the difficult child's response pattern to the new. As another example, the restlessness and shifts in attention of a highly active and distractible youngster were distinguished from "laziness," willful inattention, and lack of interest. The necessity for giving such a child periodic breaks, whether on long automobile trips or while doing homework, was spelled out in detail.

In most cases of behavior disorder in early and middle childhood, poorness of fit involved some feature of the child's temperamental characteristics as a major issue. Other factors did play a significant role in certain cases, such as a parent's difficulty in accepting a child's intellectual limitations, or in understanding the organic basis of a dyslexic syndrome. Whatever the issue, the basic strategy of parent guidance was similar. The cornerstone was always the delineation of the *specific* nature of the pathogenic child-environmental interactional process in each *individual* case, and then to tailor the guidance program *concretely* to that *individual* situation.

An essential feature of the guidance program was a systematic follow-up schedule with the parents after the initial session. Even with parents who were eager and able to carry through the schedule of behavioral change recommended to them, more than one discussion was usually necessary for this to be implemented fully. Several sessions, at least, were usually required for them to grasp adequately the concept of the child's individuality and its influence on the youngster's ability to cope with parental and other environmental demands and expectations. At these follow-up discussions, the parents' behaviors in a number of specific incidents which had occurred in the interim period were reviewed. This review, which was done in detail, was usually required for the parents to become adept at identifying those situations in the child's daily life in which modification of their techniques of management was required.

Inevitably, the guidance sessions revealed defensiveness, anxiety, or guilt in a number of parents, in addition to misconceptions, misinformation, and confusions. It was often possible, in the course of clarifying the dynamics of the behavior problem development, and of pointing the way for the parents to actively resolve their child's problem, to relieve effectively these disturbed parental cognitive and affective reactions. In other cases, these parental attitudes reflected significant psychopathology which was not amenable to the therapeutic strategy of parent guidance. The same was true of the instances in which other types of symptomatic expression of parental psychopathology, such as neurotic needs for domination, intrusiveness or passive submissiveness, served as an influential and even decisive influence on the child's behavior disorder development.

PARENT GUIDANCE SUCCESSES

Parent guidance was evaluated by qualitative clinical judgment as moderately or highly successful in approximately 50 percent of the NYLS childhood behavior disorder cases. This rating was estimated both by the indication of parental change in the desired direction and by improvement in the behavior disorder, two factors which went hand in hand in a reciprocal relationship. When the initial efforts at change by the parents brought quick positive change in the child's functioning, this then acted as a powerful stimulus for the parents to continue and extend their altered behavior and attitudes. An average of only 2 to 3 guidance sessions were required for this successful outcome.

A positive parental response to the guidance approach was found with children with all types of temperamental patterns, except for those with high distractibility and low persistence. (The reasons for this unfavorable response in this latter group will be considered in the next section.) In the successful cases, the parents were able to understand and accept the judgment that their child's disturbed behavior did not reflect any deep-seated psychopathology and that the need for change on their part did not indict them as "bad parents." Furthermore, the validity of their goals and aspirations for the child's future was affirmed. With these assurances, they were able to accept and implement the need for a modification in their approach to the child if their goals were to be achieved.

PARENT GUIDANCE FAILURES

In the other 50 percent of cases, however, parent guidance was unsuccessful, as judged by the lack of any significant change in the behavior and attitudes which had entered into the formation of a poorness of fit and behavior disorder development. In some cases, only one or two guidance discussions were attempted, because of the parent's fixed refusal to consider that his or her functioning was undesirable. In other instances, lip service was given to the recommendations for change, or apparently earnest efforts were made to follow the outlined program, but a number of discussions then revealed that nothing had changed. And in a few cases, a parent was willing to come for a number of guidance sessions but made it clear that there was no acceptance of our judgments and suggestions. One father even put it that, "I know exactly what you're going to say," then proceeded to give a caricature of the discussion in the previous sessions and continued to go his own way.

Fortunately, the failure of parent guidance did not necessarily doom the child to an indefinite continuation or even an exacerbation of psychological difficulties. This unfavorable outcome did happen in some cases, for example, Bruce (Chapter 13), and Norman (Chapter 14). In other instances, recovery from a behavior disorder occurred in spite of the failure of parent guidance, as with Nancy (Chapter 17), with the favorable consequences of her musical and dramatic talent, or with Roy (Chapter 17), with his ability to distance himself from his compulsive, pressuring and controlling mother.

The reasons for the failure of parent guidance were varied. One striking finding was the uniform failure in the four children who were temperamentally highly distractible and nonpersistent. It was clear in each case that the parents could not accept these characteristics as normal. These middle- and upper middle-class parents attached great importance to educational achievement for both their daughters and sons, and to success in professional careers or business for the boys. For both of these goals, persistence and low distractibility, i.e., "stick-to-it-iveness," were considered laudable and even essential. It was, therefore, difficult for these parents to accept the characteristics at the other extreme, nonpersistence and high distractibility, especially in boys. In this regard, it is of interest that these four cases were all boys. In a few cases, this attitude was expressed openly in the guidance sessions, with such remarks about the child as, "He lacks character" (See Norman, Chapter 14). In the case of Roy (Chapter 17), the problem was further complicated by his mother's interpretation of his "forgetfulness" in finishing a task or meeting a time deadline as willful disobedience. We might speculate that with parents espousing different sociocultural values, parent guidance for distractible children might be more successful.

In several other cases, rigid parental standards which led to excessive demands on the child could not be influenced in the guidance sessions. One example was Bert's father (Chapter 15), who could not accept the fact that the consequences of the boy's brain damage made it impossible for him to live up to his father's standards of speech, behavior, and academic achievement. As another example, Nancy's father (Chapter 17) refused to modify his expectations for quick positive adaptation to new situations, no matter how much we discussed the unrealistic nature of this demand, given Nancy's difficult temperament pattern.

Parental denial of their child's limitations also proved inflexible to change in several cases. This was especially evident in the case of Kevin's parents (Chapter 15), whose refusal to accept the extent and permanence of his intellectual retardation led them to arrange inappropriate and excessively stressful school and social settings for the boy. In other cases, one or another type of psychopathology in the parent or especially severe parental conflict, which was an essential factor in the development of the child's behavior disorder, proved an insuperable obstacle to any significant parental behavioral change. Extreme examples were Lori's father (Chapter 17) and Bruce's parents (Chapter 13). Though parental conflict was a hindrance, and sometimes a serious one, to their joint implementation of a guidance program, this was not always the case. In a few instances, as with Nicky (Chapter 17), the parents were able to put aside their problems with each other, accept our advice, and change their approach to their child for the better.

The parents who failed to carry out the guidance recommendations were not prepared to face the implication that this might be due to their own psychological problems. Either they gave lip service to the endeavor, reporting that they were carrying through the necessary changes when it was clear that this was not the case, or they "misinterpreted" our suggestions, or they minimized the problem, or they simply politely but firmly disagreed with us. They were quite willing to consider that the child might need direct psychotherapy and make the necessary arrangements, but not that they themselves might require treatment. At least several of these parents had had extensive courses of psychotherapy in their earlier years, which they referred to openly, but this also did not facilitate any self-scrutiny in the guidance sessions. To have pressed the issue of their own problems, which we tried tentatively on some occasions, would only have alienated them, with loss of whatever influence, no matter how little, we still had on the child's developmental course.

PARENT GUIDANCE IN ADOLESCENCE

As indicated in Chapter 16, the youngster's temperamental characteristics were much less involved in the pathogenesis of a behavior disorder in adolescence as compared to the childhood years. For the teenager, it was the demands of the peer group and the school which were typically most influential in shaping either healthy or pathological adaptations at this age period. In some cases, a deviant developmental course had had its onset in childhood with a pathogenic parent-child interaction, even if it was not until adolescence that the consequences became evident in the crystallization of a behavior disorder. However, in these instances, the symptoms also reflected the youngster's difficulties outside the home more than any continuing problem of relationships with the parents.

As a result, the influence of the parents, for good or bad, was no longer the preeminent environmental factor it had been in the childhood years. With this, parent guidance, even when the parents cooperated fully, did not have the same dramatic effect by itself as it did in the successful cases in childhood. Guidance was useful, and in some cases very valuable, but direct treatment of the teenager was usually also essential. One girl, Lily (Chapter 16), was an exception. Her family had moved frequently because of her father's work assignments, she lacked the environmental stability and continuity to ameliorate her difficulties with impulse control, and she became involved in a number of thoughtless but not serious delinquent acts. The parents were advised to set firm rules quietly and to stabilize the living situation for their daughter. This they did and Lily recovered quickly. In several cases the parents arranged for treatment of the youngster on their own without consulting us, so that an attempt at parent guidance was not possible.

The number of adolescent cases with parent guidance is too small to permit any definitive conclusions, but it is our impression that a greater percentage of the parents were less responsive than were those in the childhood behavior disorder series. Most likely, this reflected the thrust of our judgments that change on their part might be helpful, but would not by itself produce a dramatic improvement in their troubled teenager. However, in those cases where the parents were responsive, the guidance discussions were helpful and well worth the effort.

PARENT GUIDANCE IN CLINICAL PRACTICE

One of us (S.C.), in a child psychiatric practice extending over many years, has found the therapeutic procedure of parent guidance to be as valuable as with the NYLS families. The clinical approach has been the same, with a delineation in each case of the specific dynamics of the poorness of fit between child and environment responsible for the development of the behavior problem for which the parents sought professional help. Based on this analysis, a program of altered parental functioning, supplemented when necessary by remedial tutoring or other special therapeutic procedures, was recommended to the parents, in the same manner as outlined above with the NYLS families.

The majority of parents accepted the logic of the guidance recommendations, appeared pleased to assume the role of therapeutic allies, and attempted seriously to carry through the necessary changes in their own functioning. In some cases, only a few discussions were necessary for the parents to modify their approach to the child and for the positive effect of this change on the child's behavior to become evident. No systematic follow-up of this clinical series has been possible. In a number of cases, informal follow-up revealed a continued benign and healthy developmental course on the child's part. In other instances, the parents returned, months or even several years later, because of recurrence of the child's difficulties. In most such cases, it was evident that the parents had not sustained the necessary change in their functioning, and this was then corrected by a review of the issues as originally defined. In a smaller number of cases, the analysis of the reasons for the recurrences of old symptoms or the appearance of new ones in the child revealed evidence of more severe psychopathology than originally estimated, or of special problems on the parents' part in implementing the guidance program. Either direct treatment of the child or more extensive guidance sessions with the parents, or both, were then necessary.

In some cases, a positive parental response to the guidance program was not sufficient by itself to resolve the child's behavior problem. This occurred typically when the disturbed behavior had been present for several years or more, resulting in one or another fixed, self-defeating defensive patterns. In such cases, direct treatment of the child was necessary, supplemented by a prolonged series of parent guidance discussions.

In a minority of instances in which parents came for consultative evaluation of their child's problems, they refused categorically to participate in the guidance program. It was evident that they expected the psychiatrist to take over the burden of caring for the child. Rather than being willing to assume an active role in their child's treatment as the psychiatrist's allies, they expected to be relieved of all such responsibility. These parents did not return after the nature of the guidance program had been explained, and undoubtedly went "shopping" until they found a professional approach to their liking.

OVERVIEW

The therapeutic strategy of parent guidance, as we have formulated it, has proven an effective treatment modality in perhaps 50 percent of children with behavior disorders. If the diagnosis was made quickly after the onset of the disorder, then the guidance program in the successful cases usually required only a few discussions. If the condition had been chronic before treatment was started, with fixed defensive reaction patterns already established in the child, then direct treatment of the child was often required, in addition to a prolonged series of guidance sessions. This experience argues strongly for the value of early diagnosis and treatment of behavior disorders in children.

The usefulness of this parent guidance approach indicates the practical value of the goodness of fit model. With this conceptual framework, it has been possible to individualize the treatment approach to fit the needs of each child and to identify concretely the behavioral and attitudinal changes on the parents' part required to change a pathogenic interaction with the child into a healthy relationship.

CHAPTER 21

Continuity-Discontinuity and Developmental Stages: A Life-Span Perspective

It is tempting for mental health professionals and educators to embrace the concept of continuity in psychological development from early childhood into adult life. With such a formulation, it appears possible to predict later outcome from early life, to interpret adolescent and adult psychopathology in terms of early childhood psychic traumata, to proceed with specific intervention programs for "high risk" children with the confidence that these will definitely alter adult outcomes, and to explain poor academic achievement in terms of early childhood cognitive "deprivation."

Thus, Freud propounded the dictum that, "Neuroses are only acquired during early childhood (up to the age of six), even though their symptoms may not make their appearance until much later. . . . the events of the first years are of paramount importance for . . . . (a child's) whole subsequent life" (Freud, 1949, p. 83). And Watson (1928, p. 3) the founder of the behaviorist school which came to rival psychoanalysis as an influential developmental conceptualization in the United States, put the issue in similar terms. "But once a child's character has been spoiled by bad handling, which can be done in a few days, who can say that the damage can be repaired? . . . at three years of age the child's whole emotional life has been laid down, his emotional disposition set."

Where change and discontinuity in development are obvious and cannot be wished away, a number of strategies are employed to maintain the commitment to continuity. As in the quote from Freud above, the symptom or other behavior is assumed to be formed in early childhood, but then to have hibernated in "the unconscious" until some trigger brought it into the open at some later time. Or the changed behavior may be conceptually identified with the early childhood period, either symbolically or through the operation of one or another defense mechanism. Thus, an adult's stinginess may be explained as due to difficulties in early toilet training, or a grown-up's timidity may be interpreted as a reaction formation to childhood hostility and aggressiveness. Then there is the appeal to "common sense." In the words of a prominent child development researcher, "Along with some others, I see our apparent inability to make empirical predictions about later personality from the early years as so much against good sense, common observation, and the thrust of all developmental theories that I can take it only as an indictment of established paradigms and methods rather than as evidence of a developmental reality" (Bronson, 1974, p. 276).

But "good sense" and "common observation" have never been reliable criteria for the validity of a scientific theory. And "the thrust of all developmental theories" is now more and more influenced by interactionist formulations which challenge the possibility of finding simple linear correlations between the early years and later personality.

DATA FROM THE NYLS

The NYLS case vignettes in previous chapters indicate that the course of psychological development, whether healthy or pathological, can show striking consistency in some individuals, marked inconsistency in others, and various combinations of consistency together with inconsistency in still others. Thus, Kathy (Chapter 12) and Barbara (Chapter 13) are examples of consistent healthy developmental courses from infancy into early adult life, and Norman (Chapter 14) and Ronald (Chapter 17) show similar consistency in a pathological direction.

Marked change from one age-period to another was evident in other cases. Michael (Chapter 12) developed a behavior disorder at 4 years, from which he recovered by age 8 years. A new and apparently unrelated disturbance then manifested itself in adolescence from which he also recovered by age 22. Olga (Chapter 14) and Olivia (Chapter 17) were both cases of severe disorders developing in adolescence, with subsequent dramatic recoveries.

In other instances, unpredictable idiosyncratic factors influenced substantially, and sometimes even decisively, the evolution of a behavior disorder. Such unanticipated influences on the developmental course of a psychological disturbance resulted either from unpredictable special life events and experiences or from the emergence of new psychological characteristics in the youngster. Bernice, Nelson, and Nancy (Chapter 17) represent examples of various types of unpredictable and significantly influential idiosyncratic factors. In addition, a psychiatric syndrome which is at least partially biologically determined may emerge at one or another age-period and alter seriously the youngster's psychological course. The two cases of major depression (Harold and Sylvia, Chapter 14) represent just such an unpredictable developmental change which was crucial in both the origin and evolution of a behavior disorder. The appearance of a schizophrenic syndrome, of which there have as yet been no examples in the NYLS sample, would represent another similar new and serious pathological influence.

In other subjects, both continuity and discontinuity were evident. A most interesting example was Carl, mentioned briefly in Chapter 16. Carl requested a consultation with one of us after his first term in college because of feelings of depression and inability to cope with the academic and social situation at college. He had made virtually no friends and found studying difficult, experiences he could not recall ever having before. He had done well academically in high school, had many friends, found school enjoyable, and had a wide range of interests, including the piano. In the interview he was alert, articulate, and in very good contact. He did not appear depressed, but rather bewildered at what was happening, exclaiming, "This just isn't me!"

The anterospective longitudinal data showed that in early life Carl had been one of our most extreme difficult temperament types, with intense negative reactions to almost all new situations, and slow but gradual adaptability only after many exposures. This was true whether it was the first solid foods in infancy, the beginning of nursery school and elementary school, first birthday parties, or the first shopping trip. Each such experience evoked stormy responses, with loud crying and struggling to get away. However, his parents learned to anticipate Carl's reactions, knew that if they were patient, presented only one or a few new situations at a time, and gave him the opportunity for repeated exposure, Carl would finally adapt positively. Furthermore, once he adapted, his intensity of responses gave him a zestful enthusiastic involvement, just as it gave his initial negative reactions a loud and stormy character. His parents became fully aware that the difficulties in raising Carl were due to his temperament and not to their being "bad parents." The father even looked on his son's shrieking and turmoil as a sign of "lustiness." As a result of this positive parent-child interaction, Carl never became a behavior problem.

In his later childhood and high school years Carl met very few radically new situations. He lived in the same community and went through the neighborhood school with the same schoolmates and friends. Academic progression was gradual and new subjects were not introduced abruptly. He had sufficient time to adapt to new demands, and typically became enthusiastically and successfully involved with a number of activities. As a result, he developed an appropriate positive and self-confident self-image. He played the piano and spoke with special animation of his pleasure in this activity. Carl was asked in the interview, "Do you remember what happened when you first started piano lessons?" He thought for a moment, and a startled expression came over his face. He described how he had asked his mother if he could take lessons and she said yes — but she insisted on one condition, that he stick to the lessons for six months, no matter how he felt, and then, if he wanted, he could give them up. He consented, started, began by "hating it," felt like quitting, but stuck to the bargain with his mother. Six months later she asked if he wanted to quit. His answer was, "Are you crazy? I love it!"

When Carl went off to college away from home, however, he was suddenly confronted with a whole series of new situations — a new and different community, strange living arrangements, an entirely new peer group, and new types of faculty approaches, school schedules, and curriculum. In addition, he had begun to live with a young woman student who was making heavy demands on him for time and attention. Sexually, though, there was no problem. In our judgment, Carl was, in his first college year, as in early childhood, faced with the demands for adaptation to a number of new situations simultaneously; these again elicited his temperamental responses of intense negative reactions and withdrawal. Other possible reasons for his difficulties were explored — dependency needs for his parents, sexual conflict, anxiety over academic demands, and peer competition — but there was no evidence for any of these alternative explanations.

Only the one discussion with Carl was necessary, and this consisted primarily in clarifying for him his temperamental pattern and the techniques he could use for adaptation. Actually, he had already begun to take these steps on his own — cutting the number of new subjects, disciplining himself to study each subject daily for a specific time, attenuating his relationship with the young woman, and making a point of attending peer group activities, no matter how uncomfortable he felt. By the end of the academic year his difficulties had disappeared and his overall functioning had returned to his previous positive level. He was told that similar negative reactions to radically new situations and experiences might occur in the future. His response was, "That's all right. I know how to handle them now."

Carl was seen again at age 22 years, for the regularly scheduled early adult interview. His self-image was positive, "Basically I'm happy with myself, I'd love to have great athletic abilities, but I realize my limitations and strengths."

He had switched colleges twice because of dissatisfaction with courses and indecision as to goals. He had finally settled on his career direction, did very well at his last college, has graduated, and has been accepted in the Ph.D. program at a major university. His daily routines were irregular, he described hir..self as outgoing and sociable, but "usually need time to warm up to a new friend." His sexual life was active, without any problems. His feelings "are pretty high-keyed," but he felt he could adapt quickly to a sudden change. He remembered his first semester at college as "low point of my life, felt my life was collapsing. I was in a new environment, all these pressures, didn't know how to handle them. I was on my own, couldn't go back to my parents. Grabbed at this girl, she was available, but she was crazy." He remembered the one discussion with one of us as very helpful, but only recalled the suggestion to limit his relationship with this girl. He has not felt the need for any psychiatric help since then.

This early adult interview showed Carl to be functioning again at a strongly positive level. His difficult temperamental characteristics were still somewhat in evidence, with biological irregularity, intense reactions, and slow adaptability to new colleges and friends, though he did say that he adapted quickly to "sudden change." His mood was predominantly positive, which reflected his current positive adaptations.

Thus, Carl's behavioral functioning was characterized by one pattern in early childhood, a markedly different one in middle childhood and early and middle adolescence, a dramatic change in late adolescence when he went away to college to a functional pattern similar to that of early childhood, and a further change in early adult life to the behavioral characteristics of his middle childhood and early adolescence. Should we interpret this sequence by giving primacy to the difficult functioning in early childhood, assigning some hypothetical cause to this, which then remained "buried in the unconscious," even if not manifest in middle childhood and early and middle adolescence, only to reassert its influence on Carl's overt behavior in later adolescence? But such an explanation requires a series of assumptions for which there is no evidence from the data. Nor does it explain the sequence of responses to learning to play the piano in middle childhood, unless one is prepared to make further speculative assumptions about some presumed symbolic meaning of the piano to Carl. Finally, there is the quick and complete recovery after one therapeutic session, a recovery which has been sustained into early adult life. Another series of assumptions to explain this latest sequence would be required to maintain the thesis of some primary influential psychological force "buried in the unconscious" since early childhood.

It is a much more parsimonious explanation, and one which fits Carl's anterospective longitudinal data, to interpret his behavior at any one age-period, or with any one specific activity, as the reflection of the organism-environment interactional process. Specifically, Carl's difficult temperamental pattern made for a potentially excessively stressful response to a demand for adaptation to a number of new situations or activities simultaneously or to a radically different new situation. This is what occurred in early childhood and in his first college year, and to a much lesser degree with his piano playing in middle childhood and with his shift to a different college. The actual manifestations of this excessive stress at any age-period were shaped by his behavioral repertoire and the responses of his parents and other influential individuals in his life. In his periods of positive and serene functioning, Carl still retained the *potential* for stressful responses. However, this was not due to some conflictual pattern derived from early life experiences and perpetuated in "the unconscious," but rather to the nature of his temperamental characteristics.

Overall, in the NYLS clinical sample, for those cases of behavior disorder originating in middle childhood or adolescence, review of the early childhood anterospective data in most cases did not reveal prodromal symptoms or pathogenic conflict and excessive stress in that earlier age-period. Thus, we question Freud's dictum, quoted above in this chapter, that "Neuroses are only acquired during early childhood (up to the age of six), even though their symptoms may not make their appearance until much later" (1949, p. 83).

As to the question of continuity of temperament, this issue has been considered by a number of other workers as well as ourselves (Thomas and Chess, 1980, pp. 124–127; Ciba Symposium, 1982). The data indicate that temperament, like other psychological characteristics, cannot be expected consistently to show linear continuity over time. The categorization of temperament in any individual is derived from the constellation of behaviors exhibited at any age. These behaviors are the result of all the influences, past and present, which shape and modify these behaviors in a constantly evolving interactional process. In most cases, consistency of a temperamental trait or constellation in an individual over time will require stability in these interactional forces, such as environmental influences, motivations, and abilities. In other instances, however, environmental stability may serve to change the character of a temperamental trait rather than enhance its continuity. This is especially true of the difficult and slow-to-warm-up temperamental patterns, in which the conspicuous responses of withdrawal, negative mood and slow adaptability are evident in new situations, i.e. with environmental change. With environmental stability, the absence or infrequent occurrence of new situations will result in minimal or absent withdrawal, negative mood and slow adaptability responses. The developmental course of Carl in middle childhood and early adolescence, detailed above, illustrates this sequence.

OTHER RESEARCH FINDINGS

The data from the NYLS indicate that simple linear continuity in psychological development from early childhood to later years cannot be expected and that our ability to make predictions about later personality from the early years is at best very limited. These conclusions have also been affirmed from a number of longitudinal studies—the type of study which is uniquely suited to examine the issue of continuity over time. Thus, in a review of the 30-year Berkeley study, MacFarlane noted that "many of our most mature and competent adults had severely troubled and confusing childhoods and adolescences. Many of our highly successful children and adolescents have failed to achieve their predicted potential. . . . We did have several small groups whose adult status fulfilled theoretical expectations" (MacFarlane, 1964, p. 124). From the Topeka study, Murphy and Moriarty (1976) reported that "the relations between earlier and later forms of experience and behavior are too complex to warrant our thinking of simple causal relations between what came first and what came later" (p. 150). And from the Harvard Grant study, Vaillant observed that "the life cycle is more than an invariant sequence of stages with simple predictable outcomes. The men's lives are full of surprises, and the Grant study provides no prediction tables" (Vaillant, 1977, p. 373).

Similar conclusions are reached in several comprehensive reviews of the developmental literature (Sameroff, 1975; Clarke and Clarke, 1976; Clarke, 1978; Brim and Kegan, 1980). And, as Clarke emphasizes, our very limited ability to make long-term predictions of individual development is not "an indictment of established paradigms and methods," as Bronson (1974, p. 276) and some others would have it. Rather, "no science can predict accurately qualities which have not yet made any appearance in the development of the pre-school child, . . . No science can predict those chance encounters, opportunities or calamities which 20 years ahead can act as strong determinants of stability or change" (Clarke, 1978, p. 255).

DEVELOPMENTAL STAGES

Much of development, at least in our society, proceeds in definite invariant stage sequences. With few exceptions, the infant sits first, then stands, and then walks. Mastery of language almost always proceeds from single simple words to phrases and then sentences. Motor skills, social behavior, and task mastery all evolve sequentially from lower to higher levels of competence. The seminal studies of Piaget have also provided solid data for conceptualizing a single scheme of sequential developmental stages for cognitive development.

It is tempting, therefore, to look for a similar pattern in personality development, in which one stage would follow another in some fixed sequence. Such invariance would introduce a basic structure of continuity and stability in the process of behavioral change from one age-period to another, provide a conceptual basis for prediction, and confirm the validity of the ever recurrent search for continuity in the developmental process from infancy to adulthood.

A number of developmental psychologists and psychiatrists have offered various schemes for conceptualizing behavioral development in terms of one or another system of invariant developmental stage sequences, starting with Freud's instinctual drive model of oral, anal and genital stages. The rejection of a theoretical framework for human development based on instinct theory, even by many psychoanalysts, has led to a number of modifications of the traditional Freudian model of stage sequence which have attempted to deal with its most blatant defects, without abandoning the basic psychoanalytic framework. The most influential revision has been that of Erikson (1950), who introduced a substantial social dimension into the traditional psychoanalytic formulation of stage sequences. In another direction, Kohlberg (1964) has proposed a scheme for invariant sequences in moral judgment, derived from Piagetian concepts.

These various models of invariant psychological developmental schemes, including Piaget's, have received critical evaluations from a number of sources for their inadequate attention to sociocultural factors, the narrowness and rigidity of their formulations, their methodological problems, and the questions raised as to their universality by the empirical data provided by an increasing number of studies (see Thomas and Chess, 1980, pp. 128–131 for a summary of some of these critiques; also Gilligan (1982) for additional comments on Kohlberg's model).

In our own studies of the origin and evolution of behavior disorders in the NYLS sample, we have not found the concept of invariant stage sequences useful. So much developmental variability existed from one subject to another, so much difference in the nature of change from one age-period to another was evident, so much was the process of individual-environment interaction influenced by adventitious and idiosyncratic factors, that any attempt to impose an a priori scheme of developmental stages appeared not only futile but clearly invalid. Flavell's comment regarding cognitive development applied even more definitely to the behavior development of the NYLS group, as "tortuous and spiral-like, cyclical and recursive, sequence-violating and sequence-transforming" (Flavell, 1972, p. 343).

CONCLUSIONS

Certain fundamental theses are impressively documented in the developmental research literature (Brim and Kagen, 1980) and confirmed by our own NYLS data. Development is characterized by both change and continuity, and one cannot occur without the other. Development necessarily proceeds from the simpler to the more complex, and sequential stages can often be identified in this process. But such sequential stages are the categorization of group trends for specific populations with specific sociocultural backgrounds. Individual variability between and within groups is significant and widespread, and the search for invariant linear developmental stage sequences which are valid for all individuals is bound to be futile.

Developmental research can concern itself with the identification of patterns of change *and* continuity, as they coexist, as they interact dynamically at the same age-period, and sequentially, as their manifestations are similar or different between individuals and between groups, and as change turns into continuity, and continuity into change. From such studies we can hope to elucidate progressively the general laws that govern development, rather than be imprisoned in the blind alley search for linear continuity and invariant stage sequences.

A LIFE-SPAN PERSPECTIVE

An alternative to the conceptualization of developmental stages as universal and invariant in their sequences is provided by the formulations of life-span developmental psychology. This theoretical orientation, while its roots extend back many decades, has only begun to receive substantial attention in the past decade. As of now, the life-span perspective represents a major and rapidly increasing influence in developmental psychology.

As formulated by Baltes and his associates (1980), the first assumption of a life-span perspective is that development is a lifelong process. "The orientation in terms of growth and maturation is to assume a certain state of maturity (usually attained in early adulthood) as the end state of a developmental change process. Subsequent change, as a corollary, is often seen as decline or aging rather than development. . . . In the life-span orientation, no special state of maturity is assumed as a general principle, and therefore

development is seen as a life-long process" (p. 70). Thus every age-period is
an active one developmentally, and middle childhood should not be viewed
as a "latency period," (Thomas and Chess, 1972) and older age should not
be labelled as a "period of decline" (Schaie and Gribbin, 1975).

The life-span perspective also emphasizes a pluralistic concept of development. "Developmental change can take many forms in terms of onset, duration, termination, and directionality. Behavior-change processes associated
with life-span development do not always extend across the entire life-span;
novel behavior change processes can emerge at many points in the life course
including old age" (Baltes et al., 1980, p. 74). Baltes and his associates suggest a developmental model identifying three sets of influences and constituting
a useful paradigm in the search for causal relationships and determinants.
A first set, *normative age-graded influences*, are defined as "biological and
environmental determinants that have (in terms of onset and duration) a fairly
strong relationship with chronological age. . . . Age-graded events are normative if they tend to occur in highly similar ways (timing, duration) for all individuals in a given culture or subculture" (p. 75). Examples are biological
maturation and age-graded socialization events, and it is this type of influence which has been emphasized in most concepts of healthy and pathological
development.

It should be pointed out that even these normative age-graded influences
are not fixed and invariant in their nature and timing for all groups in a given
culture. For example, the demand in our culture that individuals assume economic and psychological responsibility for their lives comes at an earlier age
and with a different emphasis in working-class families than it does for the
NYLS subjects. For this latter group, college and even graduate school attendance are welcomed and supported by parents, who, with few exceptions,
are able to assume this financial burden. Even those subjects who did not attend or dropped out of college did so with the justification that they were
"finding themselves" and "experimenting" with life, and they knew their
parents would back them if they decided to return to school. For such a group,
the assumption of personal responsibility comes later and evolves differently than in working-class families. Similarly, this same issue undoubtedly takes
a different form and content in the sons and daughters of upper-class families.

A second set, *normative history-graded (evolutionary) influences*, "are
defined as biological and environmental determinants associated with historical time and historical contexts related to cohorts" (p. 75). Relevant to
this set of determinants is the shaping of symptoms and specific areas of demands on the child for adaptation by parental and community sociocultural
values and expectations, as discussed in Chapter 18 above. As another ex-

ample, our NYLS subjects, who in early adult life were hopeful of an academic career, face uncertainty and doubts about their future because of the current stringencies in academic budgets which would have been absent 25 years ago.

The third set of influences, *"non-normative life events,"* refers to "biological and environmental determinants that do not occur in any normative age-graded or history-graded manner for most individuals" (p. 76). These are the influences that we have categorized as idiosyncratic and unpredictable, as in the histories of Bernice, Nelson, and Nancy (Chapter 17).

Baltes and his associates suggest that development results from the continual interaction of these three sets of influences, as "mediated through the developing individual." This "mediation," which the authors do not spell out, involves the complex structure of intrapsychic factors, such as motivations, goals, value system, temperament, abilities, and defense mechanisms. They further propose that "life-long development involves the mastery of successive tasks in a series of contexts. The dialectical conception suggests that tasks and contexts derive from the interplay between age-graded, history-graded, and non-normative influences and events" (pp. 80–81).

The emphasis in the life-span perspective on the issue of context has been elaborated in a review article by Lerner, Hultsch and Dixon (in press). In this approach, the influence of context is not seen as a unidirectional environmental factor. Rather, in their words, "just as the context changes the individual, the individual changes the context." Moreover, "the context is seen as a multi-level one—having interrelated biological, sociocultural, physical environmental, and historical components" (Lerner et al., in press).

We ourselves have always considered a contextual viewpoint as essential. As detailed in Chapter 3, our data-gathering procedures in the NYLS, as well as in other longitudinal studies, have included from the beginning the requirement that the subject's behavior should be linked to the environmental context at all times. This included not only a description of the initial context in which the behavior occurred, but how the parent, teacher, other active participant, or the subject himself, reacted to the behavior, how this reaction then affected the subject's behavior, what effect this then had on the parent or other participant, and so on until a stable response pattern was established.

The significance of context is illustrated in the case of Carl, detailed above in this chapter. Without the identification of the changes in context which, in interaction with his temperamental characteristics, produced his remarkable sequential behavioral changes, it would have been impossible to understand what was happening, let alone enlighten and advise Carl.

Baltes and his associates point out that the life-span movement up to now has been carried primarily by researchers interested in adulthood and old age rather than in childhood and adolescence. "We believe that a more vigorous concern of life-span researchers with issues of infancy and childhood will be important as life-course bridges and substantive theories are built. There can be no satisfactory life-span developmental psychology without a strong foundation in infancy and childhood. Equally, there can be no comprehensive theory of child development without statements about the role of child development in the life span" (Baltes et al., 1980, p. 101). We would add that these caveats apply as much to the fields of developmental psychiatry and psychopathology as they do to life-span developmental psychology.

CHAPTER 22

The Goodness of Fit Model: Theoretical and Practical Implications

Research findings of recent years have documented the necessity for theoretical approaches and models which take into account multiple mutually interacting factors which influence the course of individual psychological development. With this trend, the inadequacy of formulations that are unidimensional and that view behavior as the exclusive result of one or another narrow set of determinants becomes more and more evident.

These findings have brought to the forefront of current theory in developmental psychology and psychiatry a number of related conceptualizations, including the interactional model (Thomas and Chess, 1980, Ch. 7), the transactional model (Sameroff, 1975), the life-span developmental perspective (Baltes et al., 1980), the biopsychosocial model (Engel, 1977), and systems theory (Marmor, 1983). These various formulations, though they may differ in their specific emphases and terminologies, all agree on the need for interacting multidimensional approaches to the study of both normal and pathological psychological development. A leading developmental psychologist has summed up the issue nicely, noting that recent research gives us a view of "the person as so complex and multifaceted as to defy easy classification and comparisons on any single or simple common dimension, as multiply influenced by a host of interacting determinants, as uniquely organized on the basis of prior experiences and future experiences, and yet as rule-guided in systematic, potentially comprehensible ways that are open to study by the methods of science. It is an image that has moved a long way from the instinctual drive-reduction models, the static global traits, and the automatic stimulus-response bonds of traditional personality theories. It is an image that highlights the shortcomings of all simplistic theories that view behavior as the exclusive result of any narrow set of determinants, whether these are habits, traits, drives, reinforcers, constructs, instincts, or genes, and whether they are exclusively inside or outside the person" (Mischel, 1977, p. 253).

THE NEXT STEP

The various interactional multidimensional conceptualizations have provided guidelines for developmental research and formulations regarding the nature and dynamics of the life course from infancy through childhood and adolescence into adult life and extending to old age. But by themselves they constitute primarily *approaches* rather than comprehensive conceptualizations of the processes of development or strategies for analyzing the specific content and dynamic interplay of the relevant multidimensional factors in specific individuals. The comment of Baltes and his associates that "life-span developmental psychology is not a particular theory but an orientation to the study of behavioral development" (Baltes et al., 1980, p. 69) applies to systems theory and the interactional, transactional, and biopsychosocial models as well. The orientation is of crucial importance, but does not tell us: how to identify the variables that are functionally significant at a particular age-period in a specific individual; what determines the outcome of the interaction among these variables so that either healthy or pathological development is promoted; how stress and excessive stress are generated and resolved; how anxiety and defense mechanisms are produced and evolve; and how the consequences of any individual's behavioral characteristics and functioning affect his adaptive capacities and defensive strategies at subsequent age-periods.

Thus, Marmor (1983) has enumerated the types of variables that have to be considered in the systems approach to the study of personality: faulty parenting; temperament; the diverse personality patterns and culturally acquired value systems and expectations of the parents; economic, racial and ethnic realities; dietary adequacy or inadequacy; the nature of relationships with sibs, extended family members, peers, teachers, and other influential individuals, and concludes, "We begin to get a glimpse of how difficult it is to accurately trace the origins of specific personality patterns at all, let alone to try to derive them from just one or two variables" (p. 856). In a similar vein, Rutter (1980) emphasizes that interactionist views indicate that, "It is difficult to make valid, broad, sweeping generalizations about human behavior. Attention must be paid to the specificities of person-situation interactions . . . it may be suggested that it is preferable to take an idiographic approach which explicitly focuses on the individuality of human beings — not just in the degree to which they show particular traits or even in terms of the traits which are relevant to them, but more generally in terms of the idiosyncracies which make each person uniquely different from all others" (p. 5).

THE GOODNESS OF FIT MODEL

We suggest that the goodness of fit model provides a most useful conceptual framework and analytic strategy for the "idiographic approach which explicitly focuses on the individuality of human beings" that Rutter recommends (1980, p. 5). We have defined this model in Chapter 2, and have utilized it in the individual subject and clinical case studies in subsequent chapters. This goodness of fit conceptualization has provided an effective framework within which to identify the specific dynamics of the organism-environment process responsible for the development of a behavior disorder in each individual case, and to trace the evolution of the disorder over time without recourse to speculative, untestable formulations (such as conflict over the repression of presumed instinctual drives), or to simplistic unidimensional explanations (such as the pathogenic consequences of maladaptive conditioned reflexes).

Poorness of fit between an individual's characteristics and capacities and the demands and expectations of the environment which leads to a pathological developmental course can arise in a number of different ways, can involve different psychological and environmental factors in different individuals, and can express itself in different interactional processes and sequences in specific cases. The identification of the pattern of poorness of fit in any single instance of behavior disorder therefore requires a multifactorial and multidimensional approach, in which theoretically relevant biological, psychological, and social influences, as well as their mutually interactional effects on each other, are identified and considered as to their functional significance in that specific case.

This does not mean that all the potentially significant etiological factors will be actively involved in every case. Quite the contrary. In one individual, one particular characteristic and one particular environmental demand may be the prime interactional determinants in the development of a behavior disorder, while in another case the significant pathogenic factors may be different, and in a third instance may differ again, and so on. Thus, in the case of Olga (Chapter 14), it was the combination of her difficult temperament and her father's critical attitude and excessive demands, coupled with her mother's inconsistent approach, that was pathogenic. In Norman's case

(Chapter 14) it was his marked distractibility and low persistence, along with his father's highly derogatory judgments of these characteristics, which were primarily responsible for the behavior disorder development. For Bert (Chapter 15) it was the behavioral consequences of his brain damage and the negative excessively stressful reactions to these characteristics by parents and peers which produced the poorness of fit, while in Kevin's case (Chapter 15) it was the unrealistic academic and social expectations of his parents, so inappropriate for an intellectually retarded youngster, that were pathogenic.

In some instances, the biopsychological deviation may be so extreme as to constitute the prime determinant of a pathological developmental course, though environmental influences may play a part in exacerbating or mitigating the symptomatology. This is illustrated by our two cases of recurrent major depression, Harold and Sylvia (Chapter 14), and would also be true for certain other conditions, such as infantile autism, schizophrenia, severe brain damage, and attentional deficit disorder.

At the other extreme are those situations in which special environmental stresses may be the prime pathogenic factors, though the characteristics of the individual may influence the nature of the specific symptoms and their severity. Extraordinary stress created by a special environmental event may be sufficient to produce even severe and protracted behavioral disturbances in most, if not all, individuals subjected to such an event. Thus, Terr (1981) has reported on the effects of the Chowchilla, California, kidnapping, in which 26 children were buried in their school bus in a hole for 16 hours. Terr interviewed 23 of the children and at least one parent six to twelve months after the event. She found that every child still showed signs of the emotional effects of this frightful experience, with varied symptoms, which in some cases were quite severe. Similarly, Erikson (1976) made a study of the psychological consequences of a sudden, terrible flood that tore through the coal mining villages in a narrow mountain hollow in Appalachia called Buffalo Creek and killed over one hundred people. He found evidences of symptoms typical of traumatic neurosis of varying severity in almost all the surviving children and adults two years after the catastrophe. He emphasized that recovery from the initial shock, anxiety, and demoralization at the destruction of the survivors' closely-knit community did not occur because the relief measures undertaken by a number of agencies were insensitive to the primary need to restore a sense of community and community support. Erikson makes a significant challenge to conventional psychiatric theory. "It is a standard article of psychiatric wisdom that the symptoms of trauma ought to disappear over a period of time, and when they do not, a peculiar strain of logic is likely to follow. If one has not recovered from the effects of trauma within a reasonable span of time, so the theory goes, then it follows that the symptoms themselves must have been the result of a mental disorder predating the event itself" (1976, p. 184). But such reasoning, as Erikson points out, would require the assumption that virtually all the people of Buffalo Creek were suffering from significant degrees of psychological disorder before the flood struck.

On a less dramatic level, in the NYLS sample, there is the case of Bernice (Chapter 12). Her severe adolescent disorder would not have escalated had her father not died suddenly at that time and left her mother overburdened and even overwhelmed at times with the sole responsibility for her four children. However, it is also true in this instance that this traumatic event and its consequences would not have been pathogenic were it not for Bernice's temperamental characteristics.

It should be emphasized that goodness or poorness of fit cannot be rated in the abstract, but only within the social context in which the individual is functioning. This issue is exemplified by the difference in the effect of the temperamental characteristic of high activity level (as distinguished from pathological hyperactivity) in the NYLS youngsters as contrasted to the children in the Puerto Rican working-class sample, a difference due to the presence or absence of environmental limitations on physical activity (see Chapter 18 for details).

It is of interest that the goodness of fit concept has been utilized by a number of other investigators of normal versus pathological child development, even though they may not use the term itself or apply the concept systematically. Thus, Murphy (1981), in discussing the data of the Topeka Longitudinal Study, speaks of "interesting examples of misfit and fit between mothers and babies. . . . Mrs.Rogers was an energetic, intelligent, devoted mother who did well with her energetic, active baby, Malcolm; but with the next baby, Vernon, who was extremely sensitive and not as responsive, the fit was not as good. Tommy's mother, by contrast, was a sensitive little lady who was not up to the demands of her very vigorous, lively, energetic baby" (p. 168). And Greenspan (1981), reporting on the findings of the NIMH clinical research study of high-risk infants and their families, comments that "the clinician must recognize the unique way a particular infant, or phase of infant development, contributes to maladaptive parental patterns. . . . Similarly, the family or extended family may reveal characteristic group patterns that undermine optimal attachment" (p. 63). He also emphasizes that "some parents who are flexible enough to respond adequately to an engaging youngster will be overwhelmed and disorganized by a youngster who is not able to engage them effectively" (p. 204).

If the influences on psychological development are multifactorial and multidimensional, and if the functionally significant factors and dimensions can vary from one individual to another, does this mean that it is not possible to formulate general principles of the developmental process that may have universal applicability? Not at all. As Rutter (1980) suggests, the apparent dichotomy between the individual case (idiographic) and the general (nomothetic) approach is in many respects a false one. "Perhaps, . . . the answer lies in attempting to derive nomothetic principles which apply to the idiographic circumstances of person-situation interactions" (p. 5). In this respect, useful analogy can be drawn with the combined nomothetic-idiographic approach in physical medicine. When faced with a case of disturbed functioning of the circulatory, respiratory, or other bodily system, the clinician knows that many possible etiological factors may be involved, and his task is to identify which of these, and in which dynamic interactional pattern, are responsible for the pathological functioning and symptomatology in that particular individual. But in so doing, the clinician must draw on his knowledge of how the general principles may apply to the specific factors that appear influential in the particular individual. It is the development of such a combined nomothetic-idiographic approach which is a basic task for developmental psychology and psychiatry, and this issue will be considered further in the next chapter.

Goodness or poorness of fit are rarely global. At any age-period for any individual, certain environmental demands and expectations may be consonant with his or her capacities and coping mechanisms, while others may be dissonant. These consonances or dissonances may even shift at succeeding age-periods, as the individual's capacities, characteristics and motivations change, and as environmental demands and expectations are altered.Such a shift from poorness to goodness of fit because of a change in the individual's characteristics is highlighted in the case of Nancy, wherein the emergence of musical and dramatic talent evoked a qualitative change in parental attitudes and expectations which led to the disappearance of her behavior disorder. A similar direction of change was produced in Bernice (Chapter 12), with the drastic alteration in environmental demands that occurred when her mother forced her to assume a fully independent and responsible position at 18 years. With this, Bernice's motivational system changed, she mobilized her talents and interests, became self-supporting and self-reliant, and launched herself on her own merits on a career which absorbed her.

If the goodness of fit model is to be useful, it must avoid the danger of circular reasoning that has bedevilled so many psychological theories. In other words, it would be very easy to explain adaptive versus maladaptive functioning as due to goodness versus poorness of fit, and then "prove" the type of fit by the type of functioning. *Independent* criteria by which goodness or poorness of fit can be determined must be established for the many factors which are involved in shaping the course of psychological development. In this regard, it is not sufficient to identify high-risk or low-risk influences, as valuable as such studies can be for other reasons. What is also required is the identification of those conditions under which such factors contribute to either a goodness or a poorness of fit, and to healthy or pathological development.

The necessity for such an approach is emphasized by the evidence that high-risk genetic characteristics (Eisenberg, 1977), early-life psychological traumata (Clarke and Clarke, 1976), and the experience of racism and poverty (Thomas and Sillen, 1972) may vary greatly and even qualitatively in their consequences from one individual to another. Approaches to the identification of the factors which can affect the influence of high-risk and low-risk characteristics have already been explored, among others, in studies of temperament (Thomas, Chess and Birch, 1968; Thomas and Chess, 1977), of mildly retarded youngsters in the community (Chess, 1980), of deaf children (Chess et al., 1980), and of differential school experiences (Rutter, et al., 1979). Such studies provide examples of the interactional-contextual research designs which can provide appropriate data for the goodness of fit model.

We have also found the goodness of fit model to be useful in the study of the origin and evolution of several significant factors in normal and pathological psychological development: self-esteem, anxiety, and defense mechanisms.

SELF-ESTEEM AND GOODNESS OF FIT

There is general agreement among researchers and clinicians as to the vital importance of self-esteem in personality development and psychological functioning, though formulations as to the definition, origin, and evolution of positive or negative self-esteem vary greatly. A good working definition of what he calls "an optimal sense of identity" is provided by Erikson, as "a feeling of being at home in one's body, a sense of 'knowing where one is going,' and an inner assuredness of anticipated recognition from those who count" (1968, p. 165). Erikson also emphasizes, as do others (Lidz, 1968, p. 267), the social context as a basic influence in the origin and development of self-esteem. "The growing child must, at every step, derive a vitalizing sense of reality from the awareness that his individual way of mastering experience is in accord with its space-time and life plan" (1950, p. 208).

This formulation of Erikson, in which positive self-esteem develops from the child's sequential successes in "mastering experience," is congenial with the concept of social competence and task mastery as primary adaptive goals (see Chapter 2). The other factor emphasized by Erikson is that the child's "individual way of mastering experience is a successful variant of a group experience" and also represents "achievement that has meaning in the culture" (1950, p. 208). This indicates that the child needs to learn what are the significant behavioral and ideational feedbacks from parents, other family members, teachers, and peers, in order to "recognize achievement that has meaning in the culture."

We would postulate, therefore, that the development of positive self-esteem or, in Erikson's phrase, "an optimal sense of identity" depends on sequential successful experiences in social competence and task mastery, combined with adequate opportunities for learning the significant values of the culture and with appropriate feedback from influential others as to successful achievement and realistic guides to the correction of failures. Unfavorable experiences with social functioning and task mastery, together with confusing, contradictory, and inappropriate environmental feedback, will, on the other hand, foster the development of negative self-esteem. This positive or negative self-esteem, as it crystallizes subjectively and ideationally in the growing child, is thus, on the one hand, the outcome of the child's life experiences. At the same time, the nature of the child's self-esteem and sense of identity then become highly influential in shaping the character of his or her goals and behavior, so that successive life experiences usually serve to reinforce the youngster's positive or negative self-esteem. This dialectic of cause and effect was dramatically evident in the cases of Carl (Chapter 21), Norman (Chapter 14), and Richard (Chapter 14). Carl, though of markedly difficult temperament, had consistent successful experiences with social functioning and task mastery throughout childhood and adolescence, with clear-cut and reasonable parental standards which were consonant with those of his peer group, and positive feedback from parents, teachers, and peers for his "individual way of mastering experience" (to use Erikson's phrase). When he then encountered difficulties in his first year away from home at college, he could not reconcile this with his positive self-esteem. In recounting his problems to us, he kept exclaiming, "This isn't me!" With this attitude, he had already begun to take appropriate steps on his own to master the series of new demands which had temporarily overwhelmed him, even before consulting us.

By contrast, Norman was bombarded, as he grew up, by unrealistic demands and criticisms by his father, who could not accept the judgment that his son's high distractibility and low persistence were normal characteristics. Even when Norman was accepted into a prestigious private school with high standards on the basis of his performance on their entrance examination, his father considered the school's decision to place him in the same grade he had just completed in public school as a demotion and a failure. Actually, this was a promotion, as this private school was a year advanced compared to the public school, and Norman had started school almost a year ahead of the usual age. However, the father transformed what should have been a successful achievement into its opposite and the boy refused to transfer to the new school. Unfortunately for Norman, as this incident illustrates, his father's judgments carried the greatest influence and outweighed the positive feedbacks he received from teachers and peers. By early adolescence, Norman had developed a markedly negative self-image and depressed mood, saying to us, "My father loves me. I guess he has to, since I'm his son. But he doesn't respect me. Let's face it, why should he?" With such a self-image, his functioning became increasingly inadequate, with quick drop-outs from two colleges, and inability to hold a job for any consistent period of time. His father's judgments turned out, sadly but inevitably, to be a self-fulfilling prophecy.

Richard (Chapter 14), in contrast to Norman, did receive positive feedback from his parents, but his experience with teachers and peers was quite different. His severe tantrums, triggered by some abrupt termination of an ongoing activity in which, with his extreme temperamental persistence, he was deeply absorbed, brought him violent disapproval and punishment by teachers and ridicule from his peers. By age 10 years these repeated experiences had crystallized into a seriously negative self-image, with his statement to us, "I know you like me, but there's something inside me that blows up every once in a while, and I don't want to talk about it." This derogatory and hopeless self-evaluation was confirmed to him by further episodes in which his persistent efforts backfired, and prevented any effective positive counterinfluence from his many successful experiences. As a result, when interviewed at age 22, he was clinically depressed, self-derogatory, and pessimistic about his future.

For the achievement of positive self-esteem, the importance of the fact that the child's "individual way of mastering experience is a successful variant of a group experience," to use Erikson's formulation, is highlighted by the four cases of behavior disorders in youngsters with easy temperament (see Chapter 16). In all four cases, the parents imposed a set of idiosyncratic standards and rules of behavior which the child accepted quickly and learned easily. But then the idiosyncratic pattern proved maladaptive with peers or school, or both, with unfavorable consequences for psychological functioning and self-esteem. In these instances the child's "individual way of mastering experience," while successful within the family, did not prove to be "a successful variant of a group experience."

A different special factor which influenced decisively the development of a negative self-image was seen in the case of Sylvia (Chapter 14). Outwardly, her progress through childhood and adolescence was smooth and successful, with positive feedback from parents, teachers, and peers. However, at about age 12, she suffered the first of a series of recurrent major depressions, most likely of endogenous origin. With this depression, and with each recurrent episode, she responded with feelings of unworthiness and self-depreciation, along with a sense of impending failure in her life activities. This extreme self-derogation occurred in spite of all evidence of successful social and academic functioning, and in the absence of any special environmental stresses. It thus appears that a biologically induced affective disorder, and undoubtedly other types of organic brain dysfunction as well, can by itself induce the development of negative self-esteem.

This formulation, which views the type of self-esteem as arising out of the specific individual patterns of social competence, task performance, and environmental feedback (with the exception of organic mental disorders noted just above), is fully consistent with the goodness of fit developmental model. As such, no speculative, untestable concepts as to presumed instinctual drive frustration of intrapsychic conflict in the young infant are required to identify the factors responsible for the origin and evaluation of a negative self-image in any individual youngster. It is rather the poorness of fit between the child's capacities and characteristics and the demands and expectations of the environment which impair social competence and task mastery and create negative environmental feedback, leading to negative self-esteem. The many different ways in which such a poorness of fit can develop have been indicated in the various case vignettes in this and previous chapters.

ANXIETY, DEFENSE MECHANISMS, AND GOODNESS OF FIT

Common to a number of influential theories on the ontogenesis of behavior disorders is an emphasis on the primary role of anxiety (Freud, 1949; Dollard and Miller, 1950; Sullivan, 1953; Wolpe, 1958). Although anxiety may be defined differently, the various theories agree in the main in viewing symptoms as a technique for the reduction of anxiety and for the insulation of the individual from it.

The NYLS anterospective longitudinal data have made it possible for us to determine the time relationship between anxiety and symptom formation. Our data do not support the view of the role of anxiety as primary. In each clinical case, a parsimonious formulation based on the goodness of fit model, in terms of objective and overtly evident characteristics of the child, patterns of parental functioning, and other specific environmental influences, has been sufficient to account for the genesis of the problem behavior. Where anxiety has evolved in the course of the development of the behavior disorder, it has been a secondary phenomenon, a consequence rather than a cause of symptom formation and expression. In addition, the removal of symptoms by a successful parent guidance procedure has had positive consequences for the child's functioning and has not resulted in the appearance of overt anxiety or new substitute symptoms.

It is, of course, true that once anxiety appeared it did affect significantly and often profoundly the subsequent course of the psychological problem and the modification and elaboration of symptoms.

A major contribution of the psychoanalytic movement to developmental theory has been the identification and analysis of psychodynamic defense mechanisms. These defensive strategies often play a significant role in both normal and deviant psychological development. However, to accept the validity and usefulness of the concept of defense mechanisms does not require a simultaneous acceptance of the psychoanalytic theoretical assumptions regarding the conflict between primitive asocial instinctual impulses and the repressing forces of socialization, which then require one or another defensive strategy for the resolution of the conflict. Thus, we do not have to accept Freud's explanation for the use of the defense mechanism of reaction formation: "The multifariously perverse sexual dispositions of childhood can accordingly be regarded as the source of a number of our virtues, insofar as through reaction-formation it stimulates their development" (1964, pp. 238–239; originally published 1905).

Operationally, defense mechanisms can be defined as behavioral strategies with which individuals attempt to cope with stress or conflict which they cannot or will not master directly. This definition does not assume any a priori theoretical formulations of the ontogenesis of stress and conflict.

Similarly, specific defense mechanisms can also be defined operationally and identified by simple inference from empirical data, again without commitment to any one theoretical scheme. For example, *reaction formation* can be defined as the attempt to cope by transforming the motivation and goal into its opposite; *denial* can be defined as the posture that the stressful environmental demands or other apparently threatening aspects of reality are really insignificant and undeserving of attention; *rationalization* can be defined as the ascription of a socially acceptable motive to behavior which has other motivations, etc. (Thomas and Chess, 1980, p. 170).

Defense mechanisms may play very different roles in different individuals and in the same individual at different times or different situations. As with

all factors that influence psychological functioning, defense mechanisms always operate as one element in the sequential interactional process that determines the course of development.

This variability of defense mechanisms in importance, continuity, and consistency has been strikingly evident in the life-course of the NYLS subjects.
Thus far, a substantial number have a consistent life history of successful direct task mastery and growth in social competence at every age-period. At
no time did symptoms of behavior disorder appear and at no time have these
youngsters resorted to any defensive strategies. In some of this group, family relationships were benign and without significant stress or conflict. In
others, however, substantial, and in some cases serious, parental discord or
pressures were prominent. The youngsters were caught up in the resulting
stress and conflict, but had the ability to face the issues directly and openly—
without defensive strategies (Kathy, Chapter 12; Barbara, Chapter 13).

At the other extreme is the group with severe behavior disorders in which
various defense mechanisms were utilized. Examples are Norman (Chapter
14), with his defensive hopelessness in adolescence and his extreme denial in
early adult life; Sylvia (Chapter 14) with her denial and projection; Bert
(Chapter 15) with his sublimation through socially constructive activities and
his denial of any psychological problems; and Bernice (Chapter 12) with her
denial and projection. In these cases, the defense mechanisms served to alleviate stress and symptoms temporarily. However, they also intensified the difficulties in coping directly with environmental demands; in the long run they
became counterproductive.

It is, however, not always possible to decide whether a new pattern of behavioral functioning which serves to alleviate psychopathological symptoms
represents a defense mechanism or a successful strategy of direct mastery.
A striking example is Olga (Chapter 14) whose sudden religious conversion
experience at 16 years was followed by dramatic improvement in her severe
behavior disorder. Was this experience an expression of a defensive strategy
of sublimation or did it provide Olga a basis for new goals and patterns of
healthy adaptive coping, which led to mastery of the life situations and environmental expectations which previously were threatening and overwhelming? Her future developmental course should provide the answer to this question.

The use of defense mechanisms is not always maladaptive and unhealthy.
An individual may at one time or another be faced with excessively stressful
demands or conflicts which cannot be mastered directly. This may evoke the
temporary utilization of a defensive strategy, which then gives the person the
opportunity to resolve the stress positively. "In these situations it would appear that the use of the defense mechanism is necessary to organize the

strengths and capacities needed for successful mastery" (Chess and Thomas, 1976, p. 520). For example, a number of the NYLS subjects in the early adult-life interview rationalized their lack of definite life-goals and their dropping out of college as necessary for them "to find myself," or "to establish my self-identity," concepts which were rather fashionable in their social peer group at the time. In some cases, this defense mechanism appeared to be maladaptive and to be reflecting and contributing to the subject's overall difficulties in functioning. In others, however, there was no evidence of psychopathology and the confusion over life-goals appeared to reflect a temporary period of indecision and conflict over contradictory values and goals. In some of these individuals, it was our judgment that the socially acceptable rationalization would give them a breathing spell to resolve their conflicts on their own, and to define and then pursue a constructive life-course.

As is clear from the above discussion, we have utilized the goodness of fit model to explain the need for the elaboration of defense mechanisms in specific subjects in the NYLS. Where goodness of fit was present and direct mastery of environmental demands and expectations was achieved, there was no need for the youngster to develop one or another defense mechanism. Where, on the contrary, a poorness of fit existed, the need for one or more defense mechanisms, whether useful or counterproductive, did arise. As with the issue of the origins and evaluation of self-esteem, this goodness of fit approach to the explanation of the significance of defense mechanisms avoids such speculative, untestable concepts as presumed instinctual drive frustration or intrapsychic conflict in the young infant.

PRACTICAL IMPLICATIONS

The goodness of fit model has a number of practical applications for clinicians and educators; several have been indicated in previous chapters. The most direct and extensive application is in the treatment strategy of parent guidance, which is discussed in detail in Chapter 19.

A number of pediatricians (Carey, 1982) have found this approach useful in counseling parents for well-baby care. The evaluation of the child's temperament and other significant characteristics enables the pediatrician to advise the parents as to the specific child-care practices which will be most desirable for their particular youngster.

Nursery school teachers can also profit by the identification of those characteristics which may make for stress and difficulty in a child's adjustment to this new situation and life experience, and modify their usual approach as needed.

In the classroom, poorness of fit may arise in a number of ways (Chess,

Thomas and Cameron, 1976). High activity children may suffer if required to sit still for long periods of time. Distractible, low persistence youngsters may be unable to learn profitably if they are expected to concentrate at length, as easy as this may be for other youngsters. Slow-to-warm-up children may perform below par in the initial weeks of the school year, and incorrect and undesirable judgments with unfavorable consequences may be made by teachers. As Keogh (1982) has put it, "UCLA research on temperament and teachability suggests that individual differences in children's temperament are important contributors to children's success at school. . . . These variations in patterns are clear contributors to teachers' views of pupils' teachability, to the estimates they make of pupils' abilities, and to the kinds of expectations they have for pupils' educational performance. Recognition of the stylistic differences in children's behavior is important for teachers as these variations are the basis of many instructional and management decisions" (pp. 277–278).

These practical implications of the goodness of fit model have not yet been developed systematically for the adolescent and adult years, as they have been for the childhood period. It is our impression that the model should be useful for these later age-periods, as well as for childhood, and that research in this direction within the life-span perspective would be profitable.

We have had many discussions, conferences, and seminars with parents, clinicians and teachers, in this country and in a number of other countries, in which we have elaborated on the goodness of fit concept and its practical application. Uniformly, we have found our audiences not only to be receptive to the general approach, but able to apply it immediately to their experiences and observations with various children under their care.

CHAPTER 23

Overview:
What We Know;
What We Don't Know

Our analyses of the origins and evolution of behavior disorders in the NYLS subjects have served to confirm and amplify several theoretical formulations in developmental psychology and psychiatry. The analyses have also identified several high-risk behavioral and environmental factors, as well as particular variables that appeared influential in shaping a favorable outcome in cases of behavior disorders in children and adolescence.

INTERACTIONISM AND THE ACTIVE ROLE OF THE CHILD

From the beginning of our own research activities, over 25 years ago, our theoretical constructs have included the concepts that the child is an active agent from the moment of birth in the organism-environment interactional process; that temperamental individuality is a functionally significant influence in development at all age-periods; and that a dynamic interactionist (or transactional) model is required. While we were by no means the first to formulate or to emphasize these ideas, they did run counter to the dominant one-sided environmentalist views and drive-reduction and stimulus-response models of the 1950s. These concepts have now entered the mainstream of developmental theory in psychology and psychiatry, thanks to the cumulative effect of the research data and formulations contributed by workers in the biological sciences, in child and developmental psychology, in social psychology, and in clinical and research psychiatry.

The case vignettes reported in the various chapters of this volume highlight the diversity of significant child and environmental pathogenic factors and the differences in their interactional patterns over time. Only an interactional model can do justice to this variability in pathogenesis. Any attempt to fit this diversity in pathological developmental course (or, for that matter healthy development) within a unidimensional theoretical framework, or one which gives prime importance to any one age-period, would indeed require a theoretical Procrustean bed.

THE GOODNESS OF FIT MODEL

As emphasized in the previous chapter, we have found the goodness of fit model to be a most useful conceptual framework within which to trace the vicissitudes of individual psychological development from infancy to early adult life. This model has also served to organize and implement strategies of treatment, especially for parent guidance (Chapter 19). In this regard, it is our impression that the analysis of multidimensional, multifactorial behavioral data within an interactional framework calls for one or another type of goodness of fit model, whether or not the term itself is used (Greenspan, 1981; Murphy, 1981).

The goodness of fit model can be compared to that of natural selection in evolutionary theory. The concept of natural selection formulates a mechanism for biological change in plant and animal species. It does not specify only one or two or three ways in which favorable or unfavorable adaptation to the environment can occur, but includes the possibility of multiple, varied and unpredictable (but nevertheless determined) types of species-environment interaction that can be adaptive or maladaptive. Similarly, the goodness of fit concept does not specify that any one pattern of individual-environment interaction is required for favorable psychological development to occur. As with natural selection, goodness or poorness of fit includes the possibility that multiple, varied and unpredictable types of interactional patterns may produce either adaptive or maladaptive functioning.

HIGH-RISK FACTORS

The psychiatric literature is replete with reports of specific factors, whether biological, psychological, social, or a combination of these, which constitute high-risk influences in the development of behavior disorders in children and adolescents (Chess and Hassibi, 1978). The NYLS findings have highlighted parental conflict and difficult temperament in early childhood as high-risk factors (Chapter 10). Divorce as such did not appear to constitute a long-term maladaptive influence for the child, a finding in accord with the Wallerstein and Kelly report that "the divorced family was neither more nor less beneficial or stressful for the children than the unhappy marriage" (1980, pp. 306–307). Hetherington (1979) and Rutter (1981a, 1981b) have also emphasized the deleterious effect on the child of parental discord as contrasted to actual separation or divorce.

Studies from several other centers have also reported significant correlations between difficult temperament in children and the later incidence of behavior disorder (Graham et al., 1973; Maurer et al., 1980). Dunn and her co-workers (1981) have found that the difficult temperament traits are significantly related to the incidence of sleep problems in first-born children following the birth of a sibling. Other reports, however, indicate that difficult temperament may not be as difficult for children and their parents from different sociocultural backgrounds. Thus, Super and Harkness (1981), in their comparative study of suburban Boston and rural Kokwet (Kenya) children, found that "one can recognize from maternal interviews in both samples dimensions of mood, adaptability, intensity of reaction, and rhythmicity. Naturalistic observations of daily behavior provide evidence that these similarities are not simply conceptual artifacts of common biases of judgment" (p. 78). However, marked differences in child-care practices and attitudes in the two samples had different consequences for the temperamentally irregular infants. "Night waking by a 1-year-old can severely stress American parents whose own daytime lives are rigidly scheduled; in Kokwet, night waking is normal and not particularly stressful" (p. 82).

In our own research unit, Korn and Gannon (in press) compared a sample of children from the NYLS with a like number from our Puerto Rican working-class sample. Behavior adjustment of the children at 5 years was rated through the use of a symptom checklist derived from the parent interviews. A significant correlation was found between symptomatology and a difficult temperament rating in the NYLS youngsters, but not in the Puerto Rican group. The most likely explanation for this finding appeared to be differences in parental child-care attitudes and practices in the two samples. The NYLS parents made many more demands than did the other group for the early establishment of regular sleep and feeding schedules, for the establishment of early self-feeding and self-dressing, and for quick adaptation to new situations and new people — demands which are especially stressful for children with difficult temperament.

Most dramatic is the report by de Vries (in press), who collected temperament data on children of the Masai tribe in Kenya. This is a primitive tribe living in the sub-Sahara region. De Vries obtained temperament ratings on

47 infants, age 2–4 months, using a translation of the Carey (1970) questionnaire, at a time when a severe drought was just beginning. With these ratings, he identified the 10 infants with the most easy temperament, and the 10 with the most difficult temperament. He returned to this tribal area 5 months later, by which time the drought had killed off 97 percent of the cattle herd. He was able to locate 7 of the easy babies and 6 of the difficult ones. The families of the other infants had moved in an attempt to escape the drought. Of the 7 "easy" babies, 5 had died, whereas all of the "difficult" infants had survived! Thus, the adaptive value of easy versus difficult temperament is indeed a matter of the goodness or poorness of fit with specific characteristics of the child's environment.

With regard to major primary depression in childhood and adolescence, the history of our two cases, Harold and Sylvia (Chapter 14), suggests that a strong family history of depressive illness constitutes a high-risk issue. This is in line with the reports in the literature which consistently implicate a genetic factor in the etiology of depressive illnesses (Allen et al., 1974; Schildkraut et al., 1978; Gershon, 1979).

As to brain damage, the developmental course of our three cases (Chapter 15) indicates strongly that the behavioral consequences of this handicap can constitute a significant high-risk factor for behavior disorder development. Again, this is in line with the clinical literature in this area (Graham and Rutter, 1968). The symptomatic consequences of brain damage vary greatly in their manifestations and severity, but we have been especially impressed with the importance of perseveration, both because of its frequency and its functional significance (Chess, 1972). As seen in our three cases, it can have serious effects on social relationships, learning and school adjustment, and can potentiate the effects of other symptoms and disabilities. Second to perseveration in the problems of management of a brain-damaged child is the presence of impulsivity, especially when it contains an aggressive component. Impulsivity, as we have seen it clinically, appears to be related to Rutter's (1981) description of the syndrome of "social disinhibition."

We cannot generalize from our one case of mental retardation (Kevin, Chapter 15), but the literature consistently reports retarded children at high risk for behavior disorder development (Menolascino, 1969). The data from our own sample of mentally retarded children (Chess, 1980) suggests that, at least in the cases of mild retardation, the major pathogenic factor may be excessive and inappropriate demands and expectations from parents and community.

It can be anticipated that children with multiple high-risk factors will be especially vulnerable to behavior disorder development, with the likelihood also of more severe symptomatology. This was evident in our subjects with both difficult temperament and severe parental conflict at age 3 years (Chapter 12), and dramatically highlighted in Barbara's case (Chapter 15), with the combination of brain damage, difficult temperament, and highly inappropriate and even punitive handling by the parents.

Our findings highlight the fact that high risk does not predict inevitably the development of a behavior disorder. Werner and Smith (1982), in their large-scale longitudinal study of the children of Kauai, Hawaii, make this same point most emphatically. "In this cohort of 698, 204 children developed severe behavior or learning problems at *some time* during the first two decades of their lives. . . . Yet there were others, also *vulnerable* — exposed to poverty, biological risks, and family instability, and reared by parents with little education or serious mental health problems — who remained *invincible* and developed into competent and autonomous young adults who 'worked well, played well, loved well and expected well'" (1982, pp. 2–3). Gordon (personal communication) has used the apt phrase "defiers of negative prediction" to designate such youngsters.

It is a major challenge to developmental psychology and psychiatry to mount serious studies of such stress-resistant, high-risk children. As Garmezy (1981) points out, this is "an area in which there exists neither a substantial body of empirical data nor a formal conceptualization" (p. 215).

NYLS HIGH-RISK, STRESS-RESISTANT SUBJECTS

A number of NYLS subjects were "defiers of negative prediction." These were youngsters who developed a behavior disorder in childhood and adolescence, where parental guidance and, in some cases, direct psychotherapy with the youngster were unsuccessful in arresting the pathologic developmental course. It appeared in these cases in the NYLS clinical sample that a pessimistic prognosis was justified. Yet these youngsters confounded our predictions by dramatic reversals in their developmental course, with recovery from their behavior disorders by early adult life. These cases include Bernice and Michael (Chapter 12), Olga (Chapter 14), Lori, Nancy, Olivia and Roy (Chapter 17). As discussed in Chapters 12 and 17, we have been impressed by what appears to have been the therapeutic value of a firm commitment to a specific career direction (Bernice and Michael) and/or the ability of the youngster to achieve emotional distancing from a pressuring and intrusive parent (Lori, Olivia and Roy). However, the question still remains unanswered as to why these youngsters developed a career commitment or emotional distancing from the parents, while other clinical cases did not. Our data do not provide any definite answer to this important question.

Favorable outcome in other cases reflected the influence of unpredictable changes within the youngster—Nancy, with the emergence of her dramatic talents in middle childhood, and Olga, with her religious conversion experience at 16 years. In two instances, adventitious factors appeared influential in preventing the development of a behavior disorder. One was Stanley (Chapter 12), who was at high risk because of difficult temperament and severe parental conflict; however, he escaped serious difficulties with a highly pressuring and intrusive mother because her destructive struggles were focused on his older brother, Roy. The other was Nelson (Chapter 17) whose adolescent drug abuse was terminated when he became a follower of an Indian guru.

The favorable outcomes in these cases do not justify any attitude of "benign neglect" of childhood behavior disorders. A significant number of cases did not improve or even grew worse in adolescence and early adult life, and it was frequently not possible in childhood to predict eventual outcome. Hence, we would recommend parent guidance and other appropriate therapeutic intervention in all cases.

WHAT WE DO NOT KNOW

In the play *Equus*, the psychiatrist muses on the causes of psychiatric disorders. "A child is born into a world of phenomena all equal in their power to enslave. It sniffs—it sucks—it strokes its eyes over the whole uncomfortable range. Suddenly one strikes. Why? Moments snap together like magnets, forging a chain of shackles. Why? I can trace them. I can even, with time, pull them apart again. But why at the start they were ever magnetized at all— just those particular moments of experience and no others—I don't know. *And nor does anyone else*" (Shaffer, 1974, p. 88).

The playwright here challenges us to explain why certain potentially pathogenic experiences do have this influence on some children, but not on others. Beyond this, why does an unfavorable child-environment interactional process lead to certain symptoms in one child, or adult, and to different symptoms in another? Why does one youngster utilize one type of defense mechanism and another a different type? Why did one of our NYLS subjects show consistency in a defensive strategy from early childhood to adult life, another change from hopelessness to denial, and another from projection to hopelessness? Why could some of our behaviorally disturbed youngsters achieve effective emotional distance from a destructive interaction with a parent, while others could not?

It is clear that we cannot look for answers to any simplistic unidimensional model, whether it be drive-reduction, stimulus-response bonds, or any other single set of determinants. We also cannot look to any single age-period where life events are all-important determinants of future development.

But we do have some partial answers. The interactionist and life-span perspectives provide valuable approaches to the posing of research questions and strategies, and to the conceptualization of data analytic schemes. The goodness-of-fit model gives us a number of answers as to the processes involved in the origin and evolution of behavior disorders in specific cases. Psychodynamic formulations enable us to understand the effect of excessive stress on intrapsychic emotional and ideational states, resulting in behavior which perpetuates and even exacerbates a poorness of fit (Sylvia and Norman, Chapter 14, illustrate this dynamic sequence, in which the defensive response to excessive stress served to intensify maladaptive behavior patterns).

However, in Emde's words (1983), we lack and need a "developmental psychopathology of transactions . . . . phase specific transactions . . . what leads to what under what circumstances . . . individual differences in family systems." Emde further emphasizes the need to study "not only individual development but the individual within a specific family." One model for such directions of research is contained in the volume *Toward Understanding Relationships*, in which Hinde (1979) reviews systematically what we know about relationships between people, and the requirements for advancing this knowledge into a science of relationships.

HUMAN DIVERSITY AND FLEXIBILITY

As we have reviewed the developmental course of our NYLS subjects, we have been deeply impressed by the diversity of interactional processes and personality outcome which have been so evident from one youngster to another as they matured from infancy, to childhood, through adolescence, and into early adult life. Equally striking has been the capacity for flexibility, adaptability and mastery in the face of all kinds of adverse and stressful life experiences. As we have put it, "As we grow from childhood to maturity, all of us have to shed many childhood illusions. As the field of developmental studies has matured, we now have to give up the illusion that once we know the young child's psychological history, subsequent personality and functioning are *ipso facto* predictable. On the other hand, we now have a much more optimistic vision of human development. The emotionally traumatized child is not doomed, the parents' early mistakes are not irrevocable, and our preventative and therapeutic intervention can make a difference at all age periods" (Chess, 1979, p. 112).

PART V

Appendices

APPENDIX A

Early Adult Life
Interview Protocol
for Subjects

Note to Interviewer: The following outline should be used as a guide for an open-ended, semi-structured interview, and not as an inflexible protocol to be followed without deviation. If the subject responds to questions in one area by discussing another area of his life, do not stop him. Make a note of the diversion and let him pursue his own direction. Make sure, however, to cover the original area before completing the interview. If the subject resists answering questions in any area, do not press him. Make a note of his reaction and proceed to the next item. Come back to the resisted area later in the interview, but if there is the same negative reaction, note this and drop the issue.

As much as possible, the interview data should concentrate on objective descriptions of behavior and events. Subjective statements and interpretations should be recorded, but not considered an adequate substitute for descriptive data. General statements should be recorded, but one or two typical specific examples should be requested.

Specific questions on temperament are scattered throughout the interview protocol rather than grouped as a separate section. In this way, data on temperament are obtained as pertinent to individual areas of functioning. For the temperament data, it is especially important that specific objective descriptions of behavior be obtained with at least several examples for each statement.

The interviewer should not feel bound to the questions as stated in the protocol below. Questions can be rephrased or modified to suit the understand-

ing or specific life style and functioning of the subject. Additional questions
can be added to illuminate in greater depth specific areas of behavior or attitude that appear significant.

Self-Image and Self-Evaluation—How would you describe yourself as a
person? Do you feel you have been changing as a person in recent years? If
so, how? What do you like most about yourself? What would you like to
change about yourself?

Medical History—Have you had any important illnesses or operations in
your life? If so, give details. Do you have frequent minor illnesses, such as
colds? If so, give details. Are you sensitive to pain, or doesn't this bother you
much? If you need an injection, or to have blood drawn, does the needle stick
usually hurt a great deal or not? If you have a cold and a stuffed nose or sore
throat, are you very uncomfortable or not?

Life Goals—Have you decided on a specific profession or vocation? If so,
what, and how did you become interested in it? What specific plans do you
have for pursuing this goal? If you have no specific goal for the future, does
this bother you?

Immediate Goals—What are your major interests or concentrations in time
in this period of your life? How are you pursuing these goals? Are you the
kind of person who sticks persistently to something, no matter what the obstacles, once you have become interested in it? Or do you turn your interest
to something else? Give me a few examples?

Daily Routines—How do you spend your day, typically? Do you tend to
follow the same routine each day or does this vary greatly from day to day?
What is a typical day for you, as far as routines go? How do you like to spend
your free time?

Biological Functions—How many hours a night do you sleep? Is this the
same each night, or does it vary from night to night? Do you get up at the
same time each morning? What is your schedule of meals? Do you eat about
the same amount each day or does this vary greatly? Do you like to try new
foods and new restaurants? Do you have the same number of bowel
movements at about the same time or not?

Special Interests and Hobbies—Do you have any special interests or hobbies? If so, what are they? How do you pursue them and how much time do
you give to them? Do you concentrate for long or short periods on such an
interest or hobby? If you are absorbed in something you are doing, can you
be distracted if someone comes in or talks to you, or are you oblivious to
whatever else is going on?

Athletics—Are you interested in any sports, and if so, which? How much
time do you give to them? Do you prefer active involvement in a sport, or
are you content to be on the sidelines or just watch? Do you need physical

activity each day, else you get restless, or doesn't this matter to you? Do you play hard to win, or don't you care if you win or lose?

Relations with Family — How do you get along with your father, mother, brothers and sisters? If there are any special problems, please specify? Have these relationships changed in recent years or not? What do you remember of how you were treated by your father and mother (and older brothers and sisters) when you were a young child? What influence do you feel your parents and brothers and sisters have had on you as you have grown up? Do you consider that your parents have been easygoing with you, understanding, sympathetic to what you needed, concerned for what you wanted, easy in their discipline and expectations, — or the opposite? Please specify. Have any other family members, such as a grandparent or uncle or aunt, been an important member of the household for you? If so, answer the same questions above for them. Do you still live with your parents? If so, why, and do you prefer this? If not, why, and how much do you miss them? If there has been a divorce, or death of a parent, what has been the effect on family and on you? Can you communicate easily with family? If not, why not?

School Functioning — Are you still attending school? If so, give details. If not, when did you finish and why? What has been the level of your academic achievement? Do you feel this level corresponds to your academic potential? If not, why not? Can you concentrate for long periods in school or with homework or do you need frequent breaks? Do you get restless if you have to sit quietly for a lecture and can't move around? If subject material is difficult do you plug away at it or give up and turn to something else? Do you prefer to study by yourself or with one or more classmates? If you are studying, do you get easily distracted by a noise or a person or not? When you moved to a new school, did you get used to it quickly, or did it take you a long time? Have you had any problems with school at any time in your life? If so, specify. Also, what was done about the problem? What are your future work plans?

Work Functioning — What jobs have you had, past and present? If you have not worked, why not? Which jobs interested you and which did not, and why? At work, do you concentrate at a specific job for long periods, or do you need frequent breaks? Do you get restless if you have to sit quietly at work for long periods? Do you plug away at a difficult task or do you stop and turn to something else? When you are concentrating on a job, do you get easily distracted by people or a noise or not? Do you prefer to work alone or in a group? When you moved to a new job did you get used to it quickly, or did it take a long time? What are your future work plans? Do you feel you have any work problems? If so, specify.

Social Functioning — Would you characterize yourself as a loner or as very sociable, or in between? Do you make new friends quickly and easily or does it take you a long time to warm up to a new person? Do you like to go to social gatherings where you will meet new people or does this make you feel uncomfortable? How many good friends would you say you have? Do you keep friends easily? If not, why not? Do you prefer to go to a movie or show or game by yourself or with a group? Do you have any problems getting along with people? If so, specify.

Sexual Functioning — Do you have a steady girl/boy friend? Can you make friends with a new girl/boy easily or not? How much do you date and what do you do on dates generally? History of masturbation, petting, intercourse. Do you have any problems with sex? If so, specify. Can you discuss sex easily with your parents? Do you want to get married? If so, when? If not, why not?

Task vs. Person — If you have a job to do or are working on a project, can you do it by yourself easily, or do you want to do it with other people? If you are busy with a task or hobby or book and friends call you, do you generally drop your task to be with your friends? Or do you prefer to continue with your task, even if you miss seeing your friends? If you are trying to figure out a problem, do you tend to do it in terms of the task itself or in terms of the people involved?

Expressiveness and Communication — Do you express your feelings easily in general or not? Do you express some feelings easily and others not? In general, can you communicate your thoughts easily to others or do you stumble and grope for words? Do you communicate easily with certain people and not with others? If you get angry or are pleased, do you express this vigorously and energetically, or quietly? Do many things irritate or annoy you, or do you take them in your stride and even cheerfully? Give examples. Can you talk easily about your deep and important feelings or not?

Adaptive Patterns — Does change or something new bother you or do you welcome it? Are you cautious about going into anything new or do you plunge in? Do you adjust quickly and easily to change or not? Give examples. If something or somebody bothers you or puts you under strain, how do you handle it? Do you plug away at it, do you try to push it away or avoid it, do you try to enlist someone else to help you or take it over, or what? Give examples.

Additional Temperament Questions — To interviewer: At this point introduce questions to obtain temperament data not obtained by the previous questions. Specific questions regarding sensory threshold will probably be necessary - sensitivity to heat, cold, sound, light, rough fabrics, skin irritation, pain. For the other temperament traits, the need for additional questions will be determined by the data obtained up to this point with each individual subject.

Substance Use and Abuse — Do you smoke? If so, when did you start, how much do you smoke and do you feel it has any beneficial or harmful effects on you? Same questions for alcohol and marijuana use? Have you ever experimented with any other drugs? If so, give details.

Psychological Symptoms — Do you get nervous, depressed, worried, easily angry. Specify extent, frequency, intensity, any relationship to specific events and people.

Psychosomatic Symptoms — Do you have difficulties with sleep, digestion, appetite? Do you get easily tired? Do you have any other symptoms, for which no physical cause has been found, such as headache, backache or palpitations? If so, specify as in "Psychological Symptoms" above.

Thought Disturbances — Do you have any unusual or special thoughts which occupy your mind? If so, specify. Do you see or hear unusual things that other people don't?

General Comments — Are there any other items we have not covered that you want to bring up? Do you think you have given me a good idea of the kind of person you are?

Interviewer's Comments — Record specific description of subject's physical appearance, behavior, speech, mood, expression of mood. Detail any unusual observations regarding subject's behavior that you have noticed. Describe nature of subject's relationship to you (cooperation, responsiveness, spontaneous elaboration, etc.)

Adjustment Rating Scale from 3-Year Parent Interview

1 = Insignificant;	2 = Mild; Happens Occasionally	3 = Moderate; Frequently	4 = Moderately Severe; Often, Regularly
	5 = Severe; On every occasion	6 = Not Applicable	

Note: additional items for any child in any category are to be noted under "Comments". If a rating is not possible because of lack of information, this should also be noted under "Comments".

SLEEP   *RATING*

Child prolongs bedtime routine by emerging, calling out, demanding servicing, etc.   _____

Child makes great commotion, has tantrums at bedtime.   _____

Child wakes up, demands servicing, climbs into parents' bed at night.   _____

Child has bad dreams or nightmares.   _____

Child wakes up family very early, despite prohibitions.   _____

Comments: _____

EATING   *RATING*

Child throws, spits out or pushes unwanted food off plate.   _____

Child is fed by parents.   _____

Child is disruptive at table, fidgets, walks away, talks incessantly,
   etc.   _____

Child has limited food preferences (finicky, eats only 2–3 kinds
   of food).   _____

Comments: _____

_____

_____

ELIMINATION

Child wets at night.   _____

Child soils at night.   _____

Child wets accidently during day.   _____

Child soils accidently during day.   _____

Child actively withholds urine or bowel movement.   _____

Comments: _____

_____

_____

FEARS, TICS, RITUALS

Child expresses fear of specific event, person, or animal.   _____

Child turns routines (e.g. bedtime) into rituals.   _____

Child has evident tic or habit.   _____

Comments: _____

_____

_____

SPEECH COMMUNICATION

Child's speech is incoherent or incomprehensible.   _____

Child talks excessively and disruptively.   _____

Child's speech is immature.   _____

Comments: _____

_____

_____

MOTOR ACTIVITY

Child is clumsy, spills, breaks, or knocks things over.   _____

Child resists outdoor or gross motor activity or equipment.   _____

Child performs poorly at fine motor activities.   _____

Comments: _____

_____

RELATIONSHIP WITH PARENTS   *RATING*
Child cries, protests, or clings to parent at separation.   _____
Child shows clear preference for one parent over the other.   _____
Child whines, fusses, and nags at parents.   _____
Child demands unnecessary servicing.   _____
Child resists necessary servicing.   _____
Comments: _____
_____
_____

DISCIPLINE
Child is fresh, rude, talks back to parents.   _____
Child is directly disobedient or noncompliant with parents.   _____
Child teases, manipulates, dawdles.   _____
Child has tantrums in response to parental demands or prohi-
    bitions.   _____
Child disregards or disobeys safety rules.   _____
Comments: _____
_____
_____

RELATIONSHIP WITH SIB
Child quarrels with, hurts, or bullies sib.   _____
Child is intimidated by or expresses dislike of sib.   _____
Child expresses preoccupation with sib.   _____
Comments: _____
_____
_____

NON-FAMILY RELATIONSHIPS
Child is timid with familiar nonparent adults.   _____
Child is too friendly with strangers.   _____
Child is aggressive and bossy with playmates.   _____
Child gets into fights with peers.   _____
Child is teased, bullied, or pushed around by playmates.   _____
Child prefers older playmates.   _____
Child prefers younger playmates.   _____
Other: _____

COPING TASK MASTERY
Child has tantrum, acts up when in stressful or frustrating situ-
    ation.   _____

RATING

Child quits easily, withdraws in stressful or frustrating situation. _____

Child is negative, says "I can't". _____

Child dislikes going to or being in school. _____

Comments: _____

_____

_____

APPENDIX C

Global Adaptation Score— Early Adult Age Period

This score is derived from a qualitative composite judgment of the individual's level of adaptation in the significant areas of functioning. These include: relationships with family, school functioning, work functioning where pertinent, level of social competence, sexual functioning, clarity of life goals and pattern of implementation of these goals, range of interests and activities, ease of expressiveness and communication, and effectiveness of coping with any special traumatic events or situations. The score also includes judgments on character of self-image, presence of significant areas of defensiveness, and evidence of psychopathology and its severity. Also, excessive substance use should be considered in rating.

General Criteria

1. The evaluation should be made in terms of each subject's capacities and goals, and not in terms of an *a priori* norm.

2. Relationship with parents may be difficult and stressful and yet represent a positive level of adaptation. This can be true if the parents, or one parent, are difficult, precipitate conflict, exert unreasonable pressures, etc. This has to be estimated and the subject's functioning judged accordingly.

3. Level of social competence again cannot be rated in terms of one *a priori* norm. A small circle of friends may be optimal for one subject, a large circle for another.

4. Absence of active sexual functioning at this age-period may be due to different reasons: a principled moral position, slow maturation, or actual inhibition. Only the last would rate as maladaptation.

5. Degree of clarity as to life goals again may vary greatly in this early adult age-period. Some may have a general direction but not a specific goal yet in that direction. Others may have clear short-term but not long-term goals, and others may have very definite and specific short-term and long-term goals. Any of these patterns may represent a positive adaptive direction or the reverse. The judgment must be made individually in each case.

6. Self-image must be judged both in terms of the subject's own statement and the correspondence of this statement to reality. Of course, if a subject expresses a negative self-image, and this appears valid, the rating has to be a negative one.

Criteria for Scores

9. Optimal or close to optimal functioning in all major areas. Clear goals with good implementation. Excellent valid self-image. No psychopathology, at most occasional fleeting episodes of mild anxiety or depression. No areas of defensiveness.

8. Same as 9, except for mild to moderately suboptimal functioning in one or two areas.

7. Close to optimal functioning in most areas, a few at moderate levels. Goals and implementation fairly good. Good valid self-image. Mild episodes of anxiety, depression or psychosomatic symptoms.

6. Moderate but suboptimal functioning in all areas, one area perhaps only fair. Fair valid self-image, or high self-rating which is excessive. Perhaps one or two areas of mild defensiveness. Mild to moderate occasional episodes of anxiety, depression or psychosomatic symptoms.

5. Like 6, except that one area may be real problem area in functioning.

4. Marginally satisfactory functioning overall, with several problem areas. Fair level of coping with special stresses. Several areas of defensiveness. Psychopathology on mild to moderate psychoneurotic level. Self-image at best is fair.

3. Periods of unsatisfactory functioning in several major areas, with much anxiety, depression and/or psychosomatic symptoms. Goals uncertain, coping level is marginally satisfactory. Several areas of defensiveness. Definite diagnosis of psychoneurosis, moderately severe.

2. Severe difficulties in functioning in a number of major areas, but is able to make marginal positive adaptation in functioning. Marginally self-sufficient. Poor self-image, number of areas of defensiveness. Moderate to severe psychoneurosis, or borderline psychosis.

1. Severely disabled, barely functional in community with much external support, or requires hospitalization at times. Severe psychoneurosis or psychosis.

Bibliography

Alexander, F. G. and Selesnick, S. T. 1966. *The History of Psychiatry*. New York: Harper and Row.

Allen, M. G., Cohen, S., Pollin, W., and Greenspan, S. I. 1974. Affective illness in veteran twins: a diagnostic review. *American Journal of Psychiatry*, 131:1234–1239.

Anthony, E. J. 1969. The reactions of adults to adolescents and their behavior. In G. Caplan and S. Lebovic, eds. *Adolescence*, New York: Basic Books.

Arnold, L. E., ed. 1978. *Helping Parents Help Their Children*. New York: Brunner/Mazel.

Baltes, P. B., Reese, H. W. and Lipsitt, L. P. 1980. Life-span developmental psychology. *Annual Review of Psychology*, 31:65–110.

Bates, J. E. 1980. The concept of difficult temperament. *Merrill-Palmer Quarterly*, 26:299–319.

Bates, J. E. and Bayles, K. 1984. Objective and subjective components in mothers' perceptions of their children from age 6 months to 3 years. *Merrill-Palmer Quarterly*, 30:111–130.

Becker, W. C. and Krug, R. S. 1965. The parent attitude research instrument: a research review. *Child Development*, 36:329–365.

Beiser, H. 1964. Discrepancies in the symptomatology of parents and children. *Journal American Academy of Child Psychiatry*, 3:457–468.

Bell, R. 1968. A reinterpretation of the direction of effects in studies of socialization. *Psychological Review*, 75:81–95.

Birch, H. 1954. Comparative psychology. In F. Marcuse, ed. *Areas of Psychology*, New York: Harper.

Birch, H. G. (ed.) 1964. *Brain Damage in Children: Biological and Social Aspects*. Baltimore: Williams and Wilkins.

Birch, H. G., Thomas, A. and Chess, S. 1964. Behavioral development in brain damaged children. *Archives General Psychiatry*, 11:596–603.

Birns, B. 1976. The emergence and socialization of sex differences in the earliest years. *Merrill-Palmer Quarterly*, 22:3–30.

Blos, P. 1979. *The Adolescent Passage*. New York: International Universities Press.

Bower, T. 1977. *A Primer of Human Development*. San Francisco: W. H. Freeman.

Bradley, C. 1957. Characteristics and management of children with behavioral problems associated with brain damage. *Pediatric Clinics of North America*, 4:1049–1060.

309

Brazelton, T. 1973. Neonatal behavioral assessment scale. *Clinics in Developmental Medicine,* *(50).*

Brazelton, T. 1978. Introduction. In A. Sameroff, ed. Organization and stability of new born behavior. *Monographs Society for Research in Child Development*, 43(5–6):1–13.

Brim, O. G. and Kagan, J., eds. 1980. *Constancy and Change in Human Development*. Cambridge, Mass.: Harvard University Press.

Bronson, W. C. 1974. Mother-toddler interaction: A perspective on studying the development of competence. *Merrill-Palmer Quarterly*, 20:275–301.

Bruner, J. S. 1973. Organization of early skilled action. *Child Development*, 44:1–11.

Burks, J. and Rubenstein, M. 1979. *Temperament Styles in Adult Interaction*. New York: Brunner/Mazel.

Burstein, B., Bank, L. and Jarvik, L. F. 1980. Sex differences in cognitive functioning: Evidence, determinants, implications. *Human Development*, 23:289–313.

Buss, A. H. and Plomin, R. 1975. *A Temperament Theory of Personality*. New York: John Wiley and Sons.

Cameron, J. R. 1977. Parental treatment, children's temperament, and the risk of childhood behavioral problems: 1. Relationships between parental characteristics and changes in children's temperament over time. *American Journal of Orthopsychiatry*, 47:568–576.

Cameron, J. R. 1978. Parental treatment, children's temperament, and the risk of childhood behavioral problems: 2. Initial temperament, parental attitudes, and the incidence and form of behavioral problems. *American Journal of Orthopsychiatry*, 48:140–147.

Cantwell, D. P. and Carlson, G. 1979. Problems and prospects in the study of childhood depression. *Journal Nervous and Mental Diseases*, 167:522–529.

Carey, W. B. 1970. A simplified method for measuring infant temperament. *Journal of Pediatrics*, 77:188–194.

Carey, W. B. 1974. Night wakening and temperament in infancy. *Journal of Pediatrics*, 81: 823–828.

Carey, W. B. 1982. Clinical use of temperament data in pediatrics. In *Temperamental differences in infants and young children*, Ciba Foundation Symposium 89. London: Pitman, pp 191–202.

Carey, W. B. in press. The validity of temperament assessments. In T. B. Brazelton and H. Als, eds. *Behavioral Assessment of Newborn and Young Infants*. Hillsdale, N.J.: Erlbaum Associates.

Carey, W. B. and McDevitt, S. C. 1978. Stability and change in individual temperament diagnoses from infancy to early childhood. *Journal of the American Academy of Child Psychiatry*, 17:331–337.

Carey, W. B. and McDevitt, S. C. 1980. Minimal brain dysfunction and hyperkinesis: a clinical viewpoint. *American Journal of Diseases of Children*, 134:926–929.

Carlson, G. A. and Cantwell, D. P. 1980. Unmasking masked depression in children and adolescents. *American Journal of Psychiatry*, 137:445–449.

Carpenter, G. 1975. Mother face and the newborn. In R. Lewin, ed. *Child Alive*. London: Temple Smith.

Chamberlin, R. W. 1976. The use of teacher checklists to identify children at risk for later behavioral and emotional problems. *American Journal Diseases of Children*, 130:141–145.

Chess, S. 1969. *An Introduction to Child Psychiatry*, 2nd ed. New York: Grune and Stratton.

Chess, S. 1972. Neurological Dysfunction and Childhood Behavioral Pathology. *Journal of Autism and Childhood Schizophrenia*, 2:299–311.

Chess, S. 1979. Developmental theory revisited. Findings of longitudinal study. *Canadian Journal of Psychiatry*, 24:101–112.

Chess, S. 1980. The mildly mentally retarded child in the community: Success versus failure. In S. B. Sells, R. Crandall, M. Roff, J. S. Strauss and W. Pollin, eds. *Human Functioning in Longitudinal Perspective*. Baltimore: Williams and Wilkins.

Chess, S. 1982. Brain syndromes in congenital rubella. Presented at Conference on Measles and Rubella at the Johns Hopkins School of Hygiene and Public Health, Baltimore, MD, Oct. 28, 1982.

Chess, S. and Fernandez, P. 1980. Do deaf children have a typical personality? *Journal American Academy Child Psychiatry*, 19:654–664.

Chess, S., Fernandez, P. and Korn, S. 1980. The handicapped child and his family: consonance and dissonance. *Journal American Academy Child Psychiatry*, 19:56–67.

Chess, S. and Hassibi, M. 1970. Behavior deviations in mentally retarded children, *Journal American Academy Child Psychiatry*, 9:282–297.

Chess, S. and Hassibi, M. 1978. *Principles and Practice of Child Psychiatry*. New York: Plenum.

Chess, S. and Korn, S. 1970. Temperament and behavior disorders in mentally retarded children. *Archives General Psychiatry*, 23:122–130.

Chess, S., Korn, S. and Fernandez, P. 1971. *Psychiatric Disorders of Children with Congenital Rubella*. New York: Brunner/Mazel.

Chess, S., and Thomas, A. 1976. Defense mechanisms in middle childhood. *Canadian Journal of Psychiatry*, 21:519–526.

Chess, S., Thomas, A. and Birch, H. G. 1966. Distortions in developmental reporting made by parents of behaviorally disturbed children. *Journal American Academy Child Psychiatry*, 5:226–234.

Chess, S., Thomas, A. and Cameron, M. 1976. Temperament: Its significance for school adjustment and academic achievement, *New York University Educational Review*, 7:24–29.

Chess, S., Thomas, A. and Cameron, M. 1976. Sexual attitudes and behavior patterns in a middle-class adolescent population. *American Journal of Orthopsychiatry*, 46:689–701.

Chess, S., Thomas, A. and Hassibi, M. 1983. Depression in childhood and adolescence: A prospective study of six cases. *Journal of Nervous and Mental Diseases*, 171:411–420.

Chess, S., Thomas, A., Korn, S., Mittelman, M. and Cohen, J. 1983. Early parental attitudes, divorce and separation, and young adult outcome: Findings of a longitudinal study. *American Academy of Child Psychiatry*, 22:47–51.

Ciba Foundation Symposium 89. 1982. *Temperamental Differences in Infants and Young Children*, London: Pitman.

Clarke, A. D. B. 1978. Predicting human development: Problems, evidence, implications. *Bulletin of British Psychological Society*, 31:249–258.

Clarke, A. M. and Clarke, A. D. B. 1976. *Early Experience: Myth and Evidence*. London: Open Books.

Cohen, J. 1982. Set correlation as a general multivariate data—analytic method. *Multivariate Behavioral Research*, 17:301–341.

Cohen, J. and Cohen, P. 1975. *Applied Multiple Regression/Correlation Analysis for the Behavioral Sciences*. Hillside, New Jersey: L. Erlbaum Associates.

Coleman, J. C. 1978. Current contradictions in adolescent theory. *Journal of Youth and Adolescence*, 7, 1, pp 1–11.

Condon, W. and Sander, L. 1974. Neonate movement is synchronized with adult speech: Interactional participation and language requisition. *Science*, 183:99–101.

Connolly, K. and Stratton, P. 1969. An exploration of some parameters affecting classical conditioning in the neonate. *Child Development*, 40:431–441.

Cytryn, L. and McKnew, D. H., Jr. 1974. Factors influencing the changing clinical expression of the depressive process in children. *American Journal of Psychiatry*, 131:879–881.

Cytryn, L., McKnew, D. H., Jr. and Bunney, W. E., Jr. 1980. Diagnosis of depression in children: A reassessment. *American Journal of Psychiatry*, 137:22–25.

Davis, H. V., Sears, R., Miller, H. C. and Brodbeck, A. J. 1948. Effect of cup, bottle, and breast feeding on the oral activities of newborn infants. *Pediatrics*, 2:549–558.

Diagnostic and Statistical Manual of Mental Diseases, 3rd ed. (DSM-III) 1980. American Psychiatric Association, Wash., D.C.

Dobzhansky, T. 1962. *Mankind Evolving*. New Haven: Yale University Press.

Dobzhansky, T. 1966. A geneticist's view of human equality. *The Pharos*, 29:12–16.

Dollard, J. and Miller, N. E. 1950. *Personality and Psychotherapy*. New York: McGraw-Hill.

Dubos, R. 1965. *Man Adapting*. New Haven: Yale University Press.

Dunn, J., and Kendrick, C. 1980. Studying temperament and parent-child interaction: Comparison of interview and direct observation. *Developmental Medicine and Child Neurology*, 22:484–496.

Dunn, J., Kendrick, C. and MacNamee, R. 1981. The reaction of first-born children to the birth of a sibling: Mothers' reports. *Journal of Child Psychology and Psychiatry*, 22:1–18.

Eisenberg, L. 1964. Behavioral manifestations of cerebral damage in children. In H. G. Birch, ed. *Brain Damage in Children: Biological and Social Aspects*, Baltimore: Williams and Wilkins.

Eisenberg, L. 1972. The human nature of human nature. *Science*, 176:123–128.

Eisenberg, L. 1977. Development as a unifying concept in psychiatry. *British Journal of Psychiatry*, 131:225–237.

Eissler, K. R. 1958. Notes on problems of technique in the psychoanalytic treatment of adolescents. *Psychoanalytic Study of the Child*, 13:233–254.

Eliot, G. 1963 ed. *Middlemarch*. New York: Washington Square Press, p. 810.

Emde, R. 1983. Discussion of Symposium: Vulnerability and invulnerability in infants, children and families. Annual Meeting of American Psychiatric Association, New York City, May 7, 1983.

Engel, G. L. 1977. The need for a new medical model: A challenge for biomedicine. *Science*, 196:129–135.

Erikson, E. H. 1959. Identity and the life cycle. *Psychological Issues I*, pp. 1–171.

Erikson, E. H. 1968. *Identity, Youth and Crisis*. New York: Norton.

Erikson, K. 1976. *Everything in Its Path*. New York: Simon and Schuster.

Escalona, S. and Leitsch, M. 1952. Early phases of personality development: A non-normative study of infant behavior. *Monographs of the Society for Research in Child Development*, 17:No. 1.

Eysenck, H. J. 1963. Behavior therapy, spontaneous remission and transference in neurotics. *American Journal of Psychiatry*, 119:867–871.

Fantz, R. and Nevis, S. 1967. Pattern preferences and perceptual-cognitive development in early infancy. *Merrill-Palmer Quarterly*, 13:77–108.

Field, T. M., Woodson, R., Greenberg, R. and Cohen, D. 1982. Discrimination and imitation of facial expressions by neonates. *Science*, 218:179–181.

Fishman, M. E. 1982. *Child and Youth Activities of the National Institute of Mental Health 1981–1982*. Washington: Alcohol, Drug Abuse and Mental Health Administration.

Flavell, J. H. 1972. An analysis of cognitive-developmental sequences. *Genetic Psychology Monographs*, 86:279–350.

Freud, A. 1953. Some remarks on infant observation. *Psychoanalytic Study of the Child*, 8:9–19.

Freud, A. 1958. Adolescence. *Psychoanalytic Study of the Child*, 13:255–278.

Freud, A. 1960. The child guidance clinic as a center of prophylaxis and enlightenment. *Recent Developments in Psychoanalytic Child Therapy*, New York: International Universities Press.

Freud, S. 1924. *Collected Papers*, Vol. 2. London: Hogarth.

Freud, S. 1924. *Collected Papers*, Vol. 4. London: Hogarth Press.

Freud, S. 1949. *An Outline of Psychoanalysis*. New York: W. W. Norton.

Freud, S. 1964. *Three Essays on the Theory of Sexuality*. (1905). In J. Strachey, ed., *Standard Edition of the Complete Psychological Works of Sigmund Freud*, Vol. 7. London: Hogarth Press.

Garmezy, N. 1981. Children under stress: Perspectives on antecedents and correlates of vulnerability and resistance to psychopathology. In A. I. Rabin, J. Aronoff, A. M. Barclay and R. A. Zucker, eds. *Further Explorations in Personality*: New York: Wiley & Sons.

Gershon, E. S. 1979. Genetics of the affective disorders. *Hospital Practice*, 14:117–122.

Gilligan, C. 1982. *In a Different Voice*. Cambridge, Mass.: Harvard University Press.

Gittelman-Klein, R. 1977. Definitional and methodological issues concerning depressive illness in children. In J. G. Schulterbrandt and A. Raskin, eds., *Depression in Childhood: Diagnosis, Treatment and Conceptual Models*. New York: Raven Press, pp. 81–85.

Glaser, K. 1967. Masked depression in children and adolescents. *American Journal of Psychiatry*, 21:565–574.

Glavin, J. P. 1972. Persistence of behavior disorders in children. *Exceptional Children*, 28:367–376.

Goldberg, L. R. 1970. Man versus model of man: A rationale plus evidence for a method of improving on clinical inferences. *Psychological Bulletin*, 73:422–432.

Goldstein, K. 1936. Modifications of behavior consequent to brain lesions. *Psychiatric Quarterly*, 10:586–610.

Gordon, B. N. 1981. Child temperament and adult behavior: An exploration of "goodness of fit." *Child Psychiatry and Human Development*, 11:167–178.

Gordon, E. 1983. Personal communication.

Gould, S. J. 1981. *The Mismeasure of Man*, New York: Norton.

Graham, P. and Rutter, M. 1968. Organic brain dysfunction and child psychiatric disorders. *British Medical Journal*, 3:697–700.

Graham, P., Rutter, M. and George, S. 1973. Temperamental characteristics as predictors of behavior disorders in children. *American Journal of Orthopsychiatry*, 43:328–339.

Greenspan, S. I. 1981. *Psychopathology and Adaptation in Infancy and Early Childhood*, New York: International Universities Press.

Haggard, E. A., Brekstad, A. and Skard, A. G. 1960. On the reliability of the amnestic history. *Journal of Abnormal and Social Psychology*, 66:221.

Hall, G. S. 1904. *Adolescence*, Vol II. New York: D. Appleton.

Hertzig, M. E., Birch, H. G., Thomas, A. and Mendez, O. A. 1968. Class and ethnic differences in the responsiveness of preschool children to cognitive demands. Monographs Society Research in Child Development, 33:1–69.

Hetherington, E. M. 1979. Divorce, a child's perspective. *American Psychologist*, 34:851–858.

Hinde, R. A. 1979. *Toward Understanding Relationships*. London: Academic Press.

Hsu, C. C., Soong, W. T., Stigler, J. W., Hong, C. C. and Liang, C. C. 1981. The temperamental characteristics of Chinese babies. *Child Development*, 52:1337–1340.

Hunt, J. V. 1980. Implications of plasticity and hierarchical achievements for the assessment of development and risk of mental retardation. In D. B. Sawin, R. C. Hawkins, L. O. Walker and J. H. Penticuff, eds. *Exceptional Infant*, Vol. 4. New York: Brunner/Mazel.

Kagan, J. 1971. *Change and Continuity in Infancy*. New York: John Wiley and Sons.

Kagan, J. and Moss, H. A. 1962. *Birth to Maturity*. New York: John Wiley and Sons.

Kagan, J., Kearsley, R. B., and Zelazo, P. R. 1978. *Infancy, Its Place in Human Development*. Cambridge: Harvard University Press.

Kanner, L. 1957. *Child Psychiatry*, 3rd ed. Springfield, Ill.: Thomas.

Kashani, J. H., Hussain, A., Shekim, W. O., Hodges, K. K., Cytryn, L. and McKnew, D. H. 1981. Current perspectives on childhood depression: An overview. *American Journal of Psychiatry*, 138:143–153.

Katcher, A. Unpublished data.

Kaye, K. and Brazelton, T. 1971. Mother-infant interaction in the organization of sucking. Presented to the Society for Research in Child Development. Minneapolis, Minn.

Keogh, B. K. 1982. Children's temperament and teachers' decisions. In *Temperamental differences in infants and young children*, Ciba Foundation Symposium 89. London: Pitman, pp. 269–279.

Kohlberg, L. 1964. Development of moral character and moral ideology. In M. L. Hoffman and L. W. Hoffman. eds. *Review of Child Development*, Vol. 1. New York: Russell Sage Foundation.

Korn, S. J. 1984. Continuities and discontinuities in difficult/easy temperament: Infancy to young adulthood. *Merrill-Palmer Quarterly*, 30:189–200.

Korn, S. J. and Gannon, S. in press. Temperament, cultural variation and behavior disorder in preschool children. *Child Psychiatry and Human Development*.

Korner, A. 1973. Sex differences in newborns with special reference to differences in the organization of oral behavior. *Journal of Child Psychology and Psychiatry*, 14:19–29.

Kovacs, M. and Beck, A. T. 1977. An empirical-clinical approach toward a definition of childhood depression. In J. G. Schulterbrandt and A. Raskin, eds. *Depression in Childhood: Diagnosis, Treatment and Conceptual Models*. New York: Raven Press, pp. 81–85.

314   Origins and Evolution of Behavior Disorders

Kraemer, H. C. 1981. Coping strategies in psychiatric clinical research. *Journal of Consulting and Clinical Psychology*, 49:309-319.
Lapouse, R. and Monk, M. A. 1958. An epidemiological study of behavior characteristics in children. *American Journal of Public Health*, 48:1134-1138.
Laufer, M. W. and Denhoff, E. 1957. Hyperkinetic behavior syndrome in children. *Journal of Pediatrics*, 50:463-474.
Le Carré, J. 1983. *The Little Drummer Girl*. New York: Knopf.
Lehrman, D. 1970. Semantic and conceptual issues in the nature-nurture problem. In L. R. Aronson and E. Tobach, eds. *Development and Evolution of Behavior, Essays in Memory of T. C. Schneirla*. San Francisco: W. H. Freeman.
Lerner, J. V. 1984. The role of temperament in psychosocial adaptation in early adolescence: A test of a "goodness of fit" model. *Journal of Genetic Psychology*, 143:149-157.
Lerner, R. M. and Busch-Rossnagel, eds. 1981. *Individuals as Producers of Their Development: A Life-Span Perspective*, New York: Academic Press.
Lerner, R. M., Palermo, M., Spiro, A., and Nesselroade, J. R. 1982. Assessing the dimensions of temperamental individuality across the life-span: The Dimensions of Temperament Survey (DOTS). *Child Development*, 53:149-159.
Lerner, R. M., Hultsch, D. F., and Dixon, R. A. in press. Contextualism and the character of developmental psychology in the 1970s. *Annals of the New York Academy of Science*.
Lewin, K. 1935. *A Dynamic Theory of Personality*. New York: McGraw-Hill.
Lewis, M. 1981. Child development research and child analysis. *Journal American Academy Child Psychiatry*, 20:189-199.
Lidz, T. 1968. *The Person*. New York: Basic Books.
Lipsitt, L. 1969. Learning capacities of the human infant. In R. Robinson, ed. *Brain and Early Behavior*, London: Academic Press.
Lyon, M. E. and Plomin, R. 1981. The measurement of temperament using parental ratings. *Journal of Child Psychology and Psychiatry*, 22:47-53.
MacFarlane, J. W. 1964. Perspectives on personality consistency and change from the guidance study. *Vita Humana*, 7:115-126.
MacFarlane, J. W., Allen, L., and Honzik, M. P. 1962. *A Developmental Study of the Behavior Problems of Normal Children Between Twenty-One Months and Fourteen Years*. Berkeley: University of California Press.
Maccoby, E. E., and Jacklin, C. N. 1974. *The Psychology of Sex Differences*, Stanford: Stanford University Press.
Marascuilo, L. S. 1966. Large-sample multiple comparisons. *Psychological Bulletin*, 65:280-290.
Marmor, J. 1942. The role of instincts in human behavior. *Psychiatry*, 5:509-516.
Marmor, J. 1983. Systems thinking in psychiatry: Some theoretical and clinical implications. *American Journal of Psychiatry*, 140:833-838.
Martin, B. 1975. Parent-child relations. In F. D. Horowitz, ed. *Review of Child Development Research, IV*, Chicago: University of Chicago Press, pp. 463-540.
Matheny, A. P. 1980. Bayley's infant behavior record: Behavioral components and twin analysis. *Child Development*, 51:1157-1167.
Maurer, R., Cadoret, R. J. and Cain, C. 1980. Cluster analysis of childhood temperament data on adoptees. *American Journal of Orthopsychiatry*, 55:522-534.
Maziade, M., Boudreault, M., Thivierge, J., Caperáa, P., and Côté, R. 1984. Infant temperament: SES and gender differences and reliability of measurement in a large Quebec sample. *Merrill-Palmer Quarterly*, 30:213-226.
McCall, R. B. 1977. Challenges to a science of developmental psychology. *Child Development*, 48:333-344.
McNeil, T. F. and Persson-Blennow, I. 1982. Temperament questionnaires in clinical research. In *Ciba Foundation Symposium 89*, London: Pitman, pp. 20-35.
Meltzoff, A. N. and Moore, K. M. 1977. Imitation of facial and manual gestures by human neonates. *Science*, 198:75-78.

Mendelson, M. and Haith, M. 1976. The relation between audition and vision in the human newborn. *Monographs Society for Research in Child Development*, 4, No. 4.

Menolascino, F. J. 1969. Emotional disturbance in mentally retarded children. *American Journal of Psychiatry*, 126:168-176.

Mischel, W. 1977. On the future of personality measurement. *American Psychologist*, 32:246-254.

Murphy, G. 1947. *Personality: A Biosocial Approach to Origins and Structure.* New York: Harper.

Murphy, L. B. and Moriarty, A. E. 1976. *Vulnerability, Coping and Growth.* New Haven: Yale University Press.

Murphy, L. B. 1981. Explorations in child personality. In A. I. Rabin, J. Aronoff, A. M. Barclay and R. A. Zucker, eds. *Further Explorations in Personality.* New York: Wiley and Sons, pp. 161-195.

Offer, D. and Offer, J. 1975. *From Teenage to Young Manhood.* New York: Basic Books.

Papousek, H. and Papousek, M. 1975. Cognitive aspects of preverbal social interaction between human infants and adults. In *Ciba Foundation Symposium No. 33, Parent Infant Interaction.* Amsterdam: ASP.

Persson-Blennow, I. and McNeil, T. F. 1981. Temperamental characteristics of children in relation to gender, birth order, and social class. *American Journal of Orthopsychiatry*, 51:710-714.

Philips, I. and Williams, N. 1975. Psychopathology of mental retardation. A study of 100 mentally retarded children. *American Journal of Psychiatry*, 132:1265-1271.

Piaget, J. 1954. *The Construction of Reality in the Child.* New York: Basic Books.

Piaget, J. 1963. *The Origins of Intelligence in Children.* New York: Norton.

Richardson, S. A., Goodman, N., Hastorf, A. H. and Dornbusch, S. M. 1961. Cultural uniformity in reaction to physical disabilities. *American Sociological Review*, 26:241-247.

Robbins, L. 1963. The accuracy of parental recall of aspects of child development and child rearing practices. *Journal Abnormal Social Psychology*, 66:261-270.

Rothbart, M. K. 1981. Measurement of temperament in infancy. *Child Development*, 52:569-578.

Rubin, R. A. and Balow, B. 1978. Prevalence of teacher identified behavior problems. A longitudinal study. *Exceptional Children*, 44:102-111.

Rutter, M. 1972. *Maternal Deprivation Reassessed.* Middlesex, England: Penguin Books.

Rutter, M. 1979. *Changing Youth in a Changing Society.* London: Nuffield Provincial Hospitals Trust.

Rutter, M. 1980. Introduction. In M. Rutter, ed. *Scientific Foundations of Developmental Psychiatry.* London: Heinemann, pp. 1-7.

Rutter, M. 1981. Psychological Sequelae of Brain Damage in Children. *American Journal of Psychiatry*, 138:1533-1544.

Rutter, M. 1981a. Stress, coping and development: Some issues and some questions. *Journal of Child Psychology and Psychiatry*, 22:323-356.

Rutter, M. 1981b. Epidemiological/longitudinal strategies and causal research in child psychiatry. *Journal of the American Academy of Child Psychiatry*, 20:513-544.

Rutter, M. 1982. Syndromes attributed to "Minimal brain dysfunction" in childhood. *American Journal of Psychiatry*, 139:21-33.

Rutter, M., Maughan, B., Mortimore, P., Ouston, J. and Smith, A. 1979. *Fifteen Thousand Hours: Secondary Schools and their Effects on Children.* Cambridge, Mass.: Harvard University Press.

Rutter, M., Tizard, J., Yule, W., Graham, P. and Whitmore, K. 1976. Isle of Wight studies, 1964-1974. *Psychological Medicine*, 6:313-332.

Sameroff, A. J. 1975. Early influences on development: Fact or fancy? *Merrill-Palmer Quarterly*, 20:275-301.

Sameroff, A. J. and Seifer, R. 1982. Sociocultural variability in infant temperament ratings. *Child Development*, 53:164-173.

Schaffer, H. and Emerson, P. 1964. The development of social attachment in infancy. *Monographs for Research in Child Development*, 29, No. 3.

Schaffer, R. 1977. *Mothering.* Cambridge, Mass.: Harvard University Press.

Schaie, K. W. and Gribbin, K. 1975. Adult development and aging. *Annual Review of Psychology,* 26:65–96.

Schildkraut, J. J., Orsulak, P. J., Schatzberg, A. F., Gudeman, J. E., Cole, J. O., Rohde, W. A., and LaBrie, R. A. 1978. Toward a biochemical classification of depressive disorders. *Archives of General Psychiatry,* 35:1427–1439.

Schneirla, T. C. 1957. The concept of development in comparative biology. In D. B. Harris, ed. *The Concept of Development.* Minneapolis: University of Minnesota Press.

Sears, R. R. 1951. A theoretical framework for personality and social behavior. *American Psychologist,* 6:476–483.

Sears, R., Maccoby, E. E. and Levin, H. 1957. *Patterns of Child Rearing.* Evanston, Ill.: Row, Peterson.

Shaffer, P. 1974. *Equus.* New York: Bard Books, Avon.

Slater, E. and Roth, M. 1969. *Clinical Psychiatry,* 3rd ed. London: Cassell.

Sorell, N. and Nowak, C. A. 1981. The role of physical attractiveness as a contributor to individual development. In R. M. Lerner and N. A. Busch-Rossnagel, eds. *Individuals as Producers of their Development,* New York: Academic Press, pp. 389–446.

Spanier, G. B., Lerner, R. M. and Aquilino, W. 1978. The study of child-family interactions — a perspective for the future. In R. M. Lerner and G. B. Spanier, eds. *Child Influences in Marital and Family Interaction.* New York: Academic Press, pp. 327–344.

Spock, B. 1957. *Baby and Child Care,* rev. ed. New York: Pocket Books.

Stern, D. 1977. *The First Relationship.* Cambridge, Mass.: Harvard University Press.

Stern, W. 1927. *Psychologic der Fruhen Kindheit, bis zum Sechsten Lebensjahre,* 4th ed. Leipzig: Quelle and Meyer.

Strauss, A. A. and Werner, H. 1943. Comparative psychopathology of brain-injured child and traumatic brain-injured adult. *American Journal of Psychiatry,* 99:835–840.

Sullivan, H. S. 1953. *The Interpersonal Theory of Psychiatry.* H. S. Perry and M. L. Gawel, eds. New York: Norton.

Super, C. M. and Harkness, S. 1981. Figure, ground and gestalt: The cultural context of the active individual. In R. M. Lerner and N. A. Busch-Rossnagel, eds. *Individuals as Producers of their Development,* New York: Academic Press, pp. 69–86.

Terestman, N. 1980. Mood quality and intensity in nursery school children as predictors of behavior disorders. *American Journal of Orthopsychiatry,* 50:125–138.

Terr, L. C. 1981. Psychic trauma in children: Observations following the Chowchilla school-bus kidnapping. *American Journal of Psychiatry,* 138:14–19.

Thomas, A., Birch, H. G., Chess, S., and Hertzig, M. E. 1961a. The developmental dynamics of primary reaction characteristics in children. *Proceedings Third World Congress of Psychiatry,* Vol. 1. Toronto: University of Toronto Press.

Thomas, A., Birch, H. G., Chess, S. and Robbins, L. C. 1961b. Individuality in responses of children to similar environmental situations. *American Journal Psychiatry,* 117:798–803.

Thomas, A. and Chess, S. 1957. An approach to the study of sources of individual differences in child behavior. *Journal of Clinical and Experimental Psychopathology and Quarterly Review of Psychiatry and Neurology,* 18:347–357.

Thomas, A. and Chess, S. 1972. Development in middle childhood. *Seminars in Psychiatry,* 4:331–341.

Thomas, A. and Chess, S. 1975. A longitudinal study of three brain damaged children. *Archives General Psychiatry,* 32:457–462.

Thomas, A. and Chess, S. 1977. *Temperament and Development.* New York: Brunner/Mazel.

Thomas, A. and Chess, S. 1980. *Dynamics of Psychological Development.* New York: Brunner/Mazel.

Thomas, A. and Chess, S. 1981. The role of temperament in the contributions of individuals to their development. In R. M. Lerner and N. A. Busch-Rossnagel, eds. *Individuals As Producers of Their Development.* New York: Academic Press.

Thomas, A. and Chess, S. 1984. Genesis and evolution of behavior disorders: From infancy to early adult life. *American Journal of Psychiatry*, 141:1-9.

Thomas, A., Chess, S. and Birch, H. G. 1968. *Temperament and Behavior Disorders in Children*. New York: New York University Press.

Thomas, A., Chess, S., Birch, H. G. Hertzig, M. E. and Korn, S. 1963. *Behavioral Individuality in Early Childhood*. New York: New York University Press.

Thomas, A., Chess, S. and Korn, S. J. 1982. The reality of difficult temperament. *Merrill-Palmer Quarterly*, 28:1-20.

Thomas, A., Chess, S., Sillen, J. and Mendez, O. 1974. Cross-cultural study of behavior in children with special vulnerabilities to stress. In D. Ricks, A. Thomas and M. Roff, eds. *Life History Research in Psychopathology*, Vol. 3. Minneapolis: University of Minnesota Press, pp. 53-67.

Thomas, A., Hertzig, M. E., Dryman, I. and Fernandez, P. 1971. Examiner effect in IQ testing of Puerto Rican working-class children. *American Journal of Orthopsychiatry*, 41:809-821.

Thomas, A., Mittelman, M., Chess, S., Korn, S. J. and Cohen, J. 1982. A temperament questionnaire for early adult life. *Educational and Psychological Measurement*, 42:593-600.

Thomas, A. and Sillen, S. 1972. *Racism and Psychiatry*. New York: Brunner/Mazel.

Tieger, T. 1980. On the biological basis of sex differences in aggression. *Child Development*, 51:943-963.

Torgersen, A. M. and Kringlen, E. 1978. Genetic aspects of temperamental differences in infants. *Journal American Academy Child Psychiatry*, 17:433-444.

Tuddenham, R. D. 1962. The nature and measurement of intelligence. In L. Postman, ed. *Psychology in the Making*. New York: Knopf, pp. 469-525.

Tukey, J. W. 1979. Methodology and the statistician's responsibility for *both* accuracy and relevance. *Journal of the American Statistical Association*, 74:786-793.

Turkewitz, G. and Birch, H. 1971. Neurobehavioral organization of the human newborn. In J. Hellmuth, ed. *Exceptional Infant: Studies in Abnormalities*, Vol. 2. New York: Brunner/Mazel.

Vaillant, G. E. 1977. *Adaptation to Life*. Boston: Little, Brown.

Vaillant, G. E. and Vaillant, C. O. 1981. Natural history of male psychological health, X: Work as a predictor of positive mental health. *American Journal of Psychiatry*, 138:1433-1440.

Vaughn, B., Taraldson, B., Chrichton, L. and Egeland, B. 1981. The assessment of infant temperament: A critique of the Carey Infant Temperament Questionnaire. *Infant Behavior and Development*, 4:1-18.

de Vries, M. in press. Temperament and infant mortality. *American Journal of Psychiatry*.

Vygotsky, L. S. 1978. *Mind in Society*. Cambridge: Harvard University Press.

Wallerstein, J. S. and Kelly, J. B. 1980. *Surviving the Break-Up*. New York: Basic Books.

Watson, J. B. 1928. *Psychological Care of Infant and Child*. New York: W. W. Norton.

Wenar, C. 1963. The reliability of developmental histories. *Psychosomatic Medicine*, 25:505-509.

Wender, P. H. 1971. *Minimal Brain Dysfunction in Children*. New York: Wiley and Sons, Interscience.

Werner, E. E. and Smith, R. S. 1982. *Vulnerable but Invincible*. New York: McGraw-Hill.

Wertheimer, M. 1961. Psycho-motor coordination of auditory-visual space at birth. *Science*, 134: 1692.

White, R. W. 1959. Motivation reconsidered. The concept of competence. *Psychological Review*, 66:297-333.

Wohlwill, J. F. 1973. *The Study of Behavioral Development*. New York: Academic Press, p. 140.

Wolkind, S. N. and De Salis, W. 1982. Infant temperament, maternal mental state and child behavior problems. In *Temperamental differences in infants and young children*. Ciba Foundation Symposium 89, London: Pitman, pp. 221-239.

Wolpe, J. 1958. *Psychotherapy by Reciprocal Inhibition*. Stanford: Stanford University Press.

Index

Active symptoms, 224
Activity, 191
Adjustment
of adults, risk level and, 111–14
of early adults, childhood antecedents
of, 130–47
highest and lowest scores in, 139–45
of high-risk subjects, 119–22
of low-risk subjects, 122–26
quantitative analyses of, 97–98
risk level and, 115
sex differences in, 90
Adjustment disorders, 53–56
in brain damage cases, 178
with depressed mood and behavior disorder, 159–60
organic personality syndrome, 172
prediction of behavior disorders from
clinical diagnoses of, 203–4
Adjustment scores
for children, 46–47
correlations between three-year ratings
and early adult adaptation, 69
for early adult subjects, 47–49
rating scale from three-year parent
interview, 302–5
Adolescents, 200–2, 229, 245–47
behavior disorders in, 56–57
clinical symptoms in, 225–26
depression cases in, 148–63

interviews with, 38–39
mastery of childhood disorders in, 238–
41
parental guidance for, 258–59
poorness of fit in, 242–43
recovery from initial diagnoses of adjustment disorder by, 204
sex differences in, 89
sexual attitudes and behavior of, 229–33
smooth expansive development in, 234–
36
substance use and abuse by, 234
turbulent but healthy development in,
236–38
turmoil in, 243–45
Adults
antecedents in childhood of adjustment
in, 130–47
depression in, childhood depression
and, 148–49
sex differences in, 90
sexual activity of, 231
see also Early adult subjects
Affective disorders, 282
Alcohol abuse, 160, 209, 234
Alexander, F. G., 219
Anal personality, 228
Animal models, 10–11
Anthony, E. J., 247
Anxiety, 243, 282–85

319

Arnold, L. E., 251
Attrition of sample, 25

Baltes, P. B., 269-72, 274
Becker, W. C., 50-51
Behavior
  clinical evaluations of, 33-36
  data collection on, 28-29
  goals of, 15-17
  interactionist model of, 20
  of neonates, 13
  observation of, 33
  quantitative ratings of, 41-42
Behavior disorders
  adjustment disorder with, 159-60
  adolescent and early adult symptoms
    of, 225-26
  in adolescents, 56-57, 200-2
  anxiety in, 282-83
  in brain damage cases, 181
  childhood characteristics and origins of,
    192-94
  childhood origins of symptoms of, 219-
    25
  in children, 53-56
  difficult temperament and parental con-
    flict in evolution of, 204-9
  distancing from parents in evolution of,
    209-12
  diversity in development of, 183-84
  dysthymic disorder with, 155-59
  in early adults, childhood antecedents
    of, 133-36
  effects of treatment on, 215-16
  goodness of fit model for, 184-86
  high-risk factors for, 288-91
  idiosyncratic factors in evolution of,
    212-15
  parental characteristics and origins of,
    195-96
  parental guidance for, 252-53
  peer group influences and origins of,
    197-99
  poorness of fit model and, 186
  prediction of, from initial clinical
    diagnosis, 203-4
  retrospective reports on, 6-7
  risk level and, 114-15
  school demands and origins of,
    199-200
  sib relationships and origins of,
    196-97
  sociocultural influences and origins of,
    202

temperament and, 186-92
Behaviorism, 5-6, 219, 261
Bell, R., 15
Biological factors
  in clinical symptoms, 226
  see also Brain damage cases
Biologically induced affective disorders,
  282
Birch, H. G., 12, 13, 62, 63, 104
Bootstrapping technique, 48-49
Borderline personality disorder, 210
Bower, T., 12, 13
Boys, see Males
Brain damage cases, 164-82, 193, 215
  clinical symptoms in, 226
  as high-risk factor for behavior
    disorders, 290
Brazelton, T., 13
Brazelton Neonatal Behavioral Assessment
  Scale, 13
Bronson, W. C., 262, 267
Bruner, J. S., 16

Cameron, J. R., 50, 92-93, 224
Carey, W. B., 30, 31, 94, 191, 285, 290
Chess, S., 6, 10, 19-20, 27, 31, 35,
  40, 41, 45, 58, 63, 94, 99, 105, 107,
  118, 145, 146, 163, 164, 177, 178, 180,
  181, 202, 223, 229, 266, 268, 270, 273,
  279, 283, 285, 288, 290, 293
Child-care attitudes, 221
Childhood and children
  as active agents in interactionism,
    287-88
  adjustment rating scale from three-year
    parent interview, 302-5
  adjustment scores for, 46-47
  adolescent mastery of problems in,
    238-41
  antecedents of early adult adjustment
    in, 130-47
  behavior disorders in, 53-56
  brain damage in, 165-82
  cognitive development of, 226-27
  correlations between three-year ratings
    and early adult adaptation, 68-80
  depression cases in, 148-51, 160-63
  Freud on origins of neuroses in, 261,
    266
  goodness of fit model used for, 285-86
  high- and low-risk, and adult outcomes,
    110-29
  as neonates, 12-14
  origins of symptoms in, 218-25

parental characteristics and, 195–96
parental data on, 30–32
parental guidance of, 251–58
peer group influences on, 197–99
prediction of behavior disorders from
  clinical diagnoses of, 203–4
ratings correlations between early adults
  and, 81–88
retrospective reports on, 6
school demands on, 199–200
set correlations between young adults
  and, 81–88
sex differences in, 90
sib relationships of, 196–97
sociocultural influences on, 202
subjective intrapsychic data on, 36–38
temperament ratings for, 41–45
temperament and causes of behavior
  disorders in, 186–92
theories of development of, 14–15
see also Infants
Clarke, A. D. B., 20, 145, 267, 279
Clarke, A. M., 20, 145, 267, 279
Clinical cases
biological factors in symptoms in, 226
sex differences in, 91–92
sexual activity of, 232
symptoms in, 224–25
Clinical diagnoses
prediction of behavior disorders from,
  203–4
psychiatric, 49–50
Clinical evaluations, 33–36
Clinical practice, parental guidance in,
  259–60
Cognitive development, 226–27, 268–69
Cohen, J., 103
Coleman, J. C., 244
Communication (speech)
in brain damage cases, 165–67, 175,
  177
by neonates, 13
parental importance placed on, 222
of sexual issues, 230
Computers, 106
Conditioned reflexes, 10–11
in behaviorism, 219
in neonates, 13
Condon, W., 13
Conduct disorders, 53–54
Conflict
in adolescents, 246
in correlations between three-year
  ratings and early adult adaptation, 72

parental, 127–28, 195–96
parental, evolution of behavior
  disorders and, 204–9
parental, in guidance failures, 257–58
parental, as high-risk factor, 288–89
symptoms as expressions of, 219–20
of values, 202
of values, in adolescents, 242
Continuity and discontinuity in developmental stages, 261–72
Correlation analyses, 64
between childhood and early adult
  ratings, 81–88
Correlations, 104
Cross-sectional studies, 8–9
Cultural evolution, 12
Cultural influences, 202
Culture, 11–12

Data collection strategies, 28–29
Death of parent, 212–13
Defense mechanisms, 282–85
Denial, 227–28, 283
Depression, 54, 192–93, 215
in adolescents, 201, 242–43
biological factors in, 226
in children and adolescents, 148–63
family history of, 290
as unpredictable developmental change,
  263
Depressive neurosis (dysthymic disorder),
  149, 155–61, 163
DeSalis, W., 118
Despert Fables, 37
Developmental stages, 261–72
Deviance, longitudinal studies of, 27
Diagnoses
of behavior disorders, 53–54
clinical psychiatric, 49–50
of depression in children, 148
prediction of behavior disorders from,
  203–4
Diagnostic and Statistical Manual of
  Mental Disorders, Third Edition
  (DSM-III), 53–54
on depression, 148, 149, 160, 161
"Difficult" temperament group, 43,
  186–89
Divorce, 288–89
Dixon, R. A., 271
Dobzhansky, T., 11
Drug abuse, 159, 213, 234
Dubos, R., 12, 22
Dyskinesia, 171

Dysthymic disorder (depressive neurosis), 149, 155–61, 163

Early adult subjects
    adjustment scores for, 47–49
    antecedents in childhood of adjustment in, 130–47
    clinical symptoms in, 225–26
    correlations between three-year ratings and early adult adaptation, 68–80
    global adaptation scores for, 306–7
    high- and low-risk, compared with at age three, 110–29
    interview protocol for, 297–301
    interviews with, 39–40
    ratings correlations between childhood and, 81–88
    recovery from initial diagnoses of adjustment disorder by, 203–4
    set correlations between children and, 81–88
    on sexual attitudes and behavior, 233
    sib relationships of, 196
    substance use reported by, 234
    temperament ratings for, 45–46
"Easy" temperament group, 43, 189–90
Eisenberg, L., 10
Elimination difficulties, 194, 220–21, 227–28
Emde, R., 292
Enuresis, 221
Environment
    extraordinary stresses in, 276–77
    in interactionist model, 185
    in life-span perspective, 271
    symptom choice influenced by, 223
Equus (play, Shaffer), 292
Erikson, E. H.
    on cultural factors in achievement, 280
    on developmental stage sequence, 268
    on identity crisis, 244, 245
    on sense of identity, 279
    on weaning, 17
Erikson, K., 276–77
Escalona, S., 104

Factor analyses, 104–5
Fathers, see Parents
Feeding problems, 220, 221
Females
    recovery from initial diagnoses of adjustment disorder by, 203
    sex differences between males and, 89–95

see also Sex differences
Fishman, M. E., 246
Flavell, J. H., 268–69
Freud, A., 219, 252
Freud, S.
    on causality in development of disorders, 7–8
    on childhood origins of neuroses, 261, 266
    on defense mechanisms, 283
    on developmental stage sequence, 268
    on goals of adult behavior, 17
    importance of behavioral goals to, 15
    interactionism of, 19
    on retrospective histories, 7
Freudian theory, 5
    see also Psychoanalytic theory

Gannon, S., 289
Garmezy, N., 291
"Generation gap," 245–46
Genetics, 11, 290
Girls, see Females
Global adaptation scores, 306–7
    sexual functioning and, 233
Global adjustment scores
    for children, 46–47
    correlations between three-year ratings and early adult adaptation, 69
    for early adult subjects, 47–49
Goals
    of behavior, 15–17
    of New York Longitudinal Study, 24–25, 183
Goodness of fit model, 20–23, 184–86, 273–79, 288
    anxiety, defense mechanisms and, 282–85
    parental guidance and, 252–53
    physical characteristics and, 195
    practical implications of, 285–86
    self-esteem and, 279–82
    see also Poorness of fit
Gordon, E., 22, 291
Gould, S. J., 66
Greenspan, S. I., 22, 277
Guidance, parental, 251–60
    goodness of fit used in, 285

Haith, M., 12
Hall, G. S., 243
Handicapped people, 194
Harkness, S., 188–89, 289
Harvard Grant longitudinal study, 7, 267

Hetherington, E. M., 289
High-risk factors, 288-91
  "defiers" of predictions based on,
    291-92
High-risk subjects
  childhood antecedents of early adult
    adjustment in, 136-37
  difficult temperament and parental
    conflict in, 205
  at three years and early adult outcomes,
    110-29
Hinde, R. A., 293
Homosexuality, 233
Hsu, C. C., 94
Hultsch, D. F., 271
Human development model, 11-12
Hunt, J. V., 22
Hyperactivity, 176
Hypomania, 158

Identity crises, 244, 245
Idiosyncratic factors in evolution of
  behavior disorders, 212-15
Impositional symptoms, 224
Impotence, 232
Impulsivity, 180, 201-2, 290
Infants (neonates), 12-14
  brain damage in, 165
  goal-oriented behavior in, 16
  NYLS data on, 29-30
  socialization of, 17-18
  theories of development of, 14-15
  see also Childhood and children
Inhibition, 232
Interactionism, 18-20, 183
  changes over time postulated in, 65
  child as active agent in, 287-88
  goodness of fit and, 184, 185
  symptom formation and, 228
  on uniqueness of individuals, 274-75
Interviews
  of adolescents, 38-39
  data collection strategies in, 28-29
  of early adult subjects, 39-40
  of early adult subjects, protocol
    for, 297-301
  of parental, 31-32
  parental, adjustment scale from three-
    year, 302-5
  on sexual attitudes and behavior, 229-30
  of teachers, 32-33
IQ scores, 26, 33, 51, 194
  in brain damage cases, 165, 171, 175-77
  risk level and, 115

Kagan, J., 22
Kashani, J. H., 148-49
Kelly, J. B., 289
Keogh, B. K., 286
Kohlberg, L., 268
Korn, S. J., 93, 95, 109, 289
Kraemer, H. C., 65, 67, 106
Kringlen, E., 30
Krug, R. S., 50-51

Language, see Communication
Latency periods, 58
Learning
  in neonates, 13
  parental importance placed on, 222
Le Carré, J., 108
Lehrman, D., 11
Leitsch, M., 104
Lerner, J. V., 22-23
Lerner, R. M., 271
Life-span developmental psychology,
  269-72, 274
Longitudinal studies
  data collection decisions in, 104
  data on continuity and discontinuity
    of developmental stages from, 267
  need for, 8-9
Low-risk subjects
  childhood antecedents of early adult
    adjustment in, 136-37
  at three years and early adult outcomes,
    110-29
LSD, 234

McCall, R. B., 66, 105, 107
MacFarlane, J. W., 267
McNeil, T. F., 93-94
Major depression, 54, 149-55, 215
  in children and adolescents, 160
Males
  failures of parental guidance with, 257
  risk level among, 115-19
  sex differences between females and,
    89-95
  see also Sex differences
Marijuana, 160, 234, 237
Marmor, J., 274
Martin, B., 31
Masked depression, 148
Masturbation, 221, 233
Maziade, M., 94
Measurement
  reliability of, 66-67
  statistical, 65-66

Men, see Males
Mendeleev, D. I., 106
Mendelson, M., 12
Mental retardation, 27, 175–78, 290
Methods
adjustment rating scale from three-year
parent interview, 302–5
danger of circular reasoning in, 278–79
early adult life interview protocol,
297–301
global adaptation scores, 306–7
longitudinal studies, 8–9
in New York Longitudinal Study, 25–40
qualitative analyses, 103–9
quantitative analyses, 63–65
reliability, validity and relevance issues
in, 66–67
retrospective reports, 6–7
set correlations between childhood and
young adults ratings, 81–88
statistical, 65–66
temperament ratings, 42–43
Minimal brain dysfunction (MBD), 164,
181–82
Mischel, W., 185, 274
Models
animal, 10–11
goodness of fit, 20–23, 184–86, 273–86
human development, 11–12
interactionist, 20
see also Goodness of fit model
Moriarty, A. E., 267
Mothers, see Parents
Motor activity disturbances, 223
Multiple regression analyses, 63–64
correlations between three-year ratings
and early adult adaptation, 68–80
sex differences in, 91, 92
Multiple regression correlations, 81
Multivariate R^2 statistic (MRV^2), 81
Murphy, L. B., 267, 277

Narcissistic personality disorder, 160
Natural selection, 11
Neonates, see Infants
Nervous system, animal models for, 10–11
Neurological dysfunction cases, 164–82
Neuroses, Freud on childhood origins of,
261, 266
New York Longitudinal Study (NYLS), 9
adolescent interviews in, 38–39
adolescent subjects of, 229–47
brain damage cases in, 164–82

childhood antecedents of early adult
adjustment in, 130–47
clinical evaluations in, 33–36
clinical symptoms in, 224
comparisons of high- and low-risk
subject at three years and early adult
outcomes, 110–29
data collection strategies for, 28–29
data on continuity and discontinuity of
developmental stages from, 262–67
data sources for, 25–27
defense mechanisms in subjects in,
284–85
depression cases in children and
adolescents in, 148–63
early adult interviews in, 39–40
goals of, 24–25, 183
high-risk factors identified by, 288–91
interactionism in, 19–20
IQ testing for, 33
maintenance of sample for, 27–28
neonatal data collected by, 29–30
parental data collected by, 30–32
parental guidance in, 253–60
Puerto Rican longitudinal study
compared with, 223
qualitative analyses in, 103–9
quantitative analyses used in, 96–100
quantitative ratings used in, 41–51
retrospective histories tested by, 6
sample over time in, 52–58
school data collected by, 32–33
set correlations between childhood and
early adult ratings, 81–88
sex differences found in, 89–95
subjective intrapsychic childhood data
in, 36–38
symptoms of behavior disorders in,
220–21
weaning and toilet training data in,
17–18
Nonaccommodational symptoms, 224
Non-normative life events, 271
Normality assumption, 65–66
Normative age-graded influences, 270
Normative history-graded (evolutionary)
influences, 270–71
Normative identity crisis, 244, 245
Nursery school, 32

Observer reports, 106
Offer, D., 243–46
Offer, J., 243–46

Organic brain dysfunction, 282
Organic brain syndrome with adjustment
    disorders, 54
Organic personality disorder, 178
Organic personality syndrome, 169,
    172, 174
Overadapting symptoms, 224

Parents
    adjustment rating scale from three-year
        parent interview, 302-5
    on adolescent sexual attitudes and
        behavior, 230
    characteristics of, 195-96
    children's distancing from, 209-12
    children's self-esteem and, 281
    of children with difficult temperament,
        187-88
    of children with easy temperament, 190
    of children with slow-to-warm-up
        temperament, 191
    conflict among, 72, 127-28
    conflict among, evolution of behavior
        disorders and, 204-9
    conflict among, as high-risk factor,
        288-89
    conflicts between adolescents and, 242
    as data source, 30-31
    death of, 212-13
    distancing from, 217
    goodness of fit used by, 285
    guidance by, 251-60
    interviews with, 31-32
    quantitative ratings of, 41-51
    ratings of attitudes and practices
        of, 50-51
    retrospective reports by, 6-7
    school demands and, 200
    sociocultural influences on, 202
    temperament of, children's temperament
        and, 192
Passive symptoms, 224
Paupousek, H., 16
Paupousek, M., 16
Pavlov, I. P., 19
Peer groups, 197-99
    conflicts between parents' patterns and,
        222
    influences on adolescents by, 242
    sociocultural influences on, 202
Perseveration, 193, 226
    in brain damage cases, 171, 174, 178-80
Persistence, 191, 257

Personality, study of, 274
Persson-Blennow, I., 93-94
Phobias, animal models for, 11
Physical characteristics, 195
Piaget, J., 105, 226-27, 268
Poorness of fit, 185, 186, 275
    in adolescents, 242-43
    defense mechanisms and, 285
    physical characteristics and, 195
    in school, 285-86
    school demands and, 199-200
    temperament of children and, 187
    see also Goodness of fit model
Prediction of behavior disorders from
        clinical diagnoses, 203-4
    "defiers" of, 291-92
Privacy, 230
Projective tests, 37
Psychiatric diagnoses, 49-50
Psychiatric evaluations, 34-35
Psychoanalytic theory, 5, 219
    on adolescent turmoil, 243-44
    childhood origins of behavior disorders
        in, 261-62
    defense mechanisms in, 283
    importance of behavioral goals in, 15
    toilet training in, 228
    see also Theory
Psychodynamics, 220
Psychological development, human
        development model for, 11-12
Psychomotor retardation, 226
Psychotherapy, 35-36
    effects on evolution of behavior
        disorders of, 215-16
Puerto Ricans, longitudinal study of, 27,
    223, 277, 289

Qualitative analyses, 103-9
    of childhood antecedents of early adult
        adjustment, 130-47
    of high- and low-risk subjects and three
        years and early adulthood, 110-29
    symptoms in, 218-28
Quantitative analyses, 1-67, 96-100
    of adjustment, 46-49
    of clinical psychiatric diagnoses, 49-50
    IQ scores, 51
    of parental attitudes and practices,
        50-51
    qualitative analyses and, 103-5, 109
    set correlations between childhood and
        early adult ratings, 81-88

Quantitative analyses (*continued*)
  sex differences, 89–95
  of temperament, 41–46

Rationalization, 283
Reaction formation, 283
Rebellion, 201
Relevance issues, 66–67
Reliability issues, 66–67
Religion, 159, 213, 215, 284
  in "defiers" of predictions, 292
  sexual behavior and, 232
Retardation, 27, 175–78, 290
Retrospective histories, 6–7
Risk levels
  childhood antecedents of early adult
    adjustment and, 136–37
  high and low, at age three and early
    adulthood, 110–29
  high-risk factors, 288–91
R^2 statistic, 81
Rutter, M.
  on adolescents, 244–46
  on idiographic approach, 274–75, 278
  on idiosyncratic developmental pat-
    terns, 65
  on minimal brain dysfunction, 182
  on parental conflict, 289
  on social disinhibition, 178, 180, 290

Sample
  attrition of, 25
  characteristics of, 26–27
  maintenance of, 27–28
  over time, 52–58
  sex differences found in, 89–95
Sander, L., 13
Schaffer, H., 12
Schizophrenia, 173, 182
Schneirla, T. C., 19
School, 199–200
  data from, 32–33
  early functioning in, 138–39
  poorness of fit in, 285–86
Selesnick, S. T., 219
Self-esteem, 279–82
Set correlation analyses, 64
  between childhood and early adult
    ratings, 81–88
Sex differences, 89–95, 99
  in recovery from initial diagnoses of
    adjustment disorder, 203
  risk level and, 115–19

Sexuality
  adolescent attitudes and behaviors,
    200–1, 229–33
  in clinical symptoms of adolescent and
    early adult subjects, 225
Shaffer, P., 292
Siblings, 196–97
Sleep irregularities, 221, 223
Slow-to-warm-up temperament group,
    43–44, 104–5, 190–91
  parental guidance for, 254–55
Smith, R. S., 291
Social communications, by neonates, 13
Social disinhibition, 178, 180, 290
Socialization, of infants, 17–18
Social learning theory, 6
Sociocultural influences, 202
  in origins of symptoms of behavior
    disorders, 220–23
Spearman, C., 66
Speech, *see* Communication
Spock, Benjamin, 26, 221
Statistical methods, 65–66, 103
Stern, D., 22
Stress
  in adolescents, 242–43
  defense mechanisms and, 284–85
  goodness of fit and, 21
  as pathogenic factor, 276–77
Subjective intrapsychic data, 36–38
Substance abuse, 159, 160, 213
  by adolescents, 234
Sucking behavior, 17
Super, C. M., 188–89, 289
Symptoms, 218–20
  in adolescence and early adult life,
    225–26
  biological factors in, 226
  evolution of, 226–28
  of neuroses, Freud on childhood origins
    of, 261, 266
  origins in childhood of, 220–25
  sexual, in adolescents, 231

Tape recordings, 108
Teacher interviews, 32–33
Temperament
  in adolescents, 201
  in brain damage cases, 180–81
  in causes of behavior disorders, 186–92
  comparisons of high- and low-risk
    subject at three years and early adult
    outcomes, 110–11

continuity of, 266–67
in correlations between three-year
    ratings and early adult adaptation,
    69, 73–77
in depression cases, 162–63
difficult, as high-risk factor, 288–90
in origins of symptoms of behavior
    disorders, 223–25
parental conflict and evolution of
    behavior disorders, 204–9
parent questionnaires on, 31
quantitative analyses of, 96–97
quantitative ratings of, 41–46
sex differences in, 90, 93–94
symptom choice influenced by, 223–25
Terr, L. C., 276
Theory, 5–6, 10–11
on adolescent turmoil, 243–44
on childhood development, 14–15
childhood origins of behavior disorders
    in, 261–62
danger of circular reasoning in, 278–79
developmental stage sequence in, 268
goodness of fit and, 184
human development model, 11–12
importance of behavioral goals in, 15
interactionism, 18–20
of life-span developmental psychology,
    269–72, 274
on symptoms, 219–20
see also Psychoanalytic theory
Thomas, A., 6, 10, 19–20, 31, 35, 40, 41,
    45, 58, 63, 94, 99, 105, 107, 118, 145,
    146, 163, 164, 177, 180, 202, 223,
    229, 266, 268, 270, 273, 279, 283,
    285, 286

Thurstone, L. L., 66
Toilet training, 17–18, 221, 228
Topeka Longitudinal Study, 267, 277
Torgersen, A. M., 29–30
Traumas, 276–77
Treatment
    effects on evolution of behavior
        disorders of, 215–16
    goodness of fit model used in, 285
    parental guidance in, 251–60
Tuddenham, R. D., 66
Tukey, J. W., 66
Turkewitz, G., 13
Twins, 28

Vaillant, C. O., 128
Vaillant, G. E., 7, 128, 267
Validity issues, 66–67
Values
    conflicts of, in adolescents, 242
    sociocultural influences on, 202
    symptom choice and, 222–23
Verbal communication, see
    Communication
de Vries, M., 289–90

Wallerstein, J. S., 289
Watson, J. B., 261
Weaning, 17–18
Wender, P. H., 181
Werner, E. E., 291
Withdrawal symptoms (of behavior
    disorders), 224
Wolkind, S. N., 118
Women, see Females
Work, commitment to, 128